CISSP EXAM STUDY GUIDE
FOR SECURITY PROFESSIONALS

5 BOOKS IN 1

NIST CYBERSECURITY FRAMEWORK, RISK MANAGEMENT, DIGITAL FORENSICS & GOVERNANCE

BOOK 1
NETWORK SECURITY FUNDAMENTALS
SECURITY ARCHITECTURE & DESIGN PRINCIPLES
BOOK 2
IMPLEMENTING CYBERSECURITY RESILIENCE
PHYSICAL SECURITY CONTROLS & CRYPTOGRAPHIC CONCEPTS
BOOK 3
CYBERSECURITY ENFORCEMENT AND MONITORING SOLUTIONS
ENHANCED WIRELESS, MOBILE AND CLOUD SECURITY DEPLOYMENT
BOOK 4
CISSP: CYBERSECURITY OPERATIONS AND INCIDENT RESPONSE
DIGITAL FORENSICS WITH EXPLOITATION FRAMEWORKS & VULNERABILITY SCANS
BOOK 5
CISSP: CYBERSECURITY GOVERNANCE AND RISK MANAGEMENT
POLICY CONCEPTS & DEPLOYMENT WITHIN ORGANIZATIONAL SECURITY

RICHIE MILLER

Disclaimer

Every effort was made to produce this book as truthful as possible, but no warranty is implied. The author shall have neither liability nor responsibility to any person or entity concerning any loss or damages ascending from the information contained in this book. The information in the following pages are broadly considered to be truthful and accurate of facts, and such any negligence, use or misuse of the information in question by the reader will render any resulting actions solely under their purview.

Table of Contents – Book 1

Table of Contents – Book 2

Table of Contents – Book 3

Table of Contents – Book 4

Table of Contents – Book 5

BOOK 1

NETWORK SECURITY
FUNDAMENTALS

SECURITY ARCHITECTURE & DESIGN PRINCIPLES

RICHIE MILLER

Introduction

IT Security jobs are on the rise! Small, medium or large size companies are always on the look out to get on board bright individuals to provide their services for Business as Usual (BAU) tasks or deploying new as well as on-going company projects. Most of these jobs requiring you to be on site but since 2020, companies are willing to negotiate with you if you want to work from home (WFH). Yet, to pass the Job interview, you must have experience. Still, if you think about it, all current IT security professionals at some point had no experience whatsoever. The question is; how did they get the job with no experience? Well, the answer is simpler then you think. All you have to do is convince the Hiring Manager that you are keen to learn and adopt new technologies and you have willingness to continuously research on the latest upcoming methods and techniques revolving around IT security. Here is where this book comes into the picture. Why? Well, if you want to become an IT Security professional, this book is for you! If you are studying for CompTIA Security+ or CISSP, this book will help you pass your exam. Passing security exams isn't easy. In fact, due to the raising security beaches around the World, both above mentioned exams are becoming more and more difficult to pass. Whether you want to become an Infrastructure Engineer, IT Security Analyst or any other Cybersecurity Professional, this book (as well as the other books in this series) will certainly help you get there! But, what knowledge are you going to gain from this book? Well, let me share with you briefly the agenda of this book, so you can decide if the following topics are interesting enough to invest your time in! First, you are going to discover what are the basic security concepts in an enterprise environment such as configuration management, data sovereignty, data protection, and why we should be protecting data in the first place. Next, you will learn about geographical considerations such as site resiliency; and then also something referred to as deception and disruption. After that, you will understand the basics of virtualization and cloud computing. We'll be also talking about cloud models, managed service providers, and the concept of fog and edge computing. Next, you will discover how to secure microservices and APIs or application programming interfaces. We'll also talk about SDN and SDV, or software-defined networking and software-defined visibility. After that, we'll talk about serverless architecture, and virtualization. Next, you will discover how to implement secure application development and automation in various types of environments. We'll also going to cover testing, staging, QA and production, provisioning and decommissioning resources. We'll also cover integrity measurement and what that means, secure coding techniques and careful considerations and planning when coding for security. Next, we will cover OWASP specifications or the Open Web Application Security Project, along with software diversity, automation and scripting. We'll also talk about elasticity, scalability, and version control in various environments that we can deploy into. After that, you will learn about authentication and authorization methods and the various technologies associated with those. We'll also talk about smartcard authentication, biometrics, multi-factor authentication, or MFA deployment, as well as authentication, authorization, and accounting, otherwise known as AAA, as well as cloud, versus on-premise requirements, as far as authorization and authentication is concerned. If you are ready to get on this journey, let's first cover what are baseline configurations!

Chapter 1 Baseline Configuration, Diagrams & IP Management

First we are going to cover security concepts in an enterprise environment. If we take a look at what we have at a high level, we have security concepts in an enterprise environment such as configuration management; we'll talk about data sovereignty, what that means and some gotchas there potentially; we'll talk about data protection, the various methods, and why we should be protecting that data; and then geographical considerations; site resiliency; and then also something referred to as deception and disruption. Every organization, enterprise, company, regardless of size, has a need to maintain standards in some type of configuration management. There's a number of reasons for this. Number one, we want to standardize the environment. The more standardized something is, the easier it is to maintain, the easier it is to find anomalies and to troubleshoot. By doing that, we can set baselines within our environment and then understand what is normal. Because once we understand what's normal, it's much easier to figure out what's not normal, what stands out, what are red flags, etc. Another side benefit is to identify conflicts and collisions. When we have configuration management at scale and we have a number of different people groups, all needing to make changes, all needing to adjust configurations, and if we have some type of collision calendar or a configuration management calendar, whether we call it a change board or a configuration management process, if we all have our processes documented, and then we review that whether it's weekly or monthly or whatever your change schedule is, we review that to make sure that some changes are not going to step on each other, cause conflicts in some form or fashion, and it just lends itself to having the organization run that much more smoothly. To put it into a definition, configuration management is the management and control of configurations. Configuration management is the management and control of configurations for an information system with the goal of enabling. And here's the takeaways: enabling security and managing risk, because that's really what we want to do. We want to enable security. We want to make sure our environment is as secure as possible. But we also want to manage risk. We don't want to unnecessarily introduce risk into the environment. Conversely, the risk that is there, we want to be aware of it and understand how to manage it. We can accept it, we can transfer it, we can pass it on. We can just say that we're willing to accept that part. It's going to cost too much to remediate, and we're just going to accept it. There's a lot of different ways to handle it, but configuration management allows us to have that line of sight and that overall big picture to understand when things change, and the more standardized that is, the easier it is to see. But just understand the basics of configuration management. The method of determining what's normal, why do we do that? Well, changes can quickly be identified then. If we have a big environment, don't think, necessarily, maybe you have a small environment with only a few computers or a few servers, maybe a few hosts, very easy to see things when they change. Once you start to get into bigger environments and you have hundreds or thousands of servers or tens of thousands of servers, it's very, very difficult to manage the snowflakes. By standardizing, we can identify changes very quickly and we can roll them back if necessary. Patches and updates can also be determined very quickly, were they successful or did they fail? We can quickly determine a success or failure and then roll back if necessary. Also, changes throughout an enterprise are documented, discussed, and then any potential collisions determined. By having that collision calendar, we make sure we're minimizing risk. We're not introducing unnecessary risk into the environment, and we're making sure that changes can be applied successfully. At the end of the day, it doesn't matter if we can roll the change back or not. It's still a pain; it still requires time and effort and resources validation teams. If we can avoid that whenever possible, it just makes for a much more smooth running operation. One of the things that we want to do when we're doing configuration management is to diagram, to understand how things work. Diagramming visualizes how things work, how they're connected, and how they interoperate. It's very timely, and it helps us to visualize and then troubleshoot, and we can understand all the dependencies and how things connect. Dependencies are identified and they're documented, inputs and outputs are understood, security risks can be discovered and then mitigated, and then applications, networking, compute, storage, all of those things, we have line of sight as to how they connect, what's dependent on each other, etc. It's a very lonely day when you have an outage, and all of a sudden you didn't realize that 15 other applications actually depended upon that application that just failed. And when your boss or your boss's boss starts asking, what about this, what about that, what about that application, what about that application? And you have no idea that even connected or talk to each other, it doesn't look good. So by having all these things diagrammed, documented, it allows us to derisk the environment. Making sure that things are stable as they can be, that we can quickly remediate when things do happen, and the more standardized, the better we're going to be. In addition to diagramming, we also have something referred to as a baseline configuration. In a baseline configuration, setting those baselines is critical to quickly identifying changes and configuration drift. When I say configuration drift, I mean over time, little things get tweaked and changed, and it gets to the point where you can't even tell where you're at anymore, what was normal, because so many things have changed. Well, if we have a baseline that we can roll back to, then we can even programmatically, every so often, reapply, whether it's group policy or some script or something to the environment that will roll those things back, so that if someone adds in an administrator where they shouldn't have been or they make a change to a policy or maybe even within the registry or in a conf file, it just depends upon the environment, what operating system. But if those changes get introduced and we don't really want them, some rogue administrator decides to do a one-off just because he thinks it may make his life easier, well, when it comes time to remediate, that person may have left that department or that role 6 months or a year prior but now we have an issue with something that they changed and only they know about, it becomes very difficult to find that needle in a haystack. So by having baseline configurations, we periodically just apply to the environment and we keep things standardized. Also when hackers or bad actors in a system or a network, what do they want to do? They want to change things. They're going to try to install backdoors, persistence or elevate privileges. Those changes can be quickly discovered, or more quickly because they're outside of that norm or that baseline. So having those things in place makes it much easier to identify. In case you actually haven't guessed it yet, the name of the game is standardization. The more standardized things are, the easier they are to maintain, to deploy, and also to troubleshoot. I really want that to be a takeaway for you. And if you don't have a standardization policy or working toward that in your environment, I highly recommend that you do so. It will make your life easier. It will reduce outages and also make troubleshooting when there is an outage that much easier. Let's change gears slightly and talk about IP address schema. And when I say schema, I mean, what is your IP address plan? Going back to what I said before about standardization, a schema allows us to have some type of standardization, some conformity around how we actually allocate IP addresses. Standardize. And then also maintain an IP address database. To an extent, we do that with the DHCP. It maintains a scope and a database of IP addresses for us. But in a large environment where we may have multiple DHCP scopes, we may have multiple DHCP agents or relay agents and servers that are acting in that capacity, it's possible to have things overlap. Or it's possible to have things that are allocated an IP address and we just don't know what that thing is, who's getting the IP address. So part of that database should be allocations and also reclamations. When we allocate an IP address, we should document who it's allocated to. Then also when we reclaim that IP address, it should also be brought back into the pool and back into our database that reflects that reclamation. A toolset or a suite of tools that can do that for us to an extent, is IP control or IP address management, IPAM. Different organizations will refer to it as something different. It may not be called the same thing in your organization if you even have it. But IP control is a way for you to simplify management, make troubleshooting easier, and then also increases security. Because we can understand at a glance what our IP addressing scheme is, and so we have, like, say, servers allocated a certain range, hosts perhaps allocated a certain range,. We may have things broken off into VLANs, or virtual local area networks, like for management IP addresses. For now, just suffice it to say that it's important for us to standardize and then also increase security. Troubleshooting also becomes easier because we have a database we can look up very quickly and say, this IP address was assigned to so and so. That assumes that we have good information in, the old saying garbage in, garbage out. We have to make sure that we have mechanisms in place to keep these things updated. But assuming all things are in play and all things are working properly, it increases security and makes troubleshooting and management much easier.

Chapter 2 Data Sovereignty & Data Loss Prevention

Next, let's talk about data sovereignty. Sovereignty, means who owns the data. When data is stored electronically, and this is something that you may or may not be aware of, it is actually subject to the laws of the country in which it's located. If you store data outside of your own country, it's possible that that data is subject to a different set of laws than what exists in your existing or your own country. Some other countries may have more stringent access rules, meaning they can access or mine that data, and you may not necessarily want that. It's important to understand these things before you start putting data in other locations. Who owns the data and who has access? Also, who can mine the data or pull things out of it. Depending upon the country around the world, law enforcement, government agencies, some countries are very stringent and they want access to all of it. Others are less restrictive and more geared toward the actual consumer or the individual person and their privacy. But those same sets of laws and policies don't exist globally, It's important understand where that data sits and what rules or regulations it falls under. Laws governing data use, access, storage, and also deletion, will vary from country to country. When you store information in the cloud, make sure you understand how that data is actually being stored, does it replicate to other data centers, are these data centers in a specific region, or are the outside of the country? Typically, you'll be made aware of those things, but just something to keep in mind. Next, let's talk about data loss prevention, or DLP. DLP detects potential breaches and also, and more importantly, the exfiltration of data. A few ways this can actually be instantiated, we have endpoint detection, that means data that's actually in use, we have network traffic detection, so data that's in transit, if it's going from one location to another, could be internal. But typically, we're doing DLP when we're having data leave our network. If it's crossing our boundary and going out to the internet, many companies will have DLP infrastructure in place that will stop that data from leaving, inspect it first, and then if it meets that criteria, we'll allow that data to go outside of the network. If for whatever reason it's determined that that data is not applicable or not permissible to leave, then it just shuts down that communication and does not let that email or that communication to be sent. Then we also have data storage, or data at rest. We can have devices that will scan in any one of these formats. It may just scan data at rest to make sure there's not PII, or PHI, health information, sitting inside file shares, network shares that are not necessarily secure. It can pull that data out, alert the user and say we found XYZ in a file store in your name or that you're showing as the owner of, it had personally identifiable information or HIPPA related or PCI data. We removed that file from your file share. It's in this quarantined location. Please double-check on it if it's valid, pull out the information you need, otherwise it will be deleted, things along those lines. There are automated methods to alleviate some of the pain associated with having to scan a very large network. Some additional methods of data loss prevention would be USB blocking. Don't allow people to insert USB devices, thumb drives into their machines, copy data, and then leave. Also, we have cloud-based and then email blocking. A lot of these things, again, are an automated process. They can scan, they can do SSL interception, even if that data is encrypted, depending upon the organization and the devices that they have in play, they can do what was traditionally called a man-in-the-middle attack. Now it's an on-path attack. But have a piece of infrastructure that sits in between the end user and who they're communicating to, and it will actually intercept that SSL traffic, unencrypt it, pull all the information out, see if there's anything that might be compromising, and then stop that communication from leaving the network. When we're talking about types of data to secure, three main ones that I want you to be aware of. We have data at rest, as you might guess, is data sitting on a hard drive or removable media. It's local to the computer, or it could be remotely on a storage area network or network attached storage, SAN or NAS, but it's data that is sitting somewhere. Next, we have data in transit, that's data that's being sent over a wired or a wireless network. A VPN connection will encrypt that data while it's in transit, again, wired or wireless. But once it actually sits on the disk, that VPN does not encrypt that data. That's where you would need data at rest. And then we have data in use, so data that's not at rest, and it's only on one particular node on a network. It's in memory on that server. Could be memory, it could be swap or temp space, but it's being used or accessed at that point in time. Even data that's at rest encrypted, once an application, once the server or an application accesses that data, it unencrypts it, brings it into memory. There are different ways to encrypt these pieces of data, depending upon how sensitive they are, and it will vary from application, it will vary from institution, perhaps regulatory compliance issues as well. But just understand the three different types and where it may fit into your environment.

Chapter 3 Data Masking, Tokenization & Digital Rights Management

With data masking, what we're doing is hiding or obfuscating some piece of data, whether it is in a database or an application, we're hiding that from someone who's not supposed to have access to that component of data. We're giving them access to some of it, but not necessarily all of it. When we're talking about data masking, there's a couple different types. So data masking can be done within applications, databases, at the individual record, row, or the entire table. We can make pieces of data available so someone can use that to test, to try communication, to see how things may work, maybe a query or setting up a development database, maybe iterating through, making changes to some databases, some tables or some applications. They need some data to test to make sure it works. But they shouldn't have access to sensitive data, so we're masking part of that out. In another area, you may hear the term IP address masking - just giving you a few different types of definitions so you're familiar with them. With IP address masking, another term for that might be network address translation or NAT. What that does is, it enables private IP addresses, the IP addresses that are not routable out on the internet, it allows us to use those internally, but then have an IP address that's public facing that masks all of the internal IP addresses. It allows internal hosts right inside of a network to communicate with the outside world without requiring them to have a public IP address or even giving away their internal IP addressing scheme. From the outside world, it all looks like it's coming through that public IP address or that range of public IP addresses. And then also understand that data masking can

19

be static or dynamic, so data at rest or data in transit, and it could be done in a variety of methods, encryption, substitution, nulling, or just zeroing out the data, tokenization. And we'll talk about to organization a little more detail here shortly. But just understand that there are a number of ways that we can hide that data or obfuscate that data from unauthorized viewing. As an example, here we have a database, we have a few databases running, a database engine, and that contains the raw data. That has the data that's actually sensitive and non-sensitive. We have a combination of different things. We have some line-of-business applications that need access to that data, but not necessarily all of it. Some applications or some lines of business may need access to everything; some lines of business may not need access to everything. They may not be authorized to view some of that. What we do is, we put in a dynamic data masking engine. This is one method of doing; it's not the only way. But it's a method that can be use. A data masking engine can be put in line in between the database and line-of-business applications. We couple that with a firewall and, in this case, a firewall with an IDS, or an intrusion detection system. We can then consider that the masked data. Those lines of business applications, when they need to access that data, it will go through the firewall, access a load balancer, and then that goes through the data masking engine so requests are handled appropriately. The applications that may need full access have it; the ones that don't get a subset, and that can be done through encryption, tokenization or nulling. Different systems, different platforms have different methods for doing that, but the end result is the same. As an example, one of those lines of business might do a query, might query the database. The unmasked query result will return good old Alice and Bob, our two old friends, but it also shows their Social Security number. That's a no-no for most areas within the business. There's no need to know that. Even though we have the data there, we don't want to make that data visible, or viewable, to certain lines of business, to certain users or groups. We also don't want to have to maintain separate databases with raw data and then the masked data. If we have to maintain multiple databases, then it becomes problematic to have things kept in sync, what's the actual source of truth. So by masking, we can maintain one database but then just mask the results. In this case, the masked query result would give Alice and Bob, that would either be encrypted or it could be replaced with something else, could be tokenized, and we'll talk about some of these methods in more detail here shortly. But just understand that the result is then unreadable to the person on the other side who's making that query. If they don't have access to that data, they don't get it. When it comes to data masking and tokenization, what we're talking about is this. A tokenization process is replacing sensitive data with a non-sensitive equivalent. The token can be single use, it can be multiple use, it can be cryptographic or non-cryptographic, meaning it's some type of cipher, or can just be replaced with something, maybe a one-time replacement. It can be reversible or irreversible. There's a number of methods to implement tokenization. Then there's two different types. We have high-value tokens, or HVTs. That can be used to replace things like primary account numbers, like PANs, on credit card transactions, and it can be bound to specific devices, so like for instance, an iPhone. It can be bound to that phone That your fingerprint or your face ID, that would be used, that's a tokenization of a credit card, the credit card information. Then we have low-value tokens. LVTs can serve similar functions, but those things actually need the underlying tokenization system to match it back to the actual PAN - a tokenization example.

Let's walk through this. The customer makes a purchase and the token goes to the merchant. The merchant passes that token along to the merchant acquirer, the merchant acquirer passes that token over the network, which is all connected through the financial network, and that data then resides inside of a secure bank vault, an electronic bank vault, in this case. The token vault is consulted to match the token with the customer. It goes back now and actually contact the bank matches things up, makes sure that that token matches with the customer to make sure it's verified. From there, the bank passes it back and says we're good to go. The network passes the token and the PAN, or the primary account number to the bank. The bank verifies funds, and authorizes this transaction. The information is passed back through the network acquirer and to the merchant to complete the transaction. It seems like a lot of things happening behind the scenes, and it is. But if you think about how quickly that actually happens in real life, you go to a point of sale terminal, you pull out your phone, whether it's Android or iOS, and you simply put it up to the card reader, it goes click and verified and the purchase is made that quickly. But the process is nice in that it keeps primary account numbers, credit card numbers, and personal information from traversing the network. It sends that token in its place. Digital rights management, or DRM is a suite of tools that is designed to limit how or where content can be accessed. That can be movies, music files, video files ort PDF documents. That was very big a while back, and it fell out of favor for a while, but there are new systems in place, and there's definitely a need to maintain some type of digital rights management to make sure that assets and products are not pirated or given to people that are not authorized to actually view them. It can prevent content from being copied, it can restrict what devices content can be viewed on, and it also may restrict how many times content can be accessed, say, for instance, on Netflix or one of the movie subscription services as an example. You can either rent a movie or you can buy the movie. If you rent it, you have access to it for a certain amount of time, and it's cheaper than actually buying it. But it's time based, so it may be for a day, a week, a month, however long, and then when that time is up, you can't access it anymore.

Chapter 4 Geographical Considerations & Cloud Access Security Broker

Another concept that I want you to be aware of is encryption. We talked about encryption before, but there's a couple things that I want to make sure you understand when we're talking about hardware-based encryption, encryption keys, and making sure that the information on our systems, whether it's a laptop, a desktop, server, those things can be secured properly. Two things I want to call to your attention. One is called a TPM, or a TPM chip, and that stands for a Trusted Platform Module. And a Trusted Platform Module, or a TPM chip, is a hardware chip that is embedded on a computer's motherboard, and it's used to store cryptographic keys that are used for encryption. We talked about encryption using public key, private key, or some type of encryption algorithm, whether it's symmetric or asymmetric. But those keys can be stored on the actual laptop, the motherboard itself. It's not an area you can access. It's not accessible to the user, but it is there to allow that cryptographic functionality in place. Something else is referred to as an HSM, or a hardware security Module. A hardware security Module is similar to a TPM, but HSMs are removable or external devices that can be added later. So both are used for encryption using RSA keys, and there are two different versions. One is a rack-mounted appliance. One is a card that would actually insert into a computer, a desktop or a server. Those things serve similar functionality but allow encryption of data on that device. When we're talking about architecting for security, there are some things around geographical considerations that you should be aware of as well, or should be in the back of your mind, at least. Where people log into can identify potential security issues. What do I mean by that? Well, logins from geographically diverse areas within a short period of time, unless, A, they're using a VPN and they're logging in from multiple locations in a very short period of time, like East Coast and then 10 minutes later, a half hour later, whatever, from the West Coast, that could be possible. There's really no reason to do that 9 times out of 10, that may raise a flag in and of itself. But logins from geographically diverse areas within a short period of time, so unless they're potentially magic or they've somehow defeated the laws of physics and can travel faster than the speed of light, then there is potentially a red flag. Those types of things should pop up. At least we should have some way of notifying or capturing those types of things and identifying, even better, alerting when those things happen. Also, foreign countries; if we're US based, as an example, and folks on our team always log in from somewhere within the US. They're not traveling abroad, but then all of a sudden there's a login from a foreign country. There should be mechanisms in place to log that and alert upon that, because that should be a red flag. Also unusual or flagged IP blocks. There are ranges of IP addresses that are known to be malicious, that are known to house spammers. Those types of things should also be logged and potentially blocked until it can be remediated or understood why this is happening. Next is something referred to as a cloud access security broker, so a CASB. What is it? Well, it helps control how we access cloud resources, so security policy enforcement points. We have on premise or in the cloud. This thing can be based in either location, and it's placed between the company, the consumer, and the cloud provider. It ensures that policies are enforced when accessing cloud-based assets. What policies are we talking about? Well, these are policies that are set by the company, not by the cloud provider, but our internal company. We may have our own methods, our own procedures, and our own standards for how things are accessed, our own security levels. This allows us to make sure those policies are enforced, such things as authentication, single sign-on, perhaps credential mapping, or even device profiling, and then, logging. All of these things, as a company, we want to make sure we have policies in place, and we can very easily make sure they're followed or enforced locally, within our own internal network. But now when we start accessing cloud-based resources we need to make sure that those policies are enforced as well. Along a similar line, we have something referred to as security as a service. Cloud providers can offer more security services cheaper, typically, or more effectively than on premise. Now that's not always the case. It depends upon the company, the size of your team, the level of expertise. But typically speaking, cloud providers operate on economies of scale, they have massive teams, typically, that have expertise in all of these areas. They can normally provide security as a service cheaper, they're more up to date, they have more resources, a deeper bench. Things like authentication, antivirus, anti-malware, antispyware, intrusion detection, they can offer pen testing services, or even SIEM services, security incident and event management services. It can offer all of these things as a cloud-based service, and it can operate strictly in the cloud, or it can also bridge into our internal networks as well. We can map authentication but we can also provide those services both in the cloud and on prem so that there's a bit of a blurring or no distinction between the functionality between those two environments. You may ask yourself, well, what's the difference between security as a service and a cloud access security broker? Well, we have cloud providers offer their services, infrastructure, resources to extend into a company's network. It's not just in the cloud; it's going to bridge into our network and blur that distinction between the two. They can provide those security services, typically at a cheaper TCO, or total cost of ownership, than the customer organization can. Again, not always across the board, depends upon the organization. Yours may be different. Whereas a cloud access security broker is going to sit between a customer's network and the cloud, and it acts as a broker or a services gateway. What it does is, enforce the customer organization's policies when accessing anything in the cloud. You can see there's a difference between the functionality between the two. Sometimes there is an overlap. Some security-as-a-service offerings may have a cloud access security-broker functionality built in, There is an overlap. But just understand the differences between those two. Can users recover their own passwords, and if so, ensure security questions aren't easily discoverable via social engineering? What do I mean by that? Social engineering can be very specific and can be very diabolical, in that someone can strike up a conversation with someone and in 5 minutes talk about their favorite dog, children's names, what their favorite car is, perhaps a favorite vacation spot, sports figure, just general conversation that seems like it's innocuous. But those things are typically, or at least a lot of times, what people will use as their password, or at least part of their password. It gives a social engineer, and a hacker, a bad actor, whatever you want to call them, it gives them a good starting point to try to guess passwords. If we don't train our users and we don't make them aware of these types of things, then more often than not, they don't know any better and they'll use these things as their password, easily guessable. So by policy, we can define if users need to call the help desk, or if they have a self-service mechanism in place to reset passwords. If they can do it themselves and make sure they're aware of some of the pitfalls and make sure it's complex enough that they can't reuse the same password over and over again or they can just increment it and say, , my favorite dog number 1, my favorite dog number 2. And then also our reuse policy, so they can't use the same two passwords back and forth month to month, back and forth. It just gives attackers and easy in into the network.

Chapter 5 Secure Protocols, SSL Inspection & Hashing

Next, let's talk about secure protocols, so SSL and TLS, two protocols that we should be aware of, Secure Sockets Layer and Transport Layer Security. These two things allow encryption or enable encryption when we're communicating between two hosts on a network. TLS is newer and it's based on SSL, and it also adds confidentiality and data integrity by encapsulating other protocols. We'll dig more into protocols itself later, but suffice it to say here that these are secure protocols that should be used whenever possible and also it initiates a stateful session with a handshake. It helps prevent eavesdropping and people jumping on the network and actually getting hold of that traffic. I mentioned before something called SSL and TLS inspection. That's an on-path type of an attack, formerly known as a man-in-the-middle attack. An SSL decryptor sits in between the user and the server. So both parties think they're connecting securely to each other, the host and also the server or the service that the host is connecting to. But they're actually both connecting to that SSL decryptor as an intermediary device. They're connecting there securely, but that device is acting as a man-in-the-middle or like on-path attack, although it's not really an attack per se because in this instance, it's actually owned by the corporation. It's just there to prevent someone from encrypting data and then sending it out of the network. They're checking it first to make sure that it meets policy. It inspects traffic to block sensitive information leakage, DLP, things like that, and also things like malware and ransomware, because that's becoming more and more common as well, where those things traverse over encrypted communication channels. Another concept I want to make sure you're familiar with is the concept of hashing. Hashing is a mathematical algorithm that's applied to a file before and also after transmission. If we hash a file, then we can tell if anything changes if we match those hashes before and after. If anything changes within the file, that hash will be completely different. There are a few types of hashing algorithms. We have MD5, SHA1, SHA2, and there's some others as well. But as an example, let's use SHA1, and we'll take a hash of a sentence. If you take a hash of that and if we change just one letter in that sentence, it's completely different. There's not even anything that's remotely the same between those two hashes. We can do that before we send something, and we can match it with how it was received on the other end. If those hashes are different in any way, shape, or form, we know that something happened. Either the data got corrupted or it was intercepted. Someone could have perhaps intercepted it, injected it with their own information, and put it back on the network and sent it to its host. These types of things allow us to verify the integrity of what we're sending. They can also be used when you're downloading something from the internet. If you go to a website and they say, here's our MD5 hash or our SHA1 hash or here is the hash. We'll let you download that file, you can run the same hash algorithm against that file, and if they don't match, well, then that you're downloading something that's not the same as what is advertised. Perhaps, again, it was corrupted or it was messed with in transit. So use that as a way to verify what you downloaded.

Chapter 6 API Gateways & Recovery Sites

From an architecture standpoint just some considerations, security vulnerabilities such as authentication, SQL injection, distributed denial-of-service attacks, and also portability between formats. Along those same lines there is something referred to as an API gateway. An API gateway can perform load balancing. It can also perform virus scanning, orchestration, authentication, data conversion, and more. Some of the things that I just talked about can be handled by an API gateway. As an example, let's say we have some back-end services, applications, data, services, and messaging, as an example, this group of back-end services, and then we have some customers that want to consume these services, mobile users, wearable users, smartphones, laptops. Well, we need some type of gateway that sits in between those two. And what's the purpose of an API? To put it very simply, if we're driving a car, we know how to drive pretty much any car out there unless it's something really funky. But generally speaking, you can pop into any car and how to drive it because how to operate the steering wheel. how to operate the gas pedal and the brake and the gear shift. You can think of that steering wheel, brake pedal, gas pedal as the API to the engine of the car. You don't have to know all the inner workings of the engine. You don't necessarily have to know it gets gasoline, does it have a carburetor, is it fuel injected, how many cylinders, any of that information. It doesn't matter which card you get into, it'll have an API, that's the same between different models of car. If we have an API that provides different functionality, the end user doesn't necessarily have to know what happens under the hood. We can change that without them even knowing it. All they have to know how to do is interact with the API. As you can see, the gateway acts as the intermediary piece. It provides that connectivity between the services on the back end and the API to the customer That all they have to understand is how does the API function. They don't need to know anything about the services on the back end. Now let's talk about recovery site options. What I mean when I say recovery site, we have a data center in location A. We need another data center that we can fail over to where we can recover to in the event of some type of disaster. Let's take a look at a few types of recovery sites and see the pros and cons. What's known as a cold site is really an empty building. This is somewhere we can fail over to. We're still going to bring in all of our equipment. We're going to have to move everything over, but at least we have a physical location. The pros, it's very inexpensive because it's just an empty shell, just a building that we have to move everything into. The cons, as you can imagine, long recovery time, could be weeks or even months depending upon the size of the organization, how much infrastructure you have to move. Additionally, all data is lost since your last backup, and do you have the money quickly available to purchase new equipment and/or services to make that move actually happen? Next we have a warm site. That's relatively inexpensive, but you can see the trend here. We have a cold, warm, and then we have hot, which we'll talk about in a moment. But a warm site is relatively inexpensive, but cheaper than a hot site. Some equipment is there, like phone, maybe the networks, but it's not ready for an immediate switchover. Recovery time could be a few days to a few weeks, again, depending upon the infrastructure, size of the company. But at least we have the bare bones are there. Next, we have a hot site. Pros, very quick to fail over and as you can imagine, a hot site is the most expensive of the three options. Infrastructure, replication, all these things

32

that we have set up or want to have set up will come into play as far as determining cost. But just understand that out of the three, this is the most expensive. Duplicate infrastructure must be acquired and maintained. We would more than likely want to make sure that the equipment that is actually there is up to date, is patched, firmware. Replication, costs money. The amount of data that we want to replicate, we may need to have duplicate of everything. And then also bandwidth and location constraints may be in place, so synchronous failover or replication. If we're too far apart, if our data centers are too far away electronically, then that synchronous replication may not be there because of latency. And then, lastly, we have cloud based. Cloud based is more or less like DR as a Service or Disaster Recovery as a Service or cloud DR. It's managed by a provider typically. It's not managed by us. We go with an Amazon or Azure or xBase or Google or whoever your cloud provider of choice may be, it's managed by that provider. They have unlimited backup capacity as far as you're concerned. There's always a limit, but that's on their side. That's for them to worry about. As far as you're concerned, if you pay for it, you have endless backup capacity. Recovery times may be slower. Again, we're going now over the internet to a cloud-based provider. It's not local. It's not on-prem speeds. Another con, there may be confusion around types or best practices. What needs to be on prem? What needs to be off prem? Should we do a hybrid model, a multi-cloud model? But assuming those things are fleshed out, it is a good option, especially for companies that don't need or want to have a lot of extra equipment on site. When we're talking about DR failing over, let's say we have a data center here in Florida, somewhere in Central Florida. Not necessarily the best location as far as hurricane protection is concerned, but not a bad choice overall. So here we have

33

our main data center. We also have a data center in Atlanta, Georgia. Geographically dispersed. We are in separate power grids. However, let's say, for instance, that hurricane that I mentioned just a moment ago starts to come up off the coast of Southern Florida. That potential is there for it to be in the same hurricane path or the path of that hurricane rather taking out both data centers if it were a large enough hurricane. The likelihood is small, but just some things to consider. When we're planning our data center locations, make sure that they're geographically dispersed enough That they can weather these types of storms, these type of events, so power grades, fuel availability, blast radius if it were some type of disaster or terrorist attack. A better option may be to move that data center far enough apart so that they're not in the same type of natural disaster type of zone. If we need synchronous replication, they have to be close enough electronically so we have very, very low latency, round trip time between the sites. If that's not an issue, you could even move it anywhere else within the country so it acts more as a failover bunker, a data ring bunker. It's going to be asynchronous replication because we're too far apart electronically to really have that low latency that we may need for certain applications. Databases, as an example, are typically very latency-dependent or latency-sensitive. But if that's not an issue for you, perhaps you have West Coast customers and East Coast customers, and all you need to do is make sure the data is available in the event of a disaster and doesn't need to be real time, this could be a great option as well.

Chapter 7 Honeypots, Fake Telemetry & DNS Sinkhole

The next concept is something referred to as a honeypot. As the old saying goes, you can catch more flies with honey than you can with vinegar, and the same thing holds true here when we're talking about looking for bad actors. A honeypot is a computer or host that's set up to specifically become a target of attack. We're making it very attractive to bad actors. We want to provide them with a landing spot, somewhere to come in and try to hack through that we're monitoring and keeping a close eye on. That way we can identify the tactics, techniques, and procedures that they're using and potentially even reverse-engineer some of what they're doing. The basics of a honeypot, we want to have it appear to have sensitive information. We also want to make sure that it's monitored, and we want to identify hackers, learn their methods and also their techniques, and then we have something along the same lines referred to as honeyfiles. It's similar in concept, but it applies to individual files versus an actual system, but it's still the same net result. It's designed to entice bad actors and to monitor their activities. Next, we have a honeynet, so similar to a honeypot, but larger in scale. A network setup that's intentionally designed for attack so that the attackers can be monitored and also studied. In this example, we have a network setup that looks very similar to a normal production network. We'll have a publicly-facing infrastructure that the hacker or bad actor would potentially come through. They'll hit our switches. We have management servers set up. We might have a honeywall, which is a firewall designed and specifically monitored with vulnerabilities in mind to allow hackers to come through. They think, ooh, I'm getting something special here. They bust through that firewall or that honeywall, and then they have access to the network that we've set up. And we may have infrastructure that is reflective of a normal production network, Linux hosts, Windows hosts. And at that point we sit back and watch what they do, understand their techniques, follow them through the network, see what they're trying to potentially get to, and it gives us clues as to how they operate and potentially even allow us to trace back to the actual location of those bad actors. Telemetry information is all of the ancillary information that's provided or created by something like, say, for instance, a Tesla car. There's tons and tons of telemetry data, all the different things around that system, electricity consumption, wear and tear on the individual components, speed, so on and so on. All of those things get fed back constantly to corporate, and then they use that data, they mine that data, and then develop patches, understand how things operate. Those types of things happen with everything, cable boxes, cell phones, I mean you name it. Everything generates telemetry data. Well, by generating fake telemetry data, we can have applications that can pretend to be useful utilities when in actuality, they're not. As an example, an anti-virus and anti-malware fake. Those things will actually pop up and claim to find fake viruses or malware. They may show report data that looks very, very convincing. And then what happens, it tricks the user into paying for premium support, i.e. virus removal. It can also install additional malware behind the scenes and actually make things worse. But these applications that are providing that fake telemetry look very, very convincing to the end user if they don't know any better. This is where training and conversations come into play, making sure that people look out for these types of things They don't fall victim. Next we have something referred to as a DNS sinkhole. A DNS sinkhole is a DNS server that supplies false results. You may think, well, that's no good. Well, it can be used constructively or maliciously. It doesn't necessarily have to be a bad thing. Although it sounds like a bad thing at first, it's not necessarily. In most cases, it's not. Example use cases, a DNS server that's operating as a DNS sinkhole can be used for good purposes, as an example, deploying a DNS sinkhole high up in the DNS hierarchy to stop a botnet from operating across the internet. And in a lot of instances, this is how they do that. The botnets that are set up and operate at large, large scales across the internet with thousands of hosts, all of those hosts will typically hit DNS for a domain name, and then they'll respond back to that domain name. Well, if we use a DNS sinkhole, that provides false results, so when that DNS query gets sent, instead of going to the proper host, we actually send it to a another host, that can effectively shut down that botnet or at least for a period of time. In a malicious instance, actors can use a DNS sinkhole along the same lines to redirect users to a malicious website. A user thinks they're visiting CNN as an example, when they think they're actually visiting the correct site. If a DNS sinkhole is in place and they're redirected to a false or malicious website, it may look like the actual website they're trying to visit, but it's obviously not the right one. But when they put in their username, credentials, even though it fails and the user thinks there's a problem with the website, what happens is the bad actor captures those credentials and then can use them for malicious purposes. In summary we talked about security concepts in an enterprise environment. We talked about configuration management, data sovereignty. We talked about data protection, some geographical considerations, along with site resiliency and also some things around deception and disruption with honeyfiles, honeynets and DNS sinkholes.

Chapter 8 Cloud Storage and Cloud Computing

In the following chapters, we'll be covering understanding virtualization and also cloud computing. We'll be talking about cloud models, we'll talk about managed service providers, and we'll also talk about the concept of fog and also edge computing, two new terms you may or may not be familiar with. We'll talk about microservices and APIs or application programming interfaces. We'll also talk about SDN and SDV, software-defined networking and software-defined visibility. We'll talk about serverless architecture and also virtualization. What is the cloud? Well, the cloud is one of those buzzwords, , quote unquote, that everyone is talking about right now, whether it be security professionals and they're talking about the cloud, or application developers need to make their applications cloud ready, or whatever the case might be, everyone is talking about the cloud. Well, the cloud, in a very basic sense, is storage that's external to a company's data center. So you're storing stuff outside of your own data center. It's accessible from the outside world, whether it be publicly accessible to everyone or only people with proper credentials, it depends upon the application, and then you also need to define is it simply storage, or is there automation behind that? In other words, is it just an application that is cloud-enabled, it sits out in some public data center, or is it something that you may offer to your internal customers and give them the ability to provision virtual machines, to provision databases, to provision some type of development environment, whether it might be OpenShift or Cloud Foundry or some type of development environment to allow them to quickly spin up that environment. That all can focus around a cloud infrastructure. And then, as we talked about before, there are different types of clouds. There are public clouds, private clouds, and then a hybrid combination thereof. Cloud, when it refers to a security posture, we need to just understand, really, are there policies in place, are there access controls, as to who can access that data? We need to make sure that we audit third-party providers to ensure that their security practices are at least as stringent as our own. Because remember, we talked about previously, our security, just generally speaking, is really only as effective as the weakest link. So only the strongest is the weakest link. That pretty much goes for anything, but it's especially important with security. It doesn't matter if we have millions of dollars in locks and controls, if on the side, attached to our network, is a third-party hosting provider, and they have abysmal security. Someone could walk right in through the side door and get into our company's network. That doesn't do us much good. We need to make sure that all of these things are lockstep with each other so that we have a consistent security posture. Something else to keep in mind, is the data copied to multiple data centers? When they replicate, most times, they're going to replicate that data to three or more data centers. Is it within the same geographic region, or do they copy that off-site somewhere, or do they copy that out of the country? It's important to understand where that data is being copied to and replicated to from a compliance perspective, but also from a security perspective. As we talk about the evolution of virtualization, cloud computing is really the next step. Cloud computing is the virtualization of infrastructure, platform, and services, and it really just depends upon what level of virtualization and what level of services are being offered to the end user. In a nutshell, it gives us automation and self-service. In a cloud platform, or a cloud environment, depending upon whether it's infrastructure, platform, or software, there is a level of automation and self-service. A user can go in and perhaps provision their own virtual machines, or provision their own databases, or they may be able to provision their own development environment, test their applications, spin up some type of test dev environment. Or they may just go in and just start using an application. It just really depends upon what platform we're virtualizing. It's a reduced time to market, and it also gives us an increased speed to develop our applications and deliver value to the business. Cloud computing is made up of a couple different services. We have infrastructure-as-a-service, or IaaS, platform-as-a-service, or PaaS, and then software-as-a-service, or SaaS. And there are a couple different variations of cloud computing. We have a private cloud, we have a public cloud, a hybrid, and then community. I'll talk about each of these in a little more detail in just a moment. Collectively, though, that's called the cloud. That is just what the cloud is. And it means different things to different people, but in a nutshell, it is a virtualized infrastructure that provides some level of service, and it gives it in an automated fashion. Let's go ahead and talk about X-as-a-Service. When I say X-as-a-Service, what do I mean by that? Well you can insert the buzzword, It means everything these days is turned into a service, as the flavor of the day. It is virtualization and commoditization of almost every layer of the IT "stack". It provides for quicker deployment along with increased HA and DR, HA being high availability and DR being disaster recovery. When I talk about these X-as-a-Service, I'm talking about infrastructure, platform, network, storage, compute, security; you name it, these different verticals are now being turned into a service.

Chapter 9 IaaS, PaaS & SaaS

As an example, let's look at Infrastructure as a Service. Infrastructure as a Service, or IaaS, allows for the distribution and consumption of resources as a service as the name implies. So multiple users can utilize the same infrastructure, hence it's a multi-tenant environment, meaning we can have multiple customers all using that same infrastructure, and it allows you to fully utilize that infrastructure because as some people are using it fully, others are not, and vice versa, so that way the infrastructure itself doesn't sit idle very long. It also allows for elastic scaling as needs and demands increase and decrease. You don't necessarily have to spin up a very large environment at first, you can spin up a small environment, have everything you need for an initial deployment, and then as things start to ramp up, as it becomes more popular, or as let's say for instance you start advertising in certain markets or for whatever reason those things start to speed up and the actual interest starts to heat up and now the service is becoming popular, you can increase dynamically the resources allocated to that service, and then when those things die down, those resources can be destroyed or taken down, leaving you with just what you need. So it allows you to pay for what you need as you go, rather than having to invest a lot in infrastructure right up front. What it does, it prices things as a utility model. It shifts the spend from CAPEX, or capital expenditures, to OPEX, operating expense. It turns it almost into a utility bill. These types of things can also either be private or public or both, you can have a hybrid model. These things can be spun up, as I said, dynamically to adjust to a specific user's needs. Something else I want to make sure that we're clear on is the fact that IaaS lends itself or leverages automation and also self-service. That's one of the milestones of that type of platform. It enables a customer to select their own hardware and software configurations and then provision their own infrastructure. As an example, we have a user who would then access a self-service portal - some website that gives them some ability to pick and choose their configurations. And then from there, they'll typically have sizes that they can pick from, in this case, a small, medium, and a large. A small might have a server with a single CPU and a certain amount of RAM and storage. A medium configuration might have double the CPU and RAM and storage. And then the large might have three or four times that amount of CPU and RAM and storage. It allows for a standardized set of offerings, which makes it very easy to set up and configure, where you can have all your changes pre-approved in change management. These are known configurations, these are known reference architectures, but it gives the user some choice so they can have small, medium, large, or whatever a combination of choices you want to provide to them, but it gives them that option. They can quickly pick and choose. They don't have to worry about configuring and racking and stacking all the things that are typically associated with that infrastructure. They go to the portal, click a few buttons, and then within a few minutes or a couple hours or whatever the approval process is behind the scenes, that infrastructure is then made available to them. It lends itself very nicely to test dev environments or POC environments where we need to spin up some infrastructure to test out an idea, or to build some type of test lab. It ultimately speeds up the time to market considerably. Next, we have Platform-as-a-Service, or PaaS. PaaS environments comprise of computational resources, typically a test and dev environment, or DevOps environment, that can be easily created and configured. In a PaaS environment, you don't care about the infrastructure underlying it. You don't care about how the servers are spun up and how they're racked and stacked, and configured, and IP'd, and access controls, and all those types of things; all you want really in a PaaS environment is to deliver a development platform to your developers They can quickly do what developers do, which is develop applications, iterate through, and deliver some type of service. There's no need to order, acquire rack/stack hardware, configure the network IP addresses, stand up load balancers, VLANS, install software; all of these things are typically associated with an Infrastructure-as-a-Service, a PaaS or a Platform-as-a-Service sits on top of that. All of those things are beneath that layer. Then as you can imagine, test environments can very quickly be created, expanded as needed, and then you can run tests, you can report, and then tear those things down on demand. It allows for a very quick iterative process, and it lends itself very well to a DevOps model. Also, multi-tenant, where many users can use the same set of resources. we don't have to buy a lot of infrastructure, and only when we're using it do we get utility out of it, if we're not using it, someone else is. If we have a multi-tenant environment, we're ensuring that that infrastructure gets utilized much more fully. Just as an example of a few PaaS providers, we have AWS, or Amazon Web Services. They have one referred to as Elastic Beanstalk, Windows Azure or Azure, depending upon who you talk to, Heroku, Force.com, and I'll go through the rest of these or you can read through the rest of these rather. They're all providing some type of Platform-as-a-Service. Some are more mature than others, and I'm not really recommending one over the other. However, we know which one is really the 900 pound gorilla in the room, but there are others and they all provide similar types of services. Next we have SaaS, or Software as a Service, and as you might guess, it's now Software as a Service, meaning we don't have to go out and buy a specific software, we don't have to turn around and install it on our individual servers, Applications that can be provided on demand. No setup, no installation, no configuration required. Much easier than buying, , 300 copies of something and going around in the old days and either sneaker-netting, , installing those things on individual workstations, or putting it on a network share and having people install, or some automated method where we're pushing it out, maybe via group policy or some type of packaging mechanism; Software as a Service, none of that is really necessary. You sign up for it, and we can either access it as a web portal or a web service, or it may download and install on our workstation. Examples might be Salesforce, Office 365, and Google Apps, those are three big ones, there's obviously lots and lots out there, but you get the general idea of what Software as a Service is and how that can make an environment much more agile. From a security perspective, these things work well; however, just understand you may or may not have control over the security that takes place with some of these types of Software as a Service providers, depending upon the agreement you have in place, depending upon where that actual software resides. Just to point out the differences between IaaS, PaaS and SaaS, we have Infrastructure-as-a-Service, you manage from the OS up, and you can see the distinction, networking, storage, servers, and virtualization, that's all managed by the vendor. You manage OS, middleware, runtime, data, and applications, That manages up the stack. Platform-as-a-Service you would manage from the data layer up. You manage the applications and the data. You don't care about the runtime, the middleware, the OS, the virtualization, the racking, stacking, configuring all of those things, you don't care about that. All you want is that Platform-as a-Service or that development environment; and then Software-as-a-Service, you manage nothing. You can see everything is provided by the vendor. Something to keep in mind if you're running a private cloud, then you are the vendor, and the customers, or your customers, are the actual managers, So depending upon where you sit in this scenario will depend upon whether you're the vendor or the manager.

Chapter 10 Managed Service Providers, Fog Computing & Edge Computing

Just to call your attention to the different types of clouds we talked about briefly before, we have a private cloud, and in a private cloud, you manage and maintain all resources. It could be IaaS, PaaS, or SaaS. Then we have a public cloud. A cloud provider manages those resources. That's going to be a hosted platform typically. You control the data, they control the actual infrastructure. Then we have a hybrid model, where we have a public and private mix. Typically, those things will start internally where a company will have a private cloud, and then as things grow, they might expand out into a public cloud, which, allows them that elastic growth where they can expand and contract as necessary. Then we have a community cloud. So, resources are shared among several groups or organizations. They may not necessarily be in the same company, but they may have common goals. Oftentimes companies will group resources so they have access to the same applications. That can be public or private, but costs for that specific cloud are spread across the members of the cloud. Next, let's talk about managed service providers, or MSPs. We mentioned them previously, but just to recap, an MSP, or managed service provider, delivers services either on-prem or at a customer's site, in the MSP's data center, or in a third-party data center, and typically, a managed service provider will provide the following things: they'll do network, application, infrastructure, and then also security. They don't necessarily have to provide all of these things, but they certainly can. When you switch over to a managed service provider, they'll either come in on-prem and manage your infrastructure, manage stuff in your data center, or, you can put it in their data center or a third party. You can think of it as outsourcing your IT department. They're going to take care of application, network, infrastructure, security, storage, compute, all of these things, or a combination thereof. Conversely, a managed security service provider, or an MSSP, they're going to do things around, obviously, security. MSPs provide outsourced monitoring and management of security devices and systems, usually in a 24x7 fashion. Again, you can think of it as outsourcing a piece or the entirety of your IT department. In this case, we're doing security. Things like firewalls, intrusion detection, virtual private networks, or VPNs, also vulnerability scans, anti-virus, antimalware, and ransomware protection, things along those lines. A lot, if not all of these things, can be outsourced and handled by a third party. There is some differences between on-prem versus off-prem, obviously. In an on-prem environment, you own the infrastructure. Whether you buy it as a capital expenditure or you're leasing it, you still, for all intents and purposes, own that infrastructure. It's your equipment. But along those same lines, you also have more control on customization and non-standard builds, so you're not relegated to just the sizes that a managed service provider or someone outsourcing may provide to you. If it's your equipment, your IT department, your everything, then you can build it however you want. That's not necessarily a good thing. We talked before about standardization and how that actually improves things like security, eliminates risk, makes administration easier, but there are instances where you may need to have a custom type of build, and this will allow for that. Also, you have more direct control over policies, management, and administration, as I just talked about. On the downside, you also have a continual upgrade and a continual refresh of that infrastructure. Typically, it's a three year or a five year cycle where you're going to swap out that infrastructure. Depending upon what it is you're replacing, it can be a pretty monumental effort, especially for a large storage array or maybe your SAN infrastructure. Things that have a lot of tie-ins and a lot of dependencies, it's much more of a task to coordinate all of these different teams and make sure that that migration goes smoothly. And then also, depending upon how your company is structured and what you have tolerance for, when you buy your own equipment, it's typically a capital expenditure, or a CAPEX expenditure. Some companies like that, some do not, it just depends upon the individual company. When we're talking about off-prem, you don't own the equipment, it's managed by the provider. Having said that, you have less control over customization, policies, and overall administration, which again may or may not be a big deal to you, depending upon what it is you want to do with that infrastructure. On the upside, there's no lifecycle or maintenance activities, That's a big one. You don't have to worry about constantly refreshing that infrastructure. You don't have to worry about patching and security. That's managed by the provider as well. Lifecycle activities, patching, security updates, anti-virus, antimalware, they actually manage. Then it's also an operating expense, or OPEX, versus CAPEX, and that's good in the fact that you don't necessarily have to buy everything up front. You don't have to buy hundreds of computers or thousands of computers, large storage arrays, SAN infrastructure, and front-load all of that expense. When you buy that in a CAPEX model, you can pay for just what you consume. When you're buying it in a third-party or an off-prem situation, you're not buying the entire storage array. You're only buying what you need. You're not buying hundreds of servers or thousands of servers. You're buying as much as you need. If it's Azure, Amazon, Google, a lot of the bigger cloud providers, they have a very mature elastic capability, so as you grow, or as you need to grow, you can grow dynamically, and then when you don't need all of that infrastructure, it can be collapsed or destroyed That you only are paying for what you need at that point in time. The next term I want to talk about is something referred to as fog computing. Fog computing, along the same lines where we're keeping the theme of the cloud, well, fog computing extends cloud computing to the network edge. It takes the cloud and it makes it a foggy bridge into the local, or at least a part of the local network, or the edge of your individual network. Edge computing we'll talk about more in just a moment as well, but with edge computing we're processing data local to where it was created, That's a subset of fog computing, so keep that in mind. Edge computing we'll talk about in a moment. That's a subset of the overall bigger picture of fog computing. Fog computing is comprised of compute, network, and storage that bridges the gap between everything being in the cloud and then also some stuff on-prem or at the edge of the customer's premise. We take a look at this in more detail. We have the edge, and in the edge environment we may have things like IoT devices, applications, telemetry, information. Those things feed edge networks and they need local low-latency processing, It doesn't make sense to send all of that data all the way back to some central processing area, in the cloud to be processed, analyzed, and then perhaps fed back to the local devices that generated that to make decisions or have some type of interaction with that device. It's a lot of back and forth traffic that's unnecessary. By having things at the edge, all of these devices, they feed into a local or an edge network that can process that in a much more expedited fashion, low latency. In between, we have the fog network, or the fog layer. That's distributing compute, storage, and

49

networking, again, closer to users for real-time processing. We have a bunch of servers and networking, and there's some storage intermixed in there as well. That bridges between the cloud and the edge. It gives us that distributed compute, storage, and networking for things that really require that real-time processing or low-latency applications. Then we have the cloud. The cloud you can think of as a very deep, very large lake that everything can be dumped into. It's great for deep data analytics and processing, also long-term storage and archiving, things like massive parallel data processing, things where we need a very large amount of compute, network, storage, big data mining, machine learning, all of these things lend themselves very well to the cloud, but not the fastest thing out there, and it doesn't actually interact with things on the edge as quickly as it could. So having things in the cloud is great for large scale, then we have an intermediate layer, which is the fog layer. That's going to be for things that are really high speed, low latency, real-time processing. Then down at the edge, that's more or less on the customer's prem, and that's bleeding into their network, so the fog will connect those two layers together. Next we have edge computing, and edge, is sometimes interchanged with fog computing. Edge and fog are sometimes interchangeable, but they're not necessarily the same thing. Edge computing puts resources close to where the data is created, and it's a subset of fog computing. Storage, compute, and network close to the edge. It is a part of it or it works in tandem with fog computing, but as we saw, it's a separate layer. The fog computing layer bridges that gap between the cloud and the edge.

Chapter 11 VDI, Virtualization & Containers

Virtual Desktop Infrastructure, or VDI and VDI provides for centralized hosting of management and desktop images. Users access their desktop from the server. A user will access their actual desktop not on their local PC or their laptop, they will in essence terminal server in to the server, the VDI server, and they will be presented with their desktop image at that point. We have a centralized virtual desktop infrastructure of a VMware vSphere server cluster. We have some link clones, they're going to be our parent image, and we have a golden image, that is, this is what we're giving to either all of our users or we're going to give one image for our developers, one image for our finance folks, one image for our call center; and then we have linked clones that have different sets of applications that are fed on top of that parent image, and then we have some type of presentation server. When that user connects to that desktop, they're either going to have persistent desktops so they can install things, they can install their own software, make their own configuration changes in the look and feel. Or it could be a non-persistent desktop, so when they log off, everything goes back to its original pristine state. The next time they log in, it looks just like it did before. But the benefits of a VDI infrastructure as you might imagine, is the fact that we can manage everything centrally. We can patch all of our desktops in one location, we can make sure that they're all identical, so they can start off with a non-persistent fashion, so every time they log in they get exactly the same desktop. We can create different policies for different groups, so that certain groups, developers, finance, or they'll get different images, but they're all the same as far as within that individual group. It makes it much easier to manage. The only thing they really need to have on their end is a lower-end terminal. They don't necessarily have to have a high-end PC. They can really have a dumb terminal, for that matter, that has no hard drive or so forth. It just has a connection to the Internet or Ethernet jack rather, out to either the local network or the Internet, and as soon as they connect to that presentation server, they're presented with a full-blown desktop. It just makes things easier from the life of an administrative perspective, also from a security perspective. There are some challenges sometimes around bandwidth and connectivity. If the connectivity between the end user and that presentation server is down or congested, then they're going to have some difficulty actually doing anything, it may halt their productivity for a period of time until that's corrected, but the benefits far outweigh the negatives. As far as terminal services go, and VDI is really a component of that, we have two different things to keep in mind here as well. We have terminal services and then we have application delivery services. If we break those into two separate entities, we have application streaming, and here we have an application streaming server. We'll have an operating system, we have app 1, 2, 3, as you might see, and those apps can individually be pushed down to the clients. They run in a virtualized container on that client. Each client has their own full-blown operating system, their full-blown PC or laptop, but the applications that run on top of that laptop or that PC are virtualized containers that are pushed out from the application streaming server. Microsoft's App-V is an example of that. We also have terminal services, which you may or may not be familiar with. Terminal services, everything runs on the server and it's simply displayed to the host. We can have a terminal server that users will use either RDP or Citrix ICA Client, or some type of remote desktop tool. They'll log into that presentation server, everything actually happens on the server, and the only thing that gets sent to the client are graphic updates, when things change on the screen, mouse clicks, keyboard presses. All they really see is the graphical representation of what's taking place on the server. We have the benefit of being able to patch everything from one central location, we can control everything from a centralized location, whether it's a single server or a server farm, we can patch everything at once, It gives us the opportunity to have things in a more secure, a more locked down environment. It depends upon connectivity, bandwidth. You may or may not have connectivity issues or challenges, but if people are working remotely, say from across the state, across the country, or perhaps even globally, if that connectivity is not there, you can halt their productivity until that comes back. So just some things to keep in mind there, but from a security perspective it offers a lot of advantages. The next concept is virtualization, and virtualization is really a big jump forward, in the last 10 years or so we've been able to virtualize pretty much everything. It started off with virtualizing workstations, this moved onto servers and storage, and then networking. All of the main areas within a typical IT department, with a typical IT infrastructure, have now been able to be virtualized, and there's a number of major players in that space that you should just be aware of. I'm not endorsing one over the other, but VMware, Microsoft Hyper-V, KVM, and Oracle all have their own virtualization platforms, and what virtualization really does, it takes the capabilities and the personality of a physical device and it converts it to a virtual representation. Meaning we can take a PC or a server, all the physical attributes, all the things that you typically associate with that server, the amount of CPU capability, the processor, the network, the amount of RAM and so on; we can virtualize that and place it into a container, if you will, onto another server. In other words, we could take 5, 10, 15, 20 physical servers, virtualize those, and put those virtual representations or those virtual containers onto a single server, in this instance, let's just say like a VMware ESX cluster. We could take a number of servers, put them onto one physical box. That's going to allow us to perform the same functions as the physical counterpart. It will lower our infrastructure costs because instead of having to buy 20 or 30 servers now, we can simply buy 20 or 30 licenses and put them on a single physical server or a cluster. So, we're going to lower infrastructure costs; however, you'll notice that we're going to increase licensing costs, the hypervisor license for those individual VMs. In a traditional server, we have the server at the bottom. We install an operating system on top of that server, and then we install our applications on top of the operating system. That's just a typical server rollout or a typical workstation. In a VMware or a virtualized environment, it works the same amongst all of the virtualization platforms. We have our server or our cluster of servers, we're going to lay the hypervisor on top, in this case, in this example it's VMware, and then on top of that, we're going to lay down individual VMs, and each of the guests are comprised of an OS and an app or multiple apps. We're in essence, taking what used to be a physical server, virtualizing that into a single container, and dropping that on top of our hypervisor. In this VMware example, we have an ESX cluster, you'll notice four servers in our cluster. We have our VMware OS on top of that, it's a virtual symmetric multi-processing operating system. We have in this example four VMs sitting on top of that. We have one with four cores, one with one, two, and then one. Each one of our VMS are individual, they're distinct entities just as if they were physical servers and they can have their own number of processors, their own amount of memory, own amount of storage and so on; and we can dynamically dial that up or down. If we find that we have a VM that's not really performing as well as it should, we can actually add more processors or more processing power, or more memory to that VM, dynamically. In some instances, depending upon the software, it might require a reboot, but regardless, we can add resources to that rather than having to go out and buy a new physical server. On the ESX cluster itself or the ESX host, we have a pooled or a set of pooled resources. CPU, memory, storage, and network, all of that is shared among all of the VMs sitting on that ESX cluster. Instead of having a physical server for every application, let's say we have five databases, instead of having five physical servers like we would do in a traditional environment, we can have one ESX cluster and then five VMS. That way each of the VMs are much more fully utilized, and the actual EXS cluster, the physical hardware, is much better utilized. We also reduce power, cooling, heating and cooling and so on. There are a few different types of, or categories of servers, virtualized servers, that we should be aware of. First is Type I. A Type I virtualized server runs on bare metal, it's a bare-metal server. And guests run on that host, which is the actual ESX, in this case the VMware ESX server, that's going to run on a bare-metal server. In other words, there's no operating system underneath of that. The VMware ESX server has his own operating system, so that gets loaded onto that bare-metal host. That host can then run individual guest operating systems. That individual guest can be Windows or Linux or some other variation, it doesn't have to necessarily be just the same type of OS that the ESX server itself is. The ESX server, in other words, might be a Linux installation or a Linux flavor under the hood. However, it could run Linux, Windows on top. Each of those is its own virtual server. It's got its own operating system, its own drivers, its own binaries, and applications. It gets a virtual NIC, or network interface card, it gets its own IP address, so for all intents and purposes, it is a separate server. It appears to the outside world as a separate, distinct entity. A Type II server runs on top of an OS. It runs on top of the OS, which runs on top of the bare-metal box, the bare-metal server. The host runs on top of an operating system, Windows or Linux, and then the guests run inside of that host. We have VMware Workstation or a Virtual Box, Oracle's Virtual Box are good examples of this. The guests run at a third layer above the hardware. In the first example, we had those guests running at the second layer above the hardware. In this instance, they run at the third layer above the hardware. We have a bare-metal server, we have our Windows or Linux operating system, and then we have VMware Workstation or Oracle Virtual Box or some other type of virtualization software running, and then inside of that we have our individual operating systems, They're distinct operating systems within that Type II virtualized infrastructure. And then to contrast that we have something referred to as container-based or containers. That is an operating system virtualization. It's very lightweight. These containers can start up in milliseconds, whereas typically, just as you would imagine with a server when it boots up and has to load the BIOS or the UEFI interface, it has to load the drivers. Then it loads the actual operating system, and then all the applications, and then the drivers inside of that. It can sometimes take 10 to 15 seconds or more up to 30 seconds or a minute, depending on how old your system is, for that operating system in that server to fully boot. Well, in a container-based world, those things can spin up extremely fast. They're very lightweight, and they can start up in milliseconds. It's a little bit different approach than we saw in Type I and Type II. We have our bare-metal server, we have our operating system, and then on top of that are containers. Those containers only really have the application and the binaries. Those data boxes contain the libraries and the binaries that the applications need to run. It's not a full-blown operating system. You can spin up containers, if you will. These containers, these little micro segments of the things that are needed for that application, they can spin up very quickly. They can expand as needed to provide additional resources, they can contract just as quickly when those resources are not necessary. It allows you to elastically expand out and provide infrastructure, provide services when the demand gets high, and then it contracts when it's not needed. In the VMware, you'll see we have our host OS, which sits on top of the server. There's a hypervisor then that sits on top of that. From there, we have our guest OS, our binaries and libraries, and then application, Application A. Then we have a separate guest that has its guest operating system, binaries, libraries, and then Application B. We can have multiple guests running on that host, or that VMware ESX server. In the container example we have our server and our host OS, and then on top of that we have something referred to as a Docker Engine in this container example. From there, we have Application A, Application B, C, and so on, each of which only contain the binaries and the libraries necessary for that application. You can deploy very lightweight, you don't have to worry about patching all the things that a typical operating system would need to be patched, and virus updates. It's only the things that are specific to that application. It allows you to expand very quickly, and those containers can also run on any operating system or any platform that has that Docker engine. You provide the binaries and libraries for that application, but it allows you to deploy to pretty much any type of infrastructure that hosts a Docker-like container system. Its very scalable, and it can contract just as quickly. From a security perspective, the advantages of this would be you don't have to patch a bunch of different operating systems, you don't have to patch individual OS's and all of these containers, you're providing a bare minimum of what's necessary to run that application. But even to take a step back for our Type I and Type II's, it's an advantage in the fact that we can patch from a centralized location. We can go to our ESX server and patch all of the hosts on that server relatively quickly - same thing if we start to have a resource contention or we understand that things are starting to slow down on a specific ESX host, we can migrate that data and those workloads. We can migrate those VMs from one ESX server to another, it's called vMotioning, and in doing so, we can free up resources on the ESX server that's exhibiting contention. It gives us the ability to scale when necessary, we can move things over. If we need to patch the actual ESX host itself, we can migrate the workloads off to another ESX server. We can then bring that ESX server down, patch it, upgrade it, do what we need to do, and then once it comes back up, we can migrate or vMotion those VMs back over again, It gives us a very convenient way to patch our systems with minimum downtime. The takeaway here, however, is to understand what is a Type I, Type II, and container-based virtualization, and the general benefits and disadvantages, as far as security is concerned, from each of these platforms.

Chapter 12 Microservices and APIs

With microservices what we're doing is taking an application and breaking it apart into individual functions. Microservices treats each function of an application as an independent service that can be altered, updated, taken down without affecting the rest of the application. It's easily maintained. Each function or each service, or microservice, is loosely coupled and extensible, It can be changed, added, increased or tweaked in some fashion without affecting the other components, and it's also independently deployable. If we look at this in a little more detail, typically considered legacy, we have what's called a monolithic architecture, and in there we had a user interface, business logic, a data interface, maybe a backend database. If we wanted to add features or functionality or change anything on that application, we had to change everything - the entire application, because it was treated as one monolithic thing. With microservices, on the other hand, we have a microservices architecture that breaks all of that apart. All of the individual main functions, business logic, data interface, all of those things now become microservices, and each of those can be developed independently, they can be deployed independently, and they can scale independently. They all talk to one another in some fashion. One can be pulled out or updated and then redeployed without affecting the rest of the application, It allows for very quick and easy updating, and also it allows the application to scale very easily. If we look at this in more detail, let's say, for instance, we have a mobile app, and then we have an API gateway, an application programming interface. Normally, that's how we'll interact with a microservice in some fashion. The mobile app may connect to that API gateway via a REST API. Conversely, we have a web browser. It's going to connect to a storefront, which is a web application. Again, it will do that over the web. Well, on the backend, via REST APIs, we're connecting to different services, different microservices, which then connect to databases on the backend. Whether we come in via a mobile app or a web browser, we're still typically interacting via some type of API between where we're at and the information that we're interacting with on the backend. Whether we come in through a mobile app, and we're doing it through a REST API, or we're coming in through a web browser through some type of web frontend, once it hits the backend and starts to go into the account services and the microservices and all the infrastructure behind, there's APIs in place that allow all of these things to connect and talk to each other, but they're also loosely coupled so that one can be pulled out, updated, tweaked, expanded or scaled or even reduced without affecting the rest. Some microservices key points, some things that I want to make sure that you take away from this, is the fact that applications are broken apart by function. No longer is it a monolithic app that has every single thing packaged together as one entity, we now break things apart. All services are created individually and deployed separately from one another. Next, each component is loosely coupled, so different groups even can develop different functions and different services. Not one group has to work on an application, it could be spread across, and each service can be changed or upgraded without affecting the others. It can even be scaled. It deployed via containers, typically, we have something like Kubernetes and Docker for orchestration, or some other type of orchestration engine, then each microservice is packaged as a container image, and then as we scale, it quickly scales because scaling is done based on the changing number of container instances. If we need more, we just spin up more containers so we can handle more load, and additionally, we can spin up or scale down each individual microservice. It doesn't have to be done across the board. If all we need is database processing or some type of interaction with maybe networking or a decision engine or a recommendation engine or whatever that service might be, that specific service can spin up independent of all the others.

Chapter 13 Infrastructure as Code (IAC) & Software Defined Networking (SDN)

Infrastructure as Code is a methodology to create repeatable processes for deploying infrastructure. What it does is it replaces static scripts, and the point is here, we're trying to move away from static scripts where everybody maintains their own repository of information of scripts and the way they do things, and more or less make it standardized and deployable across the enterprise, so code can be reused between groups. Collaboration and automation tools like Puppet, Chef, Ansible, there's a number of them out there, can speed delivery. It can make things faster, it can make things standardized across the environment, and it also reduces shadow IT, and it makes processes more secure and reduces the risk of human error. The more we can derisk the environment, the better off we are. Next, let's talk about SDN, or Software Defined Networking. What this does, much like we talked about with microservices, this decouples the management plane from the data plane. We're breaking things apart. It places intelligence higher up the stack. The switches that used to have all the intelligence in each individual switch or each individual router, now those things almost become dumb devices, and all of the intelligence is placed up at a controller at a higher level that can control all of the switches, all of the routers, all of your networking infrastructure as a single unit. It's a holistic view of the network, and programmatic tuning could take place based upon activity, on workloads. So, routers and switches, more or less become dumb devices with the intelligence handled by a centralized controller suite. We're simply moving that administration up the stack, Instead of having to go into each individual switch, each individual router and configure things, we can now do things up at a higher level and push those changes out to the entire network at once. Along those same lines is something referred to as Software-Defined Visibility, or SDV. What this is, is a "visibility fabric," in quotes, that can be in-line or out of band and monitor the entire network. So proactively responds to events and can adjust traffic, it can do traffic shaping, it can shut down ports, it can log or alert if specific things happen, it can then turn on maybe different functions, it could start to capture traffic. It could perhaps turn on some type of decryption or inspection device to inspect SSL. So based upon certain things happening, it can proactively take action to make the network more secure, more functional, guard against errors, intrusions. Next, let's talk about something referred to as serverless architecture. With a serverless infrastructure, the underlying infrastructure is abstracted from the user. When you think of infrastructure-as-a-service or platform-as-a-service, IaaS or PaaS, those things abstract the infrastructure from the user. But now we're taking it even a step further and taking all of the infrastructure out of the picture, The only thing you have to worry about is the code. So only the code is managed and deployed, and that can scale at the individual call level. We no longer have to worry about spinning up instances of operating systems or infrastructure rack and stack, don't have to worry about the server at all. All we have to worry about is the function itself, and each individual function, each time it's called, that can scale independently. So having this in place allows you to only pay for the times that the function is called versus paying for an application to be always on and waiting for requests. IaaS and PaaS as an example, you pay for the infrastructure, you turn on a virtual machine, it's on, it's generating income for the host or for the hosting provider, because as long as that is on you're getting billed for it, whether it's used or not. If it spins up, obviously there's more cost associated, but simply having it turned on has a cost. When we do serverless architecture or when we do serverless computing, all we're worrying about is processing our functions, and we only pay for when that function actually gets called. Serverless providers, as an example, there's a few big ones out there. Amazon Web Services, AWS, has one called Lambda, Microsoft Azure has functions, and Twilio also has functions. There are three serverless providers for you to take a look at, maybe dig a bit deeper and understand more under the hood how these things work. It's beyond the scope to really dig too deep into it in this book, but just understand the basics of what serverless architecture is and how that can benefit you - the pros and cons versus things like IaaS or PaaS. To put all of these in context as to who manages what and where in the stack, we talked before about infrastructure-as-a-service. The first four layers, networking, storage, servers, and virtualization is managed by the vendor, and then you manage everything above that, operating system on up. Platform-as-a-service, it goes higher up the stack, then vendor manages most of that. You manage the functions, or the code, what's being called, in the application. When we're talking about function-as-a-service, or serverless computing, which is what we just talked about, the only thing that you're responsible for, or the only thing that you manage, is the function, the call itself. Everything else, the application, the runtime, middleware, all of the rest of the stack is managed by the vendor. Then we have software-as-a-service, or SaaS, and there everything is managed by the vendor. All you do is consume that service. So just understand all of the things that make up an application or make up a service, where they fit within this continuum, what parts you manage, and what parts the vendor manage.

Chapter 14 Service Integrations and Resource Policies

Next, a few more terms that I want you to be familiar with. We have services integration and resource policies. Services integration; many cloud providers provide services like database, network, maybe AI or ML, serverless or function-as-a-service, facial recognition, communication services, whether it's audio, video or messaging. Those services integration and all the other microservices associated with that, database connectivity, Amazon, Azure, the larger cloud providers, have thousands of microservices, and they're adding new ones all the time. Their services can be integrated with your applications. The only downside to keep in mind with these things is when you build an application in a specific cloud, like Amazon as an example, if you build it completely on their microservices architecture, for all the services that they provide, it becomes much more difficult to pull that application back out of that cloud. Not impossible, but it takes a lot of retooling. So just understand services integration where it fits in with the grand scheme of things. Does it lock you into that vendor? Does it make portability more difficult? Then when it comes to resource policies, so policies can be managed on-prem or in the cloud, and they can enable dynamic resource deployment, monitoring, management, asset reclamation. All of these policies can be defined, again locally, they can be just an on-prem thing, or if you have cloud integrations, you can integrate them with services, you can integrate them with policies, standardize where possible, make it as standard across the environment as possible, and that helps reduce risk and human error. Next, let's talk about a transit gateway. A transit gateway connects virtual private clouds, or VPCs, with on-premise networks. A transit gateway controls how traffic is routed among all the connected networks in what's known as a hub and spoke architecture. If we have a number of VPCs, virtual private clouds, we have a transit gateway connecting to a firewall, or a firewall/VPN, which then connects to a customer gateway and our customer network. It allows us to connect our network with Amazon's cloud or Azure's cloud or Google's cloud, or put it in your cloud provider of choice, but it allows us to extend our network into that cloud network, and vice versa. Something else I want you to be familiar with is the concept of VM sprawl. VM sprawl is a large number of virtual machines on a network without proper IT management. This happens a lot of times because various departments and users will create their own virtual machines without proper procedures or lifecycle management. In other words, you may have a proof of concept, they may have a temporary project, or just trying things out, they'll spin virtual machines up, they forget that they're actually on and consuming resources. A few ways to avoid VM sprawl is define a virtual machine policy, so this boils down to strict IT policies around resource allocation and also their use. That will help ensure standardization and also awareness of assets. Next, create standard VM templates. Standardized templates help with providing users what they need, as well as proper naming conventions, and it makes it easier to identify VM owners, and also their purpose. Then implement lifecycle management, so ensure temporary or short-term resources are reclaimed on time to ensure that virtual machines aren't created and then forgotten about. We talked about spinning things up, and then they just sit there and consume resources. Then also, routinely audit, so auditing of the environment enables discovery of assets on the network and also works in tandem or facilitates proper lifecycle management. So don't just assume that we have these

66

things in place, we have a policy in place, we have templates in place, all is well with the world. That's great, and that's obviously a great start, but we need to routinely audit to make sure those things are being adhered to, and then if things are spun up outside of those policies or outside of those templates, we capture that and then lifecycle them properly. A VM escape is an attack that enables the attacker to escape out of their VM, hence, the term VM escape, that allows them to bust out of jail. They're going to escape that VM and access resources on the actual host server. They could potentially interact with the host server or other VM guests being hosted on that server. If we have an attacker VM, VM2, VM3, VM4. We have other guests on that host operating system. So, if that in fact happens, and the attacker in that VM is able to exploit a specific mapping function and is able to change where that mapping function points to back on the host OS, the host hardware, back on that server that it's actually running on, they can remap and jump from one VM to another. Resources on section 1 of that shared resource, they can remap from one to the other and then, in a sense, jump up into the other VM, and they can access resources in the other virtual machine, and also potentially access resources on the host itself. That's something to be concerned with. VMware, VirtualBox, Hyper-V, they're all aware of these things, and most of these vulnerabilities are mitigated as they come out. As we know, with any security threat, they're constantly evolving. You need to be aware of what VM escape is, what is currently available to mitigate these risks, and make sure that you're keeping an eye on your own environment to make sure these things are not introduced and running wild, or at least unchecked. Then you should check your own virtual infrastructure in your own virtual environment to make sure you're not susceptible to these types of attacks. In summary we talked about cloud models and their various types. We talked about managed service providers, and then fog and edge computing, the concept of each, and how they tie into cloud computing. We talked about microservices and APIs and how they function and make things interconnect, help us break large applications down into subcomponents and make them much more deployable and much more scalable. We also talked about Software-Defined Networking and Software-Defined Visibility, and then serverless architecture, and also virtualization.

Chapter 15 Environments, Provisioning & Deprovisioning

In the following chapters we'll be covering implementing secure application development, deployment, and automation. We'll be talking about the various types of environments. We're talking about testing, staging, QA and production. We'll be talking about provisioning and deprovisioning resources. We'll talk about integrity measurement and what that means. We'll talk about secure coding techniques and some things to keep in mind when coding for security. We'll talk about the OWASP specifications or the Open Web Application Security Project, along with software diversity, automation and scripting. We'll talk about elasticity, scalability, and also versioning control. Let's look at the various environments that we can deploy into. We have four we want to talk about here. We have development, we have testing, also staging, and then production. Depending upon the place you may work in, production may be all three of these for you. If at all possible, let's not have that situation. We want to have a separate environment we can test in, whether it's a virtualized environment. It could be small. It doesn't have to be an exact replication of production, but it should give us the ability to test separate from production so we don't affect things negatively. Let's talk about each of these in a little more detail. For development, that's we're going to do initiation and requirements gathering. So developers can work independently of each other in this environment. We're not necessary looking to have a big, gigantic team effort yet. We want our requirements gathered and then developers potentially working in independent work streams to that finished product. At some point, we'll collaborate and bring things together. But at the initial stages, they may be working in separate streams. The intent, is to eventually merge those streams into a combined system. Next, we have the test environment. Testing can take different forms and can be integrated throughout all phases. It's not necessarily a separate phase in and of itself. We should be testing along the way to make sure that we're meeting objectives. A testing environment is an area typically that's prior to or lower than a staging environment. Code usually runs on a single system or a very small or an isolated environment. Bugs are identified, processes and systems are modified, and resolved. This can be an iterative process that goes on and on again. The process doesn't have to be, but best results are achieved when that process is iterative. Next, we have staging. Staging is a production-like environment that we can use to test. We're going to test installation, configuration, and migration scripts. In staging, we may do performance testing. We may do load testing. We may have an application to do that. We may have a piece of infrastructure or a piece of hardware that would generate load, and we can turn it up or down, add additional users, add additional processes to make sure that our system that we're creating can actually handle that load, not just initially, but as things ramp up, as that system scales. Also any processes that are required by other teams, boundary partners, we want to test to make sure that we're not just developing in a vacuum. We want to make sure we're interoperating correctly with our boundary partners and with other teams to make sure the stuff that we do doesn't negatively impact them and vice versa. Then we have production. And production, as , is a fully functioning live environment. Most costly when errors are encountered here. This is the last place we want to encounter an error. We want to figure those things out in testing or staging if it all possible. Changes can be rolled out completely into production, or we can still do it in phases.

We can have pilot rollouts that still go into production, but it's going to a smaller group. It doesn't necessarily have to go across the board everywhere in one shot. It should go through change management. That change management board or that change management process should have a holistic view of all potentially competing changes taking place. Avoid change collisions aimed at the same system. You may work in a small environment. They may only have a few changes per night or a few changes per week. Or you could work in a very large enterprise that may have hundreds of changes or even thousands of changes per week. It just depends upon the environment, but the process is the same. There should be a group sitting on top of all of those changes to make sure that two different groups that may not even know about each other or the work that they're doing are going to impact a similar system. Additionally, they should know that the systems that are being modified, how they interrelate. That's where something like a CMDB or a configuration management database comes into play because if that is fully configured and fully populated, you can test or you can least look at the cascading impacts of changes That all the things, all the systems, applications, programs, infrastructure, how they all interrelate. If we go ahead and take a look at all these environments and we break them down or look at them and how they flow, we'll see that we have some Dev Teams here. This is going to be our development environment. We have Dev Team A, Dev Team B. And they may be working independently of each other at this point. They're not working at a cohesive system, they're working on individual components that will eventually be brought into and collaborate with to build some type of common system or some type of common end product. So from there you'll see there's a lot of interdependencies that are going on within those separate groups. They'll then take their work products and push those out to the QA Team. The QA Team then will go through its iterative testing process, and it will go through and look for functional dependencies and all the things that make the system at this point functional. It's either go or no go. It's very early in the process. They're looking at it, is it meeting the requirements at this point? From there, it gets pushed down to the test environment. The test environment does fully functional testing and system testing. You have a lot of client PCs, you'll see some laptops down here. They're going to be doing user testing, and they're testing against those databases, those systems, functionality overall. Those results get pushed up to a test results database where things are tracked. They will typically also get entered into some type of bug tracking system. That bug tracking system creates a feedback loop, and you can see it goes down and filters back into the development teams, and they can work through those bugs in an iterative process. Once it hits a certain stage, it then goes into staging. That's the final check area. That's where you'll look at all the piece parts and say, is the installation, the configuration, the scripts, any type of migration things, are all of those things fully functional? If they are, then it gets pushed into production for deployment. If not, it may go back to QA, it may go back to test. Depending upon what bugs are discovered, it may be an iterative process where it goes through this feedback loop over and over and over again, It may not be just a continuous stream from Dev to QA to test to staging the production, it may go from Dev to QA to test and back again and loop through for a number of cycles until it hits something that's then staging ready. Then from there it goes into production. Even at that point, when it goes into production, it may not go out to everybody at once. It may go on a pilot or a phased deployment. That way we're deploying to a small subset of our production users first, get their feedback, make sure everything is OK, we didn't miss anything, and then it gets rolled out to the larger production environment. Next, let's talk about provisioning and deprovisioning. What are we talking about here? Well, we're talking about commissioning and decommissioning. Bring something onto the floor or into our environment and then removing that thing from the environment. In this instance, we have a happy day - a new asset is installed. When we do that, we want to make sure we know when does that actual asset go end of life as well? We want to have an end-of-service date in mind, we want to do security scans, and we also need to have an MOP or a methods of operation for those daily operations or a runbook so we know how that asset functions and how it operates. Then also periodic auditing. We want to make sure all these things just set up. There's a cadence in place. There's processes in place to make sure that it's a methodical, predetermined process that we follow each and every time. Again, following things in a very systematic approach mitigates risk. It takes out the human error. Conversely, the sad day is when we're going to have that asset be decommissioned. We're not just going to push it off the dock and say farewell. We're going to go through a series of processes. All the data is migrated to a new platform, whether it's a server, whether it is a storage array, piece of infrastructure. Right now we're not talking about the DevOps model where we're treating servers or infrastructure more like actual livestock than pets. If something goes wrong, we don't worry about trying to figure things out. We don't log in and try to fix it. We just rip it out and put in a new one. We're talking about things here that are a little more substantial, potentially. That asset needs to be formally decommissioned. We'll determine does that data need to be migrated off to something new, or is that old data no longer needed? If so, the asset is wiped and purged as per policy. We want to use some type of wiping mechanism That data is not recoverable. Then the asset is disposed of properly. Now when we're talking about asset disposal, proper asset disposal is critical to maintain security and also to ensure that confidential data is removed. We have data wiping or purging, data wiping is different than just deleting. When we're wiping something, we're overwriting. Three, as per the Department of Defense or DOD, 5220.22-M, that is a guideline that says how many wipes or how many passes of a wiping mechanism actually secures that data beyond being recoverable. A three-pass wipe is an acceptable number of passes as per DoD standards. And then also an option would be the physical destruction of drives. We could throw them into a gigantic shredder and actually literally shred those drives.

Chapter 16 Integrity Measurement & Code Analysis

Next, let's talk about integrity measurement. It is an open source alternative that creates a measured runtime environment. We talked about TPM before. Well, this ties in with that. It creates a list of components that need to load. When we're booting our system, it's going to know exactly what needs to load and will not allow other things to load or be injected into that process. It's going to anchor that list to the TPM chip, we talked about that previously, to prevent tampering. That way it has a list. It's like when you walk into a club and the guy at the front door has a list, and if you're not on that list, you're not getting in. Well, very similar here. There's a list of things that can run. And if you're not on that list, it does not allow it. It blocks it from executing. That way it ensures that you have a secure environment upon bootup. What it also does is prevent sophisticated or targeted persistent attacks because, as we know, hackers can implement processes that will inject themselves very, very early in the boot process. It could potentially sit in the boot firmware or the master boot record of a device. As soon as that device boots up, that attack or that threat is already injected in the process, and they're already in before antivirus gets a chance to load, before other processes get to load. Ensuring that secure boot process prevents those injections from taking place, those persistent attacks from being actually injected into the system. We also have something referred to as the roots of trust. Now it's beyond the scope of this book really to dig into this, but I want you to be aware there's really three main components, a measurement, a storage, and reporting component. And what those things do, again, is tie into that root of trust or that boot process so that we know that everything that builds upon that is secure, or at least we can tell when that chain breaks down. If it starts off and the very beginning is compromised, then nothing after that can be guaranteed. So by having the roots of trust and having a measurement component, a storage component where those things are being stored securely, and reporting that we know if and when things change, it gives us the ability to start off securely and then go from there. Previously, we talked about static code analysis. That's also known as source code analysis. It's part of a code review process for something that's referred to as white-box testing. It allows you to see under the covers. It's also part of the implementation phase of the security development lifecycle or the SDL. It finds vulnerabilities in non-running code. It's static code analysis. We're looking for those vulnerabilities, either through taint analysis or data flow analysis. Data flow analysis is used to collect runtime or dynamic information about data in software while it's in a static state. Taint analysis, on the other hand, attempts to identify variables that have been tainted by user-controllable input and then traces that to possible vulnerable functions, also known as a sink. If a tainted variable gets past to a sink without first being sanitized, it gets flagged as a vulnerability. As I said, we're looking for vulnerabilities, looking for input, sanitization, looking for places where the user the ability to control that input. If they can put in something, this is where SQL injection and cross-site scripting attacks come into play, if they're able to use some type of technique, either as fuzzing or just straight up SQL injection, they can try every single possible combination of codes, letters, characters. If that is successful, that code does not get sanitized, it can crash a system or have unintended results. This data flow analysis and this taint analysis allows us to go in and really identify these things ahead of time. It's part of the defensive posture that we need to take as IT security professionals. Now does every IT security professional know all of these different things? No, not. There are areas of specialization obviously. But it's important for you to have a general concept and a general understanding, number 1, to know is this an area I want to go into. Number 2, even if it isn't, you need to have those conversations with the people that are responsible for this. And if you don't know about it, it's hard to have that conversation. As an IT security professional, it's important to have a good understanding of everything, not a deep dive, but a good understanding so who to talk to, who to coordinate with, whether they're developers, pen testers, coders, your DevOps folks, your IT security folks, your infrastructure folks, all the different lines of business . You can reach out to all these different areas, coordinate efforts, and make sure everyone is on the same page and everyone is working towards the same goal. Let's now talk about secure coding techniques. The goal of this chapter was not to make you a very highly-skilled coder. We're not deep diving into the actual nuts and bolts of coding here. But the general concepts, the general mindset behind the coding so that as an IT security professional, you can have those conversations with the DevOps folks and with the coders and make sure that these concepts are being followed. So secure coding techniques; proper error handling. We need to make sure the errors don't crash the system obviously, allow for elevated privileges, or expose unintended information. So having these discussions, again, with programmers and with coders, understand, ask the questions, show me how error handling works. Show me what happens if unintended input is entered. What happens if the system crashes? What does it actually give back to the end user? Proper input validation is another. We want to make sure that we sanitize the data to mitigate such things as cross-site scripting and cross-site forgery requests. If someone goes into a web portal, we want to make sure that data is sanitized they can't put in some rogue piece of information and get unintended results back. Also, normalization on the database back end. We want to ensure database integrity and optimization of data. Now you may ask yourself, what does this have to do with security? Well, normalizing the database ensures that there are no insertion or deletion anomalies. Downstream impacts might be if something gets deleted improperly or if something gets added improperly and now our database and our tables are out of sync, it could return unintended consequences or it could have unintended consequences and return unintended data. Normalization is key. Also we have stored procedures. We want to utilize vetted, secure procedures verses writing new code on the fly. Whenever possible, reuse code if appropriate or use stored procedures that have been vetted and are known to be secure. Next, code signing. We want to ensure that validated and trusted code is used. We want to mitigate risk from unsigned code being allowed to run because, again, if we allow things that have not been vetted, have not been signed, we don't know where that's coming from or we don't trust it. If we allow those things to run, we introduce risk, potential for malware, potential for spyware, ransomware, you name it, unintended results. Hackers can use these things to try to crash the system, inject code in the application. So unsigned code is a no no. Encrypting the data, that's going to mitigate the risk of compromise should the actual computer go missing, lost, or stolen, or the drives housing the data become lost or stolen. Then we have obfuscation or camouflage. This goes hand in hand with encryption. Masking the data, encryption is an example, to avoid detection by static code analysis. That typically involves such things as a decoder and the encoded payload. You can look at these things in one of two

78

ways. Encryption is going to obviously keep the data out of prying eyes, but it also keeps someone from potentially reverse-engineering what we're doing. If we encrypting our code or obfuscating, otherwise camouflaging that code, they can't do static code analysis against that program and spot potential errors. It goes both ways. Those two things can either work for you or against you, depending upon which side of the fence you're sitting on. And then we have code reuse and dead code. Code reuse is simply code that can be reused, as the name implies, for some future use, future project. The challenge becomes when people try to write code that they can reuse later, they start to bring in things that may not be necessary for the project they're working on. They're trying to think of future uses or future bugs they might encounter or future issues they may come up with. They try to write code that is going to counteract those things when, in reality, they're probably not going to capture all those things anyway. But by focusing on what's right in front of you, you stand a much better chance of writing a very clean, secure piece of code. Server-side versus client-side. Take into account where validation, input sanitation, where those things occur and the way those controls can be bypassed. Server-side versus client-side depends upon where those things, where those validations and those sanitizations take place. They're easier to bypass on the client side than it is on the server side typically. Where we have the option, server side is typically better. Not always. There's always exceptions to every rule. But just some things to think about, so the conversations to have with the coders when you're discussing how the applications work and how they function. Next is memory management. That's going to ensure that code calls and manages memory properly to avoid heap and buffer overrun errors. These things could cause the system to crash. They could cause system instability, data exposure. things to ask your developers, making sure you're both on the same page, making sure they've thought through these things, which they may or may not have. It's always good do actually validate. Don't just assume that because someone works on code that they knew how to do it securely. There's obvious conversations that need to be had. Then third party libraries and SDKs or software development kits. Ensure that you understand any third party, any third party's security requirements, their vetting processes, where their data is stored, interaction with other apps, data. Don't just assume that they have the same level of security that you do. Always vet that, and remember that security is only as strong as the weakest link. Make sure that there is some type of service level agreement or an understanding between companies how they vet their process, how they take security as a consideration. Is their security up to the level of yours because it doesn't matter how strong your security is if there's this week, if an attacker is able to come in through the side door through their weaker security and then pivot and come through into your application or your network, that poses a challenge, and, a breach can occur. Then lastly, we have data exposure. What types of data are exposed? If unexpected inputs are put into the system and it causes a system to crash or causes some unintended result or what errors are returned if incorrect data is entered. In other words, if someone puts in some type of string or they try cross-site scripting or cross-site forgery request or they go through some type of fuzzing exercise where they just try every single combination of characters and letters to see what happens to see if the system crashes, if and when it does crash, what types of information are returned? Does it tell you the operating system, the kernel version, all those things an attacker could potentially use to fingerprint this system. Or if the website, as an example, asked for a username and password, and they put in the wrong username, does it tell them, hey, this username is not valid. Well, that lets them know, hey, strike that from the list. That one's not valid. Let's try the next one. It allows them to brute force that versus if it simply says, hey, this was correct, you'll get an email back or an email was sent or some type of more ambiguous error message so it doesn't give them any insight into what's valid or not valid. It's all a matter of conversations that you should have with the coders and developers to make sure that everyone is on the same page. They will then understand how security factors in, and you will get a better understanding of how the applications interact with each other.

Chapter 17 Security Automation, Monitoring & Validation

Security automation it's automating the processes of implementing rules, enforcing policies, and making changes. It's based on triggers and policy violations. If things happen, or when things happen, other things will get triggered and fired off and come into play automatically. It doesn't require a security administrator to be sitting there watching a monitoring station or some type of management station to see, hey, this happened, let me shut down that port, let me turn on this service, let me audit this, or look at that. Everything is done in an automated fashion. It's repeatable, it's deterministic, and it allows for things to scale pretty quickly. It can also reduce time to remediate, again, because everything is done automatically. It can mitigate risk, because things are now repeatable. It's going to mitigate that risk of human error. The other thing to keep in mind, however, though, for every plus there's also a con, for every good thing, there's a potential exploit, It can also be exploited and shut things down Denial-of-Service attacks, if the attacker knows what they're doing, and they say, I know for a fact if I do this, these four or five things are going to happen. Well, if I flood that specific thing, it's going to cause the system, because it's operating in an automated fashion, it could cause that system to overload, to shut down ports, to really take a service down when there really wasn't a need to do that. There's a constant refinement of that process to make sure we're not over-engineering, and we're not shutting things down unnecessarily or taking measures that aren't necessarily appropriate. However, for the most part, this is a very good way to approach security because, again, it allows you to scale and reduces that human error. As an example, let's say, for instance, we have a firewall change. That firewall change is reviewed and approved by some human, so they're going to look at it and say, go for it. That change gets logged. Now here's where the automation kicks in. Instead of someone having to do all these things manually, this process can be done in an automated fashion. As soon as that change is logged, it can initiate a security scan. That scan could then go out and initiate or turn on some remote instance, some remote network scan instance, which is going to do a remote network scan, . That's going to all be done automated. It's going to then take the output of that scan, compare with a known good, and make sure that the changes were, in fact, proper, and didn't have any downstream impact, downstream effects. Then, if everything looks good, those changes are logged in the ticketing system. Instead of having to go through a process where everyone has to sign off on that workflow piece by piece, this can all be done in an automated fashion, and this can all be done in minutes instead of potentially hours or even days. Next, we need to make sure that we have continuous monitoring. Continuous monitoring is going to increase visibility. It allows us to see end-to-end what's happening within that workflow. Because when we're doing things in an automated fashion, we don't necessarily have the ability for personnel to be stopping every so often and actually catch some type of error in the process. Continuous monitoring allows us to ramp up scale and volume while still making sure we're catching any errors, quality assurance. It also reduces errors and false positives. If we're monitoring everything along the process, and we know it's a very deterministic workflow, it's going to give us the same output each and every time, any deviation from that allows us to catch it very, very quickly. It also reduces our time to resolution, because if we catch something the moment it happens, we can fix it very, very quickly. It doesn't sit there and fester or turn into something larger, have greater downstream impacts. Something that goes hand-in-hand with that is configuration validation. Configuration validation and management is key to success at scale. There are things that we need to make sure are in place to allow us to catch any configuration drift, any things that start to go off course. Things like Puppet, Chef, Ansible, and Salt are a few of the tools that are typically used in this type of environment as orchestration and automation tools to allow us to make sure we have configurations in place, and any configuration drift gets put back to its known good state very quickly. Next, we have continuous integration. This is merging developer updates continuously, daily in this case, to avoid integration challenges because if we take a piece of code and we have developers work on that in a vacuum and they spend days or perhaps even weeks working on a piece of code, and you have three or four developers working in silos, and then you try to integrate those changes back into some mainstream code base, if everyone is doing so many different changes, trying to integrate that in, it's going to be extremely problematic if not impossible. Having this very continuous stream, this iterative back and forth, code updates are done very quickly. They're integrated back into the main codebase very quickly. It allows things to move forward in a very automated or semi-automated fashion. Waiting too long integrate can cause codebase to get out of sync. That's typically a result of multiple developers working at the same time. Integrate early and integrate often. That is the key to success in this model. Automated testing processes and also a replica of production or as close as you can to production is really critical to success. What I mean by testing automation is every time a change, when you have these developers working on various pieces of code, as soon as those code changes are committed to the main codebase, that should trigger a new test that should automatically be built. A new testing process kicks off, and that automated fashion allows you to quickly iterate, quickly get a new test in place, make sure that everything is validated. That is the new normal or the new committed codebase. We can go back through the process again, introduce any other changes or tweaks and modifications, and again test it over and over again. You see the infinite loop sign. That's really what it is. It's a continuous back and forth, making sure that changes get integrated quickly and moved forward. Next we have continuous delivery. Continuous delivery is an extension of continuous integration. What it is as an automation of the actual release process, in addition to the automated testing, the continuous integration. We're taking that one step further and automating the actual release of those changes or those tweaks. These actual deciding on the release frequency, however, is a manual process, We still decide when to actually do the release. We still push the button, if you will. Whether that's hourly, daily, weekly, that schedule is determined manually. On the other hand, if we look at continuous deployment, well, that takes continuous delivery one step further and automates the entire process. All changes that pass all stages of the pipeline are automatically released to the customer. The feedback loop is accelerated, and also it allows developers to focus on building software. As they push changes, as it makes its way through the CI/CD pipeline and it passes through the different testing phases, QA, staging, tests, as soon as it passes all those things, it's automatically released to the customer. If we look at this continuous delivery versus continuous deployment, we have our continuous integration area, we have builds and test, and we're going to look at a comparison between the two. In a continuous delivery model, we have our builds and test, and it passes through the various stages, acceptance, deploy to staging. Deploy to production you'll notice is different because that's going to be a manual process. When we decide, hey, we're ready to push this change, we hit the button, deploy it to production, and then we initiate our smoke tests. On the other hand, in continuous deployment, the acceptance test, deploy to staging. Deploy to production you'll notice is the same because one was a manual process, but now we do it automatically. As soon as the change is initiated, it makes its way through the different stages in our pipeline and is automatically released to production. That way, those changes get pushed almost in real time, and feedback can also be delivered in almost real time to allow very quick and also very iterative changes to be pushed to the environment and allow modifications, enhancements to be delivered much more quickly. Now let's talk about an organization that I want you to be familiar with, and that is OWASP. And that is the Open Web Application Security Project. It's an open community that produces articles, methodologies, documentation, tools, and other various technologies in the field of web application security. I don't want to dig too deep into them at this point, but I want you to be aware of who they are and then also provide you with a link that you can dig in and learn a little more about the organization. And also, here's a link to a quick reference guide they produce to give you a quick checklist of things that revolve around web application security. https://owasp.org

Chapter 18 Software Diversity, Elasticity & Scalability

Next we have software diversity. This boils down to creating different variations internally to a program to make it harder to reverse-engineer or harder to attack because the internal workings are different each and every time the application runs or at least for different users. We're creating functionally equivalent, but internally different variants of a program. Users get diversified variants of a particular program, and it makes understanding the inner workings of the application more difficult, which in turn makes attacking that application much more difficult. There's two parts to that. One is the compiler, and the compiler takes high-level source code, and it transforms it into low-level machine code. And when it does that, it diversifies that machine code, making the attack more difficult. Each time it runs, it changes it slightly, making it more difficult to actually interact with. The attackers don't know exactly how things work. The other side of that is the binary or the binaries. Introducing randomness into the binaries, either through NOPs, or no operations, and also scheduling randomization. By doing this, we're actually not changing the way it actually works, just the timing, just the way the things operate under the hood. But all of the valid constructions, all of the valid things are still there. We're just injecting some randomness. Maybe it's timing, maybe it's scheduling, maybe it's even memory addresses. But by doing so, the attacker has no clear line of sight as to craft a specific attack for that specific operation or that specific program because every time it runs or at least for every user, it's going to be slightly different. Next, we have elasticity and scalability. This is the ability to grow or reduce on demand and reduces risk because it does a few things. It takes away stranded capital because we don't necessarily have to buy a bunch of stuff that we don't necessarily need. We don't have to buy for our maximum in other words. We know we're going to get 20,000 users once a year, but we don't have to buy equipment to scale to 20,000 users when we only have to do that maybe one week out of the year. The rest of the year, we may only have 2,000 users. It eliminates the need for stranded capital and investing more than is necessary. Then, conversely, we don't have to worry about not having enough to scale when necessary. We buy to our minimums and then don't have enough to scale when the maximums hit. It achieves really both purposes. Also, we can instantiate additional security or cloud monitoring, distributed denial-of-service protection as needed. We don't necessarily have to have a lot of these protections in place, overload if you will, all year round. We may want to do it around specific events. Or when certain things are triggered, we can then fire up additional resources to protect us or to monitor or do whatever for that period of time and then scale back when not necessary. That way we're not paying for things that we don't need. To wrap things up, let's talk about versioning control. Version control allows developers to work on projects together. A version control system will track all changes to code. As multiple developers are working on something, every change will get tracked and stored as a separate version. It maintains the history of all changes, it allows for a rollback, and it allows you to make a mistake and roll back to a prior version or also fork a specific line of code and maybe go in a divergent path. Where those forks occur, you could roll back prior to that change. Version control repositories or repos can be centralized or distributed, and GitHub is perhaps the most common version control system. If we look at centralized versus decentralized, there's two major differences. In a centralized system, we have users who will actually push all of their code, all of their changes, up to a centralized server. They must maintain network connectivity. They have to be attached to the server. Every time they want to make a change or receive a change, it goes up to the server, and then the users access the change from that centralized server. Everything is stored in a central repository. Conversely, in a decentralized environment, we have users connecting to a server. But there's a copy of the project, and all the changes and all the history of that project is actually pushed out to each individual user. They have a copy on their desktop or their laptop, It gives you additional copies, redundancy. It's also much faster because you're not relying on network speed, network connectivity. It also allows people to work offline. Two different approaches achieving the same thing. Decentralized is perhaps the more popular version. Most open source projects will be using a decentralized repository as well. Just keep that in mind. In your shop, your company, your development area, you definitely should be using some type of version control to make sure that changes are tracked, and you can also roll back when issues are discovered. In summary we talked about environments, the various environments like testing, staging, QA, production. We talked about provisioning and deprovisioning of assets on projects. We talked about integrity measurement. We talked about secure coding techniques, the Open Web Application Security Project or OWASP. We talked about software diversity, automation and scripting, and then elasticity, scalability, and then, lastly, version control.

Chapter 19 Directory Services, Federation & Attestation

In the following chapters we'll be talking about Authentication and Authorization Methods. We'll be talking about authentication methods and the various technologies associated with that. We'll talk about smartcard authentication, biometrics, also talk about multi-factor authentication, or MFA. We'll talk about authentication, authorization, and accounting, otherwise known as AAA, and then also cloud versus on-premise requirements, as far as authorization and authentication is concerned. First up is directory services. Directory services provides authorization and also authentication for computers, for users, and also for groups, so laptops, desktops and servers. A component of that is something referred to as LDAP or lightweight directory access protocol. LDAP is the language or the protocol that is actually used to talk to Active Directory. They're not one and the same. Active Directory is the authentication mechanism or the suite of tools behind the scenes that Microsoft uses for their domains and networks. LDAP is a protocol that could be used to talk to Active Directory. LDAP could also talk to other authentication services as well. So real quick, without digging too deeply into Active Directory here, we'll talk about LDAP, we'll talk about Kerberos in other chapters, but just to brief history on Active Directory. Active Directory was developed in 1999 and introduced in 2000, and it was introduced with, as you guessed it, Windows 2000. In 2003, it was built upon, and we added the ability to change the position of domains within forests, within AD forests or Active Directory forests. Fast-forward to 2008, we added Active Directory Federated Services, or ADFS. And Active Directory itself was rebranded to Active Directory Directory Services and added some additional security features like PAM or privileged access management. Then in 2016, again, fast-forwarding through some of these iterations, Windows Server 2016 released Azure AD to enable the joining of on-prem Active Directory or on-prem AD with Azure AD. This enabled SSO or single sign-on for MS cloud services like Office 365 . Active Directory or AD has been evolving since it was first introduced in 2000. As far as a username is concerned, just so we're clear, every operating system creates user names for each user of a system. Each username is assigned a unique ID. For instance, in Windows in Active Directory, that unique ID is called a SID, or a security identifier. That is actually how the computer identifies that user, not the username. Without digging too deeply into the nuts and bolts of Active Directory, the username is the human-readable form. Well, if I create that user, he gets assigned a SID. If I delete that user and then recreate him again, same usernamer, he'll be given actually a different SID, or a different security identifier. It's better to disable an account and then later on re-enable that account, if you need to give it access again. Next we have federation, and a federation is allowing access to company resources to outside parties. so we're going to federate with other groups. A trusted third party is going to be that authentication mechanism, and they're going to authenticate the client, or the host, or the user, or whatever your terminology is, so that if two people trust this trusted third party, if I trust so and so, and the person I want to give access to also trust so and so, this third party, then we can both agree that we're going to allow that communication to occur because we both trust the person that we've both authenticated to. Social media sites like Facebook, Twitter, they all provide federation services. You may have logged in at some point in time to a website, that's not really Facebook or Google, but you actually log in with your Facebook, or Google, or LinkedIn password, your Twitter password, that provides that federated service. It allows you to authenticate and then log into that other web service because you both trust whatever it is, Facebook or Twitter. A trust is something that exists between two parties, two domains to companies. Well, we have such things as a one-way trust. Well that is company A trusts company B, but company B does not trust company A. It's a one-way street. It's a one-way street that they live on. Two-way street or two-way trust rather is A trusts B and also B will trust A. Company A is going to trust company B. And in return, company B is going to trust company A. Then we have a non-transitive trust where company A trusts company B, but it does not allow that trust to extend beyond company B. Company B, in other words, could not allow companies C or D to also trust A. It's a non-transitive trust. It does not go beyond the barriers and the parameters that were initially set. Then we have a pure transitive trust where A trusts B, B is going to trust C, and so A trusts C by virtue of transitivity. If we look at this graphically, we have host A. We have host B and host C. Well host A is going to trust host B. Host B is going to trust host C. So by virtue of transitivity, host A will also trust host C. It passes through transitively through host B. Our next concept of attestation. Attestation is used to prove that a system is secure and operates from a secure code base. This includes support for a Hardware Root of Trust, and what it does is it enables a service to securely sign the attestation data to prove that the device is the originator of the request. The TPM chip, the hardware chapter we talked about previously, or a trusted execution environment, they're examples of chips, or a secure area, so let's say, for instance, a secure enclave on an iPhone, as an example, it's an area that really can't be tampered with, and what it does is establishes that Hardware Root of Trust. Everything that flows down from that can be assumed to be secure.

Chapter 20 Time-Based Passwords, Authentication & Tokens

Next, we have something referred to as TOTP or a time-based, one-time password. TOTP is a unique password that uses a time-based algorithm to generate that password. As an example, we have a client trying to log into a server, and they're going to use something called Google Authenticator in this example, but there are a number of different tools that can provide the same type of functionality. But if you look at this a little more closely, we'll see here that we have the user wants to log into a server. They're going to log in with their username and their password. That server will then turn around and challenge them with that time-based, one-time password. As an example, an app for your phone, Google Authenticator, RSA makes one. There are a number of different companies and utilities that are available, but they'll all use similar algorithms. It will create a one-time password that lasts for either 30 seconds or 60 seconds, again, depending upon the utility. That will be unique for that short period of time. It's time based. But that also is in sync with the authentication mechanism on the server. Those two numbers as they regenerate and they change every 30 seconds or every 60 seconds, it's going to change both on that application and also on the server. So once the user enters his username and password correctly and gets challenged with the TOTP, the time-based, one-time password, he's going to put in his own pin into that authenticator, which allows him to then access. It's going to pop up and give him that six-digit pin or that six-digit number. He'll in turn enter that in. Then if it matches on the server, assuming that it does, the service or the server rather will grant access to that resource. Next we have HOTP, and it's a hash message authentication code algorith, HMAC for short. HMAC-based one-time password. That's the open standard for OAuth, similar to what we just talked about previously with the TOTP, or a time-based one-time password, and we can use the Google Authenticator as the same type of tool in that example. You can have different HMAC-based one-time passwords for different services, whether you're logging into email, or a server, or Dropbox, or whatever it is that online service is, or maybe a VPN for work, that will change every X number of seconds and can be used to maintain separate accounts, separate HMACs for each individual account, and as you go in and put your password in, it will regenerate every 60 seconds, you get the one that you need and are on to that server, and it will give you access, to that service. Also something to keep in mind is the fact that SMS can be used as a two-factor authentication mechanism as well. A user registers a mobile device with a service or a website, or whatever it is you're trying to access, and then when logging in, the user will provide that username and password. But then the service, the website, or the application will send a one-time code. You'll typically verify your mobile number, either like the last four digits, or click on a drop-down button or radio button that verifies your phone number. That SMS push then takes place, and a one-time code is sent as an added layer of security. That way, it's something that , and it's also something that you have, the phone in your possession. Now you have a one-time code you can use to log into that website. A similar functionality can also be provided via an automated phone call. Sometimes you have the option of choosing an SMS text message, or you can have that same service call your phone and leave you a voice message with that one-time code. Another authentication mechanism is something referred to as a token. A token is an authentication mechanism that can identify and also authenticate. I can tell servers or resources what access rights a user possesses. It can also allow or deny access. In a simplified example, but let's say, for instance, we have a user who wants to access a resource, in this case they want to access a server on their network. Well, they've already logged into the network, they've authenticated with Active Directory. Active Directory then gives them a token, and that token says what you can and cannot access, what groups you belong to. When they go to access that resource, they pass along that token. That token, in effect, has a number of different attributes. the user SID, the group SIDs, any security IDs of groups they're actually a member of, privileges, what's their primary group, the default ACLs, or access control lists, a number of attributes that's presented to the server, the server will look at that and say Active Directory says you have access, so you may pass, and then access, is granted, or if they're not a member of the group or there's an explicit deny, then access would be denied. Another method of authentication is static codes. Static codes are backup codes, essentially, that can be created and stored as a backup, or for a one-time use. Depending upon the application or the service, you may be given a number of backup code that you can print, take offline, store somewhere safe, That way if you lose your phone or your authentication device, your authentication mechanism, Google Authenticator, or whatever it is that you had initially set up, if that's gone, you can use these backup codes to actually get back into your account. Many password managers and also security applications will enable a user to generate a list of offline or backup codes, and then again, you print them and store them offline. That way, they're there in case of an emergency. Next is the actual authentication application, which we talked about before.

But these authentication applications can create a one-time password, an HMAC password, Applications that generate a code every X number of seconds or minutes, perhaps 30 seconds or every 60 seconds, so they're in sync with the application being logged into or the web server being logged into. Your application is in sync with the one on the web server or the application you're logging into, and it will change every X number of seconds. An RSA Token or a key fob was an early example of this; however, nowadays, many Android and also IOS apps have this functionality as well. Authy is one for iOS, Google Authenticator, Microsoft Authenticator. There a number of them out there. They all work very similarly, and they can generate these passwords independent of each other. Each account will have their own synchronization and their own actual backup codes. Some might be six digits, some might be 8, some might be 10. Something similar would be a push notification. A push notification is authentication that validates a login attempt by sending an access request to an associated mobile device. When I register my account, I will link it to a mobile device that I own. Instead of entering a password, I receive an access request notification within the application itself, which I then can approve or deny. As an example, if I try to log into Gmail via a web browser, it will actually push an access request to my Gmail application on my phone, and it pops up a notification and says, hey, someone's trying to log into your account, is this you, yes or no, do you authorize it? I can either say, no, it's not me. If someone else is trying to do it, it gives me an alert. Or I could say yes, and all I have to do is push the yes button and then I log into the website. It saves me from having to put in a pin or any of that type of stuff. I just log in with my username or email address and password, and then I get a push notification to finish the process.

Chapter 21 Proximity Cards, Biometric & Facial Recognition

Let's now cover physical access control. Smart cards give us access control, and it's also a security device. It contains a small chip or an amount of memory on that card, and that card can contain information about us. It could be metadata about who we are, it could contain medical records, it could contain access, as far as like what doors we can access within a building. Also, different levels of authorization or authentication for network resources. User permissions, access information. It's alTypically combined with multi-factor authentication, such as a PIN or a password. One is something that you have, the other is something that . For it to be true two-factor authentication, it has to be from separate categories. We can set it up so that incorrectly entering a PIN or password "X" number of times can even shut that card down and render it invalid. That way, if it's stolen and someone's trying to just randomly brute force their way in, that will shut things down and not allow that to happen. Two types of proximity cards are RFID and also NFC. RFID is the earlier version, although still very much widely in use, and then NFC is the newer version. The RFID cards that most people are familiar with allow for such things as security access into a building, even passing through a toll booth. NFC, or Near-Field-Communication, is more or less the evolution of RFID. That has roughly about a 4-inch range, It makes it a little bit more secure. You have to be actually very close to the proximity device you want to scan or connect to, make a payment through. Apple Pay, Google Wallet, Samsung Pay, all these things that uses NFC type of chip or NFC type of communication allow for very close proximity, so you have to be roughly 3 to 4 inches away from the reader. You put your phone up to it, and then it prompts you to either enter a fingerprint, or a password, or something that you may have that will then make that purchase or send that payment. If someone is standing 5 feet away or 10 feet away, they're not going to be able to intercept that because the range on these things are only roughly about 4 inches. They can also be used to transfer any type of data. With the Apple platform, or iOS, it's really only used for payments, but it could also be used for transferring video files, contact information, so NFC has a lot of uses beyond just making mobile payments. Next we have a personal identification verification card, or a PIV, and that's actually issued by the United States Federal Government. It's a smart card. It has a chip, and that chip contains encrypted information about that person. It also has a barcode, and it can display various pieces of information, their photo, what branch of the service they work for, or what specific department they're involved with. There may also be things like pay grade or their rank and issue date and an expiration date. And all of these things are actually contained also in the bar code and also in that smart chip. This will grant that cardholder access to federal facilities and information systems. It's established by the Federal Information Processing Standard 201, or FIPS. These cards are used extensively throughout federal facilities throughout the U.S. Next, we have a common access card, and this is similar to the PIV we talked about previously. It's a smart card issued by the Department of Defense, and it's a general identification mechanism used for accessing DoD computers, signing email. We have a picture of the card on the front and the back. It has the barcode and a smart chip, the integrated chip that you see there. This particular card lists paygrade, rank, affiliation, expiration date, and the federal ID. On the back, it has very similar information. It has some additional pieces of information such as blood type, DoD benefits number, date of birth and so on. These cards are capable of containing quite a bit of information about a specific individual. Definitely something that can be used for authentication. Next, let's talk about biometric factors. A fingerprint scanner allows someone to uniquely identify themselves with their fingerprint, and as we know, fingerprints are, for the most part, considered unique, although, again, depending upon where you read. But for all intents and purposes, they are unique right. It measures multiple points and multiple factors on the fingerprint and uniquely identifies that person. Then we have retinal scanners and iris scanners where it actually goes in and reads the back of the eye, or the inside of the back of the eyeball, the retina, or an iris scanner looks at the pattern within the iris itself, and that will be unique to that person. We also have voice recognition where it can ask you to repeat a certain phrase or a passphrase over and over again, and it will learn your voice, and you can use that voice as your password. All of these things are great conveniences, although some of those can potentially be bypassed rather quickly. For instance, on an iOS device, your fingerprint scanner, well, if you're sleeping and someone walks up and grabs your thumb and puts it on your phone, they can unlock it pretty quickly, so not necessarily foolproof; however, that fingerprint is unique to you. It doesn't necessarily mean it can't be used to unlock your phone even without your knowledge. When it comes to biometrics, one of the first things that people think about is fingerprints. But there's also facial recognition, and that's comprised of software that can detect a person's identity based upon facial characteristics. New or 3D technologies have increased the accuracy, and also use cases range from government, commercial, and also consumer applications. There's use cases where we scan crowds at sporting events, concerts, also government buildings, and then also, once we've had actual incidents, terrorist activities facial recognition has been used to scan a crowd and try to pull people out of those large crowds and those large gatherings. Some potential weaknesses with facial recognition are low resolution photos, it's very hard to get things when it's grainy or pixelated, also changes in appearance. Whether it's a beard, a hat, scarves, sunglasses, all of those things can also inhibit facial recognition accuracy. Also, drastic changes in facial expressions can have an effect as well. Then we have anti-facial recognition technology, so reflective glasses, infrared emitting glasses, it gets a little bit crazy. But, whatever technology comes out, there's obviously a group or an industry that pops up as well to try to thwart those activities or try to thwart that technology. There's always a battle. But just understand that the technology is there currently, it's getting better and better all the time, but it's not foolproof, and we'll talk about error rates in just a moment.

Chapter 22 Vein and Gait Analysis & Efficacy Rates

The next one I want to bring your attention is vein analysis. It's a biometric authentication using the vein or the vein pattern in a human finger, so a user would insert a finger into what's called an attester terminal, like a fingerprint reader, That emits near-infrared LED. The hemoglobin in blood absorbs that near-infrared LED light, and the patterns are unique to each individual, and they're almost impossible to counterfeit because they are underneath the skin. As you can imagine, very, very difficult and potentially very painful to try to counterfeit. Next, we have something we refer to as gait analysis. This is identifying a person based upon their unique walking pattern. I can imagine in your head right now, you're saying, man, this is getting crazy. We're identifying people by every single characteristic you can possibly imagine, and the reality is, unfortunately, yes, we're becoming more and more surveilled. It has good implications and also bad implications, but something that you need to be aware of is there are new technologies and new capabilities constantly being developed. That can be things like step length, walking speed, it could be cycle time parameters like joint rotation of the hip, the knee, and the ankle, the angles of the thigh, the foot, the trunk. All of these things combined are unique to an individual. It can help to identify that person, whether just by walking singularly, or in a crowd. Potential use cases would be, before with facial recognition, would be criminal justice applications or national security applications. Three things you should be aware of. We have something referred to as a FAR, or false acceptance rate, and this is the probability that the system will incorrectly authorize a non-authorized person. It's giving someone access that shouldn't have it. Next, we have a false rejection rate, or FRR. That's the probability that the system incorrectly rejects an authorized person. That's not quite as much of an issue as a false acceptance rate, both are not good, but it's better to reject someone that should be there than to allow someone in that shouldn't, but neither are ultimately acceptable. Then next we have a crossover error rate, or CER. That's the rate where both accept and reject error rates are equal. If we have the crossover error rate, we have the error rate on one axis, and then we have the sensitivity of that application with the technology on the other axis. We have the false acceptance rate, and then we also have the false rejection rate. Well, the point where those things meet, where they're both equal, a properly-tuned system should have equal false rejection rates and also false acceptance rates. If one is higher than the other, then the system is not tuned properly, and we need to make sure that that application is functioning properly. Let's now define what the differentiation is between identification, authentication, and authorization. Sometimes they're used interchangeably, but there really are three discrete things. But, what's the difference? Identification is who you are. Sounds like a no brainer, but in a nutshell, that's what it is. That means labeling a person via a username, a security ID, via smart card, PIV, so on, but who that person is, what we label that person as. Next is authentication, and that is actually proving who you are, and that can be a username and password combo, a pin, an OTP or a one-time password, biometric data. you say I'm so and so, or I say I'm so and so, anybody could call themselves anything, but how do you prove that, and that's by authenticating. And then we have authorizations, and that deals with permissions. So once you've said who you are and we've authenticated, we've proved who we are, now what can I do? So once I prove that I am administrator, what rights and permissions do I have on that system or on that network? That's really what that points to, what you're allowed to access once your authenticated, authorization happens after authentication. Next is authentication and just at a high level, just give you a quick overview, authentication is going to be the process of validating an identity. That is proving that you are who you say you are. If you say you're user A, or user B, or user C, prove it. Let's validate that. That could be something like a fingerprint, it could be a password, or a PIN. It's something that , or have, or whatever that's unique to you that's going to validate that you are who you say you are. The concept of multifactor authentication is something you should be familiar with. Multifactor authentication is two or more pieces of information that is used to authenticate someone. It could be a PIN. It could be a password, a fingerprint or a retina scan. But here's the caveat, it must be from different categories. A password and a PIN would really only be considered one factor of authentication because both fall under something . Things like what you have, what , what you do, where you are, but it has to be from two or more categories for it to be true multifactor authentication. Next, we have authentication factors, and these are the things you have to have in place for a multi-factor authentication system to function, something that , which could be a password or some secret, then there's something that you have, and that could be a smart card, or a token, or some type of dongle, maybe a USB dongle that changes every X number of seconds, or it could be something that you are, and that refers to a fingerprint, a retina scan, some type of biometric data. To have a true multi-factor authentication system, we have to make sure that we have at least two things that are in separate categories. We may have something that , in other words, some type of shared secret or password, along with a smartcard or a token. Having a password and a pin, if we had both of those together, that's only a single factor, because they're both something that we know. We know the password. We know the pin, but yet, if we have a password and something that changes every 60 seconds, that's something that we have. If we know, a password plus that, then we have two-factor authentication. Or if we had that same password and perhaps our fingerprint or a retina scan, that again would be multi factor because we have something from something that and also from something that you are. Two other authentication factors that I want you to be aware of is, number one, somewhere you are, so that's location based, in other words. An IP address, geolocation, it could be a specific place on the map, or it could be a specific place in a building, a floor, so forth or an IP address, so you can only log in or a session is locked to a specific IP address. Then also, we have something you do, and that could be a signature, a handwriting analysis, as an example, a pattern of behavior, the way you type, certain misspellings, language or slang. This is more of an emerging field, and depending upon who you talk to, could be considered more art than science, but it has been proven to be very accurate. People typically will do the same types of things over and over again, same types of spelling mistakes, the speed at which they type, the certain words that they use, the slang. All of these things could be used to, not only identify you, but to also authenticate you. Next is authorization, and authorization defines what you're allowed to access. That happens after you're authenticated. Remember, we prove, we identify, then we authenticate, and then we authorize. That authorization occurs after you're authenticated, and it can be controlled via policy, whether it be Group Policy in the Windows environment or some other type of policy mechanism in other operating systems, and it just says who can access what. It could be such things as time of day restrictions. It could be length of time restrictions, so we could only allow someone to log into our network between, let's say, 6 A.M. and 5 P.M. That way, if they happen to come in or try to come in at midnight, as an example, they would not be allowed. Or we could say, once they're on our system, they're only allowed to be on there for an 8-hour period. If they're on there longer than that, then they get booted. Then we also have file and folder access rights. What files can I access? What folders can I access? What resources, what printers, and so on. Two other authentication factors that I want you to be familiar with, and these are relatively new and not necessarily widely accepted across the board, but two of these you should be familiar with, nonetheless. That is, something that you exhibit. And that could be a personality trait, a neurological trait. We've talked about things getting crazier and crazier when we're trying to identify people. Well, this just goes along that same path. Obscure use cases at this point, but it is something that you should be aware of, personality traits, neurological traits, something that you may exhibit that is unique to you. Then also, someone that . That could be social proof. Having a friend or a colleague vouch for a user, usually via some type of token generation. When you create your account, you may designate someone as a friend or someone that can vouch for you in the event that you lose your credentials. You can then reach out to that person, or they will be sent some type of notification that says, hey, the person that you vouched for has lost their credentials; please provide authorization to allow them into their account. You can set that up ahead of time, That way, they're a, in case of an emergency break glass type of person, that they can allow you back into your account. Lets round this section up with authentication, authorization, and accounting, otherwise known as AAA. Authentication, as we've talked about before, identifies the user and allows or denies access or challenges for additional credentials, such as a pin, or a rotating code, a one-time password that will allow you to authenticate. From there, you have authorization, so that provides things like the length of time allowed on a network, access-control lists, or ACLs, for various resource is, what you're actually allowed to access. And then we have accounting, so that tracks the start and stop time of each session, and that can be used for billing or showback. Accounting is used by ISPs, service providers to track how long you've been online and how much they can bill you for. Next, we have on-prem versus cloud requirements when we're talking about authorization. For on-prem, it's locally managed authentication - something you have direct control over. All users and resources are housed under "one roof", and it could be a geographically dispersed or a multi-building facility, but it's still under one roof as far as under that company's auspices. Then we have onboarding and off-boarding must be properly maintained and optimized to avoid shadow IT. We don't want little small groups sprouting up all over the place and authorizing their own users, giving access to resources. That should be done collectively under one management organization. And then we have IT admins must also maintain all networking, configuration, lifecycle, integration. That can be problematic, and it's also a recurring thing every few years - two, three years, five years, depending upon your lifecycle, you have to go through that exercise all over again. Then if you have your infrastructure staggered It's not all up for refresh at the same time, then it's going to be a yearly process over and over and over again. One benefit though being it's potentially more flexible and more customizable, which, depending upon how you look at it, could be a blessing or a curse. On the cloud side, we have cloud-based IAMor identity access management. That is managed by the cloud personnel with the cloud provider. It allows workers and resources to be located anywhere, because if you think about it, they all have the same experience. They're all authorizing to the same cloud-based provider, not trying to go back to the central hub or back to corporate HQ. It may be one experience if you're here, a different experience if you're somewhere else. If it's all done through the cloud, it's the same experience across the board. Then we have optimized policies for onboarding and off-boarding, Cloud providers have a very mature onboarding and off-boarding process and to make sure everybody goes through the same policies and procedures. And then administration, monitoring, and configuration of lifecycle activities are handled by the cloud provider. That in and of itself is a big time saver. You don't have to worry about managing those things in house, so that can take a lot of burden off of your internal personnel and free them up for other things like innovation and actually driving revenue to the business. In summary, we talked about authentication methods and the various technologies associated with that. We talked about smart card authentication, biometrics, the various types, facial, voice, fingerprint, vein analysis, gait analysis. We talked about multi-factor authentication and then also authentication, authorization, and accounting, otherwise known as AAA. Then we finished up with cloud and on-prem requirements as far as authentication is concerned.

BOOK 2

IMPLEMENTING
CYBERSECURITY RESILIENCE

PHYSICAL SECURITY CONTROLS
&
CRYPTOGRAPHIC CONCEPTS

RICHIE MILLER

Introduction

IT Security jobs are on the rise! Small, medium or large size companies are always on the look out to get on board bright individuals to provide their services for Business as Usual (BAU) tasks or deploying new as well as on-going company projects. Most of these jobs requiring you to be on site but since 2020, companies are willing to negotiate with you if you want to work from home (WFH). Yet, to pass the Job interview, you must have experience. Still, if you think about it, all current IT security professionals at some point had no experience whatsoever. The question is; how did they get the job with no experience? Well, the answer is simpler then you think. All you have to do is convince the Hiring Manager that you are keen to learn and adopt new technologies and you have willingness to continuously research on the latest upcoming methods and techniques revolving around IT security. Here is where this book comes into the picture. Why? Well, if you want to become an IT Security professional, this book is for you! If you are studying for CompTIA Security+ or CISSP, this book will help you pass your exam. Passing security exams isn't easy. In fact, due to the raising security beaches around the World, both above mentioned exams are becoming more and more difficult to pass. Whether you want to become an Infrastructure Engineer, IT Security Analyst or any other Cybersecurity Professional, this book (as well as the other books in this series) will certainly help you get there! But, what knowledge are you going to gain from this book? Well, let me share with you briefly the agenda of this book, so you can decide if the following topics are interesting enough to invest your time in! First, you are going to discover how to implement Cybersecurity Resilience. Here, you will learn about redundancy, geographic redundancy, network redundancy, also power and replication redundancy, so that your network can tolerate false outages and bumps. Next we'll cover how to recognize Security Implications of Embedded and Specialized Systems such as SCADA and ICS systems. After that, you will learn about security implications and attack vectors of IoT or Internet of Things devices and specialized systems such as Voice over IP, or VoIP systems. Moving on, you will discover how to secure heating, ventilation, air conditioning, or HVAC systems as well as drones, AVs, and UAVs. We'll also talk about multi-function printers, real-time operating systems, or RTOS, surveillance systems, systems on a chip, communication considerations, and then the constraints we have to deal with when trying to secure all of these systems. Next, you will understand the importance of Physical Security Controls, deterrence as well as digital and logical security on locks, vaults, and sensors. We'll also cover securing infrastructure, such as protected cabling and data access, and then secure disposal of data, such as deleting and the wiping of data. After that, you will discover the Basics of Cryptographic Concepts and you will comprehend digital signatures, the concept of cipher suites, salting and hashing. We'll also go over at a high level quantum communications and quantum computing, blockchain, steganography, and some common use cases, as well as their limitations. If you are ready to get on this journey, let's first cover how to implement Cybersecurity Resilience!

Chapter 1 Geographically Disperse, RAID & Multipath

In the following chapters we'll be talking about Implementing Cybersecurity Resilience. We'll be talking about redundancy and talking about geographic redundancy, network redundancy, also power and replication redundancy, making sure that our networks can tolerate false outages and bumps. Next, we'll be talking about the different types of backups such as incremental and differential backups. We'll be talking about non-persistence, also high availability, the general concept of keeping things highly available, whether it's via power, individual components, storage, networking. We'll also talk about diversity in its various forms, whether it's vendor diversity, technology diversity or crypto. You might ask, what's in it for me, or why should I even care about this? So by putting these things in place, making sure that we're highly available, we can survive outages or bumps, things we that didn't expect to happen, it increases our speed and increases our agility because we're not spending time troubleshooting, we're not spending time on outages, understanding what went wrong and how we could fix it next time because things won't go wrong to begin with, we'll have redundancy or diversity in place, and things to help us mitigate the unexpected. Then if things do happen, we'll understand the different types of backup, taking us back online. Secondly, we'll have a reduction in errors and outages. Those are the types of things that keep you up at night, and a reduction in that is obviously a good thing, and then next, increased resiliency and recoverability. If things happen, if something goes wrong, a piece of equipment fails, a server goes down, if we have increased resiliency and recoverability in place, it allows us to get back online quickly. Then ultimately, all of these things combine to give us peace of mind, and that's where's the name of the game. We want to make sure that we're making our environment as stable as possible and as highly resilient as possible, all the while making sure that our sanity is intact too. Let's dig into the topics that actually make this happen. When we're talking about geographically disperse, what does that mean? What we talked about before, the different types of sites. We have a cold site. It's inexpensive, but long recovery times. We've talked about a warm site, relatively inexpensive. It's cheaper than a hot site, but there is some equipment there, but not everything. There's going to be some time involved to get us actually back up and running. Then we have a hot site, very expensive because we're duplicating everything, bandwidth, power, network, compute storage, you name it. Those things have to be in place so that if we need to failover, we can do so very quickly. Then we have cloud based, or DR as a service, and that's also managed by a provider. It's going to be typically more costly than a cold site or a warm site, but allows us to get up and running quickly, and we don't have to maintain that infrastructure. The cloud provider will have that for us. As we talked about before when we were talking about HA and being out of the way of hurricanes, and having our backup data centers be in different locations so we're not susceptible to hurricanes, well, the same thing here. Let's say, for instance, we have a data center in Florida, as an example, and another one in Georgia, somewhere around Atlanta. Well, those two data centers are fairly geographically dispersed. However, if a hurricane comes through, if they're in the same hurricane path, then they could potentially be hit by the same outage. Whether it's being able to get fuel for backup generators, or a hurricane itself could do damage along a large swath of area, It could span multiple states. A better alternative would be to move

112

that data center somewhere else. If we have the ability to move it even farther out, maybe across the country, that's even better, as long as you don't have geographical mandates that say you have to be "X" amount of miles away due to latency - some applications are very susceptible to latency. The further apart you are, that latency will increase, the round trip time between sites. But depending upon your provider and your connection that may or may not be a problem. But definitely look at geographic dispersal or diversity to improve resiliency and make your applications more resilient and your infrastructure more reliable. Next, let's talk about RAID, and RAID is Redundant Array of Independent or Inexpensive Disks, depending upon where you read, either is correct. It's a fault tolerant array of disks, so data is mirrored or spread across multiple disks and parity is used to recreate the data in the event of a drive failure. If we have an example of RAID 1, the drives here are mirrored. We have Drive 1 and Drive 2, and the blocks of data are mirrored from Drive 1 to Drive 2, They're mirror copies of each other. However, there are many types of RAID, and each provide different levels of protection. As an example, RAID 0. It's important to understand RAID 0, although it says RAID, it is not fault tolerant, so we're just disk striping, so we're spreading the data across multiple disks. But if we lose any one of those disks, we would lose all the data. For fault tolerant, we need to have RAID 1 or better. So RAID 1, is disk mirroring. Then we have RAID 5, which is disk striping with parity. If we have 5 disks in RAID 5 array, it spread across the disks, let's say, for instance, we have A1, A2, A3, and A4, well, what's going to happen is we're going to create a parity stripe based upon the data that's in A1, A2, A3, and A4. We use a parity algorithm that does a mathematical calculation on the data that exists on block A1, A2, A3, and A4. Then it creates a stripe. The next one down, B1, B2, B3, there's now a parity stripe on Disk 4 instead of Disk 5. And then on C, we have the parity stripe on Disk 3, for the D stripe, we have parity on Disk 2, and for the E stripe, we have parity on Disk 1. We never put the parity and the data on the same disk. That way, if a disk fails, we can reconstruct that data. As an example, if Disk 3 fails, well, we have A1, A2, A4, and parity, so we can take A1, 2, and 4, and parity and extrapolate it out and get the data that was A3. For C, as an example, we could do C1, C2, C3, and C4, and then reconstruct the parity stripe, which was missing on Disk 3. Each one of those stripes is able to be reconstructed because we don't have the parity and the data existing on the same disk for each individual stripe. Another one you should be aware of is RAID 6. RAID 6 is disk striping with double parity. And then we have RAID 10, which is disk striping that is mirrored. With RAID 6, we have same 5 disks, but now we have two parity stripes. That gives us the ability to lose 2 disks without losing our data. Just understand the different levels of fault tolerance, the different levels of RAID, which is fault tolerant, which is not, RAID 0 is not, everything else is fault tolerant, and know that these are very much in use today, RAID 5, 6, and 10 being probably the most popular, but these are tried and true methods of fault tolerance. Next, let's talk about the concept of multipath, or multipathing. Multipathing, in simple terms, is a redundancy concept that provides multiple paths, hence the term or hence the name, from point A to point B. It's multiple ways to get to somewhere. That holds true for networking, compute, storage, applications. Multipath will have different connotations, depending upon which context you're using it in, whether it's compute, storage, applications, but generally speaking, let's look at an example here. We have a server, and this server has two HBAs, and an HBA is a host bus adapter. You can think of it like a NIC, or a network interface card, but for a Fibre Channel SAN connectivity, for a SAN, a storage area network, instead of a NIC that would attach to a typical ethernet network. This server has two HBAs, HBA1 and HBA2. They will connect to two different SAN fabrics. Traditionally, in a Fibre Channel network or a storage area network, we have two discrete fabrics that are not connected with each other. That provides for that redundancy. HBA1 and HBA2 will both be connected to each SAN fabric. That way, when it then connects to the actual storage arrays and then the disks on the back end of the storage arrays, the storage array itself may have one or two controllers or multiple controllers, and all of these things, all these different layers of redundancy, add for multipathing. When we make the connectivity and then chase the I/O from server down to the disk, we can see that we may take a specific path. In this case, we see the path here laid out. Well, if that pathway to go down for whatever reason, we could go over a different path and connect to Array Controller 2, or perhaps we may actually go out of HBA2 and connect over SAN Fabric B to Array Controller 2, or if that link is down, over Array Controller 1. You see, it gives us multiple paths from point A to point B, which in turn, as you may guess, gives us that extra layer of redundancy. That way, if there's some issue in the fabric or some issue in collectivity, we can find a different way or a different route to get from server down to the disk itself.

Chapter 2 Load Balancer, Power Resiliency & Replication

A load balancer is a device that will spread the incoming load among multiple pieces of infrastructure, and this deals with servers, storage, and network, and it can provide additional services as well. The term load balancer can be slightly different, depending upon the context that you're using it in. If we look at an example, here, we have a firewall that will sit on the perimeter of our organization, and then we have load balancers that sit behind that firewall, which in turn spread the load across web servers, database servers behind that, and storage behind that. The load balancers are going to, as the name implies, balance the load of the incoming connections that pass through the firewall onto the web servers. We have internal users that can use this as well, but then also external customers that are coming in through the internet. They'll hit through the firewall, their traffic will be load balanced across multiple different connections, multiple different web servers, which will then service customer requests, be it the database, storage. But just understand that load balancers do just as the name implies. They're going to make sure that no single server gets overrun with requests or I/O. Next, we have a few terms around resiliency and power resiliency. Let's talk about uninterruptible power supplies, or a UPS. This is a term you may be familiar with already, and it is typically a battery backup that provides power in the event of a disruption, whether it be a sag, an actual outage, it could be a brownout or a blackout, depending upon the situation. Is it just a dip in current or is it actually completely out? The length of time that these UPSs are actually active and able to supply that backup power depends upon the type of UPS, type of batteries. Next is a generator. A generator is an alternate power supply, typically will run on gas, could be propane, but it would turn itself on if a power dip or outage is detected. Some generators will automatically kick in. Other types of generators need to be flipped over manually. Generally speaking, when we're talking about a data center situation, we're looking at ones that will flip over automatically and kick on as soon as that disruption is identified. When we're talking about dual supply, we're talking about power that is supplied by dual feeds, independent of one another, so we may have an A side and a B side coming into our data center, or to our infrastructure. That way, if one side goes down, has a dip, a brownout, a blackout, we could immediately flip over to the other side, in an active passive, or we may have both sides feeding that infrastructure at the same time, and then we have something referred to as a managed power distribution unit, or a PDU, and that provides the ability to monitor and control critical factors, such as voltage, current, the power factor. These things are typically rack mounted. You'll have them inside the racks, where you have storage, network, compute and they will distribute the power. They can be monitored, they can be smart devices, or they can be just dumb devices that provide power, but we can have situations where we have both A sides and B sides, feed into that PDU, so you don't need two sets of cords going to your infrastructure. They both feed into the PDU, or you may have the load spread across multiple PDUs. Again, depending upon the layer of resiliency that you need. When it comes to resiliency, something else I want to talk about is the concept of replication. Replication, as an example, here we have, let's say, for instance, a West Coast data center, and we have some associated infrastructure. This isn't everything within the data center, but we have firewalls that sit on the outside, we have storage, databases, web servers. Then we also have an East Coast data center, firewalls in the perimeter again.

What we're doing is replicating data from one data center to the other. In that process, we may have actual infrastructure replication like, say, array to array, so we can do replication at the array level, we can do replication at the database level, and we can also do it at the application level. It just depends upon the application that you're running, the criticality of it, is a business critical, is a business necessary. Then what is your actual replication plan? There can be offsite replications, there can be replications within the data center, a four-corners approach, That you have some diversity, like to call it a sprinkler head diversity, That if a sprinkler head were to go off, the replicated data is far enough apart from each other that a single event, like a sprinkler head would not take out all the associated infrastructure, or you can actually replicate offsite, It could be to tape backup for those that are still using tape, it could be to a VTL, and it's replicated out, so we could have data that's stored on the West Coast data center, and then replicated to the East Coast data center. It's certainly not an all-or-nothing approach, so we can have certain pieces of data, but not necessarily the entire thing. We don't need an entire duplicate infrastructure, duplicate number of servers, duplicate amount of storage. You can pick and choose, and replicate just what is necessary. Then, you have another option to replicate to the cloud, so you don't necessarily have to replicate to another data center that you may or may not own, you can also send that data to the cloud, and then restore as necessary. The nice part about that is that you can restore anywhere, assuming you have somewhere to restore to. Next, we have on-prem versus cloud, and on an on-prem situation, we have infrastructure, compute, network, storage. All of that is going to be on-prem. We have duplicate infrastructure, so geo-disperse or four corner redundancy. We also need on-site personnel to manage processes, troubleshoot hardware, also back up and replication software, and then also determining the level of resiliency, the RPO or RTO, the recovery point objective and recovery time objective, and then deciding the data to be backed up and replicated. All of these things are required when we have an on-prem situation. When we're dealing with a cloud, we have infrastructure can be, spun up on-demand, and that's handled by the cloud provider, so we don't necessarily have to have that infrastructure in place ahead of time. It can be spun up elastically, depending upon how things are configured. Also replication will take place between two or more sites, and that's determined by the customer. Then also administration, security, and troubleshooting will be handled by the provider, and you can see a recurring theme here. It takes a lot of the burden off of on-prem sources and puts that on cloud resources or the cloud provider. Also, backups and replication are provided as a service, so as you're instantiating your services, applications or databases, typically it's more or less a checkbox within the configuration settings to back this information up. The backup and replication is provided more or less as a service. You'll still determine the level of resiliency, the RPO and RTO, and then what data to be backed up and replicated, that's not going to change, you still have control, and you have to make the decision over what is actually replicated.

Chapter 3 Backup Execution Policies

When talking about backup plans, what we need to be concerned with is what data needs to be backed up? What's the retention policy? Is it the same for all data? Because at the end of the day, not all data actually needs to be backed up. Some of it's not that important, some of it needs to be highly available, some of it needs to be retrievable at a moments notice, other data could be carted off to some type of cold storage, and there's varying degrees in between. Not everything has to be backed up at the same rate or even backed up it all. We need to make sure we define these things ahead of time and understand what the retention policy is for that data, and is it the same for all data? But, what's the RPO and the RTO? The recovery point objective and the recovery time objective. Then, additionally, where do the backups actually live? Are they on-array? Are they off-array? Are they in disk, or VTL, a virtual tape library, or on tape? Or they backed up off site? Each of these options have different costs associated with them, also varying amounts of speed, reliability. So depending upon the budget, how much data needs to be backed up, and how quickly it needs to be recovered will dictate to some degree where those back apps actually live. When it comes to backup execution and frequency, some things to consider are the Recovery Point Objective, or the RPO, and the Recovery Time Objective, or the RTO. So, how often do backups occur, and how quickly does the data need to be recovered? You should have SLAs, or Service Level Agreements, in place defined for these things. Also, how long should that data be retained? Next, we need to ensure that backups can occur actually within the backup window, as per the SLA, or the Service Level Agreement. A couple questions to ask there, do the backups that we have planned, do they conflict with other backups taking place? In a small environment, you may have only a few backups per day, or maybe a couple dozen. In a large environment, you may have literally thousands of backup jobs taking place each and every day. It's very important to understand what conflicts, and does that impact my SLA? Secondly, do these backups impact server performance or network performance? There's a good chance that it might, depending on how it's architected. Those backups might need to take place off hours, or whatever is defined as a slow period within your organization. Some companies will have actually separate backup networks so that it doesn't impact normal network and normal server traffic, but again, it depends upon your organization and how things are architected. All of these things need to be discovered, documented, and defined ahead of time. Let's now talk about backup concepts. There's several backup types that I want you to be familiar with. The first is differential. A differential backup is data that has changed since the last full backup. The key takeaway here is the time to backup increases over time because each day we're adding what's changed since the last full backup. Let's say we did a full backup on Sunday. Monday, not much has changed. We do a very quick differential backup. Tuesday, some more stuff has changed, so that differential now takes a little longer. Wednesday, Thursday, and so on. That will increase each day because the amount of data between the differential and the last full backup will increase. The time to backup increases over time, but the time to restore is reduced, and it only requires two backup media, the last differential and the last full backup. Those two will get you back to where you need to be. Next we have incremental backups. An incremental is data that's changed since the last incremental backup. The time to backup is reduced, but the time to restore is increased - it's the reverse. And this is because all incremental backups are required, plus the last full backup. Each day when you do that incremental, all you're capturing is the stuff that's changed since the last incremental. If we did a last full backup on Sunday and then we did an incremental Monday, Tuesday, Wednesday, Thursday, outage occurs on Friday, we're going to need all the incremental Monday through Thursday, plus the last full backup. Then we have, which is, as the name implies, all data is backed up each time. It takes the longest amount of time to back up and restore, but you capture everything at once. Then we have something referred to as a snapshot. Now, a snapshot is a point in time copy of that data, just like if you took a picture; hence, the term snapshot. What happens here is that snapshot will typically maintain pointers to the original data, rather than actually copying the data itself. It keeps track of what's changed, and those pointers allow very quick backups. You could take a snapshot literally in seconds, depending upon what type of media it's sitting on, spinning disk versus flash media. If you look at incremental versus differential, you'll see an incremental backup schedule. Here we have a backup type of incremental. Sunday we're going to do a full backup. Monday is incremental - any changes since Sunday. Tuesday, Wednesday, you can see, each day we're doing incremental backups, but what we're capturing is only the changes since the previous day. It's incrementally building upon itself. We're capturing those incremental changes. Well, if we need to restore, let's say, for instance, we need to restore on Saturday, we have to restore the last full backup, plus all the incremental. All the incremental from Monday, Tuesday, Wednesday, Thursday, Friday, Conversely, if we're doing a differential backup, well, you can see the same thing. We're going to take a backup, a full backup, rather, on Sunday, and then on Monday, we'll do a differential. That's only the changes since Sunday. On Tuesday, we do another differential. Well, guess what? All the changes since Sunday. On Wednesday, Thursday, Friday, et cetera, each time we do that differential backup, it's capturing all the changes since the last full backup. As you can imagine, the size of those differentials will increase each day, but then when it comes time to restore, let's say, for instance again, we had a crisis on Saturday, all we have to restore is the last differential, plus the full backup, it makes restoral much quicker. Let's now talk about the concept of backup environments and different ways we can get these backups accomplished. Let's say, for instance, we have a server sitting in our data center. We have two different choices, really, for connecting that to some type of attached storage. We have Network Attached Storage, or NAS, and we also have SAN, or a Storage Area Network. One is file-based, one is blocked-based. A NAS device will be presented to the server as a NAS share, whereas SAN storage is presented to the server and it looks like a local disk. That's the two different main environments. From there, on the NAS side, we could replicate that data from the NAS device to another NAS device. So, that's replication at the array level. Similarly, for SAN, we could also replicate to another SAN array. That goes back to what I was saying previously, where we could replicate at the array level. From there, we also have some additional choices. We could replicate to a tape library or back up to a tape library, or we could also back up to cloud. Along those same lines, we can do the same thing from a SAN array, back up to tape or back up to cloud. Although it's not drawn here specifically, typically, there'll be an agent that's installed on the server, and the backup will take place from the server directly, either out to tape or out to cloud. Or, we can, replicate the NAS device or the SAN device to make sure the data remains accessible. When we talk about online versus offline backups, let's say, for instance, we have a main data center, we have a lot of disks, we have a lot of information, critical information, business critical, business necessary. Well, we want to protect that data against some type of an event, whether it's a malware attack or ransomware attack. One methodology would be the concept of a cyber bunker. In a cyber bunker, what we do is we replicate a subset or potentially all, but typically a subset of our main data, we're going to identify our business critical applications, we'll replicate that data over to that cyber bunker, but the replication link only remains up while the replication takes place. In other words, we error gap that connection. The connection comes up, in other words, we turn on the ports between the two data centers only when that replication takes place. As soon as the replication is done, that link gets severed. That way, if an attacker gets into our network, they can't bridge that gap, they can't bridge that connection from the main data center to the cyber bunker and potentially infect our backups We're going to make sure those backups remain in an immutable form, tucked away from our main data, and then we may have some additional resources within the cyber bunker to do forensic analysis and help us remediate in the event of a situation, but the main concept is the cyber bunker is going to be typically a subset of our main data, it's going to be logically error gapped That it's only up while their application takes place, and then once their application is done, the link is severed. A few things to consider when we're talking about backups, specifically, around distance considerations, so backups versus high availability, backups could be geographically far away, and that can be asynchronous versus high availability, or HA, which requires synchronous speeds. What I mean by that is the placement of our backup infrastructure needs to be consistent with our idea of what we're actually accomplishing. Backups can be far away because we're not doing it in real time in asynchronous fashion. High availability, however, has to be electronically close enough so the round trip time between those two sites is small enough, that latency is low enough, so that we can do synchronous replication or even write to both locations at the same time. Next, the physical backup distance limitations. If we are backing up the tape, as an example, how long would it take to get the tapes back in the event of a disaster? There's no right answer to this one, but it's a matter of understanding realistically those timelines and those time frames. When you're doing your business continuity or your disaster recovery planning, you factor those times into your restore process. It takes 3 or 4 hours to even get the tapes on site, and it takes another 3 or 4 hours or maybe a day or 2 to restore, all of those things should be calculated into your assessment. Then recovery testing, whether it's a hot site, a warm site, cold site, the time required to recover the offsite backups, the order of recovery, that's another big one that needs to be documented to make sure we understand exactly the order of restoration because you can't necessarily restore everything at once. It has to be a specific order sometimes, application, database, middleware. Then also, are the backups that we're doing app consistent or crash consistent? All of these things have to be tested, and they should be tested as realistically as possible, whatever your business allows for, maybe once a quarter, perhaps once a year, but they should actually be tested That you don't find that out in the middle of an actual crisis that, uh, oh, our actual backups aren't even there, or they don't work, or the stuff we recovered is not actually usable because it's not in the state that can be used by the application. All of these things are critical to make sure that the recovery process is successful.

A few other concepts we need to cover that I want you to be familiar with and the first is non-persistence. Non-persistence prevents people from customizing their desktops, installing unapproved applications, tweaking settings. This is typically associated with things like VDI, virtual desktop infrastructure. We may provide desktops as an example in a VDI instance, or contractors for developers, call center agents, things along those lines, and we don't want them to be able to necessarily tweak things, to make things more difficult to configure, troubleshoot, maintain. Every time they log off, anything that was changed while that user had that session open or that VDI session open, gets lost. Next time they boot up, they're back to a clean state. So preventing them from installing or tweaking things reduces troubleshooting and prevents unauthorized installation of applications. Next, we have snapshots. Snapshots allow a user to quickly revert to a known good state or roll back changes in the event of a virus, a malware incident, spyware. Two concepts there come two rolled into one. A snapshot allows us to roll back to a known good state. We can physically take a snapshot, and some operating systems will do this behind the scenes as we install drivers. Windows as an example, will create a last known good configuration. If something doesn't quite turn out we have an issue, we can revert back to a last known good configuration. Also, if we're in the middle of say a maintenance upgrade, we're doing some things overnight, maybe doing a maintenance window, if we have an issue, we can roll back that change to get us back to that last known good state. Then we have live boot media. This concept allows for a fully operational operating system, or an OS, either on a USB drive or some type of removable media that allows the cleaning of a system, removing of malware, or you could run the operating system from that removable media for however long. It's not the optimal way to do it. You don't want to do that every single time, but it does allow you to boot up a machine off of that USB drivers and do what you need to do. Those things work well when you need to boot up outside of the actual disk that's in the computer and then use the live boot media to clean it, remove malware, spyware.

Chapter 4 High Availability, Redundancy & Fault Tolerance

Our next concept is high availability. This is two or more systems that are in sync at or near real time. We're split writing, if you will. We're writing two systems at one time or very close to real time. We can failover between systems and minimize disruption. For example, we have one site, Site A, it's comprised of some ESXi infrastructure, a couple of VMs running, some servers, we have some virtualization infrastructure as well for our SAN, VPLEX in this example. But, we can also set up another site, in this case, Site B. That way, we have the ability to VMotion between sites, we have a VMotion network between our clusters, we have a distributed mirrored volume between our VPLEXs, and then we have SAN arrays in both locations. In essence, we're writing to both locations. They're going to synchronize pretty much in real time. That's dependent upon how far away they are. If there's more than, say, 5 or 10 milliseconds of latency between the sites, it can, depending upon the application and it's tolerance for latency, that may not be feasible. But if the applications and the data centers are close enough, then you can do in real time, have that synchronous replication and make sure you have availability in both sites. For high availability, backup data centers need to be relatively close, roughly 30 to 50 miles away, if possible, low latency between locations to ensure synchronous replication of data. You don't want one on the East Coast and one of the West Coast and expect synchronous replication. Also, do I need assessment? What systems and applications actually need HA? Not all do. Also, what systems and applications need offsite DR, or disaster recovery? Because there is a differentiation between the two. A needs assessment of that specific site and the applications within that site are really what's necessary to determine because you're not going to want to do this for every single application. It's very costly because it's not really just bunkering the data from one site to the other. You're going to need all the infrastructure as well, the servers, the applications, the understanding of which order they need to be brought up in right. There's a lot of work that goes in behind the scenes to make sure this is done properly, but it's crucial for business critical applications. Because even though it's a high cost associated with these types of solutions, what is the cost of that critical application goes down? If you're making whatever, a million dollars an hour or $3 million a minute, whatever the case might be, how much does that downtime cost versus what's the cost of a synchronous replication or a high availability site close by? Along those same lines we have redundancy. Redundancy covers all areas of an application stack, so redundant servers, power supplies, RAID, NICs, HBAs. We're also talking about networking switches and fabrics and storage arrays. If you want true redundancy, and you want to say your application is redundant, well, it's not just the application, it's not just the server, all of the things that make up that stack need to be redundant as well so there is no single point of failure, so servers, power supplies, and so on. We need to make sure that if any one of those things goes down, it does not have the ability to take that specific application offline. Another way to do that is also with clustering, multiple servers operating as one. It could be MS SQL Server, it could be Oracle RAC, also hot spares. Data is copied over proactively, so a hot spare in a storage array, as an example, is a mechanism that can detect when a drive is about to fail. You're going to have spare drives in the array already, or in the server. Those drives sit there and they're not used until something starts to go bad, and The data would then be proactively copied over from the failing drives over to those hot spares, and then you either dispatch a technician to go out and swap those drives out and replace them with good drives, and then they become the new hot spares. Something else to keep in mind is the fact that that spare can be a dedicated disk or it can be space on multiple disks, so it doesn't necessarily have to be a disk all by itself. Instead of having a hot spare you could have hot space, That things are copied over to whatever space is available on those drives, and then bad space or the bad blocks on that disk are marked as such That no new data is copied over to those locations. When we're talking about hardware, fault tolerant hardware means having redundant components in case one fails so that operations can continue. Much like I just talked about at the entire stack level, now we're talking about the individual hardware component level. In this instance, we have disks, the networking cards, NICs or the HBAs, the power supplies, the fans. It's a storage array, the storage processors, the engines and the directors. All of these things need to be redundant. As an example, we have multiple servers, we have our fault tolerant network. If we start to see where something actually starts to go south, you can see the middle server, we could remotion those instances or those workloads off of the failing server onto either one of the good servers without any disruption to the business. That can't happen if we don't have redundant components inside as well. Next, let's talk about the concept of diversity. What I mean by diversity is diversity of technologies, vendors, cryptographic keys, security controls. Let's take a look at each of these individually. When we're talking about technology diversity, why do we do that? What's the point? While technology diversity is the concept of using more than one type of technology to accomplish a given task, that safeguards against things like bugs or vulnerabilities that may otherwise take down an entire system. In essence, you can think of it as not a single point of failure. It provides a method of failback and failover also in the event of an incident. We have multiple technologies we can utilize. If one doesn't work, we can either failover to the other or quickly instantiate that other technology to bring it online very quickly. Next we have vendor diversity. Vendor diversity helps safeguard against things like supply chain attacks and incidents. If we have more than one vendor that we're dealing with, that way, if one gets compromised or is not available, we have others that we can choose from. It provides vendor lock-in, so we're not tied to a specific vendor. If one is either not available or doesn't have something that we need, we can obviously choose from another vendor. Then, realistically, it gives us more financial leverage. If we have multiple vendors to choose from, then no one vendor realizes they have all of our eggs in one basket, so we can leverage or pit one against the other. In essence, the business risk of having all of our systems, our data, technology, and/or knowledge in the hands of a single vendor introduces, to some extent, a level of risk. By spreading that out across multiple vendors, we mitigate that to a degree. Next, we have crypto and control diversity. With crypto diversity, we would rotate cryptographic keys and also use technologies from more than one provider. If there's bugs, or if one is compromised, we have multiples that we can choose from, and we're not completely dependent on one technology to provide that solution. Same thing with controls diversity - Diversification ensures overlap. It also provides wider coverage. Let's take a look at that one in more detail. Antivirus, threat detection, ransomware prevention - all of these things should be following a defense in depth methodology - layered technologies. When we're talking about layered technologies, we don't necessarily want three or four different technologies that do exactly the same thing. As an example, if we have technology A. Let's say the technology A has a 75% success rate for antivirus or threat detection, ransomware protection. Technology A, hey, we're going to diversify. Let's go ahead and buy technology B. That also has a 75% success rate. Well, that's great, but we need to follow defense in depth, so let's go out and buy technology C. Well, if all three of those have the same 75% success rate, meaning they all pretty much correlate with one another, and they all find or address the same exact issues, but what happens is, we have very little overlap, That gives us a 75% success rate, but also a 25% failure rate. If those three technologies are not tightly correlated, well, then we can see, we start to spread out a little bit more and our risk goes down, because now we have three different technologies that aren't exactly similar. Something that technology A may not cover, technology B might find, or technology C might find. The less correlated they are, as we see, it becomes more spread out, then our coverage increases. Having multiple technologies is great as long as they're not identical of each other, and it seems counterintuitive, but the less correlated they are with each other, it actually spreads our coverage wider and gives us a better chance of picking up those threats, antivirus and ransomware. In summary we talked about redundancy. We talked about geographic redundancy, network redundancy, things like power and also replication redundancy. We talked about the various backup types. We talked about non-persistence, and what that means as far as recoverability, and making our data available. We talked about high availability and how that works, along with diversity, whether it's vendor, technology, controls, cryptographic technologies.

Chapter 5 Embedded Systems & SCADA Security

In the following chapters, we'll be covering Recognizing Security Implications of Embedded and Specialized Systems. We're going to start off with embedded systems, and we'll talk about SCADA systems and ICS systems. We'll talk more about what they mean and the security implications. We'll talk about the Internet of Things and how massively that's growing, and also the attack vector is growing right along with it. We'll talk about specialized systems, also Voice over IP, or VoIP systems. We talk about heating, ventilation, and air conditioning, or HVAC. We also talk about drones and AVs, and also, UAVs. We'll talk about multi-function printers, also, real-time operating systems, or RTOS. We'll talk about surveillance systems, systems on a chip, communication considerations, and then the constraints we have to deal with when trying to secure all of these systems. The main goal here is that embedded systems, they're literally everywhere. They control things from thermostats to critical infrastructure. What I want you to do is think about from a security mindset is to just realize that really everything is a target. Be aware of all the things that are around you in your environment, things you may take for granted. Obviously, the big things that everyone thinks about, router, switches, or infrastructure servers, storage, all of those things, or the main components that make up our network and make up our infrastructure are natural things to focus on. But the other things, too, the wearables, the IoT devices - all of these things become attack vectors and attack services. There are ways for hackers to get their foot in the door. As we know, once their foot is in the door, they elevate privileges, they install persistence, they maintain persistence, they can come and go as they please, they pivot, once they're inside of our network, jump from network to network and explore. They extract things of value, or they destroy, or they just sit there and wait. Different groups have different methods of operation and different goals. Some are easy to detect, some are difficult. The easiest way to avoid all of that, is to not let them in in the first place. The thing that compounds that, obviously, is the fact that these things can leave our environment, go outside of our perimeter, go outside of our safety zones, and then come back into our network. It used to be that laptops were the primary culprit for that. But now with wearables and IoT devices, things can come and go much more easily. To start off, let's talk about what actually is an embedded system. An embedded system is a microprocessor-based computer hardware system with software that is designed to perform a very specific or a dedicated function, either as an independent system or as part of a larger system. The core of this is an integrated circuit, or an IC, that's designed to carry out computation for real-time operations. These embedded systems are very scaled down. They're not like regular computers that we think of, like a laptop or desktop. They're not designed to do everything well. They're designed to do very specific functions with very low latency and to process things in pretty much real time. They don't do a lot of things good. They do one or two things very well and very rapidly. They have embedded systems for very specific functions, There's a different type of embedded system for different types of utilities, different types of functions, different pieces of equipment, different industries. When it comes to embedded systems, a few that I want you to be familiar with; we have one called Raspberry Pi; you may have heard of that before. A Raspberry Pi is actually a fully functional computer; CPU, Wi-Fi, Bluetooth, video, not a video card, but onboard integrated video, and it's also expandable.

These small devices can be embedded in a number of different pieces of hardware and can run a myriad of applications. In essence, you could connect a monitor, keyboard and actually use this as a fully functioning computer. Next, we have a field programmable gate array, or an FPGA, not to be confused with a flip chip pin grid array, also known as an FPGA, totally different thing. In this instance, we're talking about a field programmable gate array, and this is an integrated circuit designed to be configured or programmed after manufacturing. All of the circuitry are building blocks inside of the ICs that can be configured or programmed after it's built, so you buy it, it's a blank slate, and you can program it to your needs. Next, we have something referred to as an Arduino. an Arduino, at first pass, may look similar to a Raspberry Pi, but they're very different. An Arduino device is a single board microcontroller versus having a microprocessor. A microcontroller is used for very specific functions. Think of it almost like an embedded system we talked about before. It's not a general purpose computer, but they're designed for very specific functions. These types of things, as well, are stackable. The pins and the pin slots on this board, and it's designed to be stacked, so you can have different functions added onto, and there's a number of different ones that can be added and give it additional capabilities, but these things are designed for very specific functions. Some things need to be concerned with. When we're talking about SCADA, or supervisory control and data acquisition, you may or may not be familiar with that term, but it's very important that you understand what it is and the implications if these things are not maintained properly, it has a big impact or a big potential impact because these types of systems usually refer to a centralized system that which monitor and control entire sites or complexes of systems spread throughout large areas. What does that really mean? Well think about water treatment facilities, the electrical grid, the power grid, things along those lines that really encompass large areas of critical infrastructure. We have such things as an RTU, or a remote terminal unit, and that is connections to sensors, and it's going to convert that sensor information, and whatever that sensor might be, whether it's on a pipe or some piece of equipment within a larger system, that needs to give off sensors, and alerts, they might check the temperature, or the pressure, or the amount of electricity, or voltage. There's going to be a sensor connected to that. The RTU then converts that sensor information into digital data. Next is a programmable logic unit, or a logic controller, rather, a PLC. It's similar to an RTU, but PLCs are a little newer, they're more versatile, more economical, but they do the same type of function. They're going to report into a master terminal unit, or MTU. Next we have a human machine interface, an HMI, and that's going to present the data that's collected from these RTUs or PLCs to a human operator who can then act upon that specific data. They may need to adjust valves or make sure that things are within acceptable ranges. Then master terminal unit, or the MTU, is what sends information and instructions to the RTU or the PLC. And it's also going to receive instructions back and aggregate all that information. In a SCADA environment you may have some type of master control area, or like a control center, where you have all the different screens from your different systems, whether it's a nuclear power plant, or a water treatment facility, or an electrical grid, sewage system. These PLCs and RTUs are spread out throughout the entire system. They all report back to the MTU, and you have an operator that sits there and manages, and maintains, and monitors all these things. If we look at this in a little more detail, in a SCADA system we have the RTUs, they're going to be computers set up along the network, and typically these are closed off networks that are not connected to the internet, least traditionally. You'll see as we go along here, they've evolved from a non-connected air gapped system into things that are now more distributed networked or actually connected to the internet. But at any rate, we have the RTUs that are connected to our network, they all report into an MTU, we have a human interface that actually looks in and controls, and then we have people that have access potentially through the internet, it just depends. In this type of an environment, we have to be aware of the fact that we could have a remote access hacker that could get in if our machine, or network is connected to the internet, or if we have some type of access point, whether it is a legitimate access point or a rogue access point, we may have a remote access attacker who can come in with from within our network, even if it's not connected to the internet per se, if they're able to get access to the network itself, they could potentially do some harm. As you can imagine, these things are very widespread. They connect and control large pieces of infrastructure, so we want to make sure that we have these things as secure as possible. One way we may do that, let's just say, for instance, all of our SCADA systems, these terminals cannot be updated, they're just in a situation where they are what they are, we can't patch them. We wouldn't be able to apply, let's say, for instance, a host-based intrusion detection system. We wouldn't be able to put anything on the host specifically, but we could put a network-based intrusion detection system. We could firewall off the network itself, and then we could put some type of network intrusion detection system in place, so that if any type of attacker were to come in remotely or even if they're attaching to the network itself, we could detect that intrusion. We also have to discuss some SCADA security concerns. When these types of systems were first invented and first brought online, they were very monolithic. They were not connected to the internet, and they weren't really designed to be connected to anything else. They were just very self-contained systems. Security wasn't really as much of an issue as it is today. It wasn't really baked in and as big of a concern. For the monolithic, it's evolved into a distributed system, which has then evolved into networked, and you can see the progression here. From networked and then we now went into the Internet of Things, and we have access potentially from anywhere. Some security implications and some concerns would be unauthorized access, whether it be malware, viruses, we could have hacking attempts and theft or destruction of data, or at the very least, to plant something that's going to allow them to have a back door at some later point. All of these things are big concerns from a security standpoint. We also have to understand that these types of attacks can be used to degrade or destroy critical infrastructure. Two big examples; one you may or may not be aware of, the other was all over the news for many, many months and actually a couple of years now, but in 2000 in Australia, there was a sewage system that was attacked. It ended up being a disgruntled internal employee, but that person was able to in effect, shut down the sewage system and it backed up throughout parks and throughout all areas within Australia or a lot of areas within Australia. In 2010, a much more determined and a much more focused attack that was actually using code as a weapon. It was a very specific attack by either the US and Israel, but it was created as a weapon, and it was targeted specifically at the PLCs and the SCADA systems that were used in Iran's nuclear facilities by inserting malware. There was an air-gapped system, but it was on USB drives that somebody apparently had plugged in, and when they went into that specific system, it infected and downloaded some vulnerabilities and they were able to find out exactly what PLCs they needed to attack. As soon as they found out that the one that it needed, it was able to destroy up to a fifth of the centrifuges within that nuclear facility, causing the centrifuges to spin out of control. The implication of that is, or the scary part is, the malware or the actual attack reported back to the HMIs, the human machine interface, and reported back to the operators, that everything was fine. They had no idea that the centrifuges were spinning out of control until it was too late. They burned themselves out and were destroyed. It severely crippled Iran's nuclear facilities during that time period. SCADA systems have obviously great use, they have a lot of potential, but they also have a huge potential for impact if they're breached. We rely heavily on these types of things for critical infrastructure throughout pretty much all facets of society.

Chapter 6 Smart Devices / IoT & Special Purpose Devices

When it comes to smart devices, or internet of things or IoT devices, we have to cover a few things. Wearable technology is becoming more and more pervasive everywhere, as far as watches, heart monitors, fitness devices, and there's more coming. Every time you turn around, there's some new device, or some new use case; always connected, continuously feeding information about location, our habits, our health so that increases the attack vector, making interception of data easier. If you think about it, a potential concern would be, if a hacker is able to access all this data, they could, number one, compromise the data, use it for social engineering purposes; they could even sell that data, potentially, to companies that are not necessarily on the up and up, that could use that data against you for monetary gain. They could use it for social engineering, where they could go out and now develop a more complete profile of who you are and what you do, what you like. If they were to launch some type of email scam or spear phishing campaign and they were able to use your specific data, that's personal to you, it becomes much more credible to the person they're trying to contact, perhaps a friend, or an associate of yours. Next, we have home automation. Along the same lines, same thought process, that personal data can be compromised. Entry points into a user's network, and ultimately, really their life, when you think about it. Social engineering becomes even easier. The more a hacker knows, as we talked about, and again, these are all attack vectors. These are threat vectors. The attack surface starts to spread, even though they're in tiny devices that you don't necessarily think about. They have embedded systems that should be patched, firmware updates just like any other computer system, or operating system. A lot of times, these things don't have either the capability to do that, or you don't think about doing it. Well, all of those things now become a way into the network. If someone's able to hack a device, and that device connects to your home network, they can get into your network just like they would in a corporate environment. If they're able to get in, elevate privileges, pivot, jump onto perhaps, you bring your work laptop home; now they're into your personal network. They're able to use that to get into a work laptop. You take that into the office. That malware still exists. If they were able to get in and establish a persistent connection, that's another possible way into a corporate enterprise, or a corporate network. All of these things start to compound on each other and makes it even more critical that we maintain and monitor and update or patch. Now, just to reiterate for smart devices and IoT things, so as you mentioned, sensors, wearables, smart devices, facility automation devices, all of these things can make life more convenient and also more real-time interactivity, easier to manage. But as we talked about, they also increase a company's attack surface. What we need to make sure that we do is we don't allow weak defaults. Most of these things have known vulnerabilities and weak defaults, like default passwords. It's very important to change these default passwords and settings and also routinely audit the environment to understand what IoT devices exist on the network and what types of data they actually transmit and also to where. We need to make sure that we have a good understanding of what is on our network, and it's not a once and done, nor is it a set it and forget it type of process. We need to make sure we do these things with some type of regular cadence, whether it's once a quarter, once a year, every six months. It's going to apply differently for each organization, but auditing to make sure we understand what is on the network is critical. Next, we have special purpose devices. The first one up is medical devices. Medical devices pose a risk on multiple levels. They can be hacked and adversely affect a person's health, they can obviously produce a massive amount of data, that data can be used against that person, or it can be used to formulate some type of social engineering component or sold to other companies, data mined, and these devices often contain embedded systems that are not routinely patched and updated. An interesting fact is that hospitals typically have 3X to 4X. There are 300 or 400% more medical devices than they do IT equipment. If these devices aren't patched and maintained, just like we do everything else, that's a huge potential risk for compromise and for breach. Just like the 2014 NIST voluntary framework assessment, the NIST guidelines we talked about previously, the same cybersecurity policies we apply to our traditional networks should be applied to the medical devices and the IoT devices that serve up the medical and the health-related fields. Next we have motor vehicles, and as you can imagine, as these things become more and more technologically advanced, and they become connected to the internet, they can be compromised just like anything else. There's potential for sabotage or vehicle impairment, theft of customer data, again, these types of devices produce lots and lots of data continuously, telemetry information, where you're going and when, your speed your routines - all of these things could be used to go to profile against you. Also disruption in services, we can shut the car down. If a hacker successfully exploits something in the vehicle, and someone gets injured or some type of monetary damage occurs, well, there you have reputational damages, and also consumer confidence. That has an impact to a company's bottom line, investors. Getting back to the sabotage and vehicle impairment, it was a hack of a Chrysler Jeep vehicle back in 2015, and the short of it is security researchers, this was more of a controlled demo of possibilities, but these security researchers were able to hack the Jeep and commanding it to drive into a ditch. That is not good, I mean, it goes without saying. Imagine driving down the road and all of a sudden your car just takes over, and it drives where it wants to. Especially with the more autonomous cars coming down the pike, it's a great feature that's going to ultimately save a lot of lives, but hackers are always going neck and neck, the good guys and the bad guys are constantly battling to try to outsmart and out do each other. Just like any other industry, there's constant vigilance that needs to be applied to make sure these devices are secure as possible. Next, let's talk about Voice over IP, or VoIP. VoIP has actually been around since the mid 1990s. It's been around for quite a while, it's a mature technology. Many companies have switched from traditional PSTN or public switched telephone networks, which are circuit based, to modern VoIP systems, which are packet switched and traverse over the Internet. PBX systems everyone is switching from those older systems to Voice over IP systems. Voice over IP is actually a suite of protocols, and we won't dig into that too, too much. It's beyond the scope of what we're going to talk about here, but it's a suite of protocols, including MGCP, which is a Media Gateway Control Protocol or a connection management for media gateways, also SIP or Session Initiation Protocol, and the older H.323 protocol, which was introduced when VoIP first came out. It allows, as you might guess, voice and video calling over IP networks, in other words, the internet. A few VoIP concerns, however, since we're dealing with IP traffic, IP packets traversing over an IP network of the internet. We have very much the same concerns that we would have with any host connected to the internet. Eavesdropping, vishing, which is Voice over IP phishing. Well, same process, just using VoIP as the communication medium. Also, viruses and malware. Just like we have with a host on a network, viruses and malware can also be introduced here as well. Denial-of-service attacks, something called SPIT, or Spamming over Internet Telephony. We're spamming, just like we would on an email platform, we have the potential to compromise the system, and just like we would send out millions of emails, we can send out millions of bogus phone calls using a robo-dialer or some type of mechanism; it's just an new IP address on the other side of the connection. We can do a similarly annoying and very frustrating process of spam over the VoIP network instead of our traditional method. Then call tampering and also on-path attacks, formerly Man-in-the-Middle attacks, very similar to an on-path attack when a host is attaching to a server or a web server.

Chapter 7 HVAC, Aircraft/UAV & MFDs

Next, we have HVAC systems. Heating, ventilating, and air condition systems provide, as you might guess, proper temperature control, humidity control. Excessive heat can wreak havoc on electronic devices. The heat itself can cause something to overheat, or if we start messing with the HVAC and turning it up and down and perhaps creating condensation, we can create condensation, which equals water which is bad for electronics. A hacker, a skilled hacker, could go in and manipulate that HVAC system to affect computers, networking or storage. All of these things can wreak havoc on electronic devices and the networks in general. It becomes a target. If someone wants to take down a specific entity, a data center, or a company, in general, they can do so potentially by manipulating these types of networks. It's not just the computer systems - there's the ancillary systems that all make up this attack surface, and I keep using that word. It's the global picture. You have to look at the entire landscape and say, what are all the different ways that someone can get into my network? What are all the different ways someone can get access to my data or negatively affect or negatively impact my company. As an IT professional, as a security professional, we need to be looking at all of these different avenues of attack and making sure that we're protecting against them, we're monitoring, updating, patching, and shoring up our defenses using layered defenses, making sure we have multiple layers of defense for a hacker to have to get through before they get access to our corporate or proprietary data. Some HVAC areas of concern, proper humidity needs to be maintained. Low humidity can create static electricity. Static electricity is not good. A lot of electronic equipment, a lot of the circuitry inside of a computer runs on 5 volts or 12 volts, or even less. Well, if you have static electricity, if someone were to go across the carpet and have enough static electricity to actually generate a spark when they go to touch something, that could be upwards of 30,000 volts. That spark that just gives you a little bit of a bite and, jumps from your finger to whatever you're touching may not seem like a big deal, but that is enough to fry a piece of electronic circuitry on a server or a network switch or something like that. If that happens, that could potentially take down a piece of your fabric, or your network, or a critical component to an application, or so forth. It has the potential to be severely impacting. Conversely, high humidity can create condensation or moisture. Moisture is not good for electronic components. Collectively, an entire data center can be compromised if the HVAC system is purposely degraded or destroyed. These are one of those systems that we need to closely monitor. Next, we have aircraft and unmanned aircraft, or UAVs. Unmanned aircraft, just like we talked about with cars, can be compromised. Hackers, terrorists can have access, organized crime, the same types of groups that would attack a traditional computer network can do the same thing with these types of devices. Now, the scary part, or where it becomes a big area of concern, is if they're compromised, these types of devices can be weaponized to deliver ammunitions, they can drop bombs, that could crash into things, or they could be used to spy on ourselves. If a terrorist group took control of a drone, they could actually take the feed from that drone, they could spy on troop movements, ammunitions, deployments. It's especially important in military and government application that these things are highly secured, and there is a whole different level of encryption. But there are a ton of consumer-grade devices that can also be used for these same types of purposes. A bad actor could take control or intercept communications. They could disperse weapons, they could spy or snoop on targets. They can also do something called GPS spoofing, and they pony up false GPS coordinates, so the drone thinks it's somewhere else. It thinks it's in a different place than it is, it's a different time, it's a different speed. The hacker could then take control of that drone and direct it wherever they want it to go. All of the things that are created to make our lives easier to give us additional capabilities can also be used against us. It's very, very important that IT security, or cybersecurity in general, really ramps up and apply themselves to these areas specifically. Encryption is still our best line of defense, so encrypted GPS mitigates that threat. If it's encrypted, they're not able to take control and offer up false coordinates. All the military grade or government grade drones and unmanned aircraft they have that already in place. Consumer grade, though, typically doesn't, or it's not as strong, which still gives the bad actor the ability to use these devices against us. Next, when it comes to printers and multifunction devices, printers and MFDs can contain very sensitive information. People print very sensitive data from time to time, they'll copy things, so all of these things get stored on a hard drive in that system, potentially. All of these things need to be patched and updated regularly. This is a very systematic approach to IT security, we need to patch and update regularly. Especially as the network and the size of the company grows and scales, that patching becomes more and more of a challenge, especially when you have a lot of different systems, Linux and Windows variations and different flavors of OSs, all of those things have to be updated on a specific cadence. When it comes to printers, again, patch update regularly, also, use static IP addresses when possible. That alleviates the DNS cache poisoning potential, direct that prints queue somewhere else, potentially compromise that data. Next, we have firewalls. We need to make sure these things are in place and functioning properly. Also, we have access control. Who's actually logging into these things? Who's actually using the devices to copy or scan. If we have one set of credentials that everyone uses, it's going to be very, very difficult, if not impossible, for us to then go back and audit if we have to do some type of forensic procedures, some type of forensic accounting of who is doing what. If everyone's using the same account, we can't do that. Credentials access control is very important, and also, centralized printer pools. That way, we have one place to essentially manage, and audit, and update. Then also we have hard drive encryption where possible. Just like with any other system, we want to use encryption whenever possible to maintain an additional layer of security. That way, if someone grabs that printer or that MFD, puts it over their shoulder, and walks out of the data center or walks out of the office, that hard drive is encrypted. The data on that hard drive is encrypted, or at the very least, it makes it very, very difficult for them to get access to it. Nothing is 100% foolproof, but encryption goes a long way to mitigating that risk. Then, lastly, proper disposal and sanitation processes. Just like when we want to sanitize a hard drive on a computer, we would do the same thing for a printer. We want to make sure it's wiped properly and that data is irretrievable. That way, when we dispose of that device, we know for a fact that that data is gone.

Chapter 8 Real Time Operating Systems & Surveillance Systems

Next, we have to cover RTOS, or real-time operating system. Real-time operating systems are designed to process data with minimal delay, or latency. Latency being the lag time that it takes to get a response back from something. These types of systems are more concerned with very deterministic processing of data rather than with the amount of work that can be performed. In other words, rather than being a catch-all or just a workhorse that can do everything good, this does one type of thing extremely well. They lend themselves to embedded systems, IoT devices, SCADA systems. These devices, just like any other type of operating system, even though it is a real-time operating system that's dedicated to a specific task or a subset of tasks, they still need to be updated, they still have vulnerabilities, they still need to be patched. We have to take the same due diligence with these types of systems that we do with our typical computing infrastructure. Our next area for concern is the camera systems. A lot of the security cameras that are actually used for protection are wildly open. Default username and passwords, they can get access from just the open internet. They can actually be used to monitor networks and monitor the companies that they're supposed to be protecting or guarding. A lot of these security cameras are installed with a default admin username and password, and they're never changed. A quick Google search, and I'm not recommending that you do this, but thousands of these are viewable on the internet. There's websites out there are devoted to just listing all of the cameras you can go and browse through and look at all different cameras from all over the world, where the default username and passwords are in place, and you can just view the data that they're capturing. We need to patch vulnerabilities because these things get vulnerabilities just like every other operating system or piece of computing infrastructure does, update drivers and firmware, just like any other OS or just like any other embedded system. Next, we have to understand the attack vector. Compromised cameras can be a way into a network. They can first and foremost allow us to watch what's going on, so that's not a good thing, but they're connected to a network. If we're able to actually get into that camera, elevate privileges, maintain persistence, just like with any other type of computing system, that's a way into the network. At that point, it's off to the races. We also need secure disposal policies. Encrypt communication, drives, if there are drives within those cameras, sometimes they have them, sometimes they don't, and securely wipe those devices before disposing. Next we have system on a chip, or SoC. When you SoC, it's a system on a chip, and what it means, it's an IC, or an integrated circuit, that integrates all of the components of a computer or other systems, all onto a single substrate, or a single chip. In other words, it takes an entire computer, and now it takes that entire computer, and puts it down to a chip. Some system on a chip, or SoC concerns to cover are a raspberry PI; that is an example of a system on a chip. It's an entire computing system down onto a tiny little substrate, minus the data storage. Mobile devices, phones, or wearables, watches; these are all things that are systems on a chip. These devices are becoming increasingly smaller. They used to be room sized. Then they were, suitcase sized. Now they're getting smaller and smaller for hearing aids, for vision. Next it will be down to nanotechnology or nano size, so they could inject into your bloodstream potentially, and be used to very prescriptively fight disease. Embedded devices, for hearing, for sight, for health issues; as you might imagine, there's a lot of concern here. If someone's able to compromise those devices, hackers can target those systems, compromise their data or attack the host. Let's now talk about some communication considerations. Now that 5G networks are starting to roll out globally, in the US, and across the rest of the globe, some things to worry about. Some 5G security concerns. Millions more devices will come online as 5G rolls out, and that's connected cars, healthcare. Now that we have this potential for a very high speed, very low latency network, more and more things will be tightly integrated with 5G, and we're dependent upon the network for connectivity, critical infrastructure being a big one. We talked about that before, with SCATA systems where it used to be a completely air-gapped network. That's no longer the case. Many of these systems are logically air-gapped, or, not air-gapped it all. With 5G, there are potentially more security mechanisms available; network slicing, enhanced encryption, increased visibility . But it's also more complicated to manage. The handoff between networks, as devices jump from 5G, and perhaps downgrade to 4G, or even 3G, depending upon where they are. As they traverse different parts of the landscape, they may switch networks. As that switching occurs, mechanisms that may be in place for 5G, as an example, may not have an equivalent in a 4G or a 3G network; and also something else we talked about before is supply chain attacks. As the chip manufacturers and all the sub components that make up these 5G devices are made, there is the potential for supply chain attacks, where those individual devices or components can be compromised, ultimately then putting a back door into the network or compromising it in some form or fashion. A few other terms that I want you to be familiar with are two main ones, and that's narrowband and baseband. Narrowband is designed for small amounts of data transfer, typically under 10 seconds, not milliseconds, but 10 seconds of latency. Not super speedy, but we don't really necessarily care because we're transmitting very small amounts of data. It has secure mechanisms built in, authentication and encryption, but these things are designed for very small transference of data. Then we have baseband radio, and this is dedicated processors that run real-time operating systems that we talked about before, and they control radio functions within different types of devices, not usually Wi-Fi or Bluetooth, but other radio type of connectivity. Zigbee for example at first glance, may look similar in form or fashion to Raspberry Pi or Arduino, but completely different thing we're talking about here. It's a very small device, and it's a suite of high-level communication protocols used for what's referred to as a PAN, or a personal area network. They're low power, often battery powered, low data rate, low latency, and also, close proximity wireless ad-hoc network. These things are designed to make mesh-type networks within a home, as an example. It operates in the industrial, the scientific, and medical, or ISM, radio band. There are currently over 26 billion IoT devices, and that's going to just continue to rise as we go, up into the trillions eventually. These things are becoming more and more and more ubiquitous. The average home may have 30 to 40, maybe 50 different IoT devices, and you may not even realize it. You may say to yourself, well, Zigbee, I've never even heard of it. I don't have any Zigbee devices in my house, I don't really have much to worry about. I don't care about them. Well, hold on one second there, and let's take a look at what actually makes up Zigbee products, and I'll bet that you have one or more of these things in your house. Amazon Echo as an example, Belkin or WeMo systems. I won't read through the entire list, but things like Honeywell thermostats or even Philips Hue lights. I know I have dozens of Philips Hue lights in my house. Samsung SmartThings, also their Comcast Xfinity box, and then list goes on and on. There's a very good chance you may have devices in your house that use the Zigbee protocol and you're not even aware of it. Something to keep in mind is we have some security considerations when we're talking about Zigbee security. Zigbee security does use encryption, which is good, but the keys can be extracted using publicly accessible tools, That's not so good, so you can go on the internet and search for the tools, search for the processes to do these things, It is possible. And it's also possible to jam these networks and force a repairing. If you're close enough to a device or close enough to a, let's say a person's house, you could jam their front door lock as an example. And as they get a repair, you could extract those encryption keys and potentially unlock that door. Command injection, replay attacks are possible. Also, security testing tools like SecBee, from a group called Cognosec, allows for pretty easy compromise of these devices. And again, you can easily search online for more information about these tool sets and see just how easy some of these compromises can be. When we're talking about IoT devices or embedded systems, etc, these are designed for ease of use, they are designed for low power consumption, and in some cases connectivity in hard to reach or remote locations, some of that narrow band technology that I talked about. They typically don't have large amounts of compute power, nor do they typically have the ability to manage advanced cryptographic functions like anti-tampering measures so they are potentially easy to compromise, or easier to compromise. When we have these types of devices in our house or in our businesses, all of these things come into play because they make up an attack surface, power, compute or network. If we don't have very powerful devices that are using these systems, they could be easier to compromise. Also, some of these systems, embedded systems, things that are in hard to reach places or things that are not necessarily updated very often, if at all, the inability to patch. If a vulnerability is discovered, how quickly can we patch that, if it all? Also we have authentication. If they don't have a lot of compute power or anti-tampering techniques, it may be possible to force authentication or to break authentication. Also, the range, the cost, the implied trust, all of these things come into play when we're talking about decisions around whether to bring these types of devices into our networks. Bringing these things into a corporate environment may have additional implications and you have to make sure that these things are properly vetted, properly audited, and you understand exactly how they work, what data they transmit, do they phone home, how do they phone home, what protocols do they use, what authentication methods do they use. All of these things should be vetted through you and your security teams prior to rolling them out into production. In summary we talked about embedded systems. We talked about SCADA and ICS systems. We also Talked about the Internet of Things, or IOT, along with specialized systems, voice over IP. We talked about heating, ventilation, and air conditioning, or HVAC, drones and aerial vehicles. We talked about multi-function printers and some of the security implications around those devices. We talked about real-time operating systems, or RTOS, surveillance systems and the cameras that make up those systems, system on a chip, or SoC, communication considerations, and also the constraints that we have around these systems, keeping them secure, how to patch them, how to keep them updated.

Chapter 9 Barricades, Mantraps & Alarms

In this chapter, we'll be covering Understanding the Importance of Physical Security Controls. We have physical security, talking about deterrence and controls, we'll also talk about digital and logical security such as locks, and vaults, and sensors, we'll then talk about securing infrastructure, such as protected cabling and data access, and then secure disposal of data, such as deleting and the wiping of data. Another physical control would be barricades, so barricades can prevent access by virtue of them being a physical, literally a physical, barrier. They can be temporary or they can be permanent. But even if they're permanent, they can still be fixed or movable, and they can direct the flow of traffic, or they can block traffic completely. A bollard is a giant metal pole that can rise up and go up and down to the ground. It can go down flush to allow cars to pass over, or it can rise up to provide that preventive measure. Or we have what's called a Jersey-style barrier where you'll see these a lot of times on roadways and where they want to cordon off traffic, Those things are temporary, typically, although sometimes they're put up and kept in place permanently. But these are examples of two types of barriers that can be put in place, and they can either direct the flow of traffic, or they can block traffic completely. They can be in place. They can be in raised position, and they can block traffic pretty much permanently; however, if there's an emergency, they need to get an ambulance, or they need to get some type of delivery, or something closer to the building, they can be lowered, and then, traffic or a vehicle can pass over them unrestricted. The next one is something referred to as a mantrap, and a mantrap is an access control, and it's two sets of doors. A person will enter the first set of doors, which then closes behind them, and then a guard or some automated control will allow access through a second door once authentication is verified. We have one set of doors, or one door that will open, a person would walk into that enclosed area, the door would shut behind them. They either have to badge in or they have, a card reader, whether it's an RFID or NFC chip, or there may be a guard actually sitting behind a glass area, or perhaps maybe on a video camera, there's going to be some verification system that once that person is then verified, the second door will open and they can pass through. Something else that can control access is badges. Badges enable several control and visibility options, including they can provide or restrict access to individual occasions, we can badge into certain areas within the building. We can have access to one area, but not necessarily the other. They can also be revoked quickly. If someone loses access or changes roles, you don't necessarily have to go around and try to recover keys you can do that electronically via just removing access from that badge. It also provides visibility as to who is actually in the building for things like evacuations, fire drills, it makes it much easier, or at a glance, to be able to tell is everyone out of the building, who's left, because when they badge in, they're recorded, and then when they leave the building, assuming they do it correctly, they're actually listed as leaving as well. It allows for first responders to quickly identify who is in the building and who's not. Some challenges around badges, because again, nothing is foolproof, challenges are sharing and lending. It should obviously be prohibited and not allow people to share badges because again, we're now not accurately depicting who was in the building or what area they're in. Then also, if we lend badges, there's the opportunity or the chance that that could be stolen, duplicated. Tailgating should be part of corporate training, corporate policy, to not allow tailgating. In essence, someone following closely behind, you're holding the door for that person and allowing them to come in on your credentials. Everyone should have to badge in correctly, that way again, in the event of an evacuation, or fire drill, we have an accurate count of who's in the building and who's not, and then also, it just makes things more secure. If we just get in the practice of holding the door for someone, then someone who is not authorized to be there, a stranger or a bad actor could walk up, and if it's the policy to just hold the door for people, then that allows that bad actor access to the building. Next we have alarms. Alarms are common sense, but they work in tandem with other systems. They are detective, they're preventive, and they're also a deterrent. Depending upon the systems that they're working with, if, let's say for instance you have a motion detection system, as soon as motion is detected, an alarm can be sounded, so that works in tandem with that, It's a detective control type. It can be preventive in that those alarms could tie off and set off some type of workflow again where systems are locked, ports are shut down, network systems themselves could be turned off or prevented from being accessed any further, and then it could also be a deterrent in combination with signage. If people know that there's an alarm that will go off if you open this door, or if I access this system, or if I do, whatever A, B and C, if they're aware of the fact that alarms are going to be sounded, that will deter them from taking that action, typically. Combined with proper signage, it can be a very effective deterrent. If someone is truly determined to do something, this in and of itself will not fix that. A lot of people have become so conditioned to hearing alarms and hearing, , buzz and just noise in general that they don't respond to it anymore. Thieves and vandals, sometimes they understand that, if somebody hears an alarm, they're not really going to do anything, or if they do, it might take 3 to 5 minutes to realize that it's actually something significant. That gives them time to get in and get out. So don't rely solely on any one specific control type, realize that it is a combination of many things put together. Proper lighting is essential to create a safe and secure work environment. We need to make sure that we are always striving to increase safety and reduce risk by properly illuminating our workspaces. Anywhere that we have people working, we need to make sure that it's a safe environment. We also want to reduce a potential for break-ins and for vandalism and theft. It acts as a deterrent, but it won't prevent a determined thief. Preventive and detective measures are also required to give us that a triple threat. Simply having a place well-lit doesn't in and of itself prevent someone who's really determined about breaking in or doing some type of damage. As we've seen before, we have motion lights, we can have lights that are constantly illuminated, and we can have ones that are motion-controlled, If someone walks into an area, the lights come on. That in and of itself can act as a deterrent as well because they think they've been detected, for lack of a better term. Whether they're being videotaped or not, they don't know that; they see the lights come on, they think that, at least someone knows that I'm here. Working in tandem with that is signage, or proper signs. Signs are used to increase awareness and reduce risk. It's, again, a double-edged sword, It can warn of restricted areas, potential hazards, but it can also deter thieves and unauthorized individuals. We can post signs saying this area is under surveillance, this area is being monitored. We can also post signs, again, for our own employees to let them know, hey, this is a dangerous area, this is where chemicals are stored, or this is a specific area that is restricted. Make sure that we have signage in all areas anywhere where there's a potential for risk, and in other areas where we want to make sure that we let the public know, or potential vandals, thieves, let them know that the area is being monitored as well.

Chapter 10 Cameras, Video Surveillance & Guards

Video surveillance can be used to monitor access, it can be used to guard perimeters, detect motion, as well as document activity. It can also work in tandem with other mechanisms, other controls, like mantraps or remote authentication. A guard to be somewhere remote and still buzz you into an office, or a corridor, or some a place of business remotely by viewing you over a camera or some type of surveillance equipment. It can also issue alarms or alerts if unauthorized activity is detected. We can have something record and monitored 24/7, we don't have to sit there and actually watch it 24/7, but if it detects activity, it can send an alert, an email and say hey, we noticed some sounds, some movement, and you can put up zones on the different parts of the screen, and if something goes into that zone within that protected area, it can generate one type of an alert. If activities in a different zone, it can generate a different type of an alert. It can give you a little bit of granularity as to how you're alerted within the view of that camera. It also creates a record of activity for later analysis or investigation. It doesn't do much good if you have a camera sitting there, and it's not recording, or if it records over itself, every hour or every day, it should, at the very least, have a few days of runway, That you have an opportunity to go back and review, 30 days is probably optimal because that way you can go back and see some trends, or maybe pick up something that you may have missed the first time through, or if a breach or some type of unauthorized access happens, you're not necessarily going to notice that right away. If you have some time to go back and review, you can see some things that you may have inadvertently missed. In tandem with signs and other types of controls, we have guards. Guards can be a deterrent as well as a preventative control type. They can prevent access to a building or a perimeter, so they can just say you're not authorized and they do not allow access. Some guards are armed, some aren't. The guards can be on-site, and they can verify by visual sight, or they can allow access or monitor activity remotely, as we talked about before. Using video surveillance, they can look and see this is person A, this is person B, and they can tell by the visual identification via a monitor whether that person is allowed or not. So guards are a very good way to keep control and to prevent access to specific areas within your company. Next we have something referred to as a robot sentry. A robot sentry can provide 24 by 7 coverage, and these are used in such things as parking lots, garages, industrial spaces, they can be mobile, or they can be stationary. We can have guards or sentries that just simply sit at the beginning or entrance to a garage or a parking lot, and they can record the comings and goings. Or they can be mobile, and they can actually traverse through the parking lot, the garage, or some industrial space, maybe a campus. They can read license plates, they can visually inspect people walking through the premises. These things can also be remote controlled, so you can have someone at a control station who controls or maneuvers this robot through the premises. Or it can be semi-autonomous, and they just let them go, and they almost like a Roomba, where they'll just map out the location themselves, and they make their rounds appropriately. Their mere presence can provide a deterrence, and they can also deliver communications. Some robot sentries allow you to communicate through them. They have speakers. A person at a remote location can talk to someone on campus, someone walking in the parking lot, ask them who they are, or even answer questions if that person has a question as to how to get somewhere.

Generally speaking, they provide a wider range of coverage. They don't need to take breaks and all those good things other than being recharged, but they provide that presence and can also provide insight into that remote location. Another area that has the potential for deterrence is reception. A reception area, depending upon the corporate layout, the reception area can act as a deterrent and also control access, much like badges. Training is required to be aware of the social engineering tactics that some bad actors may employ. So, people who work in the reception areas should understand the different ways that bad actors may try to get past them, gather information from them. But reception areas, receptionists in general, can quickly alert security or other additional resources, as required, if something were to happen, and they also have a tribal knowledge because they work there day to day, they understand who belongs there and who is out of place. If something doesn't look they have the ability to quickly alert the proper resources, security. Next, let's talk about two-person integrity, or TPI, Two-person integrity or control. What we're talking about here is a control mechanism designed to achieve a high level of security for especially critical materials or operations. Two people must be present at all times when sensitive material is being handled, two locks on any containers containing sensitive material, and no one person may possess both keys. But these things function in military environments, nuclear facilities, even in banks. Some locks, some vaults require two keys to open the vault. It doesn't necessarily have to be something as critical as a nuclear facility, but anything that you need an added layer of security, a two-person integrity, or two-person control, makes sense. Hardware locks come in a variety of shapes and sizes and features. Some use the old-fashioned key, some are combination. Some of the newer systems are biometric devices, and that contains, a fingerprint scanner or an iris or retina scan. Something that you have, or something that you are. Those types are, I wouldn't say rare, but they're certainly not as common as the older key and combination types of locks. No matter which type you have, locks should be placed on fencing, on doors, cabinets, cages, , within your data center or within supply closets anywhere where access is restricted. And in some cases, we should even put locks on our trash cans. If we have a shredding area or something that needs to be secure, always make sure that those things are maintained because it's very easy for someone to go in a dumpster dive and pull out some sensitive information if it's not maintained properly. Next, we have biometrics, and biometrics, as you are familiar with, more than likely, is authentication based upon who you are and something that you have, whether that be a fingerprint, an iris or retina scan, a voice print. It typically ties into an access control system, which grants permissions, rights, or access once authenticated. We've seen these in a variety of shapes and sizes. That can be a single fingerprint reader. It can read a thumbprint, a fingerprint, or a whole handprint. There are also some biometrics that, like I said, can do retina scans or iris scans, they can do voice recognition. It really just depends upon the nature of the system, and it offers an additional layer of security because it's not just something that. In other words, you can't tell somebody else your pin or your password, and they go use it. It actually has something that you are, whether it be like I said, a fingerprint, voice print or iris.

Chapter 11 Cable Locks, USB Data Blockers, Safes & Fencing

When we're talking about securing physical assets, a few things to remember are cable locks. We want to make sure we secure these things to non-removable items. Common sense here, but if we don't secure our desktop or our laptop or our monitor to something that's actually non-removable, then it's very much the same as us going outside and locking our bike to an orange parking cone. You can just pick both of those things up and walk away with them. Make sure we secure these things to non-removable items. Same thing goes along with a safe. A safe is obviously there to house very sensitive or valuable information or assets, well, we want to make sure we restrict who has access to keys or the combination. It doesn't do us much good if we have a safe, we store some valuable things in that safe, and then we give everyone either the combination or a key. Doesn't do us much good, so we might as well not even have the thing. I know it sounds like common sense, but you'll be surprised. Make sure we restrict who has access to the keys or the combination. Same thing with locking cabinets. We need to make sure we restrict who has access to the keys. Typically, we're going to have things in there that we don't want everybody to have access to, so we want to limit those to a select few. That way if we only have a select few that have access to the safe, or the locking cabinet, then we only have a few people to go back to if, in fact, a breach occurs, and we can now narrow our investigation. Next, let's talk about a USB data blocker. What this does, it's a USB device that inserts between your phone or your device and a power source. It prevents hackers from accessing data on your device, otherwise known as juice jacking. We're talking about public charging stations or foreign computers, in other words, computers you don't own. If you plug into someone else's computer or you plug your phone or your device, your laptop, in this example, into a charging station, it's possible for a hacker to install some type of software, malware, viruses, that can access your device via that USB port. By having this USB blocker in place, that prevents that from happening. Malware, viruses, theft of data are prevented by using this USB data blocker device. The next one that goes hand in hand with that would be fencing. Fencing is something that we should obviously have in place around the entire perimeter of an area or a building for it to be most effective. It doesn't do us much good if we have it only around a part of our building, and they can just simply walk around the fencing and get to the rear of a building, as an example. Fencing can also have a man trap style fencing as well, so that they have to drive into an area, the fence closes behind them, they're verified, and then another gate opens up and they can pass through, so you could have that type of dual entry system in a fencing area as well. Areas inside of a data center can be fenced off as well to restrict access. It doesn't necessarily have to be just external to a company, it can also be inside of a data center. We might have an area like a caged-off area where we have some extra sensitive information, or it could be a supply area, supply closet or a loading dock. So fencing can be not necessarily for just people exterior to the company, I should say, it could also be to keep people inside the company out of specific areas as well. Fencing can be a deterrent, or it can be preventive. Depending upon the type of fence, if it's just a 2 or 3-foot tall fence or maybe a 5-foot tall fence with nothing on top, that might be a deterrent, but it's not going to prevent someone from getting over top. If you have a fence like you see here that has some type of barbed wire or even maybe worse, even some razor wire on top, well, chances are that would be preventive. I certainly wouldn't be going over a fence like that. It just depends upon the type of fence. When it comes to fire suppression, we have lots of investment. We have high dollar pieces of equipment in our data centers, in our server rooms, critical components to our business. Any data center where there is an investment in computer systems and infrastructure, we need to make sure that we have an investment in our fire suppression system as well. Fire needs three things to exist. We have heat, fuel, and oxygen. If we remove one of any of those three, then we obviously take a fire's ability to exist away, we'll put the fire out, so those things need to be there. Fire suppression systems will remove one or more of those elements, and that's what puts the fire out. If we take a look at it here, as I said, a fire suppression system removes one of the three elements that are needed for combustion. We would have canisters, we'd have sensors on the wall, and then some type of sprinkler or dispersion heads up on top. Some data centers will have sprinkler systems. Water is not the most friendly component for our data center, however, we need to have it there in the event that it's a fire raging out of control. In the event that it's a small fire or some type of preventative system, there are systems put in place, and FM-200 is one of the most widely used clean agents. It's stored actually as a liquid in canisters, there's these canisters that store typically liquid compressed with nitrogen or some type of gas, there's sensors in a control panel on the wall, and then there are sprinkler heads or dispersion heads up in the ceiling. What happens is, if heat starts to come up inside the data center, before it actually even turns into a fire, those sensors can detect, the heat itself. There's not a fire yet, it's just hot. Well, those detectors can sense that, they will then alert to the control center or the control panel on the wall. That control panel can in tandem set off an alarm, signal to our administrators but then it can also then trigger the discharge of FM-200. That quickly reaches, within 7-10 seconds, enough of a dispersion in the atmosphere or in the air to absorb all the heat. It takes the heat away out of that triangle, it takes away one of the three elements that is needed for that fire, It can absorb enough so that the fire never actually erupts. If it gets beyond that, for some reason, and it happens too quickly or the fire overruns, that's when the sprinkler heads would then kick in. There are some other agents as well, FM-200 is one. DuPont also makes FE-13, 25, and 36 that can be used to retrofit existing systems and also for fire extinguishers. It doesn't necessarily have to be a brand-new system that's put in place like an FM-200 system, but there should definitely be some type of clean agent if possible, so that you don't spray your equipment with water or some type of chemical that can be corrosive. If we can absorb the heat and take that away before the fire even has a chance to start, we're going to be in a much better position.

Chapter 12 Motion Detection / Infrared & Proximity Readers

We also have motion detection and infrared. It's a technical control that provides detective and also deterrence capabilities. It can be combined with signage, and that can be a really powerful tool against intrusion. Is going to stop everybody? No, not, but it is a deterrent. What it does is put people on notice that, hey, if you come into this area, you're under surveillance, motion detection is enabled, and what you're doing is going to be recorded. It makes people think twice about what their going to do, doesn't prevent everybody, but it's a good start. That video can be used to detect movement in real time, or it can be used for later analysis and investigation. Infrared sensors can also detect motion in complete darkness, so just because the area is not illuminated with visible light, so that allows the camera to see everything as if it were daytime. Next we have proximity readers, and proximity readers are becoming more and more commonplace. They are typically used with ID cards, and they contain either an NFC chip or some type of RFID chip. A near-field communication or some type of radio frequency ID so that you can pass your card close to the reader, but you don't actually have to be right up on it. Whether it's you show your ID card as you enter a building in the morning, maybe it lifts a gate and you can drive through into a parking lot, or perhaps maybe through some type of turnstile as you go into the building. A person doesn't need to physically touch the reader, and it works in tandem with access lists or access control systems. As you wave your badge in front of this reader, it then checks against an access list or access control list and says, yes, this person is allowed access or they're not, or it may give you certain access or access to certain areas of the building. You may be able to get into an area perfectly fine, and then you go to a more restricted area and you wave your badge again and you're not allowed access to that specific door. It gives the company itself the ability to be very granular as to what access or level of access it can grant employees as they move about and have access to certain areas within a building. We've talked about drones and UAVs before, but just to put it in the context of monitoring for physical security, a drone could provide security and monitor large areas very quickly. We have that aerial view of our footprint. Drones can also be remotely activated based on motion. We could have a drone sitting in its charging cradle or in some type of holding facility, and then as soon as motion is detected, it can release the drone, the drone goes up in the air, flies over to wherever that motion is taking place, and can record that activity or provide insight into what's going on. It can also be used to monitor sections of PDSs or protected distribution systems with a hardened cabling in a secure system that sometimes can stretch very long distances. Drones can allow the monitoring of that very efficiently. Real-time insights into security and emergency situations allowing for precise intelligence gathering, comprehensive situational awareness, depending upon the type of activity and the type of an event. Next, we have logs, and logs provide critical details required when investigating an incident, or a breach; such things as the time of incident, their credentials that were used, maybe files or servers or resources that were accessed, also any activity, and any potential methods used. If someone's trying to cover their tracks where they used some type of escalation or privileges, once they get access to a resource, they try to maintain persistence, and they try to install some type of back door, so they can get back in again, if their primary way of breaching was discovered or somehow closed off. They maintain that persistence, and they get in and try to traverse the network, perhaps hit a point where they can pivot and jump onto another network that they typically wouldn't have access to. All of those types of activities, and the resources that they use, and the methods they use, can be identified potentially, if logs are properly kept. Next to something referred to as air gaps. An air gap is a method of isolating a computer or a network from the internet or from other external networks, or other networks aside from the one you're on. It doesn't necessarily have to be just from the internet. It could be from other networks within your company. If you have a very highly secure environment that you need to make sure that there's no chance of malware or viruses being introduced, then you would set up an air-gapped network. As with anything, there is no 100% guarantee, as we've seen in the past, with things like Stuxnet and some other very highly visible and highly cited instances where malware has actually jumped into air-gapped environments, nothing is 100% certain. But anyway, it's used for critical infrastructure. SCADA systems, as an example, and I refer back to Stuxnet, where the SCADA systems were still compromised, highly secure classified networks. There are some advanced techniques, however, to jump air gap networks. That's been demonstrated. Emanations, there's actually a technology, and it's been completely demonstrated, where they can view the emanations coming off of a computer, whether it is the sound of the hard drive whirring, or even the heat being generated by the hard drive spinning up. If you're close enough to that device, you can actually pick those things up from the device and discern what's going on. You can read data from that device. It's not something the average hacker can do, but just understand that an air gap is a very good way of isolating the network, but it's not 100% foolproof. In fact, the US government, and other agencies around the world, have specific guidelines to create additional security. The US uses something referred to as TEMPEST, which protects that room, it has to be certain thickness of walls and has to have additional coding and protections, Faraday cages, and things that just prevent emanations and monitoring from nearby locations.

Emanations, FM frequencies, even some hard drives that actually a small LED light on the front that actually shows activity of that drive. You don't see that too much anymore, but it is possible, that if you have a line of sight visibility to that light going on and off as the hard drive writes, you could actually read, almost like Morse code, what's going on with that hard drive, and read data from that device. Pretty scary stuff. But, the average hacker is not going to be employing that. More than likely, you can rest assured that your home network is safe. We've discussed that an air gap is a network that is physically separated from an unsecured network, with the goal being to ensure the packets or data grams don't leave the secure network unintentionally. A few additional pieces of information, though that we should be aware of, is the fact that when we move data between networks, let's say, for instance, we have a less secure network and then a more secure network; so networks that are designed to handle different levels of classified data are referred to as the high side and the low side; low side, as you might guess, meaning the less secure; high side being very secure or more secured networks. When we're moving data from one side to the other, low side to high side is a fairly straightforward process because the high side is already able to view that information, or contain that information. However, moving data from the high side, or the confidential side, to the low side, requires more stringent processes. Those types of moves should be done manually and making sure that data does not inadvertently leak out from a secure network to an insecure network. More stringent processes, due diligence, should be put in place to ensure that that confidential data stays confidential.

Chapter 13 Demilitarized Zone & Protected Distribution System

Next, let's talk about the concept of a demilitarized zone, or DMZ. A demilitarized zone, also known as a perimeter network, or a screened subnet; so you may hear any of these terms, interchangeably. The newer, or more preferred, name, these days, is a screened subnet, but they typically consist of hosts that provide services outside of the local area network, or the internal network; such things as email servers, web servers, DNS servers. A security professional, an IT security professional or a cybersecurity professional, is not going to know every single thing about every single topic within IT security. That's like saying, oh, how to drive a car, great, go jump on that 18-wheeler. Even though they both fall under the same quote unquote category, it doesn't mean you can necessarily operate both effectively, so It's not expected that every single thing within IT security or cybersecurity, but it's a good idea to understand where all of these things fit, so you can understand architecturally how they all fit together. On our internal network, we have a number of things; Active Directory servers, DNS, servers, perhaps some type of intrusion detection or prevention systems, logging servers. We might have some database servers, and then behind that, we may have some storage; and then we also have a DMZ, or a demilitarized zone. That's going to be comprised of things we want to be public facing, but we want to secure from our internal network. We want to create a separate network, if you will, and you'll place things like your web servers, DNS, servers, your external DNS servers, mail servers, proxy servers. In this example, we have a user who wants to get to an internal network, as an example. Well the user is going to connect to the internet, ? They're going to connect via their ISP, at which point they would encounter our external firewall. Now, there, we could place an intrusion detection or prevention system, to get an idea of how many people are trying to penetrate our network, or trying to get in unauthorized. , we don't necessarily have to put it there, but we can. It can be placed in different places throughout the network. But they'll pass through the firewall. The firewall will let certain ports through, like DNS, mail, SMTP and POP and IMAP. Port 80, port 443; and then the various application servers may have individual ports that they need access to as well. We can think of this as a less secure zone than our internal network. We want to allow people to actually get into this area from the outside world, but we don't want to allow them into our internal network. We'll have another firewall between our DMZ and our internal network; and from there, again, we may choose to place an intrusion detection, or prevention, system, or we may they choose to place that on the inside; and once we get inside to our internal network, then we have Active Directory, DNS, intrusion detection and prevention systems, logging servers, database servers and storage, or our application servers. I just want you to get a general idea of how these things are laid out. The basic takeaway here, is, what is a DMZ, the demilitarized zone. Also a couple things to keep in mind; we have wireless and guest networks. We have a guest. They may have a laptop, or they may have a desktop. They may be actually someone on our network, and they want to access some external network, or an external resource. Well, how do they do that? Well, they're going to connect to a wireless access point, if they have a laptop, or some type of mobile device, or through a desktop, they may plug directly into a jack in the wall, and off they go. From there, they will access, some of the things that are laid out, a router, a switch, firewall. Well, if they're on our wireless network, they will access that wireless access point. That wireless access point will reach out to, typically, in a corporate environment, will reach out to a RADIUS server, a remote access and dial-in user service. That will authenticate that guest and give them access, or, if there's no password, it'll just let them through, but typically, in a corporate environment, you're still going to require some type of username and password. That may change every couple of weeks, every couple of months, or but they're still going to authenticate with that RADIUS server; and also a wireless LAN controller comes into play, if we have more than one wireless access point. Say we have a large corporate environment, and we have wireless access points all throughout our environment, all throughout our buildings, multiple buildings and multiple locations. Well, those wireless access controllers, or the wireless LAN controller, allow us to configure all of those wireless access points from one location. Next, we have protected distribution systems, and this deals with cabling, PDS. And a protected distribution system is a secure conduit. It can be for copper or for fiber optic cabling, and there are a couple different types we'll talk about that has monitors in place to detect any disruption to the PDS. It gives us a very secure transport mechanism. The carrier itself we can run cabling through. It's covered under the National Security Telecommunications and Information Systems Security instruction, or the NSTISSI 7003, if you want to look that up. And it was enacted December of 1996 by the Committee on National Security Systems. These types of things are in place when we're dealing with typically data carrying national security type information. There are two main classifications, and that is hardened distribution systems and then simple distribution systems. We'll cover each here in a little more detail. These are very secure access points. The cabling, it runs along this conduit, this trough that you see, but every single area, or every single point of that conduit or that carrier is sealed off. It's got epoxy, it's got very stringent guidelines as to how it's constructed. And then anywhere where there is an actual access point, it's locked, and so only specific people have access to those tie-ins, or to those areas where they can access certain sections of the cabling. First off was a hardened distribution system, or a hardened carrier, and that conduit is electrical metal tubing, ferrous conduit, or pipe. If it's going to be underground, it needs to be buried and encased in concrete. Or if it's above ground, it needs to be permanently sealed, welds, epoxy, or some other sealant. Very high secure transport mechanism. These carriers are meant to not be disturbed. There was also some guidelines that say they have to be visually inspected or visually monitored at all times if they're not buried underground. Next would be an alarmed carrier. If we're not going to have someone actually visually looking at these things constantly, then the alarm carrier gives us the ability to have fibers that actually run within the conduit that are used for monitoring acoustic vibrations. That's associated with attempted access. If someone's trying to disrupt or access any of these carriers, that fiber will detect that and then sound an alarm. That reduces the need for visual inspection and monitoring. It ties into, like I said, an automated system. An example here is that this would detect any type of vibration, it triggers an alarm, and then this device would turn around and set off some type of workflow, alerts, alarms, and send guards to the area, and so on. It can detect where along the conduit that actual disruption is occurring. Then, we have a continuously view carrier, that's another category, and that conduit is continuously viewed, as the name implies, monitored 24x7x365. Guards and security personnel will investigate any and all attempts to disturb the PDS, typically within 15 minutes. That's according to the guidelines that we talked about earlier. Those things are constantly monitored. There's someone that keeps these things up to date and views 24x7x365. National security type information. Any disruption, guards are immediately alerted, and within 15 minutes they should be on-site responding to that area of disturbance. Next, we have a simple distribution. In a simple distribution system, cables can be installed in any type of carrier, it can be made of any type of material. However, the joints and access points are monitored by personnel, and the people that actually monitor that carrier should be cleared to the highest level of data handled by that PDS. In other words, if that specific section of cabling or that carrier is carrying secret data versus top secret, or whatever the case might be, the people that actually monitor that should have that same level of clearance. In other words, someone who has secret should not be monitoring a top secret, and vice versa. If you have top secret, obviously you can monitor anything from that point down, but it should be at the highest level of data being carried through that carrier, or through those cabling. Periodic inspections are required. It needs to be continuously verified that these systems are, in fact, secure. Another environmental control that I want to call your attention to is the concept of hot and cold aisles. Data centers can contain hundreds, thousands, tens of thousands of servers, networking equipment, storage arrays, and so on. As you can imagine, all of those devices generate a lot of heat. Massive amounts of heat are generate from these devices. Even if you have in your house maybe 1 or 2 computers, maybe a server, an Xbox, PS3 or PS4, if you sit behind those things and they've been on for a while, you can understand they generate a lot of heat. Take that same amount, times that by 100 or 1000, it gets very, very warm in a data center, especially a large data center, that's why HVAC is Important. But also in tandem with that is the concept of a hot and cold aisle. So hot and cold aisles help reduce heating and cooling because, again, our compute network and storage runs more efficiently when it's cooled properly. HVAC is also going to run more efficiently when it's designed properly. Instead of simply placing equipment in a data center of wherever we can, wherever it fits, it's much more to our benefit to set it up in such a fashion that we are taking advantage of hot and cold aisles and we're maximizing our HVAC. The basic concept is to place the front of the systems on either side facing each other so that cool air can be drawn on that aisle, or infused into that aisle, drawn in from those sides, and then the opposing aisles would go back to back so that the heat blows out the back of those systems. Those will then be the hot aisles, and the hot aisles is where we'll have our HVAC pull that heat out and then either recycle it or however that HVAC system is set up. Typically, we're going to recycle that air, it's filtered. It maintains a very clean atmosphere. If we look at it a little bit more in depth, we also have the concept of hot and cold containment aisles. In a hot air containment aisle, we have an enclosed area with doors that lead in, and in the enclosed area will be the hot aisle, so we're containing the heat. That way, we can suck it out of that area and run it through our filtration system again. In the opposing aisles, which are open, would be our cold aisles. The reverse of that would be a cold air containment aisle. In a cold air containment, we actually have our sliding doors, and we keep that area of the data center, or those aisles rather, cold. By containing it, in other words, having those doors slide across, we can contain, whether it's hot or cold, we can contain that area much more efficiently. We're ensuring that our hot areas are, where our HVAC vents are, we're going to pull that hot air out, and then we're going to place cold air in, so it gets filtered through.

Chapter 14 Shredding, Pulping & Pulverizing

Let's go ahead and start off and talk about the non-digital data destruction, or things that are not necessarily data on magnetic media, flash drives, In other words, paper documents. Really four things we can do here. We can talk about burning, and we'll cover each of these in more detail in just a second, but first off, we have burning, which is, as the name implies, we would incinerate that data, that paper data, in some form or fashion. Next we have shredding, and there are various types of shredders, we'll cover those more detail in just a moment. Then we have something referred to as pulping and then pulverizing. Then when it comes to digital data destruction, we have also something referred to as pulverizing. We then have degaussing, degaussing, depending upon, where you read or who you hear pronounce it. Then we have purging, and then wiping. Let's cover each of these error more detail. When we talk about burning, documents are incinerated, it's put into a fire, whether it is simply thrown into someone's fireplace, or there are actual commercial incineration facilities, where you can put bulk documents in and burn them down to unrecoverable status. It can also be combined with other methods to increase security, such as shredding, pulping, or pulverizing, meaning we could take one of those methods first, shred it, pulp it, or pulverize that paper data, and then incinerate at the end, We would cut it up into small pieces, whether the shredding is long strip or across cut, as an example, and then when that's done, we would then incinerate those documents, At that point, there's pretty much zero chance that data is going to be recovered. Then next, we have shredding. With shredding, documents are cut into small pieces. We have long-cut shredders, which are most typically found in like residence and small office home office environments; however, those long-cut shredded documents are not considered secure because if you take enough time and you have enough people working on it or if you just painstakingly, attention to detail, you can take each of those strips, those long strips, and find out the matching pieces and put that data back together, put those documents back together, much like you would put a jigsaw puzzle back together. It's time consuming, but it's possible. They're not considered secure. Cross-cut, on the other hand, where custard into very small pieces, much like confetti, is more secure, but it's also slower and typically more expensive. If you have a bulk documents, you typically would want to take these things to some type of shredding facility that has very large-scale shredding equipment that can do these things en masse. Then we have something referred to as pulping. Pulping is a process, where those documents are put into a vat, or a bin of some sort, and then a solution is poured in, and those documents are soaked in that solution until it is reduced to what's referred to as a slurry. It's just a mush. That data on those paper documents are then at that point, unrecoverable. Pulp can be reused, or recycled. It can actually be used to make new paper. It can be expensive. It's also time consuming, and one of the challenges can be, if you have a large number of documents, you're destroying documents at a large scale, that can be also difficult to transport because, because you won't normally have those facilities on site, so you have to transfer all of those documents to that facility. Next, we have something referred to as pulverizing. Now pulverizing can be used for paper documents. It can also be used for digital media. If we're talking about storage media, as an example, the media is fed into a pulverizing machine, which literally crushes those drives, whether it's a flash drive, a magnetic disk, a spinning hard disk. It will crush that material, or those drives, into small pieces. Hydraulic or pneumatic action, much like a very heavy duty pneumatically fed shredder. It is used to reduce that media to loose fibers, if we're talking about paper, or to shards, if we're talking about storage media, it just breaks it up into small pieces. The data is not recoverable at that point.

Chapter 15 Deguassing, Purging & Wiping

Next, we have something referred to as degaussing or degaussing. There are two types here. We have either AC or DC erasure techniques, and with degaussing, if you're using AC, it applies an alternating field over time, that renders that data unrecoverable, so it takes the magnetic field on that magnetic disk and reverses it, or in some manner, obliterates it, makes it very random That the data cannot be recovered off of that drive. DC, on the other hand, will saturate the media with a unidirectional field. In either case, it's going to make that data unrecoverable. Something else to keep in mind with this process, however, is that hard drives are typically unusable after degaussing. And that is because it erases the low-level formatting that is usually done at the factory at the time of manufacture. That low-level formatting actually delineates where the tracks and sectors are on that hard drive, and the degaussing will actually remove that information from the disk. Even though the disk is wiped, there is no delineation anymore of where the tracks and sectors are, much like if you have fence posts or fence lines in a field. If there are no fences, we have no idea where to put one piece of information versus the other. With that being gone, the rewrite heads have no idea of to actually where to start and stop on that disk. It renders that disk unusable, unless, unless you take it back to the manufacturer to be low-level formatted, or you have some type of tool provided by the vendor to low-level format that disk, which is 9 times out of 10, not done. It's just cheaper just to throw the drive away. The point being after you degauss something, don't think you're just going to pull that drive back out of the degaussing machine and put it back into your computer and use it. It's a very good chance that

that drive is going to be unusable. Next up, let's talk about something referred to as purging. Purging, also known as sanitizing, removes the data, makes it unrecoverable, and also removes something referred to as data remanence. So once a disk is purged or sanitized, data cannot be reconstructed by any known methods. That's the takeaway from that process. It's typically considered a step beyond wiping of data, and it's performed in situations where highly sensitive data exists, and again, the removal of that data remanence, In other words, ghost images or little snippets of data that can be left behind that could potentially be reconstructed to reconstitute that data, It removes any of that data remanence. Next, we have wiping. Wiping is a term you may be familiar with, wiping versus deleting. When you wipe data, wiping overwrites the data x number of times, and x is a configurable number, it's a variable, but it can overwrite that data x number of times to ensure that it's unrecoverable. The number of passes, can be configured, can go from 1 up to 35 or more. In modern times with modern disks, modern hard disks, spinning drives, a single pass, a single overwrite of that data is considered unrecoverable. That is configurable, there are different methods. With SSD or flash drives, disk sanitization, what we do here is reset the NAND, the actual flash chips on the drive itself and mark all those blocks as empty. Each SSD manufacturer typically will have their own secure erase, and that's a technology run method, to have their own version or their own secure erase tool that's specific for that particular flash drive. It's effective at rendering that data unrecoverable so if that security's algorithm and the implementation of it is actually done properly. Just to dig in for a moment, some data wiping methods, there are three that we can talk about here. One is DoD 5220.22-M standard, and that's the Department of Defense standard for a three-pass overwrite. That is considered secure and makes that data unrecoverable, pass 1 writes a 0 and verifies the write, pass 2 writes a 1 and verifies the write, and then pass 3 writes a random character and then verifies the write. We're talking about wiping an entire disk and making that disk now available or properly sanitized so it can be reused or repurposed in some fashion. Next is the RCMP CSEC ITSG-06, so that's the Communication Security Establishment of Canada. The RCMP, which has a great set of tools, they're very highly regarded in the forensics and cyber-investigative space, they have a three pass as well. Pass 1 writes a 1 or a 0, pass 2 writes a complement of the previously written character. In other words, it will write a 1 if pass 1 was a 0. so pass 2 would be a 1 if pass 1 was 0 or vice versa. Then pass 3 writes a random character and verifies that write. It makes sure that that data is obliterated; it cannot be recovered. And then we have secure erase, which I mentioned, that's a single pass, and it writes a binary 1 or 0. It's going to overwrite that data. It's very fast, and it's only available, for whole disk sanitization. The other two methods, they can wipe individual files, but typically, when we're talking about making a disk available for reuse or properly disposing of assets, we're talking about wiping the entire disk, whole disk sanitization. In summary, we talked about physical security, the different types of deterrents and the different types of controls that can make that security happen. We talked about digital and logical security, the different types of locks, and vaults, and sensors. Then we talked about securing infrastructure with our PDS, or protected cabling, and then the various types of data access restriction. Then we wrapped up with a secure disposal of data, both physical data, paper data and also digital data, deleting and wiping and securely getting rid of information we no longer need.

Chapter 16 Cryptographic Terminology and History

In the following chapters, we'll be covering Understanding the Basics of Cryptographic Concepts. We'll be talking about digital signatures and the concept of cipher suites, such things as salting and hashing. We'll also go over at a high level quantum communications and quantum computing. We'll also talk about blockchain, steganography, and some common use cases, as well as limitations. Why should I really care? What does this mean for me? Well, first off, encryption is everywhere, and it can work either for us or against us, so it's imperative that we understand how it works, what's appropriate to use, and when and where, and also to make sure we understand what's not appropriate. Not understanding what's appropriate could also be costly, not just in terms of financially to the company, but to brand, reputation, customer confidence, investor confidence, your job, There's a lot of things at stake here if we don't do things properly. Even if you're not tasked directly with some of the things covered in this chapter, security is everyone's responsibility, It's very important that each and every one of us understand at a fairly deep level what these things mean, what's appropriate and not appropriate, when we should be using a specific technology or a specific algorithm and when we should not. Let's start off and cover some cryptographic terminology. Starting off, cryptography, what is that? Well, that is the practice and the study of hiding information. Cryptography is actually a pretty old science, if you will, part art, part science. It dates back 4000 years. Next, we have cryptanalysis, and that is discovering some weakness or an insecurity in cryptography, so our cryptographic scheme. We're looking for some hole or vulnerability, and so we have two competing technologies, or competing sciences, here.

We have one who is the cryptographer, and that person is trying to hide information, and then the person who's tasked with cryptanalysis, they're actually trying to discover some weakness in that cryptographic scheme. Next, we have encryption, and that is the method of transforming data, typically which is plain text, into an unreadable format. Then we have plain text, which is, again, the readable format of data before being encrypted. These are just some words that you should be familiar with when we're having our discussion on cryptography. Next we have ciphertext, and that is the scrambled "format of data" after it's encrypted. so we have the plain text, which is the human readable form. We're going to apply some cryptographic algorithm, or cipher, turning into ciphertext, and that's scrambled data then, again, is human unreadable. We'll need to have some method of decrypting that, and that's where you come in with decryption. that's the method of turning that ciphertext that we just talked about back into plain text, back into that human readable form. Next is the encryption algorithm, and that is a set of rules or procedures that's going to define how we actually encrypt and decrypt the data, and that's known as the encryption cipher. We'll talk about a few different ways of doing that, whether it's asymmetric, symmetric, block versus stream. We'll cover those in more detail in just a few moments. Next, the concept of a key, and that's a value used in the encryption process to encrypt and also to decrypt data, otherwise known as a cryptovariable. Just a brief bit of cryptography history. Cryptography is actually over 4000 years old, so it predates, a lot of languages itself. It predates computers, obviously, electronics or any technology. I don't think there was anybody walk around with iPhones or even Walkmans back 4000 years ago. Cryptography is a very old way of hiding information from one another. Then the earlier cryptographers reliable methods simply to scramble text, otherwise known as a cipher, and they use something called a substitution cipher or a transposition cipher, It didn't advanced to the point where we have mathematical algorithms like we do now in elliptic curve and quantum cryptography, which we'll talk about later in this chapter. But back in those days, in the early days, it was simply just substituting like an A for a B, moving things left to right a certain number of characters. If you look at a substitution cipher as an example, that's changing one character for another. now Caesar, otherwise known as a Caesar cipher or a shift cipher, Julius Caesar was one of the first cryptographers or one of the first people that actually, I should say, implemented cryptography, and that was the process of shifting all the letters a certain number of spaces in the alphabet, alright. As you see here, the alphabet is shifted by three spaces, It would be X, B equals y, C equals Z, and so on We're shifting everything three spaces. Next is something referred to as ROT-13, or Rotation-13, and that is a substitution cipher as well that's going to rotate letters 13 spaces. Not extremely sophisticated. If we know the encryption algorithm, in this case, ROT-13, it's very easy to go backwards. Once we have the scrambled text, we can decipher that relatively easily. Next we have something referred to as a Vigenère table, and this is a multi-alphabet substitution cipher - a poly-alphabetic substitution cipher. It consists of your message and a keyword that only you and the other person will know. You need to share that keyword, but your keyword will go on the left, your message will go on the top, and to make things more difficult to guess, you should take the spaces out of your message. We're going to have our message, and then we're going to have our keyword, and that keyword will repeat over and over again until it fills up the length of our message. If the other person doesn't know that keyword, it's going to be very difficult for them to decipher that; however, as I said with a computer, they could brute force that because in reality it's 26 to the n-1, the n being the length of the keyword, That's how many variations there would have to be in a brute force attack before you would exhaust all possibilities. But with a very powerful computer, that is very doable. A Vigenère cipher is really not considered a secure algorithm or a secure way of communicating outside of just maybe friends passing messages, but if you want to do anything that has a high degree of security, this would not be the method that I would choose.

Chapter 17 Digital Signatures, Key Stretching & Hashing

Digital signature is an asymmetric encryption algorithm. It uses that two-key system. The two keys are mathematically linked, public-key/private-key. When we're talking about a digital signature, let's use the concept of sending or signing an email. We have Bob and Alice - old friends. She wants to send an email to Bob. Bob already has Alice's public key on his key ring. Most email programs can already accomplish this and manage these keys automatically. Alice is going to go ahead and send her email. She'll use a hashing algorithm, whether it's SHA-1, SHA-2, MD5, whatever the case might be, there's some hashing algorithm in place. She will hash that email, she'll get a hashing value. She will then encrypt that hashing value with her private key. that equals a signed document, so now that document has her digital signature attached to it, which again confirms her identity, provides non-repudiation. So going forward, Alice will now send that email to Bob, and as we mentioned, Bob will have Alice's public key already on his system. When she sends that message, she sends that signed message to him, he will use her public key to unencrypt, pull out that hashing value, hash the email, make sure the hashing values match so we can be sure that the email has not been tampered with. We can also ensure that it was sent from Alice. That offers non-repudiation, and so Bob can rest assured that that email did in fact come from Alice. Next we have a concept of key stretching, and there are two things here that we should understand. One is PBKDF2, and that stands for Password-Based Key Derivation Function 2. It's up to you if you'd rather remember that or just say PBKDF2. If you want to sound really smart, use the acronym, because nobody knows what it means, but be prepared to answer if they do ask you. nothing worse than using an acronym trying to sound smart, and then someone says, what's that mean? Password-Based Key Derivation Function 2, it's part of RSA, It's a pseudorandom function applied to a password or a passphrase. That's the thing we have to understand. The whole concept of key stretching is the fact that perhaps our key is not as strong as it could be. Well, we can strengthen that by, in effect, stretching that key, whether it be a hash, a cipher, or an HMAC. We can also have something called a password salt, or a salt rather, to the password. When we salt something, we're adding some additional randomization to that password or to that passphrase. By doing that, it exponentially increases how much more difficult that is to break, brute force, rainbow tables because it's not the same thing over and over and over again. Every time it gets used, that salt changes it just a bit, so it's almost like the one-time pads, where if you rip the page off, it's not completely different. By adding a salt, salting that password, whether it's whatever mechanism that might be, that added randomness makes it more difficult. The process is also repeated many times. As we do that, let's say we go through all this process, we do a hash, we add a salt or an HMAC, that's one pass. We can do it again and again, and each time we do that, it makes it that much more difficult to try to reverse engineer that. It just makes it much more challenging, given today's resources, for someone to hack, or crack rather, that password or that hash. If in fact they do, the next time they try to do it again, it's not the same anymore. The salt has been added, so it changes it up. Ultimately, it creates a derived key. That derived key, again, is random to a certain degree, and that can be used for future communications or for subsequent communications. That pseudorandom process makes it much more difficult. Even if the person might know the passphrase or they may know a piece of the equation that would typically be passed between sender and recipient, that salting, that randomization, and the subsequent derived key makes it a different encrypted component and makes it that much more difficult for them to decrypt. Well bcrypt is another example. Bcrypt is actually something that was developed in 1999, and it was developed based upon the Blowfish algorithm. And what it does is provide key derivation functions, gives us that added randomness used for passwords. It allows us to strengthen the key, even though that key may not be strong in and of itself. It gives us some additional characteristics we can add to that key. It adds additional functions, such as salting. When we salt a password, we strengthen it by adding randomization. Just like you add salt to food to make it better, when we salt a password, we're really making it better or making it stronger, so that salt function adds that randomness. Each time it goes through, the salting is different, which makes the encryption different, so it makes it much harder to crack, and as you see, it helps to guard against rainbow table attacks. Next, let's talk about hashing. Hashing is a mathematical algorithm that's applied to a file before and after transmission. If anything within that file changes, the hash will be completely different. We have a couple options. We could use MD5, SHA1, or SHA2, and that's your choice, depending upon which algorithm you want to use; they will each produce a different result. In this example, have a SHA1 algorithm that I will apply to the sentence! I'll run a SHA1 algorithm against that, and you'll see the resultant answer. If I change one letter in this example, I'll take the exclamation point off the end of that file and run that SHA1 hash again, you'll see the answer is completely different. By simply changing one letter in that sentence, it gives us a completely different hashing answer. In the real world, if we hashed an entire file or an entire disk, if anything has changed on that disk or in that file, depending on the example, it will result with a different hash file. Whether we're trying to send something to someone, we could take a hash first and then let them hash again when they get on the other side and see if the numbers match. If they match, we know nothing's changed; it hasn't been manipulated. Or from a forensics point of view, as an example, we could dig a hash of an entire hard drive. Then anytime you want to prove the veracity of that image, we can just run a hash against that again, and as long as those numbers match, we know that nothing has changed on that hard disk.

Chapter 18 Quantum Communications & Elliptic Curve Cryptography

An out-of-band key exchange is not sent over the network. That needs to be delivered via traditional means or manually, either in person, over the telephone, via courier. I have to get that secret key to the recipient, not sending it over the network, so that takes away the ability for it to be compromised, at least electronically, if someone is eavesdropping. An in-band key exchange, by comparison, is actually done over the network as the communication session is established. It's done real time as we're setting up communication with the other person. It's typically discarded once the session is over, it's usually used for that one-time communication, but just understand the difference between in-band and out-of-band. Out-of-band is more cumbersome, but it's also a little more secure for certain types of communication because there's no chance of someone, if they happen to be sniffing the wire at that point in time, they're not going to be able to pull that information off the wire potentially. With some of our other examples, if I want to call someone up and say, hey, my secret password is XYZ, now we both know that password, we can communicate using that password that only I and the recipient know. There's always that big what-if. If someone happens to be tapping the phone or they read the mail or there's always ways that things can be sniffed, but we're talking about a real-time pulling-off-the-wire, if you will, of those secret keys while that communication session is being established, That's just the main differentiation between these two pieces. Next we have Elliptic Curve Cryptography, and this is otherwise known as ECC. This is an asymmetric encryption that uses the algebraic structure of elliptic curves rather than the mathematical backend to generate these random keys and generate these secret keys between two systems. By using the elliptical curves and using the points on those curves, we can generate strong encryption keys, but yet use a smaller key size. You don't have to rely on all the computational resources to generate those very strong keys. The asymmetric encryption normally requires a very large amount of resources. Some of these keys are extremely big, and when we're using this to in fact encrypt this data, obviously it takes a lot of backend processing power. If we can use smaller keys and still achieve the same amount of security, well, then that's a good thing. You don't really have to understand the depths of how this works for the exam, just understand that Elliptic Curve Cryptography uses that algebraic structure, and it achieves the same level of security using smaller keys or smaller key size than traditional encryption algorithms. It gives us that same level of security using less processing power. If you contrast that with perfect forward secrecy, session keys that are derived from a set of long-term keys, yet discrete in nature. What do I mean by that? Well, if one of the long-term keys is compromised, it doesn't compromise that session key or the data that it protects. That's why I said, these keys, these session keys, are derived from the long-term keys, yet they're discrete, they're not mathematically linked. If the long term-key gets compromised, it does not compromise that session key. There are some additional rules that apply to this. Keys used to protect data aren't used to derive any additional keys. That makes sure that each session key and each communication that is protected by that is discrete in that fact. The keys used to protect are not used to derive any additional keys. And then if the keys used to protect the data currently were derived from some additional or some other keying material, then that material must not be used to derive any additional keys. The takeaway here is we want to make sure that each communication session uses its own discrete set of keys that are not linked to any other keys. That way, if one session gets compromised, the long-term key gets compromised, it does not actually compromise any individual communication session. Next let's talk about quantum communications. This is obviously a very deep field, a very emerging field, and not something that's actually in common practice widespread yet, but it's definitely coming and definitely something that we want to be familiar with. Quantum communications is predicated on the fact or the principles of quantum mechanics and the various properties contained therein. One thing we should be aware of is the concept of quantum entanglement. Quantum entanglement states that two particles can be joined, or entangled, regardless of the space that separates them. It could be across the room, it could be across the country, or theoretically across the universe. Quantum entanglement of two particles separated in space. Also, communications will take place between these two parties using something called quantum key distribution, and we'll talk more about that in just a moment. That's the basics, two of the principles that make up quantum communications. That creates, that quantum key distribution, creates an intrinsically secure and totally random keying material based upon quantum mechanics. Because, as we'll talk about it later, when we use random number generators, or pseudorandom number generators, those things can ultimately be predicted, given enough time and computing power, whereas using quantum key distribution and the properties of quantum mechanics, it's completely random, there is no way to predict that. By using that completely random keying material, we start off from a very secure base, and then everything that's built upon that becomes intrinsically more secure. As an example, here we have Bob and Alice. As we talked about before, they are old friends since the start of the internet, back in the late '60s, they've been good friends. Well, Bob and Alice, they want to communicate, so they have their laptops and they want to communicate with each other using quantum communications, so they want establish a quantum communication channel. And without getting too, too deep into the process behind the scenes, there's something referred to as that quantum entanglement that I mentioned. So Bob will generate two photons using specialized equipment, those photons are entangled, one photon will be sent to Alice, and she will receive it. But now remember, those photons are entangled, so that starts off the key distribution and they're going to agree on how to communicate. Well if Eve, the hacker, Eve, is now eavesdropping. Eve is actually listening in on the communication, or trying to, well as soon as he does that, the mere act of observing that particle, which is an element of quantum mechanics, the mere act of observing something changes it's state. It's beyond the scope to really dig into that too deeply here, but just understand that the act of even looking at, or eavesdropping on that communication, changes the state of that particle. Since these particles are entangled, they're conjoined, what happens on the side that Alice has instantly also changes the particle on Bob's side. He can tell in an instant that that communication has been intercepted or is being listened in on. The act of observing or eavesdropping on those quantum particles changes its properties, instantly changing the associated entangled particle as well. That lets Bob know, hey, someone's listening in, they drop that communication, they send new particles, and they agree again. If it continues to be eavesdropped on, they know that they're not secure and they can either not communicate, or they can choose obviously to communicate in an unsecure fashion or insecure fashion, but at this point they know that someone is listening or eavesdropping on that communication.

Chapter 19 Quantum Computing, Cipher Modes & XOR Function

We're talking about quantum computing, again, an emerging field of computing, It's not widely spread yet, but it is coming, It's something we have to be prepared for. It's more powerful at certain tasks than classical computing, and it uses something called Qbits instead of regular bits, a 0 or a 1 in traditional or classical computing. Qbits are something a little bit different. Qbits can exist in one of three states, either on, or off, or both on and off at the same time, like the old Schrodinger's cat, was it alive or dead, or is it alive and dead at the same time, if you're familiar with quantum mechanics or quantum physics in any form or fashion. Beyond the scope of this book to dig into it, but just understand that quantum computing is a specific type of computing process or power that will, at some point in time, when it becomes mainstream, will in effect be able to break traditional cryptography, along with other things. It's very, very good at doing certain types of tasks because it can do almost all tasks that assigned to it simultaneously, whereas normal computers can do things and maybe parallel or serial, but they don't do every single thing at once. Even though there's some parralization. With quantum computing, certain tasks can be done simultaneously. It can break certain things that take quite a long time, if not indefinitely with today's traditional or classical computing. Quantum computing will be able to bypass that. That brings us to post quantum. We haven't even gotten to quantum yet, what are we talking about post quantum? Well, cryptographic algorithms that can withstand quantum computing attacks, so financial transactions, federal and military data, medical devices, autonomous vehicles, the list goes on and on. These things need to be secured against quantum computing. If a hacker or a bad actor is able to get their hands on a quantum computer and use it for bad purposes, they could, in effect, have a massive impact on these transactions, on these industries, along with everything else. Several years ago, NIST called for a post quantum proposal. They put the call to action out there, and they're looking for people to submit their ideas and their plans for post quantum cryptography, or cryptographic algorithms that can withstand quantum attacks. They're currently in round three of submissions, and the draft is expected in 2022-2024, somewhere in that timeframe. It's expected to have quantum-proof cryptography or some algorithms that are quantum proof, somewhere in that 2022-2024 timeframe. Next we have a concept of ephemeral key, and the very term ephemeral means temporary. An ephemeral key is a temporary key that's used only once. It can be reused during a single communication session, but once that communication session is over, the key is gone. it can also be used to derive an additional key that is used for subsequent communications. I want to contrast this with forward secrecy that we're going to talk about in just a moment. Ephemeral keys are used only one time or throughout a single communication session, however, they can be used to derive additional keys for subsequent communication. Two cipher modes that I want to touch on, first, is counter mode, or CTR, and that's a random 64-bit block that's used as the first initialization vector. these are algorithms, or methods, that are used to encrypt data. It increments a specified number for each subsequent block of plain text. That way, each block is slightly different, It gives them randomization to that encryption cipher. Second is the Galois counter mode, or GCM, and this is used with symmetric key block ciphers, it's very efficient, low latency, and it also adds data integrity. So rather than dig deeply into what these things do and how they operate, at this point, I just want you to understand what they are and the high level basics of how they function. Next we have the XOR function. XOR, or eXclusive OR, is a method to obfuscate data. What we do is we compare two binary strings of data to produce an output. Two matching bits produces a "false," or an output of 0. Two dissimilar bits produces a "true," or an output of 1. As we see here, we have two strings of data. One is the original data, which is binary. The second line here is our cipher, and in this case, it's just 1100 repeated for the length of the original data or the original text. They are dissimilar, They will produce a true output, or an output of 1. Conversely, on the very end, we have an example of 2 similar bits, two 0s, or it could also be two 1's. As long as those 2 digits match, that's going to be an output of 0, or false. The resulting output with MBR encrypted text. Without knowing what that cipher is, it could be very difficult, if not impossible, to reverse that and get the original text. As long as we have that cipher, though, we can match things up and then very quickly revert back from our encrypted text back to the original data. Let's now talk about cryptographic methods and design, and there's a few things we have to cover. First is ECB or Electronic Code Book, next will be CBC or Cipher Block Chaining Mode, and then we have OFB or Output Feedback Mode, and then CFB or Cipher Feedback Mode. Let's look at each of these individually. In Electronic Code Book, or ECB, we see here that plain text is discreet blocks that are encrypted separately, so we see here each of these individual blocks produces the same ciphertext each time. When we're doing this key, the same key is applied against the plain text. If we have the same, let's say the same sentence, and we encrypt that over and over and over again, or the same word as an example, and we encrypt that over and over and over again, that same word will produce the same ciphertext each time. ECB should only be used for small amounts of data, when we're transmitting small amounts, because we have less chance to observe a pattern. If we're going to transmit large amounts of data with ECB, it becomes very easy to distinguish that pattern over and over and over again, and out of all of the encryption methods that we're covering here, it's the easiest to crack, so, again, only use for small amounts of data. Next would be Cipher Block Chaining Mode, or CBC. The introduction of something called an initialization vector. CBC is similar to Electronic Code Book, except that CBC inserts or something called XOR, it XORs some of the ciphertext created from the previous block. In other words, the IV or initialization vector is introduced in the very first block, so it's the seed, if you will. That's introduced along with the plain text, and a key creates your ciphertext. That ciphertext is then used, or part of that ciphertext is then inserted into the stream. That insertion is referred to as an XOR process. That's inserted into the next block. Blocks are chained together, hence the term Cipher Block Chaining Mode. Each subsequent block relies on some of the encryption or some of the ciphertext from the previous block to encrypt that block and then subsequent blocks, so on and so on and so on. The XOR process is simply inserting some of the previous ciphertext from the previous block into the next block. Then next, we have Output Feedback Motor, OFB, and again, OFB similar, looks similar, but there's some nuances here. Output Feedback Mode makes a block cipher into a stream cipher. The entire output of the previous block is used as the input for the next block's encryption. As we see as we go through here, the first block is encrypted, that entirety of that block is then introduced or used to encrypt the second block. Now the way this works, and a key differentiation between this method and the next method I'll talk about in just a moment, is the fact that transmission errors do not propagate throughout that encryption process. That's the key takeaway there, Output Feedback Mode versus Cipher Feedback Mode, or CFB. Cipher Feedback Mode is similar to OFB, and that can also be implemented as a stream cipher. However, ciphertext is streamed together, and so that allows that error or corruption to propagate through the encryption process. As you go through the four methods we just talked about, just understand where the plain text starts off, where the initialization vector starts off, where that XOR process takes place, and then also the differentiation between output feedback and cipher feedback. One does not propagate errors and one does. That's the takeaways as far as that is concerned.

Chapter 20 Encryptions & Blockchains

Blockchain is an immutable, decentralized digital ledger that is distributed among a network of many computers, a peer-to-peer network. Once a transaction is recorded in this ledger, it can't be altered or removed, or at least, not very easily. It's extremely tamper resistant. This provides trust, transparency, and near real-time processing of transactions. A block is a batch of transactions with a cryptographic hash of the prior block, a time stamp, and some other information. That digital hash, as well learn just a second, links these blocks together or makes a blockchain. Editing or altering a block would change all of the blocks that follow it, and I'll talk about that more in just a moment. You can think of it as a digital ledger, much like a checkbook would be in a checking account. It is a ledger of all transactions, everything that gets done gets entered line by line into that ledger. Blockchain was actually initially conceived way back in 1991 as a timestamp for digital transactions; however, it didn't really gain any recognition or acceptance until it was adopted in 2009 by Satoshi Nakamoto, and we don't really know if he's a real person, if it's a pseudonym, or a group of people, no one seems to know for sure. But it was developed by Satoshi Nakamoto for use with Bitcoin. Everyone is familiar with Bitcoin, cryptocurrency, and sometimes folks will commingle those terms and think that blockchain is Bitcoin or cryptocurrency. They are two distinct things. Bitcoin and cryptocurrency utilize the underlying technology of blockchain, but they're not exactly the same thing. Blockchain can exist outside of cryptocurrency. Each block contains a number of different things. It contains data, it contains a hash of that data, and then also a hash of the previous block. The data that that actual block contains will vary depending upon the type of blockchain that it is. If it's Bitcoin or cryptocurrency, it'll have a certain set of data. If it's used for supply chain, or medical devices, or you name the industry, there's different types of blockchains for different types of things, each chain will contain different types of data, it's not always the same; however, the hash and the hash of the previous block, that will remain regardless of the type of blockchain that we're talking about. We have our blockchain, and you can see, we have some data on that block, we have a hash of that block, and then the hash of the previous block. Now, since this is the very first block, there is no hash of the previous block, that's referred to as a Genesis block. Next, you can see the next block in that chain has a hash of the previous block. That creates that linkage between the two blocks. It's going to have its own data, and then a hash of that data. That hash then gets passed on to the next block, and so on, and so on. That continues on for all blocks in that blockchain. If for some reason, we had a nefarious individual, a bad actor, who goes and tries to manipulate or change the data on one of those blocks, it's then going to change the hash. That hash would then not match with the block on the subsequent block, and so on, and so on. Those things immediately appear, and it would get rejected from the blockchain. The other thing to consider is the fact that blockchain is a distributed ledger, and so we have many, many people that make up this blockchain community. There's lots of people that have copies of the blockchain, and They would need more than 50% consensus, in other words, the hacker would have to go in and manipulate all of those block chains on all of those different people's computers, and actually alter the hash and alter the hash of all the subsequent blocks across all the copies, or at least, more than 50% of those copies for that alteration to actually accepted; otherwise, it would be rejected from the blockchain, That makes it a very, very secure and virtually tamper resistant method of recording digital transactions and making everything very, very transparent. Some fundamental differences of encryption methods. Block versus stream. Now, what you'll need to understand here, is that both are actually symmetric. So don't get confused and think, well, block is symmetric and stream is asymmetric. No, they're both symmetric encryption methods. I'll block cipher, encrypts in chunks or blocks of data at a time, It's not doing it bit by bit. It does it in blocks at a time, whereas a stream cipher encrypts one bit at a time. It's doing it as the name implies, streaming, in that type of fashion. With the block cipher, let's say, for instance, here we have Bob and Alice again. They keep popping up here. Well, with a block cipher, it's a fixed length group, and so a fixed length group of bits or blocks. Each block of plain text has an equivalent size block of ciphertext. If I have a 64K block of plain text, I will have a 64K block of ciphertext. So here we see Bob and Alice communicating. In a stream cipher, we have encryption taking place bit by bit, using a pseudorandom cipher digit stream, otherwise known as a key stream. In that cipher stream, each plain text digit is encrypted, one at a time, bit by bit, with a corresponding digit of the key stream, and that gives us bit by bit digit of ciphertext. It's coming through as a stream. We take the message, and if I bring up our message here, we have our original plain text message. We have our own encryption method, in this case, a 128-bit secret key, and then our resultant, encrypted ciphertext message, so as that streams through, bit by bit, we'll take the very first bit of the message, encrypt it with the first bit of our key, and go to the next bit of the message with the next bit of the key, and that will go through, until the message is complete, and that gives us the resultant encrypted message on the opposite side. The recipient will then reverse that process and then decrypt that encrypted ciphertext back into plain text. Next, we have session keys. A session key is a single-use symmetric key. If you recall, symmetric keys are what? They're very fast, that's used for encrypting all the communication in one communication session. A symmetric key, as it mentioned, is faster than asymmetric, but it can also be used with asymmetric keys. We can have the best of both worlds. We can use an asymmetric key, a public/private key platform, to encrypt the session keys. If I want to communicate a large amount of data, and I don't want to have to use the overhead and the CPU cycles and all that stuff to generate all of that public key/private key cryptography for my entire communication session, what I can do is just encrypt the session key itself using that public key/private key. Then, on the recipient's side, they'll decrypt, get the session key, and then we can communicate using those session keys from that point forward.

Chapter 21 Asymmetric/Lightweight Encryption & Steganography

Next, let's talk about the differences between symmetric and asymmetric encryption. Symmetric encryption uses the same key, the symmetric on both sides, it's going to use that same key to both encrypt and decrypt a piece of data. Symmetric keys, as you might guess, are very fast. If, we have a secret key that's used on both the encryption and the decryption side of the equation here, so same key used for both. If I have my plain text, it goes through my encryption algorithm, secret key is applied, generates some cipher text, that cipher text is sent to the recipient, they use that same key, the same secret key to decrypt and revert that encrypted, or that cipher text, back into plain text. The same key is used for both encryption and decryption, often referred to as a shared key or a secret key encryption. Is far as concerns go, key management is really the biggest concern because both parties must know the secret key. It's also very difficult to prove identity. Because if you think about it, multiple people could know that secret key. If I need to communicate with multiple parties using this encryption platform, or this encryption algorithm, and I'm using the same key, well, if I have that shared among five different people, then I don't necessarily know which one of the five sent that message because any one of those could have used that key. But conversely, if I want to communicate in an encrypted fashion with more than one person and I don't want to use the same key for each communication session, then I'd have to manage multiple keys. That becomes unmanageable, especially at scale. Symmetric is faster than asymmetric because it's a single key for both encryption and decryption. Strength is also affected by the length of the key and the number of iterations you have to go through in the algorithm. In other words, how hard is that algorithm have to work in order to process and encrypt that data? The shorter is obviously faster, but it's less secure. Asymmetric encryption, on the other hand, uses a two-key system a public key and a private key. In that instance, I have two sides of the equation here, a sender and a recipient. The sender is going to encrypt that plain text with the recipient's public key. The sender has to have that recipient's public key ahead of time, so you'll share public keys amongst people that want to communicate. That public key is then used to encrypt that piece of data that result in cipher text. The recipient then uses their private key to decrypt what was encrypted with the public key. It's a two-key system here that are mathematically linked. The public key can encrypt something. The only thing that can decrypt that is the private key. That's where we get the two-key system from. Two keys, one public, one private. In that same situation, key pair, one for encryption, the other for decryption, a public key, as the name implies, is made publicly available, so you give that to anyone. They can then use that to encrypt data back to you. A private key, on the other hand, that must be kept secret. That must be guarded at all costs. Then either key can encrypt, or either key can decrypt, depending upon what we're doing. We can encrypt with the public key, and then decrypt with the private key. We can also encrypt with the private key and decrypt with the public key if we're doing digital signatures. Messages encrypted cannot be decrypted with the same key. That's why that we have this two-key-pair system. Public cannot do public just as private cannot do private. If you encrypt with the public, you have to decrypt with the private, and vice versa. Just understand that basic concept. Next, let's talk about lightweight cryptography. This is an encryption method that utilizes low computational power or energy consumption. NIST sponsored the effort in early 2018, and it's a small footprint and designed for constrained devices, in other words, IoT devices. It has AEAD specification, which means authenticated encryption with associated data, and it means the recipient of a message can use authentication to verify the integrity of both encrypted and unencrypted information within the message. This ensures that messages are coming from where they say they are, and the content of the message has not been altered in transit. The take away being, this is a type of cryptography that's used for devices that are very small in footprint, things that are constrained, meaning they have low computational power, perhaps low battery, or perhaps places where resources are minimal. It allows for some level of security within these IoT devices. Next we have steganography. Steganography lends itself to the old Trojan horse, where you can embed something inside of something else. Hiding a document inside of another document, it's not new, it's been around for quite a while, but it can be used very, very effectively, and it's very hard to detect. Documents can be hidden inside of other documents, such as MP3 files, image files, and video files. If someone wanted to put a secret message inside of an image file, as an example, they could use a tool to embed that specific message inside of an image file, send that image file to someone else. It would use the same tool to pull that text back out of the image. Steganography is very difficult to detect, but depending upon what they're embedding, it can bloat the file size quite a bit, so checking for excessively large files can help. If you have like a 30 MG image file, as an example, well, that may be indicative that, hey, there's something inside of that image file, when pretty much every other file is a tenth of that size. Those types of things can help, but it's not foolproof. Some popular steganography tools, and again, not an exhaustive list, so we have Xiao Steganography, we have image steganography, Steghide, Crypture, and then OpenStego. And there are many other ones out there, these are just a few that I happened to mentioned and want to call your attention to. As an example, here is a screenshot of OpenStego, and you can see we can either hide data or extract data. We can also digitally watermark stuff as well, but in this example we're going to hide data and then extract it. That's what I want to actually hide inside of a ping, or png. You can see I'm going to hide a text file inside of a graphic, a nature.png. That's the "cover" file. So once I do that, I'll put in the encryption algorithm, a password, and then I will hit the button to hide data. On the other side, the person I'm sending it to, they need to have that same tool. They also need to have OpenStego running on their machine on their side. From there, they will hit Extract Data. They will then open the graphic file that I sent them, the message.png, and from there, tell me where I'm going to output the message to and what's the password. Obviously, they're going to need to know what that password is. Once they do, it pulls that text file out of the image file and extracts it to whatever directory they choose. Next, we have the concept of homomorphic encryption. With this, there are three main concepts. We have partially homomorphic encryption, and this allows a select mathematical function, or set of functions, to be performed on encrypted values. One operation, either addition or multiplication, can be performed an unlimited number of times on the ciphertext, and I'll explain more of this in just a moment. Next, we have a somewhat homomorphic encryption. This is select mathematical functions to be performed, again, either addition or multiplication, but the operations can only be performed a set number of times. Then we have fully homomorphic encryption. This is developed from this SHE scheme, or the somewhat homomorphic encryption scheme, and is capable of both addition and multiplication, any number of times, and can make secure multiparty computation more secure. What do I mean by that? Where this starts to come into play is when we're talking about cloud security. Let's say, for instance, we have a cloud provider and we have a person who wants to put some type of an encrypted data into that cloud, but they want to be able to have other parties, whether it's programs, applications or people, work with that data or do something against that data, but not actually have access to the data. What it does, is allow people to perform computations against encrypted data without actually having access to the underlying data itself. In other words, without having to unencrypt the data first. Think of it as, you're putting data into a lockbox and you're locking it. It's a public key algorithm. You can give that public key to others. They can then actually do something with that data. They can work with it. It's almost like they're sticking their hand inside of a box and manipulating the data inside the box, but they're not allowed to take the data outside of the box. You're not allowed to actually see the end result. They can do some things to it, but they can't take it out. The person who put that data in is the only one who can actually retrieve it, so they can unlock the box and extract that data. It allows for someone to put data into the cloud securely, allow other things to work against or work on that data, I should say, securely, without actually having access to the underlying data. Encryption is never unencrypted. It doesn't leave that data vulnerable at any point in time. Let's look at some use cases for common types of encryption that we've talked about previously. We have a few things. We have low power devices, low latency, high resiliency, supporting confidentiality, supporting integrity, supporting obfuscation, supporting authentication, non-repudiation, and also resource versus security constraints. When we're talking about low power devices, ECC or Elliptical Curve Cryptography is a good example. It has low power consumption, which makes it well suited for providing security for mobile devices. For low latency, an example might be symmetric key cryptography. It provides quick or low latency, uses the same key as we talked about for both encryption and decryption, previously, it's also referred to as a secret key or a secret algorithm. Next for high resiliency, crypto systems that are made public. In other words, we're putting them out to the community and letting the community vet that actual algorithm and discover vulnerabilities. there's something referred to as Kerckhoffs'

Principle, and Auguste Kerckhoffs, who was a 19th century Dutch cryptographer, he stated or his principle states that a cryptosystem should be secure even if everything about the system, except the key, is public knowledge. Assuming that any system you develop will be immediately known to the adversary or to the person who's intercepting them, but it should still remain secure, even if they know everything about it, based upon the strength of the key. So getting back to our use cases, supporting confidentiality, well encryption in and of itself, that supports the confidentiality, because if we encrypt something, we're keeping it out of prying eyes, we're keeping it from being intercepted and then read. As far as integrity goes, supporting integrity, hashes is an example that supports or ensures integrity, especially with weaker algorithms like symmetric key cryptography. As we know, symmetric keys, they're fast, but they're also weaker. Then we have the same key using for both encryption and decryption. Hybrid cryptography uses symmetric, asymmetric and hashing to provide speed, confidentiality and also integrity. We can use asymmetric keys or the public key/private key to encrypt to the initial communication. Once that is decrypted, then we can include session keys or symmetric keys, which is then used to actually encrypt the data, . That gives us a speed, and then we can hash that information to make sure it hasn't been tampered with, which supports the integrity. As far as supporting obfuscation, obfuscation or hiding how something works is really the basis of cryptography. Creating a ciphertext that is extremely hard to reverse engineer or crack is the main thing through obfuscation. We're going to hide how that thing works. When it comes to supporting authentication, caching is used to authenticate a piece of data, ensuring nothing has changed during that transmission. We can compare two hashes to make sure that data has not been tampered with or manipulated in any way. If we take a hash of something before it's transmitted, and then take another hash once it's received, if those hashes match, then we can be sure that data has not been tampered with. As far as non-repudiation is concerned, Public Key Infrastructure, PKI, provides for non-repudiation through the use of public keys and private keys. Assuming the user keeps his private key secure, data encrypted via that private key could only originate from that user. It goes without saying that that's only really as secure as keeping the private key secure. If someone were to steal someone else's private key, they could encrypt data with that private key and make it appear as though that person sent it, and then, lastly, resource versus security constraints, right. This is an age old battle between making something very secure and the cost of speed, speed to market. Application developers are challenged with balancing security and the available resources - time, money, talent to ensure that applications are as secure as possible without undue burden to the actual application, to the deployment. It is a bit of a balancing act; however, it needs to be considered from the very beginning. Security should be not an afterthought, something that's tacked onto the very end; applications should be designed with security in mind from the very beginning.

Chapter 22 Cipher Suites, Random & Quantum Random Number Generators

We have strong versus weak ciphers. This is a point in time, a line in the sand type of thing because what was strong 5 years ago, 10 years ago, or considered strong, may be completely breakable today. It's really a matter of perspective and what tools are being used against that specific cipher. Computational resources and capabilities, as we know, they continue to increase. Every day we get more power, more capabilities. In fact, Moore's law states that every 18 months computing power doubles. Strong ciphers can become weak, or weaker at least, as computing power increases. A current example of strong ciphers would be AES, or the Advanced Encryption Standard, we have 3DES, and then Twofish. Actually, Blowfish should be incorporated in there as well, there hasn't been an effective cryptanalysis against the Blowfish as of yet. Those encryption algorithms are very strong. That's not to say, however, 5 years, 10 years down the road, as we really start to increase our computational power, whether it be quantum computing, whether it be big data, some type of distributed computing system, or perhaps a technology that hasn't even been invented yet, that computing power made just skyrocket, and then these encryption algorithms may be able to be broken in an instant. But as of today, these are considered strong ciphers. A weak cipher, by comparison, would be something like WEP, or the Wired Equivalency Protocol. When it first came out, it was considered a strong cipher; however, not too long thereafter it was broken, partly because of the RC4 initialization vector, and some other factors tied into that, but again, it went from being used everywhere to, uh-oh, we'd better not use that, let's replace it with something else. And as you recall, that went from WPA to WPA2, and then, WPA2-Enterprise if we're using it in an enterprise scenario and we want to use RADIUS or some other type of centralized authentication mechanism. Some things to be considering when you're looking at your own security infrastructure, the IoT devices in your network, the encryption algorithms. Some limitations that come to mind are things like speed. How fast can we encrypt, or how fast can something be decrypted? If we have very small or minimal resources, like certain IoT devices, we need a lightweight encryption to handle that. Things like size, the size of the keys could also, in turn, be weak keys. If we're using a weak encryption algorithm or the size of the key is too small, that could pose a security risk. Also, resource versus security constraints. We talked about IoT devices and how they have minimal resources, perhaps battery power or very small computational resources, small computational overhead, well, that can work against us, so lightweight encryption or a lightweight encryption algorithm should be chosen for those instances. If someone is able to take our data offline and then launch brute force attacks against that, they really have all the time in the world to try and crack that encryption algorithm. Conversely, if we're resource or overhead constrained, we may not have the time to actually create very strong keys as it would degrade or diminish the actual ability to stream data. And also, things like longevity, predictability. How predictable is their encryption algorithm? We talked a bit about random and pseudo-random number generators and also quantum key distribution. We'll talk more about that in just a moment. Things like computational overhead. We talked about IoT devices and how the minimal amount of computational overhead available to those devices creates a potential for security risk just because we don't have the ability to really create super strong keys, hence the lightweight cryptography that's being called for currently. Also, reuse, which comes into play in a number of different ways. Is an attacker able to reuse keys or replay information on the network? Are they able to discover or pick patterns in the encryption and perhaps gain insight into the data? And then also entropy, how random is that data? If we start off with pseudo random, as something that's very predictable, or using a weak key, then it's easier to crack. Because if it's built on, air quotes here, "a house of cards", it may look like it's secure, but in reality, it's not. If it's something that's not random enough, and we have enough time, computational power, resources to sit there and bang against that algorithm or actually launch computational attacks against that algorithm, given enough time, and if there is some predictability in that, we're able to discern how the encryption algorithm is started to begin with. And then from there, everything else falls apart. That's where things like random number generators, PRNGs, which is physical hardware, which is a random number generator, or pseudorandom number generators, which is software based, those things have varying degrees of security. But again, no matter what it is, given enough time, there will become some predictability in that device. The level of entropy, or unpredictability, low entropy is faster, but it's also weaker. Again, we're getting back to some of these limitations where speed might be a factor. Well, if we have to go very fast, we may not be able to get very, very random, so low entropy is faster, but it is weaker. High entropy, on the other hand, is slower, but it's more secure, so it's a trade-off. We have to decide what's most important when selecting an encryption algorithm. Possible attacks could be analysis of the PRNG output, the random number generator output. Or we could also have knowledge of the inputs. If we have knowledge of what's actually being inputted, or how things are started, it makes it much easier to understand the encryption that's coming out on the other side. Then lastly, if we're able to actually manipulate the inputs, well then, it makes it way easier to understand what's being encrypted and how that encryption algorithm works and makes it that much easier to break. That's where something like a quantum random number generator comes into play, which we currently have now, and will become more and more common as time goes on. We talked briefly about quantum key distribution, well, that's based around quantum random number generators. It uses the properties of quantum mechanics to create truly random numbers, because in quantum mechanics everything is completely random. There is no predictability, that output cannot be predicted, it would change every time. There is complete entropy, which means that the subsequent encryption is much more secure. In the coming years, expect a lot more from quantum computing, quantum random number generation, key distribution. In this chapter we talked about a lot of interesting topics. We talked about digital signatures, cipher suites, we talked about salting and hashing, also quantum communications and the various ways that takes place. We talked about Blockchain, how that works, the public ledgers. We talked about steganography, and how that can be used to hide things within other things, and then some common use cases and also limitations.

BOOK 3

CYBERSECURITY
ENFORCEMENT AND MONITORING SOLUTIONS

ENHANCED WIRELESS, MOBILE AND
CLOUD SECURITY DEPLOYMENT

RICHIE MILLER

Introduction

IT Security jobs are on the rise! Small, medium or large size companies are always on the look out to get on board bright individuals to provide their services for Business as Usual (BAU) tasks or deploying new as well as on-going company projects. Most of these jobs requiring you to be on site but since 2020, companies are willing to negotiate with you if you want to work from home (WFH). Yet, to pass the Job interview, you must have experience. Still, if you think about it, all current IT security professionals at some point had no experience whatsoever. The question is; how did they get the job with no experience? Well, the answer is simpler then you think. All you have to do is convince the Hiring Manager that you are keen to learn and adopt new technologies and you have willingness to continuously research on the latest upcoming methods and techniques revolving around IT security. Here is where this book comes into the picture. Why? Well, if you want to become an IT Security professional, this book is for you! If you are studying for CompTIA Security+ or CISSP, this book will help you pass your exam. Passing security exams isn't easy. In fact, due to the raising security beaches around the World, both above mentioned exams are becoming more and more difficult to pass. Whether you want to become an Infrastructure Engineer, IT Security Analyst or any other Cybersecurity Professional, this book (as well as the other books in this series) will certainly help you get there! But, what knowledge are you going to gain from this book? Well, let me share with you briefly the agenda of this book, so you can decide if the following topics are interesting enough to invest your time in! First, you are going to discover what are the most important secure protocols and how to implement them. Next you will learn about host or Application Security Solutions, endpoint protection, boot integrity; along with database security concepts, application security concepts, hardening various systems, whether it's an operating system or registry. After that, we'll cover disk encryption; hardware root of trust, TPM chip and the concepts of sandboxing. Next, we'll cover how to Implement Secure Network Designs using load balancers, network segmentation, virtual private networks, DNS, network access control or NAC, out-of-band management, and port security. Moving on, you will learn about access control lists or ACLs, route security, quality of service with implications of IPv6, port spanning, port mirroring, and port taps. We'll also talk about monitoring services, file integrity monitors and how to install and configure wireless security. We'll also cover cryptographic protocols, authentication protocols, methods, and installation considerations. Next, you will discover how to implement Secure Mobile Solutions, connection methods and receivers, mobile device management, enforcement monitoring, and several deployment models. After that, you will discover how to apply Cybersecurity Solutions to the cloud, using cloud security controls, high availability, and the subcomponents, including storage, network and compute. We'll also talk about various solutions, such as cloud access security broker, or CASB, Secure Web Gateways, along with cloud native controls. Next you will discover how to implement identity and account management controls. After that, we are going to cover authentication management, passwords, trusted platform models and hardware security methods. Lastly, you will discover how to implement public key infrastructure, along with the types of certificates, certificate formats, and certificate concepts. If you are ready to get on this journey, let's first cover what are the most important secure networking protocols that you should be aware of!

Chapter 1 Secure Networking Protocols

In the next few chapters we are going to cover secure protocols, but before we get into the details of what we'll cover, let's talk about why is this important. Well, secure protocols ensure communication is safe from hackers and also from prying eyes. It's critical to securing a company's data, intellectual property and competitive advantage. Ultimately a company's footprint, their reputation, their brand, your ability to maintain a job, their investor confidence, customer confidence, all of these things wrap up into one. Secure protocols help strengthen that security posture and make all of this possible or at least help to make all of this possible. We're talking about the secure protocols, not the non-secure ones. There are a lot of protocols that are insecure. I'm going to talk about the secure versions of those protocols and why we should use them along with the use cases. As we go through the protocols, I want you to think about each of these in your own environment and say, what are the use cases? Where can I use these protocols and make sure that I'm securing the environment as much as possible? Security should always be at the forefront of our thought process and looking for ways to secure and look for secure alternatives to the way we're doing things currently. Secure protocols, whenever given the option, we should always be looking to choose the highest security possible when establishing communication over an unsecure or an insecure medium, such as the internet. Such things as FTP, we want to look for FTP secure or HTTP web traffic. We should be looking for HTTPS or HTTP secure. Same thing with SSL and TLS, which is the underlying mechanism that a lot of this security or secure communication will take place. Secure POP or IMAP. Another way to think of that is web mail. Let's go ahead and dig in a little bit deeper here and talk about networking protocols. There are three main areas I want to make sure you're familiar with just you understand how things connect when they're talking to a network. We have IP or internet protocol, and that is connectionless. It's a connectionless protocol that's responsible for network addressing, and it provides routing of packets between networks. It allows us to give a more human-readable name or an address to a specific host or a specific resource on the internet or on our internal network that allows us to route and send traffic. It's just like a house number on the block in a neighborhood. Each of those pieces make up the address of that specific house just like an IP address. Some of the IP address will denote the network. Some of it will denote the host within that network or that subnetwork. Next we have TCP. When you put those together, we have TCP/IP. Transmission control protocol, that is a connection, or anti-protocol, and that establishes connections between endpoints and also provides guaranteed delivery of packets. What happens, it sends out a packet, and there's a wait time or a time to live on that specific packet. If the host that it's sending to or communicates with doesn't respond back and acknowledge and say, I have that packet, I've received it within a certain period of time, then that packet is assumed to be lost, and the host will resend again. That's why it's guaranteeing that delivery. Then we also have UDP or user datagram protocol, and that's a connectionless protocol. It's quick, but there's no guarantee of delivery or its best effort. These three things together make up the basis of how we communicate over an IP network or over the internet. Perhaps a bit of a refresher to you, but in case you're not familiar with this, let's just cover very briefly the three-way handshake that takes place during a TCP communication between two hosts. A three-way handshake establishes that connection between two hosts. A client node sends a SYN packet, a SYN data packet, over an IP network to a server to determine if the server is open for a new connection. It's saying, are you available to talk? The target server must have open ports that can accept and initiate new connections. If in fact that's true, the server responds and returns a confirmation receipt, a SYN acknowledgement packet, a SYN/ACK. From there, the client node receives that SYN / ACK of the SYN acknowledgement back from the server, and it will respond with its own acknowledgement packet. It goes through that handshake process very quickly and establishes that communication. Now we know the basics at a high level of how that communication is initiated, let's talk about the secure protocols and the secure versions of some protocols you're probably already familiar with.

DNS SEC

First up is DNS Secure. DNS is the Domain Name System, and we're familiar with DNS is how we resolve web addresses to IP addresses. It allows us to browse the internet, type in a website, www.Google.com, DNS will resolve that through a series of servers that are out on the Internet, all the way down to the company servers, the company DNS servers within Google's domain, respond back with the host that is specific for the resource we're looking for, and then turn around and deliver that web page to the client. All of that happens very, very quickly. There is a secure version of DNS, and that is DNS Security Extension, or DNSSEC, that was designed to add security to the original DNS specification. DNS was not originally designed with security mechanisms in place. Remember, DNS was designed way back in the late 60's, and it was designed to make browsing or communication over a very large network very fast and very efficient. It's a hierarchical naming standard. Security was not a big thing back then. There may have been four or five hosts when things initially took off, so we don't necessarily know if the original designers envisioned, 4 billion, 5 billion hosts like we have today, but as things started to scale, it quickly became apparent we needed a way to secure some of this traffic. It was meant to be a massively scalable, hierarchical naming system that resolves URLs to IP addresses. All responses from a DNSSEC server, which is protected zones, are digitally signed and authenticating their origin. It doesn't provide confidentiality of the data, so it's not encrypted itself, but it does verify that the server is in fact a legitimate DNS server. It prevents such things as session hijacking and DNS cache poisoning, so a rogue DNS server can't be set up on the network and directing them to illegitimate resources. If we look at a DNSSEC example, let's say, for instance, we have a user, which is referred to as a resolver in DNS lingo, that resolver wants to connect to a web resource. Let's say for the example here we want to connect to www.Google.com, we want to browse Google's resources out on the Internet. The user would connect, type in Google.com into their web browser, it's going to contact the ISP's DNS server. Everyone that connects to the Internet has a DNS server configured, typically from their ISP. So from there the ISP would then refer that up to the root of the Internet, which is dot, the root servers out on the Internet. In a DNSSEC example, there are signed certificates that go through the chain of resolution. As we go through all these different DNS servers, every DNS server above has a signed certificate for the DNS server below. We can follow that chain of trust to make sure that nothing was intercepted or manipulated in that path. ISP contacts the root, the root says, hey, I don't know exactly where that is, but I do know the servers that are authoritative for the.com domain so I'll go check there. It responds back to ISP and it then goes out and contacts the.com or the top-level domain, asks the same question. There's a sign-in key and a digital signature of google.com, the DNS server a level below. So from there, same process, it goes back to the ISP, the ISP then goes out and contacts google.com, which is the second-level domain. It has the DNS key, and it's able to resolve that, and what's happening here is that we have this chain of trust so that everything goes back up to the root so it can be verified all the way through the chain and we know that no one has manipulated anywhere in that process, two main security issues, DNS hijacking and DNS cache poisoning. We know for a fact that everything is secure, there's a chain of trust, and nothing's been broken or compromised in that path. We can rest assured that that DNS server's response is legitimate. We can verify the authenticity of that response and know that we're connecting to a legitimate resource.

SSH

Some other secure protocols I want to talk about is SSH, or Secure Shell. Secure Shell is used for logging into remote hosts. That can be routers, switches, or servers, and it operates over TCP. Remember, we talked about TCP versus UDP. TCP is going to be a connection-oriented protocol. It's going to connect over TCP port 22. An IP address is one thing? We connect to an IP address, but there are also ports. We can put :22 at the end of that, and it would tell the host that we're connecting to we want to connect over port 22. A server, as an example, could wear a lot of different hats. It could be a DNS server. It could be an Active Directory server. It could be a video server, a mail server, you name it. All of those different services operate over different ports. By specifying what port we want to connect to, we're telling that server what service we want to communicate with. When we're talking about different use cases, Secure Shell allows us to remotely and securely log into our routers, our switches, and servers. We can open up a command prompt on a remote server and type commands just as if we're sitting at that server, but we can do that remotely. It saves us the time and energy and effort of having to go to each individual resource, sit down, either a console cable or just connect directly in person to that resource; we can do it remotely. It makes administration much, much easier.

S/MIME

Next, we have Secure MIME, or S/MIME. MIME is the Secure/Multipurpose Internet Mail Extensions. It's a public key encryption and signing of MIME data. We're sending emails, we're securing email delivery. There are some challenges; however, I want you to be aware of the protocol, but there are some actual challenges in implementation. When we're doing this, we want to send and receive, encrypted email between two hosts, a sender and receiver. Well, both parties have to have a public key/private key pair for them to communicate. That's either issued from an in-house certificate authority or from a public certificate authority. From a corporate standpoint though, that end-to-end encryption can defeat malware scanners. In practice, a company may not want to have that in place because then they can't go in and inspect the contents of that email, and they can't scan for malware because that data is encrypted. There are ways to put different types of SSL decryptors along the perimeter, and in some cases, it can strip that information off and decrypt it at the perimeter and then send it on to the recipient, but it's problematic at best, so something just to be aware of.

Secure Real-Time Transport Protocol (SRTP)

Next, we have Secure Real-time Transport Protocol, or SRTP. It's a secure version of RTP. SRTP is a security profile for RTP, or the Real-time Transport Protocol, and it adds confidentiality, message authentication, and also replay protection to that protocol. And as you may guess, is used to secure VoIP, or Voice over IP, traffic. It's great in that it has minimal effect on the actual IP quality, of that Voice over IP service. We can add security without decaying or degrading the end user experience, and that's key here. We want to make sure that when someone picks up the phone that communication doesn't sound jittery or broken up, so there's no reason to not have Secure RTP in place.

Lightweight Directory Access Protocol over SSL (LDAPS)

Next, we have LDAPS, or Lightweight Directory Access Protocol over SSL. LDAP, as we know, is the Active Directory mechanism we use to log into Active Directory services and find resources in a Windows network, and that operates over both TCP and UDP over port 636. What that does is secures traffic between the client and server over SSL and TLS, Secure Sockets Layer and Transport Layer Security. It does require all DCs to have an X.509 certificate installed. It may or may not be completely viable in your environment, or you may have a very distributed environment where you don't have everything sitting on one server. You may have a root certificate server and then issuing service below, so it just depends upon how your individual infrastructure is set up. But for purposes of our discussion, just understand what LDAP Secure is. It's a way of securing Lightweight Directory Access Protocol, or LDAP, and the ports that it goes over, 636, TCP, and UDP. Also, understand the transport mechanism and how it secures that traffic using SSL and TLS.

FTPS and SFTP

Next, we have FTPS, or FTP Secure, File Transport Protocol over SSL. And what this does, as you can imagine, is secure file transfers that use SSL for encryption, or that Secure Sockets Layer. Encryption can be turned off if other encryption is in use. So, for instance, if we have IPSec in place, we don't need to double dip here. We can turn SSL off and still have a secure communication, or secure transferring of files. And that's going to operate over TCP ports 989 and 990. Getting back to use cases, FTP is a very popular protocol people use to upload and download files all day long. If we're inside of a network or we're connecting from the outside, FTP typically, those credentials are sent in clear text, we don't want that. We want to use something that's secure. We're going to make sure we use FTPS, or SFTP. They achieve the same end goal. But in the back of your mind, we should always be looking for ways to add security to the way we do things. If we need to FTP, let's look for FTPS or SFTP. SFTP or Secure FTP, that sounds just like we just talked about. And the net result is the same, but it's a different way of doing it. It's SSH File Transfer Protocol. Before, we were doing FTP over SSL. We're using SSH. It provides for remote file transfer, access, and also management. It gives us a little more functionality, and what it does is utilize FTP over SSH. The FTP is tunneled through that SSH connection. TCP transport protocol, Transmission Control Protocol, connection oriented. We're going over TCP port 22.

SNMP v3

Next, we have SNMP version 3. Simple Network Management Protocol has been around for a while. There's versions 1 and 2, did not have security baked in. And since we're talking about secure protocols, we're looking for version 3. SNMPv3 allows for remote management and reporting of IP devices. All the different IP devices within our network, we can turn on SNMP, set up our community strings, and go out and have a management server, and then all of our clients, or the things we're communicating with, we can set up alerts. We can configure some devices. We can report on others to see if that device is up or down. If there's an alert, it can send a trap to that management server and allow us to report very quickly on the state of our environment, or the health of these different devices. Communication protocols can be intercepted and manipulated, it can potentially lend itself to a breach or release some type of denial of service or some other type of, degradation to our service. SNMPv3 will encrypt that data. Earlier versions didn't provide encryption, Wherever possible, if we can use SNMPv3, encrypt our data, encrypt our communication, we just take one more thing off the table that hackers were able to use or try to leverage to breach or otherwise to create performance for the end user. SNMP, whether it's version 1, 2, or 3, is going to utilize UDP port 161 by default.

SSL/TLS

Next, we have SSL and TLS. SSL and TLS is Secure Sockets Layer/Transport Layer Security. And just you're aware, SSL is the older implementation. TLS is newer based on SSL. What it does is adds confidentiality and data integrity by encapsulating other protocols. It's not a method of communicating in and of itself, but it's a way for us to add security to other protocols? We can encapsulate that data, and we can add confidentiality and data integrity by encapsulating other protocols. Confidentiality and data integrity are two prongs of the CIA triad, confidentiality, integrity, and availability. It initiates that stateful session with a handshake. As an aside in your environment, make sure all servers are patched for the Heartbleed Bug. That was an SSL/TLS vulnerability that hackers were using and leveraging out in the wild, Very important that all your servers are patched to avoid that vulnerability.

HTTPS

Next, we have HTTPS. HTTP is web traffic, so authentication of the visited website, as well as privacy and integrity of that data exchange. It allows us to connect securely to a web address or to a web resource, a web server, communicate with that web server, and that communication is encrypted. So our ISP doesn't see what we're doing. Hackers or someone else that's sniffing that traffic, they don't see what we're doing. It also provides that integrity and the authentication. We know that the person or the website that we're connecting with is in fact the website that we are looking to connect with. It's not a fake or a forgery. By the same token, the client could also authenticate to the server, although typically we're just worried about connecting or authenticating and verifying the integrity of the server that we're communicating with. It also protects against eavesdropping and man-in-the-middle attacks. If you see MITM, that abbreviation is for man in the middle, which means someone is injecting themselves into that communication. Remember the old example of Bob and Alice. The hacker injects themselves into that process. Bob thinks he's talking to Alice, but he's talking to the hacker. The hacker then relays that information to Alice, but he's manipulating that data along the way. Man-in-the-middle attacks can be remediated or protected against using encryption. Also bi-directional encryption of the communication between the client and server; we're encrypting communication, both ways, between the server to the client and also to the client to the server. Also just

227

you're aware, it's TCP, TCP communication protocol over port 443.

Secure POP/IMAP

Next, we have secure POP and IMAP, so accessing webmail. When we talk about POP, or Post Office Protocol, or IMAP, we're talking about accessing webmail. We're doing that securely, again, using SSL and TLS. It's a way of encapsulating that data. Post Office Protocol, or POP, POP3 is the latest version. That's going to be TCP port 110 for normal traffic or 995 for SSL. Internet Message Access Protocol, or IMAP, that's going to be IMAP4 being the latest version, and that is TCP port 143 or 993 over SSL. We're talking about different ways we can secure our networks. If we require and mandate that we always use secure versions of POP and IMAP, we can cut down on eavesdropping. Mail, webmail specifically, is a big target for hackers because if they're able to access someone's email and scour through that, they can get a lot of information about who their friends are, the way they communicate, the words the verbiage, the language that they use. Then they can craft emails to other people and make it seem very convincing that it's coming from that person because they've gone through a bunch of emails. They know what they're interested in. They know what sites they visit, what resources, what they just bought. All of these things can put up a profile on a target or a victim, and then as that attacker crafts an email that's specifically geared towards that target, it seems very convincing. It's much more likely that that person will click on a link that's in that email or do some type of action or take some action on that email. And then as soon as they do that, boom, malware is installed on that system. It can go out and started downloading other pieces of software. It could potentially become a zombie in a larger botnet, or it could communicate back to some command-and-control server, allow a hacker to come in, gain a foothold on that system, start browsing through our network, find a way to jump over a pivot, jump over to another network, start accessing resources. As soon as they start to gain relevant privileges, install a back door and gained persistence, and then off to the races at that point. Let's see how much information we can possibly exfiltrate or steal from this network. Depending upon the type of hacker that they are, they may be very slow and steady, very stealthy, very surreptitious in their exploration of data, and they sit there for weeks or months or years where they could very quickly want to get in and get out or try to destroy data, and try to take the company down. It could be a very quick process, or it could be very long, and by the time we realize it, they're already in our backups and everything else. If we've got to restore, it's too late. All of these different things, securing our FTP traffic, securing our web traffic, Voice over IP traffic, and so on, all of these different things, as we secure them, we're doing what? We're building up a defense in depth. A layered defense. The more locks on the door, the longer it's going to take a hacker or someone who's trying to do harm to the company, it's going to take them longer and longer and longer to unlock all of those locks before they can get in. That gives us the opportunity to identify and notice that the breach is occurring or make it Difficult that we may not even notice, but it becomes such a laborious process that they just give up and go somewhere else where they may have an easier target.

Use Cases
We talk about different use cases. I don't want to dig in depth into each one of these and go off on tangents, but I just want to quickly bring these to your attention and have

you think in the back of your mind, where can I tighten up security? Where can I add security or secure protocols in each of these different instances? More importantly than the individual protocol, understand why would you want to secure that type of traffic. Voice and video; we talk about time synchronization. Every computer or every host on that network needs to synchronize their time. It's important for directory services, for other applications that everything is in sync. Typically, in large environment, all of those devices will sync to an internal time synchronization server. Smaller environments are where individual users may go out and sync to a time server out on the internet? One of the military servers, that may or may not be the case, depending upon your specific environment, but it's important that those things are secure because, again, every piece of communication can potentially be hijacked, some type of man-in-the-middle attack or some type of data manipulation to corrupt data, denial-of-service attacks where you simply get in and try to infiltrate the network itself. All of these things should be triggering thoughts in the back of your mind, how can I secure these types of traffic? Email and web browsing. We talked about HTTPS. We talked about IMAP and POP secure and File Transfer Protocol. We talked about FTPS and also SFTP. If a hacker is able to sniff the network and monitor that traffic and they can browse our FTP servers or upload and download our content, they can, again, build a very detailed profile of what's important, perhaps steal intellectual property or things they're not supposed to have access to. But aside from the obvious, stealing data, they can build a profile and get very, very good very, very quickly of what's inside of our network, the applications, the services, the users, maybe the locations even. All of these things can be potentially gleaned from the files that they're able to download or even upload, viruses, malware. That

230

defense-in-depth mindset will go a long way to securing the environment. The same thing with directory services - every time you log into a network, every time we browse for a specific resource, all of that communication is potentially going over unencrypted. We want to make sure we encrypt whenever possible. Remote access - we talked about Secure Shell. That should be a standard. It should be a given. There should not be a way to access hosts in an insecure fashion. Telnet, as an example. Get rid of it. Turn it off. Make sure it's disabled everywhere. Use SSH so that communication is then encrypted, whether you're protecting to router, switches, servers. Same thing with domain name resolution - DNS traffic over port 53. DNS traffic is a favorite for hackers to exfiltrate traffic because everybody has it. Everybody has DNS traffic internal. You also need to then go out to an external DNS server when you want to browse web resources. So firewalls will always have those ports open, and traffic can go very easily in and out of the network, or over port 53. Monitor for that. Monitor for excessive amounts. Baselining. Make sure that we understand what's normal. What are the normal packet sizes, what's normal data flow? That way, when there are very large spikes, it should be raising red flags. Wherever appropriate, secure zone transfers, making sure we don't have rogue DNS servers on our network. Security should be in place from the get-go. Talked about routing and switching, we talked about Secure Shell and ways to securely access all of these different devices within our network. But think about the additional ways you can secure routing and switching. We talked about port security, making sure we don't have rogue access points and rogue switches, Wi-Fi access points on the network. All of these things should be configured to check in or authenticate on the network. Then also, devices on our network that can scan for rogue access points to make sure that no one is just plugging into our network and trying to set up some evil twin or some rogue access point to either give out fake DNS information, fake DHCP information, man-in-the-middle attacks and more. Network address allocation, DHCP, same thing. We want to be monitoring to make sure that people are not trying to instantiate fake or malicious DHCP servers on our network. If we have DHCP security set up properly, those servers will check in, and if they realize there's already a DHCP server on that subnet, they'll shut down and not serve us requests. Then lastly, subscription services - that can mean a lot of different things depending upon what company and what industry you're in. Just think of all the things we've talked about so far and how you can secure whether it's a website, a service, or an application, how you can secure those individual piece parts. In summary we covered two main areas. We covered protocols and use cases. For protocols, we covered such things as DNS Secure, or DNSSEC, SSH, and S/MIME. We talked about SRTP, LDAPS, and FTPS, and also SNMPv3, SSL, and TLS. Also, HTTPS and secure POP and IMAP. These are all things that you're probably familiar with in their insecure versions, and we talked about the secure versions of these protocols to help strengthen that security posture and make the overall security footprint of your company stronger. Some use cases we talked about where voice and video, time synchronization, things like email and web and file transfer, along with directory services and remote access. Also, domain name resolution, routing and switching, network address allocation, and also, subscription services. Things that is useful and used every day within your organization, the ways you can avoid some common pitfalls, and also, again, strengthen those specific areas within your organization.

Chapter 2 Host or Application Security Solutions

In this chapter we'll be talking about Host or Application Security Solutions. We'll be talking about endpoint protection. We'll talk about boot integrity; along with database security concepts; application security concepts; hardening of various systems, whether it's operating system, registry; we'll talk about disk encryption; hardware root of trust and also the TPM chip; and then wrap up with the concepts around sandboxing.

Antivirus
When it comes to antivirus, they can detect viruses, malware, in some cases ransomware or crypto-malware, root kits. Well, AV software can be standalone. It can also be agent based or network based, and it can also be cloud based. In this specific instance, we're talking about host-based antivirus, which means it's going to run as an agent, typically, on that server or that PC or laptop. It can scan data on access, and it can also periodically scan the entire file system, much like their network counterparts or cloud-based counterparts. They can do things when you click on a file, when you go to save a file, or you can have it run every so often, maybe once a day or once every hour, and it will scan the entire system. Then if it finds something, whether it's a piece of malware, a virus, it will either quarantine that specific piece of code and then send some type of an alert, an email, or it can send it off to a NOC or a SOC, a security operations center, and it can also report back the details of that specific piece of code back to the company's headquarters, whether it's Microsoft or Trend Micro or McAfee. It can send that information back so that it can be aggregated and correlated across all customers in the

environment to see if that specific type of outbreak, whether it's malware, viruses, worms, if that's being seen in the wild.

Endpoint Detection and Response (EDR)

When it comes to securing systems on our network and within our environment, it's important that we have endpoint protection in some form or fashion, so applications and tool sets known as endpoint detection and response systems, or EDR systems, or sometimes they may even have threat detection in there as well. You might see endpoint detection and also threat detection and response, so it could be ETDR as well. Well, these things have a number of key features. Endpoint detection response key features are they monitor and collect activity on endpoints. It's not just an AV program, or an antivirus program. They can do additional things like monitor and collect activity, understanding when things are launched, how they're launched. They can then analyze that data to identify threats, patterns, or indicators of compromise, or IoCs, and then automatically respond to identify threats, to remove or mitigate them, and notify appropriate teams, security personnel. And then lastly, forensics and analysis tools to research threats and also search for suspicious activities. An endpoint detection program, or an EDR, may be a standalone application, or could plug into a larger system, like a SOAR system, S-O-A-R. We've talked about SOAR systems before, but just to reiterate, we have a SOAR platform that can do a number of things. It can gather information from event logs. It can gather things from our security incident and event management or monitoring tools, our SIEM systems, and then also EDR systems, endpoint detection response. All of those things can feed into a SOAR platform, which in turn can then do some automation for us, whether it be ticketing, IT ticketing, change control. It can open up tickets to

234

remediate certain things that it finds. And then also controls, like alerting or whitelisting and blacklisting. If we whitelist an application, it means allow only this application, or only the ones we have whitelisted. Or if we blacklist an application, it means allow everything except for the ones that are on the blacklist. Whitelisting would be deny everything except what's on the list, and then blacklisting would be allow everything except for what's on the blacklist? Alerting, whitelisting, and then also third-party tools. That SOAR platform allows us to integrate a number of different things, including EDR systems and automate to a much greater degree.

Data Loss Prevention (DLP)
DLP, or data loss prevention, detects potential breaches and exfiltration of data. Especially in the age of PCI we want to make sure that we are capturing any attempts to exfiltrate data from our network. It does endpoint detection, things that are in use, network traffic, things are in transit, data in transit, and then also data storage, or data at rest. It allows us to understand, is someone storing credit card information? It might scan the network and look for things that have a series of nine digits separated by dashes. That might be a Social Security number. Or it may have 16 digits or whatever numbers represent a credit card. Things that might be personally identifiable information and things that are a no-no to store from a PCI standpoint, it will search for that and make sure that we're not storing data that we're not supposed to be storing in insecure locations. Then also, when things are attempted to be exfiltrated or stolen or removed from our network, it will capture those things as well. Additional methods we can use these DLP technologies to identify if someone's trying to remove data from our environment, we can do USB blocking, we can do cloud

based, and we can do email, we can check all of these things as well. Is someone inserting a USB drive into a computer and trying to pull data off the network? Are they doing it from a cloud instance? Are they trying to upload things to some type of cloud storage or cloud application? And then, of course, email, self-explanatory, is someone trying to email something that they should not be emailing? The types of data to secure, we have data in transit, data that's being sent over a network, whether it's wired or wireless. A VPN connection will encrypt the data while in transit, wired or wireless. That could be a good thing or a bad thing. It's good because we're not sending data that could be compromised, so it saves us from being sniffed on the network. But if we're trying to detect what's being sent, it blocks that from our view. You have to take that into consideration. VPNs and encryption can work in our favor or they can work against us. Next we have data at rest, data sitting on a hard drive or removable media, Local to the computer or remotely on SAN or NAS storage, so that's data that's sitting there. And then we have data in use, data that's not "at rest," and only on one particular node or a network. It's being used in some fashion. It could be a memory resident piece of information, swap/temp space. We want to make sure we're protecting against all three of these categories to make sure data's not being exfiltrated or stored improperly on our network.

Next-generation Firewall (NGFW)
When it comes to firewalls, we have a general understanding of what a firewall is and what it does. But one thing you may or may not be familiar with is the concept of a next-generation firewall, or an NGFW. A next-generation firewall, they go beyond traditional firewalls and what we know a traditional firewall to do, such as stateful packet inspection or VPN services. Well, next-generation firewalls

also offer advanced services like deep packet inspection, so it goes much deeper into the packet than a traditional firewall. Also, it can offer application firewalls. We can block things based on application based on the application itself, not just an IP address or a packet type? We start to move up the OSI stack. Also, things like intrusion detection and also intrusion prevention. We can do things like TLS and SSL inspection where we can decrypt packets, inspect what's inside that packet, and then send it on its way. And also, things like bandwidth management. Next-generation firewalls can combine the functionality of several different appliances or several different platforms into one device or one piece of equipment. As an example, a few next-generation firewall vendors and this is not in any specific order, and it's not an endorsement of any one product over another. I'm just giving you an idea of some of the vendors out there if you want to do a little more research on your own. We have vendors like Fortinet or Forcepoint. Also, Palo Alto Networks, SonicWall, Barracuda. Cisco also makes some next-generation firewall. Check Point advanced threat protection. Checkpoint was one of the very first VPN and firewall manufacturers out there. Also, Sophos, Juniper Networks, and the list goes on and on? These are not an exhaustive list, it's not an endorsement of one over the other. Just to give you an idea of what's out there if you want to do a little more research on your own.

HIDS/HIPS
HIDS and HIPS, host-based intrusion detection systems or intrusion prevention systems. They're similar in function to the network versions, the network intrusion detection or prevention systems; however, they run on a specific host. They don't cover an entire network. They cover a specific host. Like their network versions, they can detect anomalous

behavior, and they can alert on that specific behavior. The difference is, this is a host-based, so it's running on a specific host, one system, not an entire network or a subnet or a specific part of a company. It's on a single host. When we're talking about host-based intrusion prevention systems, again, similar functionality to the network versions. They can take similar action or similar functionality to the detection systems, but they can then take action, shut down a port, run a script, do some type of workflow, in addition to alerting administrators. Very similar functionality we can run these things on a grand scale in a network environment, or we can run them specifically on individual hosts.

Host-based Firewall
When it comes to firewalls, we talked about a few different types. And in this case, we're talking about a host-based firewall. Firewalls, as we know, will typically block traffic based upon port, protocol, IP address, or perhaps application. Most server-based OSes and client-based operating systems will contain some type of virtual private networking, some type of host-based firewalls, some type of antivirus checking. You have some of these host-based tools built in to most operating systems. Then, of course, you can download free versions. You can download commercial versions. You can install enterprise-wide versions, all of which have different use cases and may fit in different environments for different reasons. But they all function generally the same way. They're going to manage and alert on some type of crossing the threshold, some type of trigger. Whether that is a port, a protocol, IP address, you can allow certain things that pass through, and you can restrict others. On host-based systems, we'll typically do that by restricting applications. You can go into that server's built-in firewall and say let these 4 or 5 or 10 or however many applications

through and block everything else. Applications can be whitelisted or blacklisted. When you whitelist an application, you're saying here's the 5 or 10 or 15 applications that I'm going to allow to run. Conversely, if you say application blacklisting, you can say go ahead and run everything except for these 5 or 10 that I explicitly deny. Its two different approaches. One allows everything except what you say not to. The other one says block everything except for the 5 or 10 that I explicitly allow.

Boot Loader Protections and Secure Boot

Talking about boot loader protections, and what is a boot loader protection? Well, it's made up of a couple things here. We have secure boot; we have a measured launch; IMA, or Integrity Measurement Architecture; and then, of course, our BIOS, or UEFI, and we'll talk about each of these in more detail. Secure boot is a feature of UEFI, that allows only signed boot software to load. UEFI is Universal Extensible Firmware Interface. It's a new type of BIOS. You can think of that as the BIOS in newer systems. It allows or enables a very secure booting mechanism. If code is not signed properly, then it will halt the boot process. If we go through the steps here, firmware boot components, it's going to be digitally signed, and it's going to be digitally signed by the maker of that laptop or that piece of hardware, typically, all. It can only run certain OSs or certain boot files. It can locked down so it can only run a specific type of operating system. That firmware boot component is digitally signed, as I said it, comprised of a boot manager, again, digitally signed. It'll pass on to winload functionality, again, checks certificates, goes to the Windows kernel startup, and that will interface with the AV software initialization, and, again, checking certificates to make sure everything along the way is signed properly. That passes it back to the kernel startup, goes into additional OS initialization, passes over to boot-critical driver installation, loads our drivers, necessary to boot the system, passes it back, and then, of course, we see the windows login screen. Anywhere along that process, if those digital certificates are not on the up and up, if they've been tampered with or they're just missing, then the boot process would halt. That prevents things like root kits and pieces of malware, spyware that try to load onto the system before the actual operating system, before the antivirus software loads. If something tries to tamper in that boot sector or some type of pre-boot startup malware, this will fix that. This will prevent that from happening because it's going to alter the digital certificate. In a nutshell, when that PC starts, the firmware's going to check the signature of each piece of boot software, including firmware and drivers. If the signature's are good, the PC will boot. If not, it's going to halt that process. Not all systems have this, and you can add additional certificates in. If we have an operating system, for example, that is not included in that initial list of digital certificates, it is possible to add that in after the fact and give additional options, as far as booting that piece of equipment.

Measured Launch
Boot components have been measured, and what that means is they've been identified cryptographically. We have a hash against those things. The cryptography hashes are checked at boot to validate each component. It's part of what's called the Intel Trusted Execution Technology, or Intel TXT. And what it also does is provide a detailed log of everything that happens before the load of that actual antimalware software. If we have to go back and try to understand what happened, something got installed on our system, some piece of malware got introduced, we can go

back and check this log and see exactly where that happened. As you can imagine, it will aid in our troubleshooting and overall analysis.

Integrity Measurement Architecture (IMA)
And then next we have IMA, or Integrity Measurement Architecture. IMA is an open source alternative that creates a measured runtime environment. It creates a list of components that need to load for that operating system or for that PC to boot up. It anchors that list to what's called a TPM chip, the Trusted Platform Module. It anchors it to that chip to prevent tampering. That way, if anything changes, any type of malware tries to install and it will alter those files if they don't match, then it prevents that boot.

BIOS/UEFI
Next, we have the BIOS or UEFI, universal extensible firmware, it's an alternative to the traditional BIOS. It offers a few advantages. We can boot from disks larger than 2 TB. It's also CPU independent architecture, CPU independent drivers, so we can work whether it's on Mac, Linux, Windows system, it's not dependent upon the operating system. It's also a flexible pre-OS environment offering options of Boot menu, network boot. It gives us that secure boot environment if we need it and gives us just more options than a traditional BIOS would allow.

Hashing
Hashing is a mathematical algorithm that's applied to a file before and after transmission. If anything within that file changes, the hash will be completely different. We have a couple options, we could use MD5, SHA1, or SHA2, and that's your choice depending upon which algorithm you want to use, they will each produce a different result. In the

real world, if we hashed an entire file or an entire disk, if anything has changed on that disk or in that file, depending on the example, it will result with a different hash file. Whether we're trying to send something to someone, we could take a hash first and then let them hash again when they get on the other side and see if the numbers match, if they match, we know nothing has changed, it hasn't been manipulated. Or from our forensics point of view as an example, we can take a hash of an entire hard drive, and then anytime we want to prove the veracity of that image, we can just run a hash against that again, and as long as those numbers match, we know that nothing has changed on that hard disk.

Salt
Password or passphrase salting is random data that is used as an additional input into a one-way function or hash. It defends against dictionary tax and/or rainbow table attacks. What we're doing is adding additional information to our password so that it creates an additional level of randomization, makes it harder to guess, makes it harder to bruteforce. This adds additional complexity and also makes it much more difficult to try to guess.

Secure Coding Techniques
The goal of this chapter is not to make you a very highly skilled coder. We're not deep diving into the actual nuts and bolts of coding here, but the general concepts the general mindset behind coding so that as an IT security professional you can have those conversations with the DevOps folks and with the coders and make sure that these concepts are being followed. When it comes to secure coding techniques and proper error handling. We need to make sure the errors don't crash the system, allow for elevated privileges, or

expose unintended information. In having these discussions, again, with programmers and coders, understand, ask the questions, show me how error handling works. Show me what happens if unintended input is entered. What happens if the system crashes? What does it give back to the end user? Proper input validation is another. We want to make sure that we sanitize the data to mitigate such things as cross-site scripting and cross-site forgery requests. If someone goes into a web portal, we want to make sure that data is sanitized so they can't put in some rogue piece of information and get unintended results back. Also, normalization on the database back end. We want to ensure database integrity and optimization of data. You may ask yourself, what does this have to do with security? Well, normalizing the database ensures that there are no insertion or deletion anomalies. Downstream impacts might be if something gets deleted improperly or if something gets added improperly and our database and our tables are out of sync, it could return unintended consequences, or could have unintended consequences, and return unintended data, so normalization is key. Also stored procedures. We want to utilize vetted, secure procedures, verses writing new code on the fly. Whenever possible, reuse code if appropriate, or use stored procedures that have been vetted and are known to be secure. Next, we have code signing. We want to ensure that validated and trusted code is used. We want to mitigate risk from unsigned code being allowed to run. Because, again, if we allow things that have not been vetted, have not been signed, we don't know where that's coming from, we don't trust it. If we allow those things to run, we introduce risk, potential for malware, potential for spyware, ransomware, you name it, unintended results. Hackers can use these things to try to crash the system, inject code into the application. Unsigned code is a no-no.

Encrypting the data, that's going to mitigate the risk of compromise should the actual computer go missing, lost or stolen, or the drives housing the data become lost or stolen. Then we have obfuscation or camouflage. This goes hand in hand with encryption. Masking the data, encryption is an example, to avoid detection by static code analysis. That typically involves such things as a decoder and the encoded payload. You can look at these things in one of two ways. Encryption is going to keep the data out of prying eyes, but it also keeps someone from potentially reverse engineering what we're doing. If we're encrypting our code or obfuscating otherwise, camouflaging that code, they can't do static code analysis against that program and spot potential errors. It goes both ways. Those two things can either work for you or against you, depending upon which side of the fence you're sitting on. Then we have code reuse and dead code. Code reuse is simply code that can be reused, as the name implies, for some future use, future project. The challenge becomes, when people try to write code that they can reuse later, they start to bring in things that may not be necessary for the project they're working on but trying to think of future uses or future bugs they might encounter or future issues they may come up with. They try to write code that is going to counteract those things, when in reality they're probably not going to capture all those things anyway. But by focusing on what's in front of you, you stand a much better chance of writing a very clean, secure piece of code.

Server side versus client side
Take into account where validation, input sanitation, where those things occur, and the way those controls can be bypassed. Server side versus client side depends upon where those things, where those validations and those sanitizations

244

take place. They're easier to bypass on the client side than it is on the server side, typically. Where we have the option, servicer side is typically better., not always, there's always exceptions to every rule, but just some things to think about, so the conversations to have with the coders when you're discussing how the applications work and how they function. Next is memory management. That's going to ensure that code calls and manages memory properly to avoid heap and buffer overrun errors. These things could cause the system to crash, they could cause system instability and data exposure. Things to ask your developers, making sure you're both on the same page, making sure they've thought through these things, which they may or may not have. It's always good to validate. Don't just assume that because someone works on code that they know how to do it securely. There are obvious conversations that need to be had. Then we have third-party libraries and SDKs, or software development kits. Ensure that you understand any third-party, any third-party's security requirements, their vetting processes, where their data is stored, interaction with other apps or data. Again, don't just assume that they have the same level of security that you do. Always vet that and remember that security's only as strong as the weakest link. Make sure that there is some type of service-level agreement or an understanding between companies, how they vet their process, how they take security as a consideration. Is their security up to the level of yours? Because it doesn't matter how strong your security is; if theirs is weak, then an attacker's able to come in through the side door through their weaker security and then pivot and then come through into your application or your network. That poses a challenge, and of course a breach can occur. Then, lastly we have data exposure. What types of data are exposed? If unexpected inputs are put into the system and cause the system to crash or cause some unintended result, or what errors are returned if incorrect data is entered. In other words, if someone puts in some type of string, they try a cross-site scripting or cross-site forgery request or they go through some type of fuzzing exercise or they just try every single combination of characters and letters to see what happens, to see if the system crashes. If and when it does crash, what types of information are returned? Does it tell you the operating system, the kernel version, all those things an attacker could potentially use to fingerprint the system, or if the website, as an example, asks for a username and a password, and they put in the wrong username, does it tell them, hey, this username's not valid. Well, that lets them know, hey, that one's, strike that from the list. That one's not valid. Let's try the next one. And it allows them to brute force that. Versus if it simply says, hey, if this was correct you'll get an email back or an email was sent or some type of a more ambiguous error message it doesn't give them any insight into what's valid or not valid. It's all a matter of conversations that you should have with, the coders and developers to make sure that everyone is on the same page. They will then understand how security factors in, and you will get a better understanding of how the applications interact with each other.

Chapter 3 Coding, Fuzzing & Quality Testing

We have static code analyzers; we have dynamic analysis; other words, fuzzing; we have stress testing; sandboxing; and model verification. Secure coding concepts, some things to keep in mind. Application development is often a balancing act between time to market and security. There are the developers and the general IT folks, and then there's the security folks. But we're all working on the same team, and we're all trying to do the same things, so it's important that we all work together. Building for security, that's going to add to development time. That's the general consensus, or the general understanding. But here's the key part. If you don't have time to find the vulnerabilities, guess who will? The bad guys. It's very, very important, it's crucial, in fact, that we spend the time, we do security up front, we incorporate security from the get go, not as an afterthought, not as a bolt-on. It should be done from the beginning. And the old adage is, if you don't have time to do it the first time, what makes you think you're going to have time to go back and do it a second time? If you can't do it once, how are you going to have time to do it twice? Some additional things with secure coding, error and exception handling. We need to look at what does the application do when it encounters an error? Does it continue running? Does it restart a process or a chapter? Or does it completely crash? And what type of data is exposed when it crashes? Does it give that attacker the ability to elevate privileges and get in and then do all the things that they typically would do, install persistence and go on from there, or does it give away information that tells about the type of operating system that it's on, the kernel level, some information that the attacker can use to then further dig into that system? Also input validation. It's important that we validate and sanitize what is entered at the client side or the server side, depending upon, again, your coding mechanisms and your preference. But either way, that needs to be processed and sanitized before it's passed and executed upon. That's going to allow us to mitigate attacks, cross-site scripting attacks and also SQL injection attacks, two big ones that can be avoided or mitigated if we sanitize that input properly. Metasploit, Exploit-Me, there's browser add-ons, Netsparker, there are a number of different tools out there that can allow an IT security professional to do these types of tests ahead of time. You can either throw them up to the wind and just use your best guess and hope that this stuff works and nobody tries to get in and nobody's able to get past your defenses. Or you can be proactive and use these tools and think like an attacker, think like a hacker, and start running tests against your own systems. If you don't have the expertise, bring in a pen testing team. But it's important that we test these things, we try to break things along the way so that we get to it before the attackers do.

Static Code Analysis

Static code analysis is also known as source code analysis. It's part of a code review process for something that's referred to as white-box testing, so it allows you to see under the covers. It's also part of the implementation phase of the Security Development Lifecycle or the SDL. So it finds vulnerabilities in non-running code. It's static code analysis. We're looking for those vulnerabilities, either through taint analysis or data flow analysis. Data flow analysis is used to collect runtime or dynamic information about data and software while it's in a static state. Taint analysis, on the other hand, attempts to identify variables that have been tainted by user-controllable input and then traces that to possible vulnerable functions also known as a sink. If a tainted variable gets past to a sink without first being sanitized, it gets flagged as a vulnerability. We're looking for vulnerabilities, we're looking for input sanitization, looking for places where a user has the ability to control that input. If they can put in something, this is where SQL injection and cross-site scripting attacks come into play. If they're able to use some type of technique either as fuzzing or just straight up SQL injection, they can try every single possible combination of codes, letters, characters, and if that is successful, and that code does not get sanitized, they can crash the system or have unintended results. This data flow analysis and this taint analysis allows us to go in and identify these things ahead of time. It's part of the defensive posture that we need to take as IT security professionals, does every IT security professional know all of these different things? No, of course not. There are areas of specialization, but it's important for you to have a general concept and a general understanding, number one, to know, is this an area I want to go into, number two, even if it isn't, you need to have those conversations with the people that are responsible for this, and if you don't know about it, it's hard to have that conversation. As an IT security professional, it's important to have a good understanding of everything, not a deep dive, but a good understanding, so you know who to talk to, who to coordinate with, whether they're developers, pen testers, coders, your DevOps folks, or IT security folks, your infrastructure folks, all the different lines of business, you can reach out to all these different areas, coordinate efforts, and make sure everyone is on the same page and everyone is working towards the same goal.

Fuzzing

Fuzzing is intentionally trying to crash a program or an application by providing invalid, unexpected or random data. Fuzzing is a set of tools. It's not a specific application, it's a suite of applications. It can be one or a dozen or more. Each hacker, each attacker, each forensics person, they all have their own toolsets that they like to work with. It's used by application designers and testers internally, as well as hackers on the outside, but if we're going to use it internally, it helps us to find bugs and defects, also security holes in our applications. It allows us to identify things we didn't account for. Hackers, they'll use fuzzing techniques as well. They'll look for zero-day vulnerabilities, and a lot of hackers will go out there and they'll gather up these zero-days and they'll sell them on the dark net, they'll hoard them, sell them to companies, sell them to security companies or perhaps rogue states or nation states. There are three-letter agencies within the U.S. government that buy these zero-day vulnerabilities from various hackers, so they'll hoard them as well. And then these hackers will also sell them to the bad guys. It's a very effective toolset, it can yield some great results, it can be used for good or bad, but it's important for us to use those same techniques to identify things internally. Whether we're trying to crash applications or websites, we want to make sure we get to our vulnerabilities before the bad guys do. There are a few fuzzing applications out there. One that makes it easy for you, there's a Linux distribution called Kali Linux. They have a suite of fuzzing tools built in, al. Also, CERT has one called BFF, or the Basic Fuzzing Framework, that you can download from the web link, and that allows you to bring in a full suite of fuzzing applications. Whether you go Linux distribution or you download a framework ahead of time, it allows you to install and use the same types of tools that these hackers use. I urge you to become proficient in what these things do, or at least develop on your team someone who is proficient in this so that you can then coordinate their efforts.

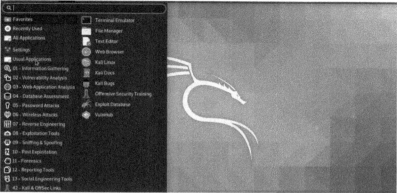

Here we have Kali Linux, which I downloaded from their website, and I'll bring up their actual web page within the actual VM that I'm running here. This is a virtual machine, so it's a little bit slower than it normally would be, but if you were to go out to Kali's website, which is kali.org, this is a reincarnation of BackTrack, which is a pen testing tool and a Linux distribution that's geared towards security. If you're familiar with BackTrack, this is the newer version of that toolset, so Kali Linux. And from there you would go to Downloads. If you're running VMware, this is a great way to get up and running quickly. You click on that and it will bring you over to this web page from Offensive Security, and then from there you can download custom ARM images and also VMware images. You would just pick one for your specific VMware flavor of choice, and from there, once you install it, which is what I have running here, you're up and running with Kali Linux and you can explore all the things that it has to offer. Under Applications down under Kali Linux, this is where all the good stuff, this is where all the magic happens. It's out of the scope of this book to go into any of these in any depth, but I wanted to make you aware of where they're located and how to get your hands on a copy of Kali Linux

You can explore on your own. From the fuzzing testing tools that I was referring to, that would be under Vulnerability Analysis and then down under Fuzzing Tools.

You see there's a number of ones available. There's also Database Assessment tools, Reverse Engineering, Stress Testing, Exploitation Tools, so there's a lot of stuff here, If you're interested in digging in, I highly recommend that you download this application, or this distribution of Linux, and then start exploring the applications that are inside here, so I just want to make you aware of where these things were located.

Additional Secure Coding Concepts
Stress testing is placing load on the system or the application. We want to see where the performance and the

usability breaks down, where that application either crashes or simply can't perform anymore. We can test via automated processes with like LoadRunner or Iometer or use some type of appliance like a load dynamics device, some piece of hardware, and we can stress test whether it's an array, whether it's an application, a server. We can see where things fall apart. We can turn up the number of users, the number of connections, the number of processes that's being processed at once. We do that to simulate where is that going to break down in the real world. If we have 5 users, it's great. If we have 500, it's a little iffy. If we have 5000, it falls apart. Well, we need to know that ahead of time, before we put into production. We put an ad on TV and all of a sudden we have 10,000 users trying to hit our website at the same time or hit our application at the same time, and it falls apart. It's not good for our reputation or for consumer confidence. Not to mention, if it doesn't fail gracefully, it could expose information and be a security risk. Next, we have sandboxing. Sandboxing is isolating the application from other systems so that we can test without impact to other applications to production. We've talked about a few ways to sandbox. We can isolate the networks logically or physically, we can use VMware or some other type of hypervisor and virtualize that environment. It allows us to just as segment that off from the rest. And then we have model verification. This is testing to verify that the product or the application that's produced aligns with the proposed model. Does it do what we said it's going to do? Does it behave in the way that we thought it's going to behave? Because it's possible to build something that's going to behave or interact with other systems that's totally different from what you thought it was going to do. Model verification is critical to make sure all the boxes are checked and make sure that we understand all the downstream impacts and how this specific application or this specific system interacts with everything else that's in production.

Peripherals Security

Peripheral security is something we typically think of, a mouse or a keyboard, what's the harm? Well, wireless keyboards, wireless mice, all of those things can be sniffed potentially. The average environment, maybe not a big deal, but depending upon how critical your infrastructure is or how crucial your job function or the industry you're in, all of those things are attack vectors, so they need to be considered, Wireless keyboards, wireless mice, displays, we've talked about emanations from displays before, such things as TEMPEST-proof rooms, Faraday cages. Also, Wi-Fi-enabled MicroSD cards, we have a camera digital device, a lot of those things days have Wi-Fi-enabled SD cards, you can upload pictures and data from that SD card directly. Well, all of those things are potentially open for compromise. Hackers are getting into everything, embedded systems, Internet of Things, even cars on the highway. It's important to always understand that every single thing in our environment is a potential attack surface, we need to remove things we don't need, and then the things that are left, we need to make sure we monitor, update, and patch. Same thing goes with printers and MFDs, the multi-function devices, external storage devices, and digital cameras. All of these things contain data that, if not either removed or strictly controlled, the access is strictly controlled, data can be pulled off of those devices if they're accessed or if they're compromised. When we talk about updating, just the overall peripheral security, a few things we should be doing, some common-sense things, and that is update and patch. We need to make sure we keep all of our systems and all the peripherals patched and updated. Just because it's an embedded system, or an appliance, doesn't mean it shouldn't be monitored, patched, and updated. Then we need to make sure we physically secure devices. Treat peripherals like any other asset. They could contain sensitive data, so don't let things walk out the door. Make sure you have an eye on things in a way to monitor, whether it's barcodes or sensors or what have you, make sure we can keep an eye on all of our assets. And then, require credentials to access, Printers or copiers, and don't just let anyone access your resources. Make sure they have to badge in or put in some type of access code so that way you can monitor who is using those resources. Last but not least, we should definitely require encryption of removable devices, external storage, or Wi-Fi connectivity, whenever possible. All of these things combine to help to strengthen our security posture and mitigate risks as much as possible.

Hardening the Environment

When we're talking about hardening the environment, I'm talking about open ports and services, locking things down that we don't need, and making sure that it is secure as it can possibly be, and still be useful. There is a fine line, you can lock things down much to the point where it's not useful anymore or people have to write down passwords, usernames and have sticky notes everywhere. It is possible to overdo it, but in this instance, let's talk about what we can do proactively to harden the environment. When you build your systems, your servers, desktops, even mobile devices, develop the mindset to do an analysis of the environment, of that application, of that device and see there are a lot of things there that we don't need. We can turn those things off. It's never going to do X, Y, Z, so we don't need to have that service listening, we don't need to have that service active because as we remove or disable services, shut down ports, we're doing what? We're shrinking the attack service. So open ports and services is one and there are things within the registry, and the registry in a Windows system at least, is sort of like the DNA of the system, it has all the fine-grained controls, it allows you to shut certain things off and make things harder to access or just disable services. Disk encryption we've talked about before as well. We need to make sure we're covering our bases. And if, in fact, a piece of equipment gets stolen, removed out of a car, out of the data center, out of a storage closet, and if the disk is encrypted, it's going to be much more difficult for that bad actor to access the information on that disk. And then OS hardening, just like we talked about with open ports and services, we want to remove unnecessary services at the OS level as well, shut down things that aren't necessary, remote desktop protocol, as an example, there are many more, but that's just one. If we don't need it, then shut it off. That removes that ability or shrinks that attack service. Next is patch management. We need to make sure that we do that religiously, and that goes for third-party updates and also auto update. Auto update may or may not be something you want to do in your environment and larger environments. We want to do things on a cadence. We want to be able to download those updates offline, test them in a very small group, do some regression testing, make sure they don't break anything, and then roll them out systematically to the environment at large. That way it gives you the opportunity to phase things in, and that way you don't just automatically update something and have a break. It's not to say you can't automate the process, but you just don't want to automate patching without testing it first.

Common Ports

When we talk about ports and services, there are things called common ports. It's beyond the scope of this book to go into all of the reports. There are over 65,500 ports. The first 1,024 are defined by RFC or request for comments, and they're known as the well-known ports. They're defined by typical applications. But these are some of the ones that you should be familiar with, port 20 and 21 for FTP as an example, port 23 for Telnet. Here's an example of one you may or may not need. If you don't need to Telnet your service or into your server or your desktop, then disable that service. It just shrinks that attack surface. If you go down the list and look at things like, as an example, Internet Relay Chat, port 194. Well, this isn't 1985. People don't use IRC anymore. If you need in your environment, great. Keep it up. But if you don't, block those things at the firewall. Block those things at the individual host as well. By doing so, we're removing or at least shrinking the attack surface. Is it foolproof? No. But why give attackers or bad actors more fuel for their fire, more ammunition. Shrink it as much as possible; help to make things more secure.

Registry Hardening

When we talk about registry hardening, registry being the DNA of the operating system, at least on the Windows side. An example of some registry hardening settings, configure permissions, deny anonymous access as an example. Deny remote registry access as an example. If you need that in your environment, then by all means don't do that, but this where it comes down to an analysis of each individual environment. Everyone's going to have different needs. Everyone's going to have different working parameters or guidelines or guardrails that they have to operate within. Make sure that you configure your permissions appropriately. But make them as restrictive as possible and still being useful. Also, I would disable access to registry editing tools at the host level as well. That way, someone can't go in at the host and start editing the registry. That goes for disabling the command prompt and also PowerShell access if it's not needed. There might be instances where you do need that, and if so, then by all means keep it enabled. But by doing that, by making people local users on the machines, taking away access to certain things that allow them to bypass some of the controls you're putting in place, it makes the system more secure. It reduces your troubleshooting and shrinks the attack surface. And then Whitelist and blacklist applications. The difference between whitelisting and blacklisting. Whitelisting is we have a list of acceptable applications. Everything else is no go. If you only have three applications on that list, then they're the only three things that we can run. Conversely, if you have a blacklist, we can run everything except the ones that are on the blacklist. It's just two different approaches to achieve the same net effect.

Self-encrypting Drives (SED)
Self-encrypting drives, also known as SED drives. These things are very much like a typical disk drive, except they have additional functionality. They can self encrypt and they maintain that information on the disk itself, so you don't need to maintain third-party encryption keys. Encryption keys are self-contained in the drive's firmware, and they're maintained separately from the CPU, which, again, reduces the attack vector. That's the name of the game here. We want to shrink the attack vector as much as possible. There's something else that I want to make you aware of, and that is the Opal Specification, and that deals with self-encrypting drives. It was created by the Trusted Computing Group, or TCG, and it's a security subsystem class that specifies how

data is encrypted on the drive. If we look at this in a little more detail, this is a very high-level overview of how it works. But you have your host interface in which you input plain text, you have your plain text that you want to encrypt onto the storage device. We have what's called a KDF, or a key derivation function. That's how we're going to create the key-encrypting key, the KEK. That key-encrypting key, usually a password, an authentication PIN here or a password, is then used to create what's called the MEK, or the media encryption key. We're taking a key, a master key, if you will. It then unlocks the media encryption keys and allows that data to be unencrypted or encrypted, depending on which way it's going in, whether you're writing it or reading it from disk. You don't need to necessarily understand the nitty-gritty of how it works, but just understand at a high level that self-encrypting drives are secure. They're a little more secure in the fact that we don't have to maintain third-party encryption keys. They're also more efficient in that we don't have to worry about the CPU or burdening the CPU with additional cycles to have the software or a software layer encrypt and decrypt the data. It's handled at the actual drive level, and those keys are stored in the firmware. That makes it very secure. It gives you very good throughput and takes that latency out of the process of the software layer, having to do the encryption and decryption, which puts additional cycles onto the CPU. By removing all of that, we make the encryption process more streamlined.

Hardware Root of Trust

Next, we have a concept referred to as the hardware root of trust. What does this mean? Well, you can see that it goes up the stack from the hardware to firmware, Hypervisor, operating system, up to the application, and what that means is that root of trust begins with systems that are inherently trusted, just like we have PKI and we have certificate authorities and root certificate authorities, that same level of trust needs to be there. If something is compromised at the very low level at the base hardware, if the BIOS of a system are compromised, then how can we trust anything that sits above that? If the BIOS itself is not inherently trusted or inherently secure, then we can trust as we go up that stack and test that the other things in that stack can be secure as well. A few concepts regarding that hardware root of trust, it needs to be secure by design, it also needs to perform security-critical functions like the TPM chip, as we mentioned, as an example, or boot firmware is another example. There are two NIST guidelines I'd like to call your attention to, NIST SP800-147, which is BIOS protection guidelines, and then NIST SP600-155 which is BIOS integrity measurement guidelines. Those two guidelines I encourage you to download and look through. They'll give you some additional information around the general concept and how that applies within your organization.

Hardware Based Encryption
Next up, and a few things that you should be aware of here, TPM being one of them, the Trusted Platform Module and TPM is a hardware chip that's embedded on a computer's motherboard. Typically, you're going to see these in laptops. They're used to store cryptographic keys used for encryption. The TPM chapter is built onto a motherboard. The takeaway here is it cannot be added later. If your desktop or your laptop or whatever the device is does not have a TPM chip, you cannot add it later. It's built into the motherboard itself. Conversely, we have HSM, or the hardware security Module. It functions in much the same way as a TPM; however, this can be external, or it could be

plugged into a server or a laptop. It is something that can be added later. Imagine that we have a network device, a network-based hardware security chapter, and this is used for storing and generating keys for encryption. Whether you have a PKI on your network or you're looking for some type of encryption technology, this can do that at the network level. There's also cards that can be plugged in to a specific server. HSM, the takeaway would be it's similar to TPM. The hardware security chapter is very similar to the Trusted Platform Chapter; however, HSMs are removable or they're external. They can be added later. That's the takeaway. TPMs are built in, HSMs are not. Both are used, however, for encryption keys, encrypting rather, and using RSA keys. Next, we have USB encryption. For the most part, when we say removable media, we're talking about USB or thumb drives. It's the same type of thing. Encrypting the contents of our USB drives, it prevents that data from being accessed if stolen, or if someone maliciously tries to copy data onto a USB drive and hand it off to someone else, that data's encrypted. The receiving party can't do much with it unless they have those decryption keys. Then we have hardware-based encryption around hard drives. Encrypting the entire contents of a hard drive, that provides that data at rest encryption, and it guards against data leakage if lost or stolen. Again, someone smashes the window or breaks into a place of business and steals computers, steals laptops, that data is inaccessible. It's also used in conjunction with the TPM or HSM chapters. These things help generate the encryption keys in a very secure environment. That way, if it gets lost or stolen, there's not much you can do with it. As an example, we have BitLocker. This would give us an entire or full disk encryption. We can turn on, go into our control panel, and turn on BitLocker at the drive level, where we have multiple drives, and ensure that those things are encrypted and, of course, inaccessible if they were to be either stolen or fall into the wrong hands.

Sandboxing

Sandboxing can be used in a couple of different contexts. In this specific context, it's isolating code, upgrades, and testing from the production environment. In other words, we're operating in a closed or a walled garden, so we can test changes, and we can do things without affecting production. We can do such things as test code changes, we can roll back changes very quickly, we can also regression test against various applications, or execute and even observe malware. We can purposely allow malware to do its thing, but it's in a sandboxed environment, we're observing it, trying to reverse engineer it, or at least see what it's doing, what's the payload? Sandboxing in an environment allows us to put those walls up and operate safely. When we're talking about sandboxing applications, it isolates the application from other user data, resources, you can think of it as virtual environments within your device, a mobile device, laptop or desktop. It can prevent malware and viruses from interacting with the application or with other applications, and each application has its own environment on the host. That prevents an application crash from affecting other applications running on the host. It's not anything that's revolutionary, but it is a tried-and-true practice that allows us to operate securely without affecting other applications. And we can do it sandbox from a network perspective, we can do it from an application perspective, we can do it to test code and roll back changes, or we can create live environments that each application can live in on a specific device, separating those applications from each other. In this chapter, we covered endpoint protection; we talked about boot integrity; and database security; along with application security, hardening, and the importance of doing that around ports and services, the registry, OS; we talked about disk encryption; we talked about the hardware root of trust, along with a Trusted Platform Module; and then we also talked about sandboxing in a few different contexts.

Chapter 4 How to Implement Secure Network Designs

In this chapter, we'll be talking about Implementing Secure Network Designs and we'll be covering such things as load balancing, we'll be talking about network segmentation, we'll talk about virtual private networks, DNS or domain name service, we'll also talk about network access control or NAC, also out-of-band management, and then wrap up with port security. A load balancer, as the name implies, balances the load between devices. A load balancer can be put in place in a number of areas. It could be a server. There could be other devices as well. It can be hardware. It can be software. It just depends upon price point, functionality, how extreme the load balancing needs to be. If it's a small environment, a server may be fine. If it's a large environment, very high volume, then you're going to need a dedicated appliance. If we have a number of users, there's the external network, and then there's a load balancer in place, and it can be one or more. It doesn't necessarily have to be a single device. It could be multiple load balancers. In this instance, let's just say we have web servers, and it's going to balance the load and determine, which is the best performing server at that specific point in time, and I'm going to send the load to that server. It may go in a round-robin fashion. It may use some algorithm to determine, but depending upon the load balancer itself, it's going to determine in some fashion, which is the best server or the best device to send that load to. It allows you to spread it out across. And as a load starts to pick up, as websites become more busy, it can spread it out so that no one server gets completely overwhelmed. A few terms I want to make sure you're familiar with regard to load balancers. As far as scheduling is concerned, we have two terms, affinity and round-robin. Affinity means if we have multiple servers, that a load balancer can serve traffic too. Well, if it has affinity in place, then the server that initially serviced the request for a host, it will use that same server for the entirety of that session. It's not going to just completely just go to the next available one. It locks into that server, and as long as that session is active, that post will communicate over that load balancer into that server, so the host to server will take the same path through the load balancer. In a round-robin fashion, we may have multiple load balancers. We may have multiple servers to get through to the back-end database or the back-end application. While in a round-robin fashion, it will pick the next available or the next best one in line, It won't necessarily wait or lock into a specific server and hold communication throughout the entirety of that session. It will go to the next available one. When we're talking about active-passive dealing with load balancers, that refers to the fact that we may have multiple load balancers. Even load balances have load balancers. The load balancer itself is operating in an HA or a highly-available fashion. The active-passive nature means one load balancer is handling or servicing all that traffic. There's another load balancer that's acting in a passive state, and it's monitoring what the first load balancer's doing. It's keeping track, but it's not doing anything. It's not actively servicing requests. Its job is to jump in in case the primary load balancer were to go offline or have some type of failure. In an active-active capacity, we have both load balancers servicing the load or it might have multiple, three or four, however many are in this configuration. But for this example, let's say we have two load balancers. Well, if they're acting in an active-active fashion, they're both servicing the load, spreading it evenly. The downside of that is in an active-active situation, both load balancers end up servicing requests near their maximum capacity. If one load balancer were to go down and there's no other load balancer to take over, then we'll start slowing down and customers will notice a degradation in service. In an active-passive fashion, one load balancer is servicing everything. If it starts to go down, the other one kicks in and takes over, so there's no noticeable difference, no noticeable degradation to end users. And then the last one I want to cover is virtual IPs. A virtual IP, or a VIP, is an IP that sits in front of all of the actual IPs that the load balancers use, so that way the end user doesn't necessarily need to know the IP addresses of the individual load balancers. All they need to know is the one, and it will cycle through and make sure that it goes to the proper load balancers behind the scenes. That way you don't have to change things. If you add additional load balancers or you switch things up behind the scenes, end users, all they need to know is they have to connect to that virtual IP address.

Security Segmentation Models

Let's now talk about segregation, segmentation and isolation. We have a few security or segmentation models I want to call to your attention. First is physical. We can physically separate or segment nodes or hosts on a network. We can also do that logically with something called VLAN, or virtual LANs, virtual local area networks. We can also do it with virtualization, so an isolation model or a segmentation model. Then we also have air gapped, meaning there is no connectivity to the internet or to the network at large. So, what do I mean by that? Well, with physical or logical, we have devices that are all on the same segment, the same Ethernet segment or the same LAN, the same local area network. And in this example, you can assume that they're all connected to the same switch, so that is a physical connectivity to the network. Well, we can also logically separate those networks. We can take that same layout, but we can use something called virtual LANs, or virtual local area networks, and group them accordingly. We can have a VLAN10, we can have a VLAN20, and in this case, a VLAN30. What that does is separate those devices out. What it does is create separate broadcast domains, separate security domains, and it reduces the chatter. Let's look at another example. Imagine that we have a multi-floor building. We have wiring on each floor that goes back to a home run, and it goes down between floors. We have devices on the first floor and a switch, we have devices on the second floor and a switch, and then devices on the third floor and a switch. It's not the only way to wire, not the only way to do it, but in this example, we have each floor going to a wiring closet. In that wiring closet, a switch, and then those switches are connected via home runs. They're all physically located in different locations. Well, we can also group those together just like we did in the previous example. They don't have to be sitting next to each other. We can group them again logically, VLAN10, VLAN20, and then VLAN30. In other words, if we had groups of computers that may be on different floors, let's say we have finance people that sit on all three floors or HR or our graphics department we can group them within our switches. We make sure that all the switches have the same VLAN associations, and that way they're grouped logically together. Those VLANs can group hosts that are in different locations, into logical groupings. That creates smaller collision domains and it reduces chatter. As an example, if you have a very large cafeteria, everyone's talking. It's very hard to understand because everyone's talking. Everyone's clashing into each other. They're colliding the conversations. If I took all of those people in that cafeteria and separated them out into five different rooms or in this example three different rooms, well, I have one third of the amount of people in each room, so the chatter is going to be less, so the collisions are less. It helps increase efficiency. Then also it can be used to create security boundaries to segment traffic so that one host doesn't necessarily see broadcasts and doesn't see traffic designated for hosts in another VLAN.

Virtualization

Virtualization is a method of segmenting or isolating, so we can keep a host in a sandboxed and isolated environment, meaning it's separate from the host that it's sitting on. We can also allow for snapshots. We can quickly revert changes, we can use virtualization to isolate or segment. We can do all of our testing. We can test changes, we can even test viruses or malware to see what it does without affecting the rest of the network and without affecting the host that it sits on. It also separates the guests from the host, the guest from the hypervisor. If we have Hyper-V, or VMware, or KVM, or virtual box, or whatever the case might be or whatever our virtualization technology is, this allows us to keep those individual guests separate from the host. Other devices may be virtualized as well. We can virtualize other infrastructure, such as routers, switches, load balancers, firewalls, and we'll talk more about that when we get into SDN, but the nice part is those things can be instantiated or spun up on demand, so as a load increases, we could spin up additional load balancers or, if we have applications that need specific firewalls, instead of having to go through the normal change process and buying equipment and racking and stacking and all the things that are associated with physical infrastructure, we can do it virtually, very quickly, spin that device up, use it while we need it, and then we can tear it down just as quickly.

Air Gaps

An air gap is a method of isolating a computer or a network from the internet or from other external networks, or other networks aside from the one you're on. So, it doesn't necessarily have to be just from the internet, it could be from other networks within your company. If you have a very highly secure environment that you need to make sure that there's no chance of malware or viruses being introduced, then you would set up an air gapped network. As with anything, there is no 100% guarantee, as we've seen in the past with things like Stuxnet and some other very highly visible and highly cited instances where malware has jumped into air gapped environments, nothing is 100% certain. But it's used for critical infrastructure, SCADA systems, as an example, and I refer back to Stuxnet where the SCADA systems were still compromised, highly secure classified networks. There are some advanced techniques, however, to jump air gapped networks, like I said, that's been demonstrated, emanations, there's technology and it's been completely demonstrated where they can view the emanations coming off of a computer, whether it is the sound of the hard drive whirring, or even the heat being generated by the hard drive spinning up. If you're close enough to that device, you can pick those things up from the device and discern what's going on, you can read data from that device. Pretty advanced stuff and it's not something the average hacker can do, but just understand that an air gap is a very good way of isolating the network, but it's not 100% foolproof. In fact, the US government and other agencies around the world have specific guidelines to create additional security. The US uses something referred to as TEMPEST, which protects that room, it has to be a certain thickness of walls and has to have additional coding and protections, Faraday cages, and things that just prevent emanations and monitoring from nearby locations. Emanations, FM frequencies, even some hard drives that have a small LED light on the front that shows activity of that drive, you don't see that too much anymore, but it is possible that if you have a line of sight visibility to that light going on and off as the hard drive writes, you could read, almost like Morse is code, what's going on with that hard drive and read data from that device. Pretty scary, but the average hacker is not going to be employing that. More than likely, you can rest assured that your home network is safe.

East-west Traffic

East-West traffic is data moving between devices within a data center. More and more traffic is being generated days East-West, just as a side note, with less and less traffic going North-South, meaning entering or exiting the data center. Again, depending upon your data center in your company, you may refer to North-South traffic as traffic leaving the top of rack and going to another area within the data center. Sometimes terminology can be co-mingled depending upon the company, the data center, but generally speaking, East-West is within the data center, North-South is exiting or entering the data center. Traditional firewalls and monitoring look normally or traditionally at North-South traffic. Our firewalls are on our perimeter, and we want to guard against what's coming into our networks and what's leaving the networks. That lack of visibility can add to an attacker's ability to move laterally around in a network undetected. Once they get into the network, once they penetrate our defenses, there's normally not as much tooling and not as much visibility into the movement within the data center, the thought being that once you're inside the network, it's a trusted environment. We'll talk more about zero trust in just a moment, but understand that that lack of visibility can allow an attacker to move around virtually undetected, at least for a period of time. How do we combat that is we implement network monitoring to identify that East-West threat or the East-West traffic. An IDS, or an IPS, or a network IDS, or network IPS system combined with tools like Suricata or Zeek, again two open-source recommendations, not the only things out there and not an endorsement, just giving you some ideas of things to look at, but Suricata and Zeek can identify malicious activity and can integrate with other systems as well, again these intrusion detection and prevention systems, and they can be leveraged to identify that malicious activity and take steps to mitigate it.

Zero Trust
Keeping with that theme, let's talk about zero trust, which I mentioned just a moment ago. Zero trust in today's world, castle moat philosophy where everything behind the firewalls was thought to be safe is no longer valid. That is not the recommended way to do things anymore. We need to take a more granular approach. Internal and external traffic should be monitored nothing implicitly trusted, whether it's internal or external. Micro-segmentation and granular access, providing only the levels of permission required. In other words, we don't just assume if you're inside the network, you're good, go ahead, don't necessarily worry about it. As we talked about, that allows an attacker to go around and move around, laterally jump networks, peruse the parking lot, and see which car they want to steal. We don't want that. That micro-segmentation, granular access, locking things down to only give people the level of permissions required, which sounds familiar. We do that anyway, typically with ACLs on resources like file shares, but we also want to make sure that we do it at the resource

level, the servers, the storage arrays, data protection, so on. A couple of tools we can leverage would be MFA, or multi-factor authentication, IAM, identity access management, and then we can leverage orchestration and analytics along with encryption. All of these more modern toolsets and these technologies, combined with detection and prevention tools, can lock down the environment enough so that it's not an easy target for an attacker or a bad actor, but we still need to make it usable, for our internal users. It's a fine line, but just understand the old way of doing things is not applicable or should not be applicable in today's environment.

VPN

The next thing I want to talk about is a VPN, or a virtual private network. A VPN is going to be something you should probably be familiar with. But if not, I'll give you a very good understanding here and the general concepts of what a VPN does. A VPN creates a virtual private network across a public network. You could be sitting in a coffee shop, for instance, very securely tunnel from that coffee shop to your corporate environment and access corporate resources without worrying that someone is potentially sniffing the traffic, accessing or picking up a sense of information like usernames, passwords. There are a couple of components of a VPN that we need to be aware of. Tunneling protocols such as L2TP, or Layer 2 Tunneling Protocol, and also PPTP, Point-To-Point Tunneling Protocol, and then IPSec, or IP security. What do these things mean? Well, there are separate components that make up the VPN because there are two components that we need to talk about. There's the tunnel, and then there's the encrypted data that passes through the tunnel. When we're establishing a VPN connection, the first thing we do is establish the tunnel, and then you establish the secure connection or the encrypted connection between the two endpoints. Security comes from the tunneling protocol and the encryption combined, and that's very important to understand. You can't have security unless you have both of those things in play. You need to establish the tunnel and then establish the security with encryption that passes data through that tunnel. Just because you have a tunnel established, if you don't have the encrypted communication taking place over that tunnel, then it's not going to do you much good as far as security is concerned. Many VPNs use something referred to as two-factor authentication. RSA is a very good example of that. They're one of the bigger vendors recently acquired by EMC. And RSA can provide hardware and software tokens, and what happens is every 30 seconds, or so, the number on that token or that Django, as it's called, will change. That number is in sync with the VPN concentrator or the VPN server back at the corporate headquarters, back at the endpoint. There's an authentication mechanism that keeps both of these in sync. Every 30 seconds that number changes on both the endpoint and also on the token. When you go to establish your connection, it's going to ask you for that username and perhaps your PIN or a password if you're going to use something like an RSA token. It will ask you for that. You have two things, what you have and what you know. You know your username and the token is what you have. That's going to change every 30 seconds, making it much more secure. Even if someone steals your laptop and they know your username, they still won't be able to gain access or get into a VPN connection and get back to the corporate headquarters because they don't have what? They don't have that PIN or that token that changes every 30 seconds. They're going to have to physically take that RSA token as well. Then even if they have the RSA token, they'll still need to know your PIN because once you put your PIN in, then, of course, the token will pop up. It's an extra layer of added security. With VPNs, many companies provide VPN access to their remote employees, so it allows corporate access to resources from an offsite or remote location. Depending on how things are set up, it can be given complete access to the network. Once you VPN in, once you make that connection, you could have complete access to the corporate network, or access can be restricted to only certain parts of the network. Depending upon how that VPN administrator sets things up, a person dialing in or VPN-ing into the network can have access maybe to only a certain subnet or a certain set of files and folders, a certain server. Here's an example of two different types of VPN connections. We have a VPN connection between two corporate networks, and it's a VPN connection in a tunnel, and you have a VPN router on both networks? Pretty much in these instances, a lot of times, it's set up as a constant connection, and then we have a VPN connection from a remote user. In this instance, that user is sitting out on the internet, again some public network. It could be a home office or remote office, some coffee shop somewhere. In other words, it's somewhere outside of the corporate environment proper. That person connects to their ISP. Now they have internet connectivity. When they initiate that VPN connection, it connects them to the corporate environment. They establish the VPN connection, the tunnel, and then the communication is secured over the public internet. They don't have to worry about someone being able to sniff their traffic.

Split Tunnel
In a split tunnel situation, we have an outside or an external user who is external to the company network or the

274

corporate network. Imagine that we have our 10.x network that's our internal corporate network. The user who is sitting external, maybe their home, at a coffee shop, some remote location. While they want to access those corporate resources, but as a company, it doesn't make sense to have that user go into our corporate network and then back out again to access external resources. So by using a split tunnel, we make sure that that external user accesses our corporate resources over the VPN so they have secure access to company resources, but then, when they want to reach external resources, they do Directly without going through the corporate network.

IPSec and Transport Encryption

Next, we have something referred to as IPSec, or the internet security protocol, and this allows us to encrypt communication over the internet over that insecure or unsecured network. There is two components here we have an authentication header, an AH, that provides authentication and integrity that does not encrypt the data, it just allows you to prove that you're communicating with who you think you're communicating with and that the data has not been manipulated or somehow tweaked while in transit, someone then pulled off the wire, manipulated it, and put it back on, so it proves authentication and integrity. We have the original IP header, the TCP section, and the payload. This is a data packet. What we're doing is adding an authentication header. No encryption as the AH only offers integrity, so it proves authentication and integrity. If we want to encrypt that data, then we're going to need something referred to as the encapsulating secure payload, or ESP. That provides also confidentiality, along with optional integrity checking, so it adds a header, a trailer, and an integrity check value, or an ICV, so that works as such. So now we have that data packet, the original header, we're going to add in an ESP header, the encapsulating secure payload, TCP is the transport protocol, the actual payload, which is the data that we're sending, it's going to an ESP trailer and ESP authentication, so that's going to give us a fully secure data pack as it traverses over that unsecure medium, and that's encrypted, which provides data confidentiality.

VPN Concentrator

We've talked about VPN several times before, but in this specific instance, we're talking about a VPN concentrator, and that has the ability to create large numbers of VPN tunnels. It's not just a single tunnel, a single point to point. A concentrator can do numerous tunnels, typically used for site-to-site architectures. In this example here, we have a site-to-site VPN, and we have two networks? We have a secure network on one side, a secure network on the other side, and in that tunnel, we have multiple VPN connections going through that tunnel, because we have VPN routers that are concentrators on either side of that tunnel. Conversely, we have a remote access VPN where we have a single person, maybe a remote teleworker or a very small office where we have one person or a single tunnel going from that remote location into the corporate internet. You'll still have a VPN concentrator on the one side, but then you have an ISP being used from the guest or the host or the small office on the other side, and they'll be going through that VPN tunnel. It's a concentrator, because even though that specific location may only have one tunnel going through, you may have multiple remote locations. So it has the ability to create multiple tunnels at once.

Chapter 5 Network Access Control, Port Security & Loop Protection

NAC or Network Access Control or Network Admission Control, depending upon, where you read or what context it's being used in, it refers to a set of policies that define a minimal set of requirements each device must have before being allowed on the network. We want to make sure that if someone pulls out their laptop and tries to connect to our network, it's going to check and say, hey, do you have this level of firmware, do you have this level of virus or anti-virus patching, do you have, all these different required security patches maybe for the OS, and if you don't, well, we're not going to let you on the network, so it does a check before it allows that access. This becomes more and more important as BYO devices become prevalent within the environment, people bring their own laptops or their own mobile phones. A couple applications that can help with that, I'm just giving you some examples, Good Messaging, Mobile Iron, and Airwatch are three mobile device management tools, or MDMs, that allow us to make sure that those devices are in compliance before they're allowed to connect to the network. Devices can be denied access, or they can be placed in what's called a secure zone until those minimum requirements are met. It may give them a cordoned-off area and says, you can connect to our network in this little safe space, and from there you can download the required patches or the required security fixes, applications, and until you do that, you can't go anywhere else. It gives them a chance to remediate the issue. Once those things are done, it will check again, and if they meet compliance, then they're allowed onto the network. Network Access Control can also be implemented in one of three ways. We have what's called a permanent agent, and that's persistent, that's persistently installed on the host device, and runs continuously. From an enterprise perspective, this is the best option, because we know for a fact that it's installed on that device we can tell what's going on all the time. From the end user perspective, they may or may not want that, especially if it's a BYO device. They may say, I don't want someone snooping on my device or potentially, pulling data off that I don't know about. Well, that's a choice you have to make within your own environment, but permanent agents are typically preferred at an enterprise level. And then we have a dissolvable agent. This is one that runs in a portal. A user will connect, it will download the agent, and it's going to run once. It will then disappear. If they need to use it again, it can be either re-downloaded or it can be fired back up again, but it doesn't run continuously in the background. Then we have agentless, which can come in a few different forms. In this instance, it's embedded within Active Directory, and that NAC code verifies that the host complies with access policies, typically when they join a domain, when they log on or when they log off. Normally it will trigger and will run or scan that device when one of those three things happen.

In-band vs. Out-of-band Management

Network devices can be managed and access both in-band and also out-of-band, depending upon preference, architectural decisions or limitations. In-band means traffic can be examined in real time, so it means we're accessing via the production network typically. Access is provided over common protocols, Telnet or SSH. And if we have an opportunity or a choice between Telnet and SSH, we should always choose SSH. Telnet is not encrypted, so therefore not secure, whereas SSH is an encrypted connection. Also with in-band, we're closer to the point of entry into the network, typically. Also less to manage and reconfigure when inserting into the network. We don't have to do a lot of rerouting or trying to move traffic around to access those devices out-of-band. Conversely, out-of-band, more reactive in nature versus real time, so we're not monitoring that traffic in real time. It has to go up to some external or out-of-band management device or some type of analytic device to monitor that traffic - not in real time. It also requires additional design or redesign to enter into or insert into the network and requires additional upstream provider components to provide similar security. The in-band is going to be less intrusive, less to manage and less to reconfigure. You get the idea. If we have the option between both, in-band's going to be less work; however, if the primary network goes down, our access goes down. So out-of-band gives us another way to access those devices. If we can't access the device via our primary or production network, we still have that access out-of-band, which gives us remote functionality. We don't have to drive to the data center or drive to wherever that location or that device is located, saving us time and effort. Then the last on our list is that endpoint compliance is not as granular, meaning client traffic is sent to a common VLAN. As an example, when clients enter our network and they want to be quarantined or checked for compliance, they're going to be sent to a common VLAN versus monitored in quarantine real time and separated from other clients entering the network. For a little more detail on in-band access control, here we have a client that is accessing an access switch. That access switch contains such things as a Policy Enforcement Point, or a PEP, an authenticator, and a Policy Decision Point. This is for granted access, network access control, to our local area network. When we're doing in-band, that functionality is typically incorporated into the switch or some other device that's placed inline on our production network. To access the switch to go through this decision making process, the Policy Enforcement Point, the authenticator, and the Decision Point, it decides, does that client meet our specifications? Are they allowed to access the LAN? If that were an out-of-band process, then it would have to go out to some external device outside of our typical network, traffic would have to be rerouted, a client may get a different IP address while they're being authenticated, and then rerouted back onto the corporate LAN once they're authenticated. It adds some additional overhead and some architectural designs, just something to keep in mind. It's in our best interest if we had the opportunity to have both in-band and out-of-band management and access. If for some reason our primary network or our production network goes down, we still have access to those devices. Another example of out-of-band access will be an out-of-band NIC, so a separate interface for management networks, whether that is a management VLAN or a separate physical network. It's used for lights out management. That way, we can monitor and audit or log. We can also use the patch, install operating systems or troubleshoot a host that is offline and won't boot. Typically, we can remote into a desktop or a server using RDP or some type of remote connection software. But if that actual device won't boot or is not operational, and therefore the remote desktop software or the remote control software is not functioning, we're dead in the water. If we have an out-of-band NIC that has a lights out functionality or lights out feature, we can still access as if we're sitting at that PC or at that server. That gives us the opportunity to manage, patch, reboot, even when the server at the OS level is down. It saves us a trip to the data center.

Port Security and 802.1x

The next concept I want to talk about is about port security in 802.1x - securing physical access to the network. What do I mean by that? Well, we want to control the ability of someone to just walk into our environment, whether it be at a kiosk or retail store or a library or a school, or even within our corporate environment, we don't want necessarily someone to be able to walk up, pull out their laptop, pull out a Cat 5 cable, plug it into the wall and get access to our network. One way we can do that is through something called port security. This is particularly applicable to things like kiosks, and schools, and libraries, but not necessarily throughout an entire environment as it becomes a little bit unwieldy at that point, but for specialized situations that we want to control specific access to specific ports, port security is definitely a good fit. What we can do is configure a switch so that it only learns one MAC address per port We can keep attackers from sending multiple fake addresses, someone can't pull out their laptop, plug in and then just start bombarding our network with fake MAC addresses, because, if you recall, when we have our devices and it connects to a switch, that very first time it does, it goes out and tries to get an IP address via DHCP, or it may have one hard-coded. It's going to try also to ARP for some resources. It might go to DNS, it might go to whatever the case might be, trying to resolve a URL. Whatever action is taking place, it's going to put datagrams or data packets onto the network. As soon as it does that, the MAC address of that device is attached to that datagram, and then it gets recorded within that switch, whatever switchport it's connecting to. The switch, which is a Layer 2 device, will learn or memorize the MAC address and associate it with that port, and so the switch will learn over time all of the devices that are connected to it, what MAC addresses are associated with which ports, so that way when information comes in, it knows what port to send that information out of. It's a very directed process. Broadcasts will go out of all ports, but if there is traffic between PC 1 and PC 2, as an example, PC 1 is connected to Port 1, PC 2 is connected to, say, Port 10 in this example, it will only go in Port 1 and only out of Port 10, so that way it keeps things more secure. However, we have malicious individuals or malicious activity that can take place, where someone could flood a specific port and overrun the MAC table on that switch and bring it down. By setting port security and allowing only certain MAC addresses, or in this case one MAC address per port, we negate that ability for someone to do that type of activity. We can also use that in conjunction with something called 802.1x to strengthen security at the wall jack, with school settings as an example, or a kiosk. We have something called 802.1x authentication, which is EAPOL, or Extensible Authentication Access Protocol over LAN, or local area network. That Extensible Authentication Access Protocol gives us the ability to say, when somebody connects to our wall jack, we're not going to allow them to communicate until they authenticate with the network. In this example, they're going to authenticate with something referred to as a RADIUS server, it's an authentication server. In this schema it's a multi-part process. The client in this case is referred to as a supplicant. The client is going to initiate a request, they're going to plug into a wall jack, let's say, as an example, they take out their laptop, and they plug it into the jack. They're going to say, can I communicate, can I get an IP address. The switch is going to say, no way, not until you authenticate. It will only allow EAPOL traffic to pass through that port. It will send it off to the authentication server, all of these things have to be configured in place so that this process takes place properly, but once it's set up, that port will not be activated until the authentication process is complete. The supplicant will send information over to the switch. The switch will then forward it on to the authentication server. Once that authentication server validates, once the credentials are validated and verified, in other words, the client is authenticated, the authentication server sends that information back and says, yes, you can communicate. The port is wide open, and of course the supplicant, or the client in this case, can communicate on the network.

Loop Protection and Flood Guards
When we're discussing ensuring availability on our network, another concept that you need to be familiar with is loop protection and flood guards. We talked about securing physical access to the network. We want to make sure that the network is available for someone to securely access. By ensuring availability via flood guards and loop protection, we have a couple concepts we need to talk about. Loop protection is a Layer 3 context. Remember, Layer 3 deals with IP routing and with the network. It's the network layer of the OSI model, and routers live with this layer. Layer 3 deals with, routing IP packets across the network. As those IP packets travel, every time they cross over a router or every time they hop, they decrement with something called a TTL, or a Time to Live. Every time they cross over a router, that TTL will decrement by one. An IP packet, has a finite lifespan to live on the network. If it lives too long, then the packet gets dropped. In other words, if it doesn't reach its destination in a certain amount of time or a certain number of hops, it gets dropped. And that's specifically designed to prevent packets from just endlessly looping around the network. As an example, we have a couple networks separated by some routers, and in a normal fashion, the packet will just traverse those routers. Every time it crosses over, it decrements by one. The TTL will decrement. The

routers know how to get from point A to point B. The packet goes from one network to the other. In a misconfigured situation, however, we have that packet, it would traverse the network, and it would just loop endlessly. If it were to do that and just loop forever, we would have a flood, and it would bring the network down. If the routers aren't configured properly, and they don't exactly know where to send the packet, router A thinks it should go here, router B thinks it should go somewhere else, it's going to get in a looping scenario. And if we didn't have that TTL in place, the Time to Live, every time it crosses over one of those routers it decrements, if that weren't in place, that packet would loop endlessly forever. And then as the next packet were to come onto the network, there'd be no room left. There'd be no bandwidth. As you can imagine, very quickly, that network would get overrun. By having that TTL in place, we negate that scenario from occurring.

Chapter 6 Spanning Tree, DHCP Snooping & MAC Filtering

In the layer 2 space, we don't have the TTL benefit. We don't have the ability to decrement. Layer 2 of the OSI model deals with things like switches and bridges. In layer 2, we have something referred to as a Spanning Tree Protocol, or STP. This accomplishes the same thing as a loop protection. It just does it in a different fashion. Spanning Tree Protocol is typically unable to prevent layer 2 loops, so switches can also prevent ports from flooding the network by clamping down once broadcasts hit a certain percentage. As an example, we have two switches. We have information that needs to pass from point A to point B. But if we have switches, which are multi-port bridges, and information comes in one port, goes out another, if the switch doesn't know exactly which port to send it out of, you can get in a looping situation. If switch A sent out Fa0/1 to switch B Fa0/1, and then switch B sent Fa02 out to switch A's Fa0/2, you can just see, we get in this looping fashion. What we have is the concept of an election. That election takes place between things called a root bridge, a designated bridge, and a root port. The root bridge is the center of the network. The designated bridges or the designated bridge are forwarders. They're going to send data to the root bridge, and then the root port is the port that sends data toward the root bridge. And if we didn't have the ability to shut down the non-necessary ports, we would just get loops all over the place. It doesn't mean those other paths aren't available. It just means they're not active. If we have a failover situation where that path becomes inactive or fails, the switches would then failover and activate those ports. It might take a few seconds, maybe 15 to 20 seconds potentially, depending upon the size of the network. But, a certain amount of time for all those things to synchronize and go through this process until all the other paths come up. But the network would, as you can imagine, it would heal itself. It gives us the ability to clamp down and not have these looping situations, but it doesn't take those other ports out of play. It just puts them in a non-active state. If it identifies that something needs to be brought up, maybe another port is down, it will bring those ports back up. It might take a little bit to converge so that everyone knows about the path so that all the switches know how the network is laid out. But once those ports come back up, the network will heal itself. At any one point in time, we only want one path from point A to point B., incidentally, root bridges are designated by the lowest MAC address, typically. As you can imagine, the lowest MAC address is going to be more than likely the oldest device on your network. You don't want to necessarily let the automatic process take place and allow that root bridge to be elected automatically because it's more than likely going to be the oldest device, and you might have, the least capability on that device. By manually selecting the root bridge, you can pick perhaps a more beefy switch or a newer piece of equipment so that we can ensure just a higher level of stability within the network.

DHCP Snooping
DHCP snooping sounds like that might be something an attacker or a bad actor might do, but DHCP snooping is a layer 2 security technology that monitors for rogue DHCP servers. What we're talking about is an actor will be on the opposite end of this specific technology. They would try to install or implement a DHCP server, a rogue DHCP server that hands out IP addresses, binding that MAC address to an IP address and giving them the ability to potentially compromise that system. Switches can be configured to

prevent malicious or malformed DHCP packets. You can in essence turn that on so that if it detects malformed packets or malicious packets or it's coming from a server that's not a trusted or already configured or preconfigured DHCP server, then it would drop that packet. When a violation is detected, the event will be logged and alerts should be generated for further follow up or action, security personnel should be alerted and they should follow that up to see hey, what's going on on the network? Why is there a rogue DHCP server? Why is there someone that we don't know about trying to hand out DHCP packets?

MAC Filtering

MAC filtering, or Media Access Control filtering predefines which Media Access Control addresses can connect to a router or an access point. MAC addresses reside at layer 2 of the OSI model, and it's a 48-bit hex number that's burned into the NIC, or the network interface card. That won't prevent a skilled hacker from spoofing an allowed MAC address. A hacker with even a modest amount of skills and the toolsets can monitor or sniff the wire, understand what MAC addresses are valid, and then spoof the MAC address to allow themselves onto the network. With regard to MAC filtering, here we have a copy of Wireshark, and we're capturing packets on the network. From there, we can expand that out and dig down and see the MAC addresses of hosts communicating on the network. MAC addresses are very easy to spoof. Tools like Kali Linux, which we talked about briefly, and Wireshark can allow an attacker to scan a network and discover valid MAC addresses. Using things like aireplay-ng or aircrack-ng, we can send what's called deassociation packets to the client and then connect in that clients place. These tools exist. It's not something that you have to be particularly skilled for. If you have the distribution of Linux, Kali Linux, in this case, a lot of these tools are already built in, or you can go out to the web and download these tools. These things can be done manually or even faster via scripts. It can take literally a matter of seconds to sniff the wire, grab a valid MAC address, send a deassociation packet, reconnect as that client, and then you're on the network. The takeaway being, don't develop that false sense of security and think, hey, I have MAC filtering in place. Only authorized clients can connect. Well, as we see, that's very easy to bypass. Always remember the mantra of defense in depth. We have to place multiple locks on the door so that if they are able to bypass one is to have another and then another and another to get through. Hopefully with enough locks on the door that we can make enough noise that we can hear them trying to come in or they'll say this is too difficult and then move on to somewhere else. In summary, we talked about load balancing, we talked about network segmentation, virtual private networks. We talked about DNS, along with network access control, or NAC. Also talked about out-of-band management and also port security.

Chapter 7 Access Control Lists & Route Security

In this chapter we'll start off with network appliances. We'll talk about access control lists, or ACLs, along with route security. We'll talk about quality of service along with implications of IPv6, port spanning and port mirroring, along with port taps. We'll also talk about monitoring services and then file integrity monitors. First, let's talk about the concept of a jump server. A jump server is a server that's used to connect to devices in remote networks, typically used to perform admin tasks in a network with limited connectivity. What do I mean by that? Well, there might be issues with firewalls, with bandwidth, you may have a remote office or an area of your existing network, or your local network that you can't get to very easily. You may have firewalls in place that will block a lot of the tools that you may need to do work in that subnet, but normally, you can remote into a server, you can open up the ports to allow remote connectivity, an RDP session, or a Citrix session, or open up some type of VDI desktop, in that specific subnet, and then you can do all your things local in that subnet. So, the only thing it's passing through the firewall is your remote connectivity traffic. Everything else is taking place as if you were sitting in that subnet. The jump server allows you to perform those tasks without having to worry about punching holes in the firewall, and then additionally, from an admin's perspective, a lot of times when you have like vendors come in, or you're doing some type of work, patching or upgrading, you don't want to necessarily tie up the admin's workstation or laptop doing those remote tasks, especially when it comes to maintenance work or patching. By utilizing a jump server, you can have a vendor or someone you're working with also remote into that server, and they can work off that local server rather than the admin's workstation, or the admin's laptop. It serves a dual purpose and allows connectivity, but it also allows you to perform tasks without tying up your workstation. Some security risks will exist potentially if it's not configured and maintained, if it's bridging networks? If you have a jump server that's sitting between two networks, which is typically not good, a dual-homed machine, typically that's going to be a no-no, but if the jump server is maintained correctly, if it's patched properly, if it's maintained just like any other server on your network, then you should be in pretty good shape, but just understand that security risks do exist. If it's a remote office, and it's something that you forget about, and you don't patch, and you don't maintain regularly, well, that's going to pose potentially a security risk, so keep those things in mind.

Proxies

Let's talk about proxies and the difference between a forward and a reverse proxy. As far as forward proxies are concerned, which is what we're typically used to, a forward proxy normally have a number of clients that are trying to access some type of internet resource. What they're going to do is forward the requests to the proxy. The proxy then goes to the internet out to the external resources. What it does is potentially speed up access or the appearance of speeding up access for clients internal to the network and everyone attaching to the proxy. If someone else is already contacted that resource previously and that content has not yet expired on the proxy, well then the client will retrieve most if not all of that information from the proxy rather than going out to the actual resource. Some content is dynamic. Some things need to be refreshed constantly. Not everything will be retrieved from the proxy potentially. Again, it depends upon the resource being accessed. But it does a few things.

It speeds up or potentially speeds up the access, but it can also act as a network address translation or a NAT device and hide the actual IP addresses or the internal IP addresses of the clients inside the network from external resources. So from any one of the websites that they see on the web servers, what they see is a request coming from the proxy server. They never see the actual internal clients requesting that access. They'll see the public-facing IP address of the proxy server, but not the internal IP addresses of the resources on that internal network. Conversely, there's something referred to as a reverse proxy, otherwise known sometimes as a load balancer. We have external resources, clients from the outside, wanting to connect to some internal resource, whether that be a web server or a database server. We have all the external clients coming in from the internet. We're going to hit the reverse proxy or load balancer. This could be one server. It could be a pool of servers. What it does is then take that request and then forward it on to the appropriate resource. It could be four servers. It could be 40. It could be 400. It just depends upon the size of the network and the resources. The reverse proxy or the load balancer will then take those incoming requests and distribute that request onto the available resources, and it will do so in a very programmatic fashion. Some load balancers or reverse proxies are more advanced than others. Some do it in more of a round-robin fashion where it just distributes the load across one server, then the next, then the next. Others have advanced algorithms where they'll be able to tell dynamically which server is least busy and will forward the request to that resource. Next, we have something referred to as a transparent proxy. A transparent proxy is an intermediary system that typically sits between a user and a content provider. It can be multi-purpose as well. It can do caching. It can do filtering, which is content filtering or application filtering, websites or services. It can allow or deny based upon type of content or a specific type of website or a service. And it can also provide gateway functionality, which is rule based, typically requiring registration or user acceptance. A lot of times in public spaces, coffee shops, you'll see these captive portals, that are, in effect, a gateway, a transparent proxy, that requires a user to register in some fashion, maybe a username, or at least accept some type of end user agreement to provide access. The transparent proxy gets its name from the fact that an end user doesn't have to configure anything. Typically, with a proxy, a user will configure something within their browse or to point to a proxy server. With a transparent proxy, there is no configuration needed. As soon as that user attaches to the network, whether it be Wi-Fi, the requests are automatically intercepted by that transparent proxy, and then some type of application filtering or content filtering is applied, or the user's prompted to register or accept some type of end user agreement before they access the network.

Web Security Gateways
Security gateways or a proxy server with advanced features, such things as virus scanning, it could prevent connections to inappropriate sites like peer-to-peer networks or file sharing sites, data loss prevention, which is a big thing nowdays, so if it determines or it can sense, does this communication contain nine digits maybe with two dashes, maybe a social security number, or does it contain 16 digits for a credit card number or, so it can identify different types of traffic and block that from escaping the network. Or you can block connections to inappropriate sites, peer-to-peer, file sharing, dropbox, box.net. A lot of users, even in the corporate environment, will use these types of services like Dropbox to

share files back and forth, primarily because it's easy, but the downside of that is, there is no governance around that? A lot of companies want to restrict access to those types of sites so they can much more tightly control what types of data is leaving their network. You can also block things like ActiveX controls, Java applets, third-party cookies, malicious websites have a lot less chance of infecting or doing damage in a corporate environment if those attack vectors are mitigated. Activex control, Java applets, a lot of times malware or misbehaving sites utilize or leverage those specific technologies to inflict harm on users. It can also enable granular access to websites so that you can access the website, but maybe not all of the website? In other words, you could access LinkedIn, for instance, but not allow someone to do a job search or you could allow people to access Facebook, but prohibit them from posting content or playing games.

Chapter 8 Intrusion Detection and Prevention

The next thing is going to be intrusion detection and prevention. This is another security concept. We have an IDS and an IPS, NIDS and NIPS. Network intrusion detection system or prevention systems vary a little bit in how they operate. There is a lot of commonality, but then as far as the lack of action that they take, this differentiates the two. They can be used to log alert or take action when suspicious activity occurs on the network. Depending upon how they are configured, they can either simply detect that there is activity taking place and I'll go ahead and log it, or they could take action and say, as soon as this happens, do A, B, and C. They may reset a TCP connection, they may block a port, they may kick off some type of a forensic data capturing activity We have active systems that can take action to prevent an attack, or we have passive systems that simply record and perhaps utilize that data for later analysis. In terms of the difference between IDS and IPS, the network part aside, just generally speaking, we have intrusion detection systems and intrusion prevention systems. IDS has been around for quite a while, fairly common, and it's easy or relatively easy to set up, but as you may gather from what we've talked about already, it simply logs, alerts, and events, so it detects the intrusion, it doesn't necessarily do anything with it, it may alert an administrator or something, but it's not going to kick off any preventative measures. So it allows for a reactive response and further research into malicious or suspicious activity. An IPS, or an intrusion prevention system, is a newer platform, it's been around for the last few years, but it enables prevention. Such as perhaps blocking an IP address, blocking a port, resetting TCP connections, their TCP/IP connections, those types of things. It takes some type of preventive measure to shut down that communication or shut down that action so that malicious activity is halted in its tracks. The downside with an intrusion prevention system is you could have a false positive that could ultimately block legitimate traffic. Worst case scenario, let's just say, for example, you have an IPS set up, and if it detects malicious activity, go ahead and block port 80 for 5 minutes. Well, you could have legitimate traffic that comes in, maybe just a heavier than normal workload that comes in that IPS would falsely identify that as malicious traffic when it's not, shuts down the internet traffic over port 80 shuts that down for 5 minutes, well, you've just created a Denial of Service against yourself. Those things have to be set up with care, as that they do have the potential for false positives, but it also gives you the ability to prevent things, when in fact, you do have malicious activity taking place. The different components of intrusion prevention and detection systems; I'm going to go through a list but this is more just for your informational purposes than anything, but we have a couple components that you need to be aware of. We have alerts. an alert is a message generated from something called an analyzer and the analyzer indicates anything that it may deem as interesting traffic or an interesting event has occurred, so that alert might be an email, that alert might be a pop up on a screen. In some form or fashion, it's going to alert us that something has occurred. The analyzer processes data collected from one or more sensors. The sensor collects data or triggers data and then it looks for suspicious activity and the analyzer is going to take that data and look for what it deems to be suspicious or malicious activity, it could be deterministic, or it could be rule-based. We could just say, hey, if it meets this signature, than it's probably malicious, go ahead and fire off some type of alert or some type of action. The data source itself is the raw data that's being analyzed. That could be log files, it could be audit logs, system logs, network traffic itself, it just depends. It depends on the system and it depends upon how it's configured. Then we have something called an event. An event is an indication, that something suspicious has occurred, it could be malicious, it could be suspicious, it could be a false positive, but in some fashion, the system has determined that this needs further investigation, so that can trigger an alert or notification. Or if it's confirmed and it is malicious activity, then that event would become an incident. Next we have a component called a manager, and the manager is the intrusion detection system console, that's the piece of software that comes up on your screen and that's what you use to manage the system. Next is a notification, which is the process by which the operator, which is someone who is working the system here, they are alerted to an event or an incident. The operator, as I said as a user, it could be an admin, someone that's responsible for that intrusion detection system. They're actively working the system. They don't necessarily need to be sitting there. They could be alerted remotely, email, but there is someone that's responsible for the operation of that system. And then the sensor is a primary data collection point for that intrusion detection system, or the IDS. A sensor could be a device driver, it could be baked into a piece of firmware on a system, or it could be a separate physical device that's attached to a network that collects data, so it could be a separate device collecting data and then processing that in real time.

IDS/IPS Component Workflow
If we look at the components of an IDS system and how they all fit together, it may make a little more sense. We have a data source, we have a couple sensors, we have the

analyzer, the active response and then a manager, and then the administrator and the operator. There are security policies that will tie all of this together. The security policies dictate what action is taken. The administrator and the operator may also analyze some of this data for trending and reporting purposes. And an active response could trigger some type of action, whether it be shutting down a port or whether it be resetting connections. The data source has some type of activity, the sensors will pick up on that, and it will generate an event. That event goes to the analyzer to be analyzed, is this something that I need to be worrying about, and if it is, it generates an alert to the manager or the management console. That console sends a notification to the operator or the administrator, depending upon, who's who, that can be used for trending or reporting purposes only. We just want to know about it, we're not going to do anything at this point. Or it could send off an active response and say, wait a minute, we need to do something here, that's when it triggers the shutting down of a port or resetting of a connection.

Four Approaches to IDS
There are four approaches that I want you to know about as far as IDS systems are concerned. We have behavior-based detection. That's variations of behavior, increased traffic, policy violations, something that's just out of the norm. We have signature-based IDS systems, and that's going to use attack signatures and audit trails. In other words, look for traffic that looks like it might be IP spoofing or might be cross-site injection, or it might be somebody hammering, doing a port scan on our external firewalls. It could be a thousand different things, but there are going to be signatures that it's going to be looking for. They're not necessarily as robust has some of the other systems because

if the signature doesn't exist or if it's a brand new, let's say, for instance, a zero-day exploit or a zero-day threat, meaning there is no signature defined yet, then those things are vulnerable to be bypassed. We have anomaly detection IDS systems, and, again, similar to behavior based in that it learns what's normal, then it looks for deviations from that baseline. In this instance, over time it's going to learn, 30% workload is normal for this specific segment. All of a sudden, if it's 60 or 70% above workload, all of a sudden we've got a ton of IP connections coming in, well, that's not normal. Go ahead and kick off some type of trigger or some type of an alert. It just depends upon what's normal for that specific environment. What's normal for one may not be normal for another. Then we have heuristic IDS, and that's going to utilize algorithms to analyze data traffic as it passes through. It's not signature based in that it has a certain set of parameters that it looks for. It has some type of internal algorithm that's going to depend upon the system so it will vary from place to place or from system to system, but it's going to use that algorithm to analyze the traffic as it passes through the system in real time and then make a determination at that point.

Network-based IDS
When you have network-based IDS systems, you can place those in a couple different places within the network. You can place them in front of your firewall, you could place them behind your firewall, or you could do both. For example, if I have an IDS system placed in front of the firewall. People from the internet are trying to get into my network, whether it's web servers or there's some type of a public-facing component that they can access. Rather than have them hit the firewall first, and then if they pass the muster, and they pass through the firewall, then if I hit the

IDS system and I start analyzing traffic, well that's great, I have a reduction in the amount of stuff I have to analyze, but I don't get a good indication or a good idea of potentially who's banging against the firewall, who's potentially trying to initiate some type of an attack. Conversely, if I do what I have here in the picture and I have the IDS system placed in front of the firewall, well, I'm going to get a lot more traffic to analyze, but I'm also going to get a better indication of attacks against that firewall. If you want to look at the best of both worlds, you would place an IDS system in front of your firewall and behind. That way you get a good indication of everything that's banging against the firewall. Some gets in, some doesn't. Once it passes through the firewall, then you have a secondary IDS system that can dig deeper and look for variations in policy or anomalies, depending upon the type of system. that's going to write out to some type of an event data database, and there's lots of different ones out there, and then typically, that's going to pass those types of things, once it has a trigger for an alert or notification, up to the network operations center, or a NOC, depending upon the size of the environment, you may or may not have a NOC in place, or you may use a third party for that purpose. But then the NOC is going to either take some type of remediation immediately, they may have some steps, they have some NOC analysts that will say, hey, if this happens, do ABC. Or they may page out a person who's on call, if it's after hours, or engage a specific team to come in and take some action. It simply just depends upon the size of the company.

Security Device Placement
When we're talking about security device placement, we have things like sensors, collectors, correlation engines, filters, proxies, firewalls, VPN concentrators, SSL

accelerators, distributed denial-of-service mitigators, aggregation switches, and taps and port mirrors. I'm just calling all of these things out you're aware of what they are and understand that any of these things, for the most part, can be placed in various places within the network. They could be placed internally. They could be placed on the perimeter. They could be placed in a DMZ on a firewall in either location or in multiple locations. In the case of sensors, as an example, you may have sensors all throughout the network on many devices, both internal and external, and they may all feedback to your intrusion detection or prevention system to let you know if somebody is trying to get into the network in some fashion or people are logging in when they're not supposed to, doing something that they're not authorized to do so. Collectors are along the same lines. Sensors and collectors, correlation engines, they all take that information and they correlate across multiple devices to show you a common timeline to help identify trends. Filters, proxies and firewalls, are typically going to go on the perimeters. They will filter content, they'll filter access requests. Proxies, as we know, will aggregate requests internally. And then that way, the person requesting a website or some resource internally if someone else just recently requested the same thing doesn't have to go out to the internet to that device. I can pull it from the proxy. Firewalls, we know what a firewall does. It blocks based on port or protocol or some type of application and only allows things through that we want to allow through. VPN concentrators, we talked about. SSL accelerators or load balancers can again be placed in front of say a web server, could be placed in front of an application server, and they can be spun up dynamically if we're using something like SDN so that we can add additional resources when we need them. Same thing with DDoS mitigators - it can detect automatically when we're having a denial-of-service attack and it can shut down ports or take some type of response to mitigate that threat. Aggregation switches will aggregate data from smaller switches, you'll have a small network and an aggregation switch that will combine a number of small networks. They could be placed anywhere throughout the network, depending upon how your network is architected, whether it's a mesh, a full mesh, a core edge. Then we have taps and port mirrors. And what it does is place that switch or that port in what's called promiscuous mode. That way you can mirror the traffic on another port, and typically that's done from mirroring or auditing or forensic investigations you can mirror all the traffic on a specific port and then analyze that without affecting the traffic on the port itself.

Chapter 9 Firewalls & Unified Threat Management

What's the actual purpose of firewalls? Well, a firewall is, generally speaking, designed to isolate one network from another. It can be hardware or it can be software based. It can be either. It can be a standalone device, or it can be an integrated device integrated into some other equipment, in other words, routers or switches. Whether you're a small office or a home office, you may have a small Netgear or Linksys or even a Cisco router, that combines a lot of functionality together. You can have a firewall. It can do NAT, or Network Address Translation, and, of course, routing functionality as well, perhaps even switching. It just depends on the size of the network, how specific you want to get. There are different devices that can perform very specific functions, or there are integrated devices that can perform a lot of different functions together. If we have a diagram of outside users outside of the firewall, and you see the firewall denoted by a brick wall. And, incidentally, the term firewall historically came from buildings that were built very close to one another, and in order to prevent fire from jumping from one building to another when they were very close together, think like row homes, for instance, they would build these brick walls in between these different buildings to prevent that fire from jumping from one to the other. That brick wall would act as a firewall, to prevent fire from jumping from one building to the other. The same concept is carried over here. And that's why you typically see a firewall being illustrated as a brick wall. As you can then imagine, firewalls are typically used to block or limit outside traffic from entering a network. Whether it's corporate, medium-sized office, small office, or a home office, they all serve pretty much the same types of functions. However, firewalls can also be placed internally, inside of a network to segment one area from another. For instance, you may have a large corporate environment that has different areas that you don't necessarily want them to communicate, or they shouldn't communicate, from one to the other very easily. You can punch holes in the firewall to allowed traffic. But, generally speaking, these things are cordoned off from one another. For instance, if you have a PCI Secure zone, like say you have a very large enterprise that has some typical day-to-day workers, and you may have an R&D department, you may have an accounting department, a finance department, PCI Secure means it contains credit card information and some type of personally identifiable information. You want to have that information cordoned off from the rest of the network. The finance folks don't necessarily talk to the R&D or maybe the graphics department, just to prevent internal browsing of those resources. A firewall can be put into place between those segments on your internal network as well. It's important to understand, and just to recap very quickly hardware vs. software, firewalls can either be hardware or software based. They can be standalone devices or integrated into other devices, like routers and switches. Even if it is a hardware-based solution, it's still going to contain software, you can't just run it on hardware by itself. There has to be some software running behind the scenes. You can drop it onto a server and have that server function providing firewall functionality. Or it can be a separate, standalone piece of hardware. However, that hardware is still going to contain software or firmware. What are some types of firewalls? Well, we have packet filtering firewalls, and packet filtering firewalls allow or block traffic based upon a specific port, HTTP traffic as an example, web traffic that typically comes in over port 80. FTP, or File Transport Protocol, that's generated on port 21 typically. You can configure the firewall to allow web traffic but don't allow FTP traffic or allow DNS but don't allow NetBIOS or time lookups or whatever the case might be. You can break it down by port by port by port and get very specific, get very granular. Doing it based just on port, there's not a lot of intelligence there. It just simply looks at the port, and then it will either allow or block the traffic at that point. Next, we have proxy firewalls. a proxy firewall is going to be dual homed, which means it's going to have two network interfaces, typically one on each network or on separate networks. It's going to segment internal users from the outside world, and it can mask the IP address using something called NAT, or Network Address Translation. That gives an added layer of security because the outside world won't know who is communicating. All they'll see is the address of the proxy firewall. And a proxy can also cache requests to improve perceived speed. If you have multiple users as an example that are accessing the same website, well, the first person to access that website or that URL will go out and pull it down from the web or from whatever resource it's getting it from. Subsequent requests, as long as that information is still sitting in the cache on that proxy server, so the next user goes out to that same web resource? Instead of going out to the web out to whatever resource they're getting it from, they'll get it directly from the proxy server, from the cache. It gives the perception that things are faster and that your network is all of a sudden more responsive. The next type of firewall is something referred to as a stateful packet inspection firewall, or SPI. An SPI firewall examines the packets and keeps the packet table of every communication channel. So, in other words, it has more intelligence than a simple packet filtering firewall, and it does a deeper dive, examines what's inside. SPI tracks the entire conversation, so it gives you an increased level of security because it only allows packets from known active connections. In other words, if someone's trying to spoof or jump into the middle of a connection or a conversation, an SPI firewall understands that. They say, hey, wait a minute. I don't know who this is from. I haven't seen this before. This is in the middle of a conversation. There's no initiation. There's no back and forth to establish that connection. This just came out of here, so I'm going to drop that. It drops the packet. It gives you that added layer of security. It's better than simple packet filtering, which only looks at the current packet. However, it's possible to attack by overloading that State Table. As you go through all of these different types of routers and switches and pretty much any type of infrastructure or equipment in our network, just understand that nothing is foolproof. There's always going to be a way, there are always going to be hackers that are trying to somehow penetrate that device, crash it, and get elevated privileges. Nothing's foolproof. That's while we're all employed and how we all eventually make the big bucks. The battle goes on and on and on. Check Point Software introduced the concept of a stateful inspection or stateful packet inspection firewall in the use of its FireWall-1 software, which was introduced in 1994. So, it's been around for quite a while.

Web Application Firewalls

A web application firewall differs from a network firewall in that it operates at the application layer of the OSI model. Web application firewalls, or WAF, operates at application layer 7 of the OSI model. That's, the application layer, and it's designed with very specific or granular rules for web servers. And these types of firewalls can analyze traffic to prevent typical web server type attacks, such as, SQL injection attacks, cross-site scripting attacks or forged HTTP requests. Any time you see a website that has a form that you can fill in, very skilled hackers, can craft either a cross-site scripting or SQL injection attacks, and they'll write SQL code that they'll use as the code in the form. It may ask you for your name, as an example, on a web form. Well, instead of putting in your name, the hacker will try to put in some type of long SQL code, some SQL query, and if it's formed correctly, it can crash that server. If the server's not protected against that, if it doesn't sanitize that input properly, then it can initiate some type of SQL query on the back end and perhaps crash that web server or crash the website, return some type of information, or even give some type of increased elevated privileges to the server. That's why these types of firewalls are in place, to understand these things as they come in in real time, analyze what's happening, and shut it down before it has a chance to do any harm., some well-known web application firewall vendors, just for your own knowledge, are things like Cisco, Citrix, Barracuda Networks, F5, and eEye. There are probably 30 or 40 more well-known vendors, but these are just a few to give you an example. If you wanted to dig a little bit further, these are just some of the major players in that space. As an example of a firewall, there's one from Check Point and they run the gamut from small firewall appliances, and it gets bigger and bigger as we go on. We have an entire chassis system with blades installed. They can range from very small software-based implementations, to small hardware-based implementations, and on up. Depending upon the size of the company and the enterprise, they can go from a few hundred dollars up to tens of thousands of dollars and more.

Unified Threat Management (UTM)
We've talked about VPNs, and firewalls, and intrusion detection and prevention systems, and all of these different

things as individual pieces of software or individual applications, but there's also something referred to as a UTM, or Unified Threat Management suite. That's a multipurpose suite of tools, and it does things such as firewalls, network intrusion detection or prevention systems, gateway anti-virus and anti-spam. It can provide VPN functionality, content filtering, load balancing, and also DLP or data loss prevention. These newer types of tools can pretty much do everything and take the place of all of these individual components. The advantage being you have a single pane of glass that you can look at all of these things, and you can correlate events across all these different applications much easier as well. It makes troubleshooting and also incident or event investigation much easier. If you haven't taken a look at these yet, I highly recommend that you look at some of the UTM software that's available and see if it fits within your environment. It could save you some time and effort in deployment, troubleshooting, patching, and also incident or event management.

Content Filters

A content filter can be hardware or software, and its purpose is to limit or restrict access to certain types of content. Inappropriate material, it could be malware, viruses, could be worms or trojans, and also things like spam or spyware. Misconfigured devices can overblock or allow content that should, in fact, be filtered. Additionally, these things can also violate censorship laws and regulations, depending upon your location or what you're filtering. Content filters are, in fact, valid. I'm not saying they shouldn't be there, just that an extra level of due diligence should be placed on them to make sure that they're configured properly, that they're blocking what they should be blocking, We don't develop that false sense of security.

Something else to keep in mind is that these things can be built into firewalls, UTM devices, or they could be standalone software. They don't necessarily have to be a specific separate device. They can be built into things like firewalls and Unified Threat Management, or UTM, devices.

Implicit Deny and ACLs

It's a firewall access control list, or an ACL, and it specifies what type of traffic is allowed. If it's not on the list, it denied access. Much like if you go into a club, or a restaurant, or some VIP event, and you walk up to the front door and the bouncer standing there all intimidating and you read off your name and say, hi, I'm so and so and he looks on his list and says, nope, you're not on the list. You're not getting in. Well, as frustrating as that might be, that's the same concept here. You walk up and your name is on the list, yeah, good for you. You can go in the front door, but if you're not explicitly allowed, then you're implicitly denied.

Route Security

Routers connect networks together and external routing protocols like BGP, or border gateway protocol, are inherently insecure. They were created years ago back when security wasn't a major concern. The main emphasis, at that point, was connectivity and getting everyone connected together, security and all the different types of threats that we face today weren't top of mind or even a consideration back then. What I'm talking about here with BGP specifically, it consists of autonomous systems, or AS groups, groups of systems that are managed by the same administrative system, Misconfigurations and deliberate route hijacks can result in outages. It's possible for someone to misconfigure their system and advertise routes that shouldn't be there and create outages. Typically, it's not necessarily a direct attack, although it can be, but oftentimes the outages that have been experienced in the past have been a result of misconfiguration on the systems. It's beyond the scope of this book to dig deeply into this, but I do want to call your attention to the NIST publication, NIST SP1800-14, which proposes securing BGP and they talk about things like route origin, validation, and also resource public key infrastructure, or RPKI. What it does in a nutshell is put some security guardrails, on the BGP protocol and only allow secure or preauthorized systems to communicate with each other and not allow rogue systems or misconfigured systems to advertise out on the internet so we can prevent some of the things that we've seen in the past. Unfortunately, this has not been widely adopted yet, but the proposal is out there, so I would encourage you to read more deeply if you want some more information on that specific topic.

Quality of Service (QoS)
QoS, or quality of service is a set of technologies to ensure critical applications or services have a certain level of performance. We're talking about packets that are marked to identify service types. You may have audio, video. You may have critical applications like in a medical facility or finance applications or things that just need a guaranteed level of bandwidth. It will reserve bandwidth for those applications, and then everyone else gets what's left. So routers prioritize packets, and they'll create virtual queues to ensure bandwidth. They put the most important applications to the front of the line. You can almost think of it like as a fast pass, if you would. If you've ever been to Disney World or some of these amusement parks, you have the concept of a fast pass you don't have to wait in the line or wait in the queue. This is a very similar type of scenario where we will mark the packets that we want to push to the front of the

line. The things we're talking about with quality of service, things like bandwidth and latency, the amount of bandwidth or how big is the pipe that they can go through. Latency being how much delay is there. Packet loss usually resolving around the fact that the network is too congested and the packets time out, so we lose those packets. Then something referred to as jitter, which refers typically to audio and video, where we have packets that arrive out of sequence or out of order, and it can make audio calls sound scrambled or digitized or it can create skipping in streaming applications. By ensuring quality of service, we make sure those applications that need that level of performance get what they need. Then as more and more IoT devices, or Internet of Things devices, come online, having bandwidth for real-time monitoring, as an example, becomes more and more important. Things that need real-time performance, real-time monitoring, so we need to make quick action or quick decisions based upon that information, QoS comes in handy because it allows us to guarantee a certain level of performance for those applications and for those devices.

Implications of IPv6
Now let's talk about the implications of IPv6, or Internet Protocol version 6. So, IPv4 addresses, which have been around since the dawn of the internet, the mid-60s, late-60s, IP version 4 is a 32-bit addressing scheme. With that, roughly 4 billion IP addresses when it first came out, we thought, that's going to be more than we'll ever need, not a big deal. Well, as it turns out, as more and more devices have come online, we're running out of IP addresses. So, NAT, or network address translation helps to a degree. We could put a bunch of internal IPs behind one external IP. But as new devices come online, IoT devices, that problem will only continue to expand. And in some parts of the world, we've

already run out of IPv4 addresses. IPv6 is natively enabled on most devices nowadays, so the issue is, the implication is, it's often overlooked and can mean open door if it's not secured properly. Sometimes if it's not configured properly, if it's not something you think about, you may say, well, I have IPv4 rules in place, I have things locked down, I'm good. But if IPv6 is enabled on the devices and it's not secured, it's just as is out of the box, well, that could have some security implications potentially. Security policies often aren't uniformly applied, from IPv4 to IPv6. Meaning the things that we have locked down with version 4, we don't necessarily have the same level of parity, or the same level of lockdown, when it comes to v6. That false sense of security in the IPv4 is locked down, it's filtered, but again, IPv6 could be wide open to attack. Another thing is with IPv6 being relatively new, although it's been around for a while, it's relatively new as far as actual adoption is concerned, that lack of experience with countermeasures against IPv6 hacks and attacks, so subject matter expertise is not as widespread, and hacking tools are taking advantage of IPv6 vulnerabilities. It's becoming more and more of a problem if we don't start to lock down these devices and make sure that things are turned off if we don't need it, or if we are using it, that it's secured properly. Hackers are taking advantage of this because the majority of the hacking tools that are out there are being upgraded, they're being patched, and, new versions coming out, just like regular traditional software or commercial software, they're upgrading their stuff as well. As new technologies come online, those tools are updated as well to take advantage of vulnerabilities in that new technology.

Port Mirroring, Port Spanning, and Port Taps

Now let's talk about the concept of port mirroring, so also known as port spanning or SPAN, or Switched Port Analyzer. What it does is a switch sends a copy of all network packets seen on a port, or it could be an entire VLAN, to another port to be analyzed. In other words, if you recall how a switch works, where it maintains a MAC table, a MAC table or MAC addresses of all the hosts attached to that switch, and it knows what hosts live on what port. It only sends traffic out of the port that that host is connected to, so it helps to reduce traffic. When we're doing port spanning or a Switched Port Analyzer, we can copy all of the data off of a port, or the entire switch or an entire VLAN, and send that to another port and it can be analyzed, so intrusion detection systems, trouble shooting, we could use it for forensics, we could use it for user monitoring. Those things are in play to allow us to identify and monitor or dig into the packets on a specific port or a specific VLAN. As an example, if we have a switch, there are four ports on the switch, and then we have four computers attached to that switch. This is a traditional connectivity scenario. We have all of these different devices connecting to a switch. When we're talking about port mirroring, well, we have the same devices. Let's say, in this case we have three devices connected, and they're connected to that device via ports 1, 2, and 3, well, then we're also going to have a monitoring device on port 4, and that will utilize port mirroring. In the first scenario, the computer attached to port 1 wants to communicate with the computer on port 3. Well, since the MAC table exists on that switch, it knows where those two hosts live, and it only sends traffic out of the port that that host lives on, so that way it's reducing traffic and it helps make things more secure. But in the second scenario, you'll notice that all the PCs, or all the hosts connected to the switch, like they're communicating, well, all of that traffic gets sent out of port 4 to the port mirroring device, and it allows that port mirroring device to capture those packets, analyze those packets, and do whatever it needs to with that information. A similar concept would be port taps. In this instance we have East/West traffic, we talked about that before, traffic occurring inside the data center. All of the devices attached to the switch, if it needs to communicate to another network within our data center, it would send that to the router and then off to its destination. Well, a similar concept to port mirroring is something referred to as a port tap. In this situation we would insert a tap inline between those two devices, and that tap would then go out to out-of-band security or monitoring tools, so it would be placed inline and then capture all the packets and do it in real time. It's quicker and it's more efficient than doing port mirroring, where you don't have the potential of duplicating packets, doing it inline. However, it may or may not be applicable for your environment. This can work for Ethernet networks and then also Fibre Channel networks, but when we do these types of activities, they can be disruptive, so these things have to be planned out ahead of time to make sure that we don't disrupt connectivity between applications, between hosts and servers, but just two concepts to keep in mind that we can use to monitor traffic on a network.

File Integrity Check
A file integrity check protects against tampering by ensuring a file has not been modified. You can look at a few different things or a few pieces of metadata to understand if that file's been tampered with. You can look at credentials. You can look at privileges and security settings. You can also look at the content, the actual content of the file itself, attributes in size or hash values. If any of these things don't match, that's going to be indicative of some type of tampering, an indicator of

compromise, perhaps the first steps in a larger breach. This might give you some advanced warning that someone's coming in, and they're starting to manipulate our files. We need to jump on this quickly, see if we can lock this down, perhaps follow what's going on, maybe even let that person do whatever it is they're doing for a short period of time while you monitor them you can then get a better understanding of who it is, where they're coming from. What happens is it's going to compare a current good state. It's going to take a baseline of that system, the file system, individual files. Typically it's going to run a hash against those files. If anything changes within that file, that hash value will be different. It's going to compare a current state against a known good state. If they don't match, then that's indicative of some type of compromise or tampering. As an example, Windows has something built in called the System File Checker, you can run that by running SFC. SFC will scan the integrity of all protected system files, and in this case it will replace ones that it finds either corrupt or changed or modified in some way with the correct Microsoft versions. You can do SCANNOW, VERIFYONLY. You can have it scan and then automatically repair what it finds, if it finds anything. Or you can say, go ahead and scan, but just verify only and report back to me. Don't repair anything yet. In the example down below, you have sfc /SCANNOW, or you can say VERIFYFILE, and you can point to a specific file You can check just one file at a time, not necessarily your entire file system. Or you can say, VERIFYONLY, and if you find anything, report back. That way you can take some further action if necessary. I summary we covered network appliances. We talked about access control lists, or ACLs. We talked about route security along with quality of service. We also covered the implications of IPv6, port spanning, port mirroring, and port taps, along with monitoring services and file integrity monitors.

Chapter 10 How to Install and Configure Wireless Security

In this chapter, we'll be talking about installing and configuring wireless security settings. We'll be talking about four main areas. We'll talk about cryptographic protocols, authentication protocols, also methods, and then installation considerations. Let's first cover some wireless definitions. WEP, or Wired Equivalency Protocol, was originally designed to provide security equal to a wired network. If you're familiar with WEP at you understand that it doesn't provide security at all anymore. It can be cracked within minutes or sometimes within seconds if you have the tools. Vulnerabilities have emerged, and this has since been deprecated. It's not recommended for a secure environment whatsoever. If you have no other choice and you have older legacy equipment in your environment that needs to communicate, in other words, make it backwards compatible, then you may have to have WEP. It's better than nothing, but not in the grand scheme of things. Anyone with an off-the-shelf-set of hacker tools or penetration testing tools, can crack WEP encryption relatively easily. The alternative to that, or the newer standards, would be Wi-Fi Protected Access, which is WPA or WPA2. WPA itself was based upon WEP, and it was used as a stop gap. WPA has also been cracked relatively quickly. WPA2, which is the newer standard, it fully implements 802.11i protocol, and that provides for additional security enhancements. We'll talk about why these things are so insecure, why we had some of these vulnerabilities to begin with. Then, for definitions sake, I want you to understand that Wireless Application Protocol, or WAP, not to be confused with wireless access point, which is also referred to with a WAP acronym, Wireless Application Protocol, that deals with

315

mobile devices and providing mobile devices with internet connectivity. It's a suite of protocols similar to TCP/IP. But, it deals with mobile connectivity. It uses Wireless Transport Layer Security, or WTLS, similar to regular TLS that we would have seen in the TCP/IP suite when we're dealing with encryption or HTTPS, as TLS or SSL, as we spoke about in the previous chapter, and it provides for authentication, encryption, and data integrity.

WEP/WPA/WPA2

To define this a little bit further, with WEP, WPA, and WPA2, the standard WEP, used what was referred to as an RC4 stream, and it was a 24-bit encryption. The length of that encryption key is what led to its insecurity or its vulnerabilities. That IV, or the initialization vector, it's vulnerable to an IV attack, meaning that 24-bit encryption was not long enough. So, packet injection can crack WEP in literally several seconds. And what it boils down to is that initialization vector, 24-bits long is just too short. Every so often it has to repeat. There are only so many different combinations of initialization vectors that it can send. As communication takes place over any length of time, if someone's sitting there sniffing the wire for a period of time, they'll see that initialization vector. That's a hard one to say. They'll see that repeated every so often, so they'll be able to pull that off the wire because that IV, or the initialization vector, is static, and it's reused, and it's part of the RC4 encryption key. You already have a piece of the information once you understand what the initialization vector is, and it's also set in clear text. You have three or four pieces of the puzzle to begin with, and if you use standard penetration testing tools, those tools allow you to crack that encryption key very, very easily. It's not recommended for any type of secure environment. It should be avoided unless, backwards compatibility is needed.

WPA and WPA2 Security

As you move on to WPA and WPA2, WPA, or Wi-Fi-protected access that partially implements the 802.11i standard. It was a stopgap. It uses something called Temporal Key Integrity Protocol, or TKIP for Short and what it does is it takes a 128-bit wrapper, and it wraps that WEP encryption. That 24-bit encryption that we've already talked about as being too small, and it's reusable every so often, or it is reused every so often, it's too small. Well, with WPA, it wraps that entire encryption packet within 128-bit larger encryption packet. It generates a second key based upon the MAC address of the sender and the serial number of the packet. It mixes this key with the Initialization Vector, it mixes it with the IV, and it creates a per-packet key. It's more secure than WEP, but it's still using RC4 encryption, and it's backwards compatible with WEP. We know it is not considered a secure protocol because, again, it's been cracked very easily, again, using off-the-shelf tools. If we move to the next one, WPA2, that fully implements to 802.11i standard. That uses something called CCMP for enhanced security, or the CC-MAC protocol. It's Counter Mode Cipher Block Chaining Message Authentication Code Protocol. CCMP, it's 128-bit AES encryption algorithm. It's not backwards compatible with WEP, but it is much more secure. Having said that, is it completely secure? Is it completely foolproof? Well, the answer is No. That has also been cracked. Given enough time and if you have enough of a skilled hacker on the other end of sniffing that traffic, it is crackable. Wireless security examples. Well, WPA and WPA2 can use something called a Pre-shared Key, or PSK, or Enterprise Authentication. Pre-Shared Keys, if you have a home office or a small office

317

home office, or a SoHo network, or a small business, you may be already familiar with Pre-Shared Keys. It means you have some password on the client. You have a password on your Wi-Fi router or your access point. As long as those two things match, then you can connect to the network. Enterprise uses something called RADIUS, which is an authentication server, and digital certificates. You have to have that certificate, and you have to have an account on that RADIUS server or some way to authenticate to that RADIUS server, so it provides for an even greater level of authentication. If we have a laptop that may again connect to a wireless access point. That wireless access point, if we're using Pre-Shared Key, all I need is that secret or that Pre-Shared Key on the laptop and on the wireless access point, and as long as they match, we connect and off we go. If we're using RADIUS, you'll see the laptop will connect to the wireless access point, or in a larger environment, you may have multiple wireless access points, in which case you would use a wireless LAN controller, and that way you can set up your information and your configuration once and push that out to all the wireless access points within your network. You can do that in one shot, so it just makes the management easier. But, you would connect to the wireless access point, which would forward your connection request over to the RADIUS server. The RADIUS server would check to see, is this person able to connect or authenticated to connect? Because if I can back up one, if we use a Pre-Shared Key, as long as we have the secret on both the laptop and the wireless access point, it connects. We don't know who it is that's connecting. If we're using authentication or Enterprise Authentication, then we have to authenticate with that RADIUS server. It's going to authenticate the user, as well as the laptop. This gives us a greater level of security.

WPA3

Before we get too much further along, let's talk about WPA3, which is the newest version of WPA and for all intents and purposes will replace WPA2. WPA2 is still very much in play, but WPA3 is making its way into the marketplace and into all the newer gear that's being released. WPA3 adds AES-GCMP, which is Galois/Counter Mode and also security jumps up from 128-bit SAE, and we'll talk about that in just a moment, to 192, which is optional for personal use. In actuality, it's 256-bit encryption, but the way things flush out when it's all said and done, it ends up being 192. SAE stands for Simultaneous Authentication of Equals, otherwise known as Dragonfly key exchange with forward secrecy feature, meaning If someone captures this traffic and then tries to brute force it maybe six months, a year, and whatever down the road, they're not going to be able to do anything with it. That forward secrecy prevents brute force attacks and prevents someone from trying to decode that data at some future date. Key features, brute force protection. Also individualized encryption for each user using unauthenticated Diffie-Hellman Pairwise Master Key. In a nutshell, it's referred to as a PAKE, or a Password Authenticated Key Exchange. That provides mutual authentication and negotiates a fresh session key each time someone connects. That forward secrecy, is a prevention of offline dictionary attacks. If we look at this in more detail, it was released in 2018, and WPA3 is the successor to WPA2, and it offers several security enhancements. So 256-bit in actuality, but the overall effect for Wi-Fi is effectively 192-bit. Simultaneous Authentication of Equals, or SAE, You hear that term come up over and over again. Add that acronym with an abbreviation to your toolbag as well, also known as the Dragonfly key exchange with forward secrecy feature, as we've talked about. And then perhaps one of the biggest advancements is Opportunistic Wireless Encryption, or OWE, which protects unsecured networks such as libraries or coffee shops, airports or hotels. This will replace unencrypted open networks. So OWE will provide individualized data encryption to users connecting to public open networks to protect against eavesdropping. Each user gets their own distinct encrypted session without them having to do anything. On open networks, an attacker connected to that network, could read or even modify other users traffic. HTTPS to an extent can provide protection against some of this stuff on an open network, but OWE uses an unauthenticated Diffie-Hellman key exchange during that association, resulting in what's called a Pairwise Master Key, or a PMK. And they use that to derive, then the session keys, and that's unique to each user. Each user that connects gets that unique session key. There's no provisioning required, and the encryption process is entirely transparent to users. The users would see and join the Wi-Fi network as they would any typical open network as they've done in the past, but they don't have to do anything additional to get that encrypted connection. So OWE is a big improvement over current open wireless networks. Then just keep in mind, we use SHA-2 for each input. And then Wi-Fi Easy Connect is another big advancement that uses Device Provisioning Protocol Secure, or DPP Secure, and that will replace WPS, or Wi-Fi Protected Setup, so it makes things much easier. Using your smartphone, you would scan a QR code on that device and then automatically pair any new devices that would connect it to the network, so it makes provisioning much, much easier. Then lastly, WPA3 is not susceptible to the KRACK attack like WPA2 was. WPA2 was susceptible to something called the KRACK attack, which came out in roughly 2017, and it rendered WPA2 vulnerable. WPA3 is not vulnerable to that same attack due to the way they use Simultaneous Authentication of Equals, or the SAE key exchange.

Wireless Security Examples

Let's take a look at a real-world example of how a hacker could gain access in an environment. Let's say, for instance, we have our two wireless access points that we have. Well, if someone wanted to come in, they could set up what's called a rogue access point. They could issue a Denial of Service against our existing wireless access point, take it offline or make it so that it can't respond to requests. They could put a wireless access point using something called open authentication, which means there is no password required. The laptop, whoever's sitting at that laptop, they would connect to that wireless access point, otherwise known as an evil twin. That's a term you should be familiar with or you should remember. But an evil twin is there to fool someone connecting to the network. They think they're connecting to the wireless access point. Even though they have credentials to connect to the legitimate wireless access point, that's going to be DDoSed so they can't connect. They're going to connect to the evil twin. It's using open authentication, which means they don't need a username and password to connect. They're connected. And if we are in control of that wireless access point, of that evil twin, we can set it so that it pops up some type of authentication message. The user sitting at the laptop would think, something must have happened; it's prompting me for my credentials. They'll go ahead and put in their username and password, or they'll do that several times. We just keep putting up fake messages until we capture enough information that we can be pretty confident that we have what we need off of that user. Then we can just disconnect and off we go. In that case, we could very easily compromise that communication. We could capture everything, or we could have it connected to the network and let them pass through and connect. We could just sit there and monitor everything that they do as that communication passes through the wireless access point. Just be advised that those types of things are, in fact, possible. You could be sitting at a coffee shop, and someone could do something similar to that. It doesn't necessarily have to be in a business environment. It could be anywhere that you would connect using a wireless access point.

Wireless Security and Pen Testing Tools
There is a number of off-the-shelf penetration testing, or pen test, tools that can quickly compromise insecure wireless protocols. We're talking about WEP and even WPA and WPA2. There are some tools, Kali Linux is one, or it used to be called BackTrack. There's some off-the-shelf scripts that can do packet injections and things that allow them to very quickly break those types of encryption protocols., what would happen is, it allows you to do network sniffing, Even if a specific wireless access point is not broadcasting, it's SSID. Even it's not broadcasting it can still sniff the wire because those things are being transmitted in the clear. Even though your laptop may not pick it up and say, hey, there's a wireless network available, it's still being broadcast, and if you have the tools, you can gather that information. It'll allow you to locate all the wireless networks and show what types of encryption they're using, what types of protocols, if they're open or secure, whether it's WEP WPA. And once you find one, you can then capture the packets on that network to capture the SSID. From there, you can send out what's called a deauthentication packet, or you can knock those clients off the network. By deauthenticating them, then they're going to reconnect pretty much away. As

they're reconnecting, you're going to capture those packets, and you'll be able to capture the actual login. It's encrypted, but you'll be able to capture the packets and you can identify that as login attempts because it's what's called a four-way handshake as they reconnect. And once you have that information, then you can brute force your way in or dictionary attack or hash attack to discover that password. If it's something simple, you can get through that relatively quickly. If you're using more secure passwords or a stronger password with like uppercase, lowercase, special characters that wouldn't necessarily be in a dictionary, then it could take longer. It could take days, hours, weeks, months, just depends upon the strength of your password. Having said that, there are other tools available that can bypass even having to crack the password. Most routers, especially the home office and SOHO routers, have what's called WPS. It allows you to do a push button on either side and automatically configure the client and the server, or the client and the wireless access point, rather. There are insecurities or some vulnerability within WPS, the PIN that it generates, that it can go out and attack that at the wireless access point and crack the WPA or WPA2 password. There are some tools available that do not take an extreme amount of knowledge to utilize. You need to be aware of these things. You need to make your networks as secure as possible.

EAP, PEAP, and LEAP

The next sets of concepts I want to cover are EAP, or Extensible Authentication Access Protocol, and then two variations of that, PEAP and LEAP. EAP, or Extensible Authentication Access Protocol, is a set of authentication frameworks for wireless networks. What you need to understand is that there are five different types of Extensible

Authentication Access Protocol that are in existence, two that we need to know for the exam that are adopted by the WPA and the WPA2 standard. We have EAP with TLS. We have EAP with Pre-Shared Key, and we have EAP with an MD5 hash. Those three have been deprecated. The two that we need to be aware of are LEAP and PEAP. Let's cover that in a little more detail. LEAP stands for Lightweight Extensible Authentication Protocol, and this one is not in use, but we need to be aware of what it is. It's a proprietary protocol developed by Cisco, and it was a stopgap to WEP insecurities, and it lacked Windows support. It was not in use or used by the Windows environment. It was strictly for Cisco environments. That itself is why it doesn't have the wide acceptance or it's been deprecated. It's easy to configure, no digital certificates, which is great. But it's also bad because it's easy to configure and there are no digital certificates. You have a lot of insecurities there. Clear text transmissions. And, it has since been deprecated. The one that we need to be focused on is PEAP, or Protected Extensible Authentication Protocol, and that was jointly developed by Cisco, RSA, and then Microsoft. Cisco develops the networking protocols. RSA deals with security. And then Microsoft with the operating systems. This joint effort ensured that it is in use or wide adoption throughout the IT and the tech community. It has Windows support, and it uses digital certificates on the authentication server. It gives you that extra layer of security by authenticating saying, I'm not going to just connect to any rogue access point, like we mentioned previously with that evil twin. If we're using PEAP, that will prevent that from happening. We have to authenticate to what we're connecting to, to the wireless access point and then ultimately to the server. It's going to establish an encrypted channel between the client and the server via a TLS tunnel. It gives us that extra layer of protection.

802.11x Wireless Protocols

Let's now talk about IEEE 802.11x wireless protocols. What we're talking about here is wireless communication and 802.11 standards operate either over 2.4GHz or the 5GHz radio frequencies. Over time, we've gotten an increase in speed for the most part, and we've gone from 1 Mbps or 2 Mbps up to 14 Gbps, theoretically. 802.11 was the original standard, and that was 1 Mbps or 2 Mbps, and that operated over the 2.4GHz frequency. Next was 802.11a, and that was a big jump. That was 54 Mbps over the 5GHz frequency. Then the next iteration of that was 802.11b, and that dropped down to 11 Mbps and operated over the 2.4GHz range. But wait a minute, that's a step backwards. Why are we doing that? Well the big difference between the two is the fact that 5 GHz has a much shorter range than 2.4 GHz. So for those devices that needed very high speed or high throughput, you could in fact use 802.11a, but the range was much shorter than it was with 802.11b. That's the big difference is the range. 802.11g, however, was a big jump up, and that gave us pretty much parity with 802.11a as far as throughput, 54 Mbps. But it had the advantage of operating over 2.4 GHz with an expanded range. Then we jumped to 802.11n up to 600 Mbps, again a huge jump, 2.4 or 5 GHz. Then, up until recently, 802.11ac was the latest and greatest with throughput up to 1.3 Gbps. That operated only over the 5GHz network. And we have 802.11ax, also known as Wi-Fi 6, and that can theoretically go up to 14 Gbps, although, in reality, probably a lot less than that, at least for. But as devices get better and the frequency range expands, we'll see speeds approaching that 14,000 Mbps or 14 Gbps. it operates over 2.4GHz or 5GHz range. You may also see something referred to as 802.11i. That's often referred to as WPA2, and that provides for additional security enhancements focused on authentication. But it does not refer to speed or frequency like the other things we just mentioned.

RADIUS Federation

A concept I want to make sure we're clear on is RADIUS Federation. We've discussed what RADIUS is, remote access dial-in user service, and federation is simply connecting systems or combining systems. A RADIUS federation connects a common system of authentication and credentials database. It uses RADIUS servers to connect these systems wirelessly. Additionally, because it's a federated system, it can be used by multiple applications or platforms.

Wi-Fi Protected Setup (WPS)

WPS is designed to make it easy for devices to join Wi-Fi networks with minimal effort. Devices without screens or keyboards are ideal for this. Some printers, as an example, they can easily join a Wi-Fi network by pushing a button on both devices, one on the actual printer, in this case, and then the access point on the other. Or some devices without that push button functionality will have a hardcoded pin, usually on a sticker somewhere on that device. Even though WPA2 encryption is used, assuming the actual wireless access point is using WPA2, it's very secure. As of the time of this writing, it has not been cracked. It's considered very, very secure. However, the WPS pin can be easily cracked. That pin is eight characters long, but only seven of those characters are used. The eighth character is a checksum. The first three and then the last four are in two separate groups. It ends up being fairly easy to brute force crack given the power of today's PCs.

Captive Portal

When we're dealing with public or open Wi-Fi networks, the concept of a captive portal comes into play. You may have been in a coffee shop or some location, a hotel, where you've attempted to log on to that Wi-Fi network and then you get some pop-up that says, before your able to access the network, you need to either agree to our acceptable terms of use, or you need to put in your username and password. It might be your last name and your room number or whatever if it's a hotel. Once you put in those credentials, then it allows you access to the network. That captive portal in quarantine or put you into a walled garden and say, you can't get any further until you authenticate. Once you do, then it allows you through, and you can have full access to the internet. Well, those types of things are vulnerable to different types of attacks, again depending upon the implementation. But one example would be packet sniffing. If a hacker sits on the network and is sniffing the packets, once you authenticate, again, it just depends upon the sophistication of the captive portal and of the network itself or the tool that's being used. But if it's simply just looking for authentication by, like say, username and password, well, it knows your IP address, and it knows you're MAC address. Once you provide those credentials, it says you're authenticated, off you go. Well if someone is sniffing the network and they get your IP address and the MAC address, they could then, in turn, spoof both of those pieces and make it look like it's you. As soon as they hop on the network with that IP address and the MAC address, well the captive portal thinks that they're already authenticated, and it allows them to go through as well. That's one method. Or they could put up a fake captive portal. Again, if you're in some type of coffee shop, there may not even be typically a captive portal in place. But you, as the unsuspecting user, would not necessarily know that if you see a pop-up and says hey, you need to put in your username and password, 9 times out of 10, people don't think twice about it. They just go out and start putting those things in. Well those things could, in fact, again, be captured by someone sitting there just being malicious and capturing this information to get usernames, passwords, or whatever other things are trying to gain from a credentials point of view.

Installation Considerations
When it comes to installing Wi-Fi on our networks, some installation considerations to take into account. We can do things such as site surveys, which are a walkthrough of a facility to visually confirm locations, potential hotspots, impediments, maybe brick walls or some other things that could impede the flow of our signal. We can visually inspect those things to make sure that we have those accounted for. We can also generate things called heat maps, and that is typically done with software and some type of analyzer to visually show where signal is weak or non-existent you can add additional hotspots or access points. That's used in conjunction with Wi-Fi analyzers, that is, again, hardware and software that allows a tech to walk a site and identify areas of weak signal and what channels are best. It will show what devices are attached to what channels, which are better than others, and will allow you to switch channels potentially to find the best one for that specific device and improve the overall quality of the signal for a specific device.

Access Points/Wi-Fi Security

Let's now talk about some concepts around securing your network from things like access points, Wi-Fi security. So rule number one is to disable SSID broadcast. That's not a foolproof method. It doesn't mean someone still can't find you. But why give out extra information if you don't have to? Disable the SSID broadcast. It's the Service Set Identifier, the Wi-Fi network name, in other words. Also, it doesn't provide security. This SSID can still be sniffed. However, let's not give away too much information. Next, use something referred to as MAC filtering. We talked about a MAC address before, with MAC filtering, we pre-select what MAC addresses can connect to the Wi-Fi network. It still doesn't make it completely foolproof because people can do MAC spoofing just like they do IP spoofing. If they can sniff the network or if they explicitly know the MAC address ahead of time, it's possible to spoof that MAC address and then still connect to the network. Also, common sense administration. Always change the default admin username and password. I know it sounds ridiculous, but in all honesty, if you do a quick bit of research, you'll find that common usernames and passwords, literally password or password123 are out there, and they're very common, so people don't take the time to secure their networks. Also, we want to make sure we use the strongest encryption and authentication available. In other words, don't use WEP when we have WPA or WPA2 available. Keep things up to date and use the strongest encryption and authentication possible. Also, keep access points up to date with patches and firmware. There are a lot of home networks, small office networks, mid-sized companies, they install a router or Wi-Fi access point, and then they forget about it. They don't go back and touch it again. Make sure those default usernames and passwords are changed. Make sure they're locked down. Make sure you use the strongest encryption possible. But just like any other computer, any other device, make sure we keep things patched and updated. Next, we want to make sure we have antenna placement and signal strength flushed out. Antenna placement is critical for proper coverage, so it should be placed near the center of the area to be covered, and antennas can be internal or external. There is not one type that's better than the other. It depends upon the manufacturer, and it also depends upon the type of router. However, there are always new models coming out, and you can also add additional access points within a Wi-Fi network to extend coverage. Next, we have antenna placement and signal strength. Antennas can be omnidirectional or unidirectional. Omnidirectional provides coverage in a 360-degree fashion, whereas directional antennas focus the signal primarily in one direction, usually over longer distances. If you have an area where you want blanket coverage everywhere, then an omnidirectional antenna is your best bet. If you have somewhere where you want to broadcast coverage or direct coverage to one area but not to the sides or not behind you, as an example, then a directional antenna is your best bet. Something else to consider is antenna signal strength. Antennas are rated in terms of gain value or dBi numbers. A wireless antenna with a 10 dBi would be 10x stronger than a 0 dBi. Some routers, some wireless routers provide control over that. You can turn the power levels up or down, depending upon the environment. Some out-of-the-box routers may not have that functionality, but you can download hacked firmware that can give you that additional functionality. It's there, but it's not exposed via the common, out-of-the-box user interface. We can combine with site surveys to identify optimal placements. You can take devices and walk the site, and determine where the signal strength is going to be best. Additionally, you can also identify where there's going to be dead spots. You may need to position your antenna so that you account for those dead spots, or you may add additional access points to the network.

Band Selection/Width

When we're talking about Wi-Fi connected access, there are two main bands that you connect with. You have 2.4 GHz and also 5 GHz. 2.4 GHz was the earlier band. It's 100 MGz wide, and it spans from 2.4 GHz to 2.5 GHz. Just 14 channels and used by many devices outside of just Wi-Fi collectivity, such as microwaves, baby monitors, Bluetooth, wireless video cameras. In reality, only channels 1, 6, and 11 are separated from each other with enough space or enough frequency in between to not overlap. That's an important consideration to keep in mind when you're doing channel selection, especially if you have multiple access points within the same building, or if you have neighboring Wi-Fi access points, perhaps from other companies or neighbors, and you want to make sure you're not overlapping and getting a diminished signal, not having frequencies overlap. In 'order to do that, you would pick channels 1, 6, or 11 to ensure that you have some distance between you and the next set of channels that you'd want to use. On the 5 GHz range, we have 25 10-MGz channels, and the bonding of channels is possible within the 5 GHz range. So 802.11n bonds 2 20-MGz channels, and also 802.11 ac bonds 4 20-MGz channels. 802.11n, would give you 40 MGz of bandwidth, 802.11ac can bond 4 20-MGz channels for a total of 80 MGz of bandwidth. If we look at this in a little more detail, the 2.4-GHz channel frequencies, channels 1, 6, and 11 are far enough apart, there's a 3-MGz space in between those channels, so they don't overlap. If you're looking for the spread that has the most channels without overlapping, these are the 3 that you should pick, 1, 6, and 11.

Fat vs. Thin Access Points and Stand-alone vs. Controller-based

Fat or thick access points have everything needed to manage wireless clients, so all the intelligence and all the management features are in fact built in to the actual client. Multiple access points need to be managed individually, so that's the downside. The upside is it's easy to install. It's great for small offices or small environments. We have everything we need. We don't need additional hardware. However, if we have multiple points as our environment starts to grow and we have more than one access point, they need to be managed individually. A thin access point is just the radio and the antenna and can be managed via a central switch. As you may have guessed, multiple thin access points can be managed and configured centrally. We have the benefit of being able to do everything at once from a centralized location. If we have a large environment or one that has many access points, that very quickly becomes an advantage. When we're talking about stand-alone versus controller-based, it's very similar to fat vs. thin. Stand-alone access points provide everything required to service clients. They do, however, have limited encryption, typically no load balancing, and no enterprise class functionality. Not to say that some don't, but typically we have less functionality, less features, less encryption than we do with controller-based. To compare and contrast the two, it's very similar when we're talking about stand-alone versus controller-based, it's very similar to fat vs. thin with regard to features and functionality and ease of management. One, it's very easy to set up, it's very self-contained, but it doesn't scale very well. Stand-alone access points are usually found in smaller environments. Typically much less expensive, a little bit easier to configure on one-by-one basis. But as we start to scale, that becomes a little bit unmanageable. For stand-alone controllers, well suited to smaller environments, contain everything needed to manage clients updates and patches, however, need to be done individually. That's where it starts to become unruly. If we have multiple access points, we don't want to have to go around and do that to every single one, especially if we have dozens or potentially hundreds depending upon the size of our environment, especially if we're in between multiple buildings and we have some type of geodispersement. Also no load balancing and limited redundancy. Also, we have limited IDS or intrusion detection functionality. Conversely, with controller-based, we have enterprise-level features and also scalability. Access points are configured and managed centrally. Again, as that starts to scale, that becomes a big deal. Updates and patches are distributed from a central location. It's much easier to manage at scale. Load balancing and redundancy also between access points. As we move throughout an environment, it has the ability to load balance or to find the best or the closest access point, the one that can service the client the best. Also, we have more full-featured IDS functionality. Something to keep in mind, the fat client or the thick client and also the stand-alone controllers very well suited to small environments or medium-sized environments that work well. However, as we start to scale, we want to able to manage things from a central location. In summary, we various cryptographic protocols and the underlying information for each. We talked about a number of authentication protocols, including the relatively new WPA3 and its associated authentication protocols and some of the benefits of WPA3. And we talked about the various methods and then installation considerations, including site surveys, heat maps, Wi-Fi analyzers, antenna placement.

Chapter 11 How to Implement Secure Mobile Solutions

In this chapter we'll be covering Implementing Secure Mobile Solutions. We'll be talking about connection methods and receivers, along with mobile device management, also enforcement and monitoring, and then deployment models. At a high level, we want to talk about connection methods. We want to talk about mobile device management concepts, also talk about enforcement and monitoring, and then also deployment models. There's a lot of information in each of these categories, and it's important to understand that we have a good concept or a good understanding of how these things tie into our overall security posture. Mobile connectivity is a big deal. Everyone is mobileadays, we have remote workers, teleworkers, so it's important that we understand how this fits into the big picture. Let's go ahead and dig in and talk about connection methods. There's a lot of ways that we can connect to our corporate networks. We can connect via cellular, Wi-Fi, SATCOM, not as common as some of the other ones, but for military installations, SATCOM is a big deal. Also Bluetooth, NFC or near field communication. We also have ANT or ANT+, which connects health devices and gym equipment. Also Infrared and then USB. There's connection concerns and security concerns with all of these different methods of communication. If we take a look at each of these individually, there are some unique challenges that we face. To start off with cellular, cellular or mobile phones in general have numerous potential security risks, not the least of which, if we have a cell phone that we're carrying around in our pocket that connects to our corporate resources. If we have no password or no pin on that device, if we leave it somewhere, if it's lost, stolen, or somehow compromised, anyone could pick up that device and have access to corporate emails, corporate resources, or more depending upon what is on that device. It's important that we make sure all of our devices have passwords or pins, and we'll talk more about that later as far as mobile device management so we can force that. If someone's using a device to connect to our corporate resources, we can make sure that they do, in fact, have a password or a pin. Also, unpatched operating systems or applications. If people download applications to their phone, or even if we push applications out in a corporate setting, if we don't update those applications or update the operating system on the phone, it's just like any other operating system or any other application. The phone is no different or a cellular device or mobile device is no different than a PC, laptop, server. They need to be patched and updated periodically. Next, you have jailbreaking or rooting. It's very popularadays, especially with iPhones, to jailbreak that device or gain root access to that device so they can install their own applications. They can bypass the App Store, download things or increased functionality or turn on features that may not be readily accessible from the stock or the factory OS. Jailbreaking is a definite security concern for IT professionals or security professionals because those phones are no longer managed or manageable. Those phones are able to bypass our security settings, and they can install whatever they want. When you bypass the app stores, especially in the iOS space, those things are very well vetted. They have security guidelines and best practices they must follow to even be admitted into these App Store. When you bypass that and you go to your own app stores, these off-on-the-side jail broken app stores, people will create their own apps and add functionality that is not vetted as thoroughly as it would be in the App Store. You run potential security risks by having that in the environment. Then, we have unauthorized applications.

They can either jailbreak the phone from the Apple Store perspective of the App Store perspective, whether it's Apple or Android, or they could install unauthorized applications from a company perspective, meaning the company says you can install applications A, B, C, and D, but the person goes in and installs their own applications. That could potentially bypass the security because IT security, again, doesn't know what ports they go over, what things they access, or what mechanisms they have in place that could potentially be a security risk. As an IT professional, we should mandate or have a list of what applications can and cannot be used on those corporate resources. Then last but not least in this category, everyone's favorite topic is malware. Malware is everywhere, laptops, PCs, desktops, servers, so on. It also exists in the mobile phone space or the cellular space. If you have a mobile phone, iOS is not as susceptible, but it still exists. Android much more so because it's more of an open environment. People can create apps not necessarily through a rigorous vetting process like they have in the Apple Store. But malware exists on both sides. Don't develop a false sense of security and say oh, I have an Apple device. I'm completely immune. There is malware. There are potential security risks with every device. Some methods to secure our mobile devices and our cellular communication in general would be authentication or two-factor authentication. We want to make sure that we authenticate. We put in a username and password. We want to make sure we have a pin or some type of biometrics, thumbprint or fingerprint of some sort, or a two-factor authentication. If we're going to go connect to a specific service, a lot of those services will offer a two-factor authentication. Typically that means they will send an SMS or a text to that phone, you'll need to have the password. Then you'll also need to verify that you're on the phone that was registered with that service. They'll send a password to that device via text. You'll put that text password back in, and that's the two factor. That way someone has to have your phone in addition to being able to try to access that specific resource. There are some other ones out there like context-aware authentication, which we'll talk about in a bit that offers a little easier experience, less friction involved. You don't have to have the device and go through an extra couple of steps by getting that pin or that text from the website or the resource to put back in again. We'll talk about those in just a minute as well. But then we want to also make sure that we verify and authenticate downloaded applications. We need to make sure that if we download something from the App Store or from the internet or from wherever that we have a mechanism in place to verify and authenticate that that application is authorized by the company, is not manipulated or somehow tainted or tampered with prior to delivery. Also, make sure we put in anti-malware software just like we have on a PC or laptop. We want to make sure we have anti-malware and antivirus software on those mobile devices. That way we capture the malware before it gets a chance to take a foothold within our system. Also, we have firewalls. It's a good idea to have a firewall in place if you're in an environment where the risks necessitate that. Everything we talk about within IT security in general, there's a risk/reward. There's a what's the chances of it happening? What's the actual damage if it occurs? What's the likelihood of it occurring? The annual loss expectancy and the single loss event. A lot of things go into play when we're talking about risk analysis. Does the amount of effort that's going to have to be put in place outweigh or justify the actual action? In other words, to put it another way, if we have to spend a thousand hours or say a million dollars for some type of security solution, but the actual thing that's preventing might only cost us 10 hours and maybe $1000 to remediate, well then it's not worth it. We have to have that risk return mentality. Then it goes without saying, we need to have the ability to do a remote disable and/or remote wiping. Most phones have that ability already built in for the individual users, and then there's a corporate or an enterprise mechanism that allows that as well. If that device is lost, stolen, compromised in some way, we can number 1 locate it. We can look on a map and geolocate that device. Or, at the very least, remote disable that device so they can't use it or remote wipe it. All the data is completely removed from that device. And then last but not least, we need to make sure we have encryption in place. That way, if for some chance, the remote disable or the remote wipe doesn't work or is inaccessible, well then we can make sure, at the very least, that the data is encrypted on that device. Someone would need to use a biometric mechanism like a fingerprint or username/password to get into the phone. They couldn't use a third-party tool to extract that data.

Securing Wi-Fi
When it comes to securing Wi-Fi, a couple main things that we should be aware of, and you're probably familiar with some of this, but just to reiterate, we need to make sure that we are disabling the SSID. None of these are foolproof, none of them are going to stop an experienced attacker from doing what they're doing. But disabling the Security Set Identifier, or the SSID, more skilled hackers from finding the network, but it will prevent clients who are just casually browsing from discovering your network. You're going to eliminate some of the casual ones that could eventually end up becoming problems. You're not going to eliminate the experienced hackers, however. Next is MAC filtering. MAC filtering predefines which Media Access Control, or MAC

addresses, can connect to that router or that access point. it will not prevent a skilled hacker from spoofing that MAC address, but it does keep the casual browsers, the casual, lower-level hackers, or miscreants, or, whatever you want to call them, from attaching to your network, because you're going to say only these MAC addresses are allowed. If they're skilled, they will be able to spoof that MAC address and then connect anyway. And then, Require Security Connectivity Protocols, we want to make sure we're using the most secure protocol available. No WEP, no WPA. If it all possible, require WPA2-PSK with AES, or Advanced Encryption Standard. That uses a pre-shared key with AES. That's currently considered the most secure standard, there are some other ones you can do at enterprise level, but they have to contact a RADIUS server, or they have to have a certificate, but for the average user, especially for a home environment or a small office, a medium-sized environment, WPA2 with a pre-shared key using AES, make sure you don't use TKIP, use AES, that's considered most secure.

Near Field Communication (NFC)
Most commonly, we're seeing near field communications in use for things like contactless payment systems, the iPhones, Android devices, Apple Pay. All those types of things have the NFC infrastructure in place, but it does pose some security concerns, things like eavesdropping, data corruption or manipulation, or interception. Just like with any communication, there's always that potential for a man-in-the-middle attack or someone to intercept that communication. With near field communication or NFC, they're hampered because of the fact that it's a very close-range technology. They have to be very close to you to be able to do any of those types of things anyway. However, that's not to say that someone can't sit next to or stand next

to some type of payment checkout system and gather information, try to manipulate that data or intercept the communication. Don't just assume just because, I only have to be maybe a foot away that I'm safe. No, someone could be standing nearby or they could have some type of device placed nearby that could intercept that communication. Some ways we can prevent some of that is by establishing secure channels. If those secure channels are established and that communication is encrypted, then we thwart a lot of those efforts. Even if they do intercept that communication, they're not going to able to do anything with it because, that communication is encrypted.

Additional Areas of Concern

Some additional areas of concern are common attack vectors like intercepting data, man-in-the-middle attack, and data corruption. These things can apply to any type of communication interaction between two devices. Some additional areas of concern are common attack vectors that are common to any communication mechanism. Like intercepting data, man-in-the-middle attacks or data corruption. These things apply to things like satellite communications, Bluetooth, we're going to talk about Bluejacking and Bluesnarfing in another chapter, ANT or ANT+, which is the connection between health and gym equipment, heart rate monitors, and then infrared devices. We need to disable unnecessary or unneeded services and ensure that devices are patched, updated, and encrypt communication where possible. With things like satellite communication, there are some vulnerabilities. Some of them are embedded and maybe not easily upgraded, but it's important that we understand that every type of communication has its own unique challenges, and there are common exploits, or at least in concept, among all these different types of communication mechanisms. SATCOM used by government installations, military installations, very important that we keep those things patched and updated. Make sure that we understand that vulnerabilities do exist. Just because it's a military grade, whatever, it doesn't mean it's impervious or immune to viruses, malware, and the targets or the information they're trying to get at. They would be considered typically high value targets. Bluetooth, if you don't need it for anything, turn it off because they are susceptible to things like Bluejacking and Bluesnarfing. But, as new devices come on board, smartwatches that have that connectivity, while there may be an opportunity for hackers to exploit that, currently not as much of a problem. Infrared, a lot of laptops, especially the older ones, have infrared built in. Some of the desktops have infrared built in. If you don't need that, which typically you will not, then turn that off because even though it's a line of sight communication mechanism, it is exploitable. It is vulnerable. You can use infrared ports to gain information or gain access to a system. Turn those things off. We want to harden our systems by disabling unnecessary things. Because the more things that are there, the more things that are exploitable. If we don't even know that they're turned on or we don't know that they're in play, then we're not going to monitor them, and they're going to fall out of compliance over time and then introduce additional vulnerabilities into our environment. Disable unnecessary services, harden our systems where possible.

MicroSD HSM

A MicroSD HSM offers the same features as PCIe-based HSM chapter that we find in servers. It can be used to encrypt communication, to encrypt storage, for key generation or for digital signatures. It can also provide, depending upon the type of card, it can also do true random number generation, provide TRNG functionality, and then also cryptocurrency use cases, we can use it as a cold wallet of sorts and encrypt those transactions. A MicroSD HSM can be used for all of these purposes, can be mobile, and be moved from device to device, and give the same levels of encryption and security that we find on servers and bring that to the mobile environment, assuming your device can handle a MicroSD card.

Mobile Device Management (MDM, MAM, and UEM)
Next let's talk about mobile device management, and three things here, we have MDM, or mobile device management being software that enables the provisioning of mobile devices, application of policy, remote wiping, and some security policies that we can push down via certificate to these mobile devices and provision them, whether it be a corporate owned device or a BYO device. Next, we have mobile application management, or MAM, and this is more granular control over mobile devices, especially BYOD Devices where policy enforcement can be set at the app level along with application containerization, meaning we can apply policy to a specific application, but not affect the rest of the applications on a user's device. We can even control what can be copied between applications on a device or if things could be uploaded to the cloud based upon policies pushed down from mobile application management software. Then we have unified endpoint management, or UEM, and this is an evolution of MDM EMM, which is enterprise mobility management, and also, MAM, or mobile application management. UEM combines the features of these different types of technologies along with being able to manage desktops, laptops, Internet of Things devices, pulling all of these different feature sets under one umbrella.

SEAndroid

Next, we have security enhanced Android, or SEAndroid, and this is an SELinux, or a security enhanced Linux kernel security chapter and its purpose is to provide a mechanism for supporting access, control security policies among other things, and when I say that, I mean things like mandatory access control where we mandate that things must happen in a certain fashion, it's not discretionary, it's mandatory, and it was originally developed by the NSA and released to open source in December of 2000, so it's been around for a while, and it's been part of the Android code base for quite a while as well. The takeaway here is it restricts actions that installed software can take with the end goal being to enhance security on that device. We all know the Android app store has some vulnerability issues, but guess what, Does the iOS app store, so there are vulnerabilities on both sides of the fence, so it's a bit of a religious argument as to which side or which camp you're in, but understand that both sides of the fence, whether it's iOS or Android, both try very hard to make things as secure as possible, and SE Android, or security enhanced Android, is one of the mechanisms put in place to help achieve that goal.

Device Security

Mobile devices pose a number of challenges? We've talked about some of those. What if that device is lost or stolen? What if it is compromised while on public Wi-Fi, or how about asset tracking? Do even know where all of our mobile devices are? Do we even have a mechanism to know if they've been lost or stolen, or perhaps going into areas where they shouldn't be going into? Do we know our mobile devices? Do they have applications that they're supposed to have or ones they're not supposed to have? And what mechanisms do we have in place to manage that and prevent that from happening? There are some ways that we can enforce that. Corporate policies need to be enforced. Let's start with policy-based enforcement, strong passwords, we're going to require that via policy. It's not just a recommendation, we're going to require it. We'll push it out with our mobile device management software, group policy if we're talking about Active Directory environment, we want to ensure that we're pushing out that strong password and/or a pin requirement. We want to make sure that we require lock screens and screensavers so that that phone is not used within whatever 30 seconds, a minute, minute and a half. Then that lock screen kicks in, or if it's a desktop or laptop, and then a screensaver kicks in. That way, if they walk away, we can be assured that that resource is secured. Then, disabling unnecessary services. This goes, of course, for iPhones and Android devices, mobile devices, in general, but it also goes for laptops and desktops. We want to make sure that we disable things we don't need. Then application and software control. We want to make sure that we have policies in place and mechanisms in place to make sure that only approved applications are installed and then software control so that the ones that are installed get updated and patched on a routine basis. Everyone knows there is nothing worse than reaching into your pocket, expecting to find your phone, and then all of a sudden, I've lost my phone, or you think you lost your phone You start searching everywhere, you start opening drawers, looking in your desk, and so on, all over the place, your heart stops, everything comes to a screeching halt and then you reach into your other pocket and realize, oh, thank goodness it's in my other pocket. And all of a sudden, everything is with the world again. All of our lives are wrapped up in our phones today, everything from personal information, banking information, personal photos to corporate access, corporate resources, and corporate emails. We want to make sure that we have these things locked down and secure, and we have the ability to remote wipe them or disable them if they're, in fact, lost. For device security, we want to make sure we have a few things in place. We want to have full device encryption, we want to make sure that the contents of that device are not able to be retrieved by an unauthorized person or persons, so full device encryption, even if they remove that hard drive or they connect that phone to some specialized device, we don't want them to have access to that data. Next, we have remote wiping. If in fact, that phone is lost or stolen, we want to have the ability to push a button and remotely wipe that device. Even if it's off the network, the command is issued, and then once that device attaches to the network, the remote wiping would take place. Next, we want to make sure we have GPS enabled or some type of location services, whether it's find my iPhone, or find my Mac, or some Android equivalent, we want to make sure that GPS is enabled We can see where that asset is geographically. We can geofence and say it's not allowed to leave this area, or if it goes into this area, please alert us, that way we can have secure areas that people should not be going into or we can pre-define areas they shouldn't leave and then be alerted, it goes both ways. And then we have mobile device management. In general, we need to have some software and some infrastructure in place to manage those mobile devices, and there are a few different ways to do this. We can either manage the entire device or we can cordon off a piece of that device, so if someone wants to use their own personal phone or their personal device, we can install MDM software on that device and cordon off a piece of that device for corporate use. That way, it's encrypted and it has remote wipe capabilities, and we don't affect the rest of that person's personal information of personal phone, but regardless of how you do it, mobile device management software is critical because we have people using mobile phones and mobile devices more frequently than they're using computers nowadays or laptops. Mobile devices are very much a part of our corporate infrastructure just as much, if not more, than PCs, so they need to be secured appropriately.

Application Security and Key Credential Management
When we're talking about application security, we want to make sure that we have such things as authentication, we need to make sure that applications are only allowed if they're authenticated, they are vetted either through some type of external process like an app store, or an internal process through our company. Some corporate process that says you're only allowed to install these 4, 5, 10 whatever applications, anything else is denied. Next, we also want to make sure we have geo-tagging. We want to have the ability to say this person is either in an area they're supposed to be or they're not, and if that phone travels in and out of an area or is lost or stolen, we can be alerted very quickly. Next will be biometrics, application security, we should have some method of requiring some type of biometric login for very secure applications. The iPhone has one built-in, Android devices are similar, where they have a fingerprint reader. Yes, you have a fingerprint reader to get in to the actual phone itself, but then certain applications require an additional level of authentication before the application will open. We can enforce that as well. Even if someone left their phone unattended and someone were to come by and pick that phone up while it was unlocked, they still couldn't get into those applications where we deem them to be highly

secure, because they'll need that additional authentication like biometrics. Next, push notification services. If we have a large environment, it's going to be very unwieldy and certainly not scalable to have someone go around and talk to one person at a time and say, by the way, update your software; hey, by the way, update your software, and on and on and on, not scalable. In a small office, sure, we can stand up in the front of the room and say, everyone, update your iPhone or update your software. In an environment with multiple offices, thousands of employees, not scalable. Push notification allows us to push out to everyone in one shot, hey, update that piece of software, update that application, we can push notifications out across the board. We've talked about encryption. We want to make sure that our devices are in fact encrypted, and a lot of these things are built into the newer devices, so they become less and less of a of a management issue. The iPhone, Androids can be encrypted. IPhone by default is fully encrypted. That way, if the device is lost or stolen, it's a lot less likely that that information will be compromised, and also key or credential management. Let's take a look at that a little more deeply. With key or credential management, we want to manage the device content, access, and authentication. That is critical to providing a secure environment. The company needs the ability to manage the devices and control access. Digital certificates are often used to authenticate. It pushes down a certificate, so if you want to connect to the corporate resources, there is a certificate that's going to push down a profile to your phone, and it's going to mandate certain things. Maybe the screen saver will kick in or the device will lock after a certain number of minutes, or you can only access these specific types of applications, or you'll need this to connect and authenticate to our Wi-Fi; whatever the case might be. That way you have the ability to control with some

347

granularity how people access and connect to your corporate resources.

Authentication

Then we're talking about authentication, securely connect to corporate resources. Again, we talked about PKI, that public key infrastructure helps to manage how people connect, and if they don't have the certificate, they don't have the authentication, they don't connect to our resources. Also, enforce password policies. We can make sure that people don't use the same password over and over again. We can make sure they change passwords every X number of days, let's say every 45 days. We can also enforce password history and also complexity requirements so that they can't use the same password, maybe say five passwords deep. That way they can't just reuse two passwords back and forth over and over again. We can also say their password has to have some type of complexity. In other words, it has to be maybe capital letters and lowercase, alphanumeric, or special characters or it may have to be a minimum length or a maximum length, so all of these things can help make our environment more secure. Then also, VPN or two-factor authentication. If they want to connect to corporate resources remotely if they're out in the field, coffee shop, they need to VPN in, and that way is over an encrypted secure channel. Even if that communication is, in fact, intercepted, it won't be readable to the hacker or to the person doing the interception. The VPN encrypts that communication. Then also, two-factor, RSA, as an example. Rather than just putting in a username and a password to connect to a VPN, you might have also a two-factor, which means they have to have an RSA token or some type of digital token that says every 30 seconds or every minute, this is going to change so that way the person trying to connect to that VPN, and ultimately to our corporate resources, needs to know their username and password, but also has to be in possession of that token or that two-factor device, whatever that might be. As an example, Google authenticator allows you to manage that two-factor authentication and for a number of services, Gmail, Dropbox, lots of different things can use Google authenticator to manage those keys, and of course, there are other companies, like I mentioned, RSA and a few others that can do the same thing.

Chapter 12 Geo-tagging & Context-Aware Authentication

Geo-tagging is important for a number of reasons. Pictures and documents can be tagged with the GPS coordinates of where it was made. A lot of people don't realize that when they upload pictures to social media, as an example, or they send that picture to others, there is a mechanism in place, it's called the EXIF data, E-X-I-F, if that data is not removed from that photo before it's uploaded, then that data is sitting there, and that person can use an EXIF tool to extract that information from that photograph. It's a potential security risk, as it allows someone to pinpoint that location. You can see here under the details, if you look down towards the bottom, it shows the GPS coordinates of where that picture was taken. The details being latitude and longitude, and also even the altitude of where that's at. Someone can punch in those coordinates and see exactly where that picture was taken. If it's a selfie with your girlfriend or boyfriend or whatever, probably not a big deal. But if it's a military installation and you're taking a picture of some type of battlefield location or government location, or something that has some type of security around it, and you don't realize this and you upload it to whatever, Instagram, social media, send it to someone else, and that other person uploads it to some social media, and that picture gets passed around versus text or instant message, or some other mechanism, that EXIF data is there. That is potentially a big security risk. There's software that can be used to remove EXIF data before things get uploaded, that comes down to corporate policy. You can have a policy in place that says, any photo that needs to be uploaded to any social media should have that information removed. That way it can't be pulled off for any reason.

Context-aware Authentication

Next, you have context-aware authentication. This is a type of two-factor authentication or 2FA, that provides for a more "frictionless" experience. It uses pre-defined rules to determine authentication, or if a more stringent challenge should be used. What do I mean by that? We can set it up to be based on things like device fingerprinting, geo-location, geo-fencing, or geo-velocity. What that means is when you register that device, it's going to look at the device itself. Where are you located? Are you East Coast, West Coast in the US? Outside of US? Where are you on the globe? Also, device fingerprinting. Let's say for instance it's a laptop. Well it can look at your browser, it can look at what fonts are installed, the browser version, drivers, screen size; all these different things that are unique, and when you combine all of those things together, it makes your device very unique against all others, because nobody has exactly the same thing; software, fonts, applications, security settings, screen size, color, depth. All those things go together to make a fingerprint, so that could be one thing. Also geo-location, like I mentioned, where are you located? Geo-fencing. Are you going to leave or enter a certain location? Or geo-velocity, meaning who checked in at say 2:00 in the afternoon on the East Coast, and then you're accessing the same website from 3:00 on the West Coast; that geo-velocity means, it's not feasible that person could've traveled across the country in an hour, or three or four hours. It's not feasible, so it would deny access. What happens is you can automatically allow things to occur if those things met, it's the same IP address or the same device fingerprint, or the same geo-location; you can allow them to just get in with the username and password. Or you can say if they fail any one of these pre-defined rules, then I want to challenge them additionally. Then you might ask for a pin, a two-factor authentication, an SMS text be issued or something. That way, it's frictionless up to the point where it can't verify via this context or authentication mechanism, I'm going to challenge you with some other thing, and then if they pass that, they're given access. If access fails any of the pre-defined rules, then the user can either be denied access out and say, nope, you don't gain access, or, we can be prompted for that more stringent authentication.

Enforcement and Monitoring
When it comes to enforcement and monitoring, there are number of things we need to be aware of, and I'm just going to touch on these briefly just you're aware that they exist and you have to make sure you keep eyes on these things. And that's things like third-party app stores. You have to make sure that our devices are not jailbroken or we restrict access to third-party app stores. We only want the people going to either the app store from Apple or Android, Google. Or we may have an internal company app store and only allow the applications we want them to have, and we would deny access to every other app store or every other download possibility. Next, also rooting in jailbreaking. We need to understand that people will try to root and jailbreak phones. When they do that, they're going to bypass security mechanisms. We need to make sure we have things in place to detect when those devices try to connect to our network and deny access. Also side-loading, custom firmware, carrier unlocking, or firmware over-the-air updates. All of these things should be prevented by corporate policy so that people can't bypass our security. We should make sure we have things in place. If we're going to have a corporately managed mobile policy and mobile infrastructure, we need to also make sure we have the corporately managed

enforcement mechanisms so they if any of these things happen, people try to do their own firmware updates outside of what the corporate policy allows, they try to do carrier unlocking, any of those things should be denied and alerted so that we can go back and investigate further. Why is this person trying to do this? Also, we have camera usage. Some areas don't allow camera use on the phones, so they'll have them either disabled or they require phones without cameras, which is becoming more and more difficult nowadays. Pretty much every phone has a camera, but we can disable that so that people can't take pictures inside of our secure locations. Also, we have SMS or MMS. You want to make sure you understand how those things are being used, understand the security implications. People can text pictures, they can text PDF documents, they can text screenshots of data. It's up to each individual company, do you want to allow or disallow SMS and MMS. Also we have external media. We want to have policies in place to either allow or somehow restrict that external media usage, flash drives, USB drives, thumb drives. Do we want to allow people to be able to plug in and copy data or not? And then we have USB OTG or on the go. This is where USB devices, typically you have a PC and then say a disk drive, a master/slave configuration. Well USB on the go allows both devices to change roles. You can have two devices that typically wouldn't connect with each other be able to connect, and one takes the master, one takes the slave role, and transfer data between the two. There's potential to take a USB drive and plug it into a non-PC device or vice versa and transfer data back and forth. Do we allow that, or do we not allow that? And then recording microphones, that can be a big one. People could potentially go in and turn on a microphone on a laptop or turn on a webcam or so forth and record information without the person knowing. Actors will do that all the time, not to mention people intentionally doing it. You could have someone sitting in a meeting and turn on, record on their laptop, record the contents of that meeting. You may or may not want to allow that depending upon your environment. If in fact that's an issue for your environment, then you can disable that via policy. And we have also GPS tagging. We want to make sure that people are aware, and some of this is with training, that people are aware that GPS tagging exists with photos, with documents, so that they understand what is applicable. They understand what's advisable to send and not send and also the security implications when they do these types of things. And then also policies in place for things like Wi-Fi direct or ad hoc. We want to remove any rogue devices from our network. We want to scan for that and have infrastructure in place that detects when rogue devices are connected. We can even have it set up so that it scans for the manufacturer address. The first half of the MAC address defines the actual manufacturer. We can have policies in place that goes out and scans the network so that if someone were to plug in a Linksys or an ASUS or NETGEAR router, we can scan for those things. In other words, everything in our environment is, say, Cisco, we could scan for any non-Cisco routers or access points connecting. And if that happens, immediately shut that part down, send out an alert, and then have security investigate further. And then we have tethering. Do we allow devices to tether or not to tether? In other words, can someone take a laptop that doesn't have a cellular device inside and tether that to their phone? But that could be potential security risk because someone can then copy the data or send the data from their laptop over a carrier device that's not being monitored through our corporate infrastructure. There are potential security risks involved with that. It's a company choice whether we want to allow that or not. WE also have payment methods. Payment methods are one that has some potential for abuse, If we have the ability to do that in our environment, we need to make sure we secure those resources especially well because that's a big target for hackers and thieves.

BYOD Concerns and Deployment Models
Next we have BYOD concerns, BYOD or bring your own device. That's great for employees because it allows personal choice. You can have whatever device you want and use that in our corporate environment. It's a security challenge, however, for employers because they need to understand the nuances of many different platforms, patch management, lifecycle management. If we have two or three phones that we manage, it is very easy to understand what needs to be managed, the lifecycle of each of those devices, how to patch them, how to keep them updated. If we have 30 different devices, especially if we don't have that exact device in house, then there's nuances to that device that we're not aware of. It's important that we understand how those things function, how they need to be patched. BYOD challenges occur with monitoring, patch management, security leaks, access to data. It saves the company money. They don't have to invest in all of those mobile phones and mobile devices. But there's a trade-off. It comes down to personal choice. As a company, you need to decide which method is best for you. And then we have COPE, corporate owned, personally enabled. This bridges the gap by providing corporate-owned resources that employees can use for personal tasks. Some companies will give you a corporate device and say you cab only use this for corporate work, for corporate endeavors. More and more companies are saying we'll give you a device, we'll give you a phone. You can use it for whatever you want, but understand that we're going to

355

monitor it. We're going to take ownership of it. We have the ability to remotely wipe it whenever we want if you feel that's lost, stolen, compromised. We own that device. There's trade-offs. It bridges the gap, but doesn't necessarily reduce costs because you still have to buy all the devices. But it also keeps people from bringing in their personal devices, so it gives you the ability to manage a little more tightly, but still allow them to use the device for personal tasks. And then we have CYOD, which stands for choose your own device. Again, a variation on the same concept. You have, say, five different devices that you can choose from. It gives them some choice, but the company owns that device, and it's still used and managed and falls under that corporate policy. And then we have two other deployment models. One is corporate owned, and that's the traditional. The company owns the equipment, and they dictate and monitor everything about that piece of equipment, what applications are installed, how it's used, how it's accessed, and, of course, they monitor everything. It also incurs the biggest cost to the company because they have to buy everything. Then we have also VDI or virtual desktop infrastructure. This is where a company provides a thin client to a user where the actual desktop resides on a centralized server. The device or the thin client that the person uses, it can even be a remote desktop session on a full-blown laptop. It doesn't necessarily have to be just a thin client. But the end user uses some mechanism, thin client or RDP connection, to a VDI server, and their actual desktop is then brought up on that VDI server. The nice part about that is all the desktops are essentially managed. They can be patched very quickly. They can be updated and also monitored or shut down or new instances spawned very quickly. That works great in instances where you have a lot of remote workers, perhaps contractors, offshore resources. You can give them a VDI instance very quickly, and then you can either maintain persistent desktops or non-persistent, non-persistent being every time they log on, they get a brand new desktop just like it's the first time they've used it. It will have the applications that they need, but it's a fresh install. Or you could have a persistent desktop meaning when they save things on their desktop, they save the configuration, the look and feel, that stays. That way when they log off and they log on the next day, all of those things, all of these changes they made the modifications will stay. That's better for developers and people that have a lot of customizations that they need. Otherwise, if you have, like, say, teleworkers or telemarketers or people that just do very repetitive tasks that they don't have any specialization or customization needed, then that non-persistent desktop works just as well.

Additional BYOD Concerns
Some other BYOD concerns, just something to think about, is data ownership. When you have people bring their own devices, who owns the data on that device? Again, all of these things should be called out in policy. People should sign off on this. They should read through your policies and sign off when they agree to connect their personal device to the corporate network. There should be some language and definitions around data ownership. Then next we have support ownership. Who's going to support the device if something goes wrong? Patch management. Who's going to push patches out? Is it the user, is up to them to do it, or is the company going to push patches out to make sure that it maintains a certain level to connect to that corporate resource? Same thing with antivirus management. Also, forensics. Do they have access to the entire device, to only a piece of the device, or do they have access at all? Again, it

should be called out within your corporate policy. When it comes to privacy, does the user have any expectation of privacy? If it's a corporately owned device, they don't. But if It's a personally owned device, and they're attaching to corporate resources, there needs to be a clear definition of what is considered private data and not. That's where mobile device management software comes into play. You can cordon off or restrict or containerize a piece of that phone for corporate use, and everything else stays outside of corporate purview, in theory. And then we have onboarding or offboarding. What policies, what training does someone have to go through when they join a company, and then also, when they leave a company? Next, adherence to corporate policies. They have to read a policy that says, you're going to adhere to our policies. It seems a little redundant, but you as a company need to make sure your policies are in place and then also make sure the person has read those policies and agrees to them. Otherwise, they shouldn't have access to that corporate resource. And that leads into user acceptance. You need to make sure they read the policies and then accept. Also, infrastructure considerations. What infrastructure is required to support these BYOD devices? If I allow someone to bring whatever model and version of a device they want and connect to our resources, connect to our corporate environment, should I, as the company, also have a copy or a duplicate of that device? If it's a Galaxy, whatever, S8 as an example, do I need to have an S8 on hand so I can support, understand patch management and lifecycle management of that device. That's, again, cost considerations. And then legal concerns, the legal considerations around acceptable use, which we have here, things they can and can't do, places they can and can't visit, who owns the data, support, and all these things fall under that acceptable use policy. Then last but not least, on-board cameras and on-board videos. In most environments it's not a big deal, but if you're a government installation, a highly secure environment, a factory or a plant, maybe it has highly explosive chemicals, or is potentially a valuable target for hackers or terrorists or, cyber criminals, organized crime, then as a company, you may say, I don't want anyone taking any video or any pictures inside of our environment, maybe inside of a data centre. All of those things need to be spelled out in our acceptable use policies, signed off, reviewed by legal, and signed off by the individual before you gain access to the network. In summary, we covered four main topics at a high level. We talked about connection methods. We talked about mobile device management concepts. Also talked about enforcement and monitoring. And then we talked about deployment models, keeping yourself and your workforce secure while on the move or at a remote location.

Chapter 13 How to Apply Cybersecurity Solutions to the Cloud

In this chapter, we'll be talking about Applying Cybersecurity Solutions to the Cloud. We'll be talking about cloud security controls, talking about high availability, and the subcomponents, including storage, network, and compute. We'll talk about various solutions, like a cloud access security broker, or CASB. And we'll also talk about Secure Web Gateways, among other things, along with cloud native controls. As we start talking about cloud and cloud security solutions, we need to define what's the main reason or one of the main attraction points to going to the cloud. Security is one component, but also high availability. Let's talk about high availability across zones. What we'll see here is that we have availability zones or failure zones. We have a primary site which will be on-prem in this example, and then a failover sight that lives in the Azure cloud. We have duplicate resources, if you will. So high availability ensures that a resource (and whether that's an application, a service) remains available even when some of the subcomponents fail, whether it be network, storage, compute. We need to architect to make sure that if any of those things fail that we have failover capability to able to move that over to alternate infrastructure. Most cloud providers can enable HA across various pieces of infrastructure when initially creating or after installation. You don't necessarily have to pick that choice away; it can be instantiated after the fact in most cases. Applications need to be architected properly, however, to take advantage of these failover capabilities. It's not magic, we don't just pull a legacy application from an on-prem or something that's old or oldish, it could be a year old, but that's ancient in IT times, things move so fast. A legacy application, you can't just necessarily take it from on-prem, drop it in the cloud, and magically it's HA. It has to be architected to take advantage of failover capabilities, and wherever possible, have the data abstracted above the infrastructure layer, that persistence lives at the application, not necessarily the failover between the subcomponents - storage, compute. If we architect it properly, we could pull a server in and out, and the end user should not even notice. In this case we have resources that are grouped into what's called availability zones, which can be in the same data center, that's not optimal, but it's possible, we could have like four corner redundancy, as we call it. But what we talk about when we're saying availability zones is to have them in separate locations. That way, if one area goes down, even if a datacenter goes down, we can failover to that alternate facility very quickly, and keep things up and running.

Resource Policies

Resource policies enforce organizational standards and compliance. It can also control access to resources and allow access and control what actions may be performed. Not just allowing access to a facility or to a location or to a specific application, but then at a very granular level, say what specific actions can be performed. Also, what types of resources are allowed? Examples are what size VMs could be created. As an example, you might have a self-service portal or a service catalog for your end users where they can spin up resources. While you can set policy to say you have T-shirt sizes, you can have a small, medium and a large - the different sizes and what that means, it will be different for each organization. There is not one size fits all. But by implementing these resource policies, you can deploy and manage your resources in a very standardized way, the one-off applications, the one-off server, or infrastructure, or switch that's not like everything else and it needs to be cared for, managed differently than every other piece of infrastructure. The more we have standardization, the more we have things identical, then the less we have to troubleshoot. If something goes bump in the night, we can pull that out, put a new piece of infrastructure in. You know exactly how it's configured because they're all the same, and it can reduce our troubleshooting time quite drastically.

Secrets Management

When we're talking about the cloud and we're talking about DevOps, secrets can be thought of passwords, keys, APIs, tokens used for applications. The tools and methods for managing digital authentication credentials, secrets. It's just another word for digital authentication credentials. Some things to keep in mind with proper secrets management. Let's take a look at that. Proper and secure storage is critical. Cloud providers offer native secrets management tools. AWS has something referred to as Secrets Manager, Google Cloud Platform has KMS, or Key Management Service, and Azure has something called the Key Vault. There's also third-party secrets management platforms, such as CyberArk, and also HashiCorp has one called Vault. It's critical to have those things properly secured and not stored with your code. It's possible that unauthorized people could have access to those credentials. A few best practices are using resource policies and secrets management to enforce standards and also compliance. Best practices would be to authenticate all access requests that use non-human credentials, APIs. Also, enforce the principle of least privilege. We've always advocated for that in an on-prem environment. It's even more critical when we start talking about cloud and cloud resources. We need to make sure that we have the least privilege necessary People can access and do what they need to do, but not Much that that access can have unintended consequences. Also, enforce role-based access control, or RBAC, and then regularly rotate those secrets and credentials. The ones that I mentioned from Azure, from Google, and from AWS, they have auto rotation capabilities, so it's not something that you necessarily manually have to do; it can be done programmatically. Then also, automate the management of those secrets, and then apply consistent policies. Whether it's on-prem, whether it's on the cloud, or whether it's between multiple clouds, you might be a multi-cloud environment, make sure those policies are consistent across the board, and then track access and also maintain a comprehensive audit trail. It's very important to able to audit and then also go back if something happens to be able to go back and see what exactly happened and why. Remove secrets from code, from configuration files, and from other unprotected areas to make sure that that stuff is not there. So following those best practices will go a long way to making sure that's secure and keeping it from unintended access when in the cloud.

Storage in the Cloud

When it comes to storage, whether it's on-prem or in the cloud, there's three main options, and this pertains to the cloud, as well as on-prem. We have block storage, which can be thought of as local disk? It's either SAN Fibre Channel, or iSCSI. So from a host point of view, that storage appears as a local disk. And then we have file, which is network attached storage, and that's going to give you either CIFS, or SMB, or NFS. Whether it's a Windows box or a Linux box, typically you'll have CIFS or NFS or SMB and NFS. Then we have object, which is relatively new. That's synonymous with S3, although that's not the only object protocol. But S3 is the main one that everyone knows about and most people design, too, so that stores data as objects. It has objects, the metadata about that object, and a GUID. Those three things are stored together in buckets. When it comes to storage and making sure that things are secured properly, a couple things to keep in mind. We want to make sure that we define and then also audit who has permissions to the storage, and, the actual infrastructure as well, not just the file shares or the exports, the actual physical hardware of the infrastructure, or the virtual hardware, but the underlying infrastructure, not just what's exposed to the end user, along with the files and folders, objects. Then encryption. We want to make sure that the data that needs to be encrypted is encrypted, whether that's encrypted at rest, whether it's hardware or software-based; hardware-based will typically give the best performance, software-based usually will have overhead. Then key management. If we need encryption, it's important to understand what impact, if any, that encryption will have on the performance of the disk. Because in some instances, depending upon the piece of infrastructure, encryption can place an extra load on that data. And then also key management. Are they self-encrypting drives? You have a third-party key management platform? All of these things need to be taken into consideration when designing and architecting your encryption strategy. And then replication. Will the data need to be replicated, either on-site between arrays within the data center or within a location, or off-site? Are you replicating to a remote location, are replicating to the cloud? All of these things have funding implications. Then retention policies will also have an impact on the amount of storage required, the funding required. Then we have data sovereignty. If we replicate that data out of a specific location, perhaps a specific geographic location, are there data sovereignty implications? It's important that we understand those things. Then also, when we replicate, are we replicating to a read-only copy, making it perhaps an immutable copy to guard against ransomware? Or is it going to be a fully read-write copy, more of like in an HA environment? And then, we have high availability. High availability costs, location, additional requirements, such as network and compute, the architecture of the application may need the change, so all of these things should be taken into consideration when you're designing your storage, architecting your needs, and just understanding general implications around funding, the amount of infrastructure you need.

Virtual Networks

When we're talking about moving our infrastructure to the cloud or instantiating to begin with, maybe we're starting net new in the cloud, the networks that we'll set up are going to be virtual networks. Virtual networks are created much like physical networks, it's the same concept, the same layout. It's designed to segment traffic and secure communication. Virtual infrastructure is created for various roles. We can have things like load balancers, NAT devices, network address translation devices, traffic managers, Quality of Service, or QoS, managers, also firewalls and secure zones. All of the things that we would see in a physical world or physical infrastructure, there are virtual counterparts, and those things are typically set up in a self-service fashion when we're talking about cloud infrastructure or cloud resources. As an example, imagine if we have a virtual network, this is an example of a virtual network in an AWS instance, or an Amazon Web Services instance. A Virtual Private Cloud, or a VPC, is set up, and as an example, we have a internet gateway, we have a NAT gateway, we talked about that before, a bastion host, which is otherwise known as a jump server. That gives us something to remote into to then access infrastructure behind the firewall. Also the concept of availability zones, we have availability zone 1, 2, and 3, and these are set up to provide us with failover capabilities, whether it's HA or just failover in general, so that if one instance goes down, or one piece of infrastructure goes down, we can failover to another availability zone. That gives us resiliency and makes sure that our applications continue to run even if individual components fail. Availability zones, and then you also see we have public and private subnets, public subnets meaning things that are accessible to the public, private subnets meaning things that are behind a firewall or behind some type of gateway, and then the concept of segmentation, we're segmenting our network, public and private. We're also doing segmentation to give us additional failover capabilities, to reduce chatter, to segment, perhaps, different types of infrastructure or different groups, maybe one group should not talk to or should be cordoned off from another group for security reasons ? You have a number of different components here that we're talking about, but all of these things are set up virtually. They're all set up via a self-service portal when you instantiate within, whether it's AWS, or Azure, or Google, or any of the cloud providers, they have these self-service capabilities that allow you to click a few buttons, and then turn on this infrastructure. It's very convenient. You can provision infrastructure and resources very quickly, and duplicate what you could do, or what would take weeks or perhaps months in a physical world, if you have to go through acquisitions, and RFPs, and then go through your supply chain, and go through all the different hoops that you would typically have to go through to have infrastructure provisioned, you can do in a matter of minutes in the virtual world.

API Inspection and Integration

APIs being, application programming interfaces. A Gartner report recently said that by 2023, over 50% of business to business, or B2B, transactions will be performed via real-time APIs. What that means to us as security professionals is that securing those APIs is going to become more and more important, critically important as things go on, because more and more businesses will be conducted, not necessarily through a GUI front end, not necessarily through any type of human interaction, but through APIs, so if those things are compromised or not secured properly, that could lead to some pretty catastrophic results. Just to give you some examples of how things can be secured, so here we have a user that will send a request, they're going to click on something, but behind the scenes, it's going to be connecting through to an API. So the raw request goes through and then we have things set up that will parse through that request and make sure that it's valid. As it parses through that request, it then takes the key and value representation and runs it through a filter in real time to identify all the things that are being passed through the API. Before it reaches its destination, it's going to go through a parser that then goes through it line by line and says, this is valid, this is valid, this is valid, and you'll see as it goes through it may identify something that's malicious or not constructed properly, and it will deny that. This type of security mechanism you can almost think of as a firewall for an API. It allows things to pass through that are valid, but it will parse through each individual piece of this, and if it finds something that's not legit, or malicious, it will block that request.

Growth of Enterprise Cloud Application

We have user-led, business-led, and IT-led. The reality of it is, again, according to some recent reports, is that roughly 30% of enterprise apps are user-led, about 68% are business-led, meaning roughly about 98% of the cloud applications are led by either business or by users. Only about 2% or maybe a little bit less than 2% are led by IT. What that means is if IT is not in the loop, we have a lot of shadow IT possibilities, a lot of things that can go around IT, so it's important that IT get in the middle of this so they can become the broker to make sure that things are secured properly because if it's business-led or user-led, what's their goal? They want the application, they want the usability, they want the functionality of that application, they're not necessarily thinking about the security implications, so it's important that IT get out in front of this and not be a gating factor because if IT or if security makes things too difficult, what happens? Users just find a way to go around it, we have to make sure that we get in front of it, but we're also an enabler of that technology, not as a service? If we constantly say no, that won't work, you can't do this, you can't do that, can't do this, they'll just stop asking and they'll find ways to get around us. They'll pull out their credit card and they'll just buy the app or they'll provision it via some Software as a Service or a cloud app and we never even know about it. It's important that all these things tie together and that IT gets in front of these things.

Cyber Kill Chain in the Cloud
Cyber kill chain was developed by Lockheed Martin back in 2011. It's based on the military concept of a kill chain. If you understand how things work like the steps that an attacker would need to get from beginning to end and you understand the different points within that process, then you can develop defenses. Like any chain, if you break a link,

then the chain falls apart. What we're doing here is looking for ways to break the links in that chain. Starting off, we have recon. When we're doing recon, it's probing for a weakness, harvesting login credentials or info that can be used for a phishing attack, as an example, and when we're talking about the cloud, publicly available information on company staff, executives, LinkedIn, Facebook, social media networks give out a lot of information. The reconnaissance process allows them to garner a lot of information about their subject. And then we talk about weaponization, step two in the cyber kill chain. Weaponization is creating the deliverable, a deliverable payload, using an exploit in a back door. Based upon publicly accessible information, a lot of times it's easy to create or easy to craft a message, whether it's malware, spyware, ransomware, we could put that in a malicious piece of email, a phishing attack and craft it so that it's very, very specific to the user, we're weaponizing and delivering that payload. Next is delivery. Sending the payload to the victim, a malicious email was quite often the attack vector, but often vulnerable users are discovered via social engineering and publicly available information. Also, Cloud services start to make this more and more efficient because the URLs, certificates are familiar to the user. If they have their weaponized payload delivered via a cloud hosting platform, that URL is familiar to the user, they don't necessarily look at it and question it, they just see I know what that is, and they click on it and then it gets delivered. Next, we have the exploit, so that's executing code on the remote system. Cloud services make this more effective or easier to exploit because popular cloud services are typically whitelisted, so they're allowed to get through the firewalls a lot of times. Instance awareness would help mitigate this step because the platforms and the tools we have that are instance aware can differentiate let's say, a corporate Gmail, or a corporate cloud services account, and a personal cloud services account, so you can allow some things through and not others, rather than just whitelisting everything. Next, would be installation. Installation is installing malware on the target asset. Again, with many cloud providers being whitelisted, this allows attackers to typically evade detection. Instance awareness, again, I'm mitigating control. If we can identify what's corporate and what's personal, we can block the personal accounts, so anything that an attacker would use as an example would be deemed personal or not corporate so it will be blocked, but it would still allow internal users to access these cloud services because it would be identified as a corporate resource. Next, you have command and control and this CNC is creating a channel and persistence where the attacker can control the system remotely. The cloud is great, but it has the potential to make things a little bit easier for the attackers as well, so cloud services make this challenging due to them being trusted in many environments and many popular applications can assist in masking that communication channel. They can use those communication platforms that are typically allowed in an organization, they can use them to deliver their payload and a command and control back and forth. Then we have the action in the cloud, persistence becomes more problematic because the attackers can move laterally across cloud services, they can escalate privileges, potentially encrypt data, or take services offline, they can also steal data or exfiltrate, and then instantiate new instances of cloud resources for things like crypto mining or crypto jacking, a distributed Denial of Service, botnets. It's important that we understand the steps in the kill chain, and then we develop defenses and then break the link in that chain somewhere along, the earlier the better, before it gets to step seven. They're getting what they came for.

Compute in the Cloud

When it comes to compute in the cloud, we have the concept of security groups, so controls like IAM, or Identity Access Management, things like secrets management, which we talked about, ACLs, or access control lists, and the concept of least privilege all become even more important with cloud resources. And why is that? Well, in the cloud, we have a much bigger attack surface. Cloud-based resources and cloud providers are, of course, big targets for hackers. And also, we have the concept of multi-tenancy. We have multiple clients that exist in the cloud, and that gives attackers a much wider berth to go after. You may not even be the target of a specific hack or a specific intrusion or breach, but if you're on the same infrastructure or shared infrastructure with other applications that are managed by groups or organizations that are the target of a breach, then you could potentially be impacted as well. So keeping all of these different pieces of the puzzle secure, as you can imagine, become even more and more important. Then we have the concept of a dynamic resource allocation. With the cloud, one of the big benefits and one of the attractive value props, or value propositions, is the ability to spin up resources on demand, but that also brings security, automation, and cost implications if not managed properly. In other words, if we spin things up and then forget about them and they just run, and run, and run, well, it does the bill. That gets higher and higher as well. Also, automation. If we spin things up and don't necessarily check it, and it just runs, and runs, and runs, and perhaps creates instances or creates load, or test, or whatever the automation is set to do, again, every time we run any process, we use any CPU, any cycles, any ingress or egress of data, all of those things incur costs. We need to make sure that someone's looking at those things, audits them periodically, and generally make sure that things are architected correctly and that we're not using too much resources because one of the whole benefits of the cloud is that we don't need to buy all the infrastructure up front. We need just as much as we need for that specific purpose, and then we can scale as required. The corollary to that being we tear the things down when we don't need them anymore so those costs don't continue to increase. Then we have instance awareness, understanding the differences between personal, corporate, and partner instances of cloud services, and then apply security policies accordingly. Instance awareness is a technology that's incorporated in some secure web gateways, next gen secure web gateways. It's an understanding of the difference between a personal account and a corporate account. A user at a company could have a personal and a corporate version of a cloud service. Typically, those things get whitelisted because you need access from the corporate side. However, if that user has a corresponding personal account, that would get through as well. That gives the opportunity or the potential for them to save things to their personal account, bring things in from their personal account. With an instance-aware technology, you can differentiate and block certain things that you don't want to get through. And then we have the concept of virtual private cloud, or VPC. A VPC endpoint, the same thing we talked about before. All of these different things, IAM, secrets management, ACLs, concept of least privilege, all of these things become more and more important for all the reasons we talked about previously. VPCs, or virtual private clouds, they're very, very convenient, they give us our own little mini data center, in the cloud. All of the things that we would take into consideration when designing a real data center, we need to make sure we do so in the cloud as well, and even more so because I said we have a multi-tenant environment where we have other companies and organizations that are sharing infrastructure with us, so security becomes important across the board. You're not controlling just your piece of the puzzle. Then container security, very much the same concept as dynamic resource allocation. We can spin things up on demand, but in doing so, we bring about security and automation and cost implications. If things are not managed properly, then we have the potential for costs to spin out of control or at least become larger than we anticipated.

Cloud Access Security Broker (CASB)
A Cloud Access Security Broker, or a CASB, it's a security policy enforcement tool or mechanism. It can be either on-premise or it can be in the cloud, and it's placed between the company or the consumer and the cloud provider. It ensures policies are enforced when accessing cloud-based assets, and allows us to make sure that we have a consistent set of policies between what we have onsite and what we have in the cloud. Having those things consistent gives us an added layer of security because we can ensure that things are going to be treated the same way, whether they're onsite or in the cloud. Authentication/single sign-on, as an example, credential mapping, device profiling, and also logging. All of those things should be consistent between both environments. That way we don't have discrepancies between the environments and perhaps miss something, thinking that we've configured it, but we only configured it on one side and not the other.

Application Security
Some other security considerations, application security - when we're designing these things, who can access the application? That sounds like a no brainer, but we have to

make sure that we're not giving access to those who don't need it. Also, what dependencies exist and are those dependencies secured? Because it doesn't do us very much good to put a very expensive lock on the front door, but leave the back door wide open or a side window open, you get the idea. We have to make sure that all the interdependencies between applications are secured so we don't have a weak link in that chain. APIs, endpoints, single sign-on, we need to make sure all of these things are secured properly. Also, what technologies are used to defend against attacks, is it a cloud access security broker, is it a next gen secure web gateway, which we'll talk about in a moment, instance aware tools. We need to make sure that we're applying them consistently and that they're configured properly. Some of these tools have lots of bells and whistles and lots of knobs to turn, and if they're not configured, it gives us a false sense of security. It's very important that we apply consistent policies across the environment, but that we also understand what each of those policies do.

Next-gen Secure Web Gateway (NG-SWG)
Next-generation secure web gateways or next-gen SWGs. What this does is combine the features of multiple cybersecurity tools, such things as a cloud access security broker; DLP, or data loss prevention tools; activity controls, We can control at a very granular level who can do what and what specific activities they can and can't do; also instance-aware, we talked about being able to differentiate between corporate or personal or vendor or partner accounts and services, and then block or allow accordingly; and then some other things, like traditional secure web gateway functionality, API checking, policy enforcement, compliance enforcement, all those good things. All of those things combined make up a next-gen secure web gateway

just understand what that tool is and the various features that it provides.

Firewall Considerations in a Cloud Environment
Next, let's talk about some firewall considerations in a cloud environment. Traditional firewalls performed IP filtering and packet inspection. They were able to identify threats at the perimeter, but they don't differentiate between corporate versions and personal versions of services. This is where instance-aware things come into play. Traditional firewalls did not address that. And then we have cloud-based apps, like Software as a Service, and APIs introduce new challenges. Again, many more points that are publicly accessible, which means many more points that are, of course, targets for attack. Cloud access security brokers, also multi-cloud nuances. If you use each individual provider's firewall services, well, there's nuances between, so the configurations may not necessarily be consistent between environments. Also, multi-tenancy, that brings up different challenges as well simply because you have a lot of different groups that are utilizing the same infrastructure. Also, support, reskilling staff, change management, governance. All of these things come into play and, of course, should be a consideration when looking at firewall providers should you allow the cloud provider to also do on-prem firewall protection. All of these things should be thought about and considered when choosing firewall options, providers. There's a lot of nuances, there's no or wrong answer, and there's no one answer that's going to fit everybody. So, this is an area that will depend upon your specific organization. And then we also have DDOS, or distributed denial-of-service mitigation. Being able to detect in real time or close to real time and then scale as needed to be able to respond to different OSI layer attacks and then reroute

traffic as necessary to reduce impact or drop it into a black hole? Then virtual firewalls, Firewall as a Service. These things enable granular segmentation? We talked about segmenting different areas, or micro-segmentation even, as needed around specific servers, applications, and services. You can segment at the subnet level, or you could scale down and get very granular and segment or firewall off at the actual application layer.

TCP/IP and OSI Models
The OSI model is a reference model designed to illustrate and standardize communication protocols, methods and devices. There's seven layers to the OSI model: application, presentation, session, transport, network, data-link, and physical. There's an OSI model, and then there's a TCP/IP model which breaks that into four layers instead of seven.

Application Layer, Protocol Layer, and Volumetric Attacks
If we have an attacker that's going to go ahead and create a botnet. They're going to infect a bunch of PCs out on the internet. And what they do with that botnet is send a bunch of HTTP GET requests to a web server, or to a target server. And in doing so, we're doing it at volume here with a bunch of hosts all sending these GET requests, and each time they do that, it spins up resources at the target. The attack is aimed at the OSI layer 7, for web servers. In a nutshell, the HTTP flood overwhelms the target system with requests that ends up exhausting resources on that target, and it takes it out of service. It makes it unable to service legitimate requests. Next, we have protocol attacks, and here we have the attacker with a bot, and what they're doing is aiming this at layer 3 and layer 4 of the OSI model, specifically targeting firewalls and load balancers. An attacker overwhelms the target with requests. In other words, they send the requests,

the victim responds, but they never get the final confirmation from the attacker, so that just leaves it open. It never closes that connection, and it just exhausts resources. They send a bunch of SYN packets to the victim. The victim responds, but they never get the final confirmation. As that continues on and on, those requests build up. The victim or the target system just eventually runs out of resources. Next, we have volumetric attacks. Here we have an attacker, again, with his trusty bot and we have a bunch of DNS resolvers out on the internet. That attacker will use the bot or the botnet to send a bunch of requests over to DNS resolvers, but I have a fake or a spoofed IP address. The IP address will be that of the victim. That way, when a DNS server responds with the response, or the answer, to that request, they're sending it to the victim instead of to the bot. That goes over and over and over again. As the attacker spoofs DNS queries with the IP address of the victim, the DNS responses get sent to the target and eventually overwhelm, or consume, all of the target's bandwidth. They can't answer their own requests, they can't originate requests, and they get taken offline. They have no bandwidth left to do legitimate activities.

Cost

Costs are always a factor no matter what organization you're a part of, and at first glance, it usually appears that the cloud is cheaper than on-prem, and in many instances, it is, but like with everything within IT, there is a big old depends, in air quotes. If you spin up a bunch of resources, but you don't use them, its uptime, you have things up, you're not using them, you're still paying for them. If you do that same activity on an on-prem situation, you're not paying for that other than just the power, but you're not paying for all of the different sub pieces of that that you would be paying for in the cloud. Also, elastic expansion is great, but if you don't tear those things back down when you don't need them, costs continue to increase. Also, data ingress and egress depending upon the application, how much data goes in and out, you can be charged for all of that. Depending upon the application, depending upon what resources you have on-premise already, it could be cheaper, it just depends on the situation, how often you need it or how busy it is. Also CapEx versus OpEx, that's an organizational preference. Some organizations are very CapEx friendly, some are very CapEx adverse. In other words, some would like to spend capital so they can depreciate the asset, all those like to do it as an OpEx, or an operational expense, so again it just depends upon your organization. There is no or wrong answer there.

Cloud Native Controls vs. Third-party Solutions
There are some nuances, and there are some pros and cons. With cloud-native controls, we have integration with the cloud provider. They are their native controls, so they work well across the board. To that point, security features are typically integrated with the other services that cloud provider offers. One potential downside, maybe, maybe not, is that the cloud provider, since it's their own tools, you and your team will need specific skills. A general set of skills typically don't apply because they're very specific to that cloud provider, and they may change from provider to provider, and also a bit of vendor lock in when you're looking at migrating or perhaps using multi-cloud environments. Then not necessarily always designed to be the most cost efficient. Not saying that they are, not saying that they're not, but they don't necessarily guide you along the way. There are services you can get, like well-architected solutions and things like that to make sure that you are

378

doing things in the most efficient way possible, but if you're doing it on your own, it's more of a self-service environment, you're not always going to necessarily design the most cost-efficient architecture, understanding when to take things up and down. With third-party solutions, you can manage similarly across clouds, so the same toolsets can be used no matter which cloud you're in, for the most part. Optimizations exist to reduce costs wherever possible, because they're not tied to a specific provider, so they try to make things as financially optimized as possible. And then additional security features around API access, privileges, secrets managements, you may have toolsets or features or functionality that don't exist with a cloud-native solution. It may or may not, depending upon the solutions that you choose. Then integration with other non-native applications, services, and automation. Third-party toolsets quite often are designed to work with a very wide range of tools of other third-party tools that aren't necessarily cloud native, so it gives you some options and potentially features that you wouldn't get in a cloud-native control or a cloud-native service. That doesn't apply all the time, of course. The cloud solutions are getting more and more full-featured every day. The big three come out with new services almost daily, so that becomes less and less of a distinction. And then tools typically work in a multi-cloud environment. If you're going to do all your work and you're never going to leave AWS or a Google Cloud platform or Azure, then great. If you're going to stay there forever, then that's not necessarily a concern. But if you do want to have a multi-cloud environment, maybe Cloud HA, the tools that you choose then become more critical. In this chapter, we covered a lot of great information dealing with cloud and cloud security, talking about cloud security controls, such things as high availability. Also, storage, network, and compute, the big three when it comes to the meat of any application or service. Also talked about various solutions like cloud access, security brokers, Secure Web Gateways, incidence aware. Then we talked about the pros and cons and the nuances between cloud-native controls and third-party toolsets.

Chapter 14 How to Implement Identity and Account Management Controls

In this chapter, we'll be covering implementing identity and account management controls. We have three main areas in this chapter. We have identity, we have account types, and then account policies. When it comes to identity, a few things to talk about. We have identity providers, or IdPs, and an identity provider stores and manages a user's identity. Something that which could be a username, or a password, or perhaps a PIN. Something that you have, which would be a badge or a smartphone. Then something that you are, a fingerprint, a retina scan, or some other type of biometric characteristic. This is used to authenticate users, otherwise known as principals, or other devices. It could be a laptop, a tablet, some other type of device. And then using two or more attributes to identify a user would be, as we know, multi-factor authentication. Depending upon the system that you're using, it may be that you only provide one of those three, or it could be multiples if it's a multi-factor authentication system. authentication factors, something that a password or some type of secret, something that you have, could be a smart card, could be a two-factor token, a PIN, or something that you are, like we talked about, a fingerprint, retina scan, some biometric characteristic. Then multi-factor authentication, two or more pieces of information used to authenticate, a PIN, a password, or a fingerprint. Also something to keep in mind is it must be from different categories. A password and a PIN, for instance, would only be one factor because both fall under something that you know. So for it to be multi-factor authentication, it should be from two different categories.

IdP Example

Here we have an IDP example, and we have Alice and she wants to access a ticketing application. Let's say it's a ticketing application for her work, and it is perhaps cloud based or uses an IDP or an identity provider. So she's going to attempt to access that application. It's going to realize that she's not currently signed on. What it does is it then goes out to an SSO provider or a single sign-on provider, and it will issue a request and say hey, can you let me in? Well, the single sign-on provider also realizes hey, she's not logged in. I can't authenticate her yet. It's going to prompt her to log into that application. It will then send her an SMS code, a username a password along with an SMS code, so it's going to be a two-factor authentication. Once Alice provides that information, it sends it back to the SSO provider who then will query an IDP. It'll issue what's called a SAML request to the IDP. A SAML request is a security assertion markup language, and it's a standardized way to tell external applications and services that a user is who they say they are. It doesn't authorize, but it authenticates. It sends that SAML request to the IDP. The IDP within authenticate, send that SAML response back to the SSO provider or the single sign-on provider who, in turn, then sends that SAML assertion back to the ticketing application and saying yes, Alice is who she says she is. Go ahead and let her log in to the application. When we're talking about attributes, an attribute is a piece of information about a user. It could be a username, an email address, a physical address. It could also be things like a company association, a role, a specific title, or contact info. There's many other things as well. These are just some examples of attributes, but these are what's contained potentially inside of an IDP record.

Certificates, Tokens, and SSH Keys

Digital certificates are electronic credentials that are issued to people, computers, and other electronic devices. Typically, people, or laptops, desktops, smart phones. They're used to authenticate and provide non-repudiation or to enable secure communications. It can also be applied in certain circumstances to IoT devices. Next, we have tokens. A token can have various uses, typically to authenticate an ID token, or to grant access to an API or some type of web application, which would in this case be called an access token. That's the two main types, ID tokens and access tokens, and we've talked about tokens in more depth in other chapters, so no need to dig in too deep here. And then we have SSH keys. They're used to securely authenticate when connecting to servers over SSH using a public key/private key certificate. As an example, if we are logged into Kali Linux, we have a terminal session opened, and from there you issue the command ssh-keygen, and that will generate a key that you can use to then connect securely to a remote system over SSH. If I open up that key file that was just generated, we see here's our private key, and then we can also take the corresponding public key, upload it to that server, and then use that to then securely communicate or connect with that session. Using tools like PuTTY or some other way to connect to a remote system, we can import that public key and then use it to securely connect and encrypt that communication to that remote server.

Certificate Issues
Certificate issues can result in people having access to a resource that they shouldn't have. If our certificates aren't correct, someone is able to have access to a rogue certificate or get one issued that they shouldn't have issued and they can have access potentially to resources they shouldn't have. Mechanisms need to be in place to quickly recall or replace a

compromised certificate or a compromised certificate authority. We also need the ability to rotate keys and certificates and also keep track of how resources are secure. Keeping everything in a giant spreadsheet is not going to cut it, for a small environment, maybe, but at any type of scale, that's not going to be manageable. If that spreadsheet gets lost, if the keys get lost, if things aren't backed up, we could potentially lose access to those backups, or those resources, or whatever the case might be that we're talking about. We need to make sure we can secure that properly and also refer back to it when necessary. Many organizations don't have the infrastructure to quickly invalidate a compromised certificate. If a certificate authority within their network gets compromised, all the certificates that are issued by that certificate authority should also be recalled. If there is no infrastructure and no mechanism to do that, then you're potentially putting all those assets at risk. As an example, if you're not familiar with the certificate hierarchy, we start off with a root CA, a root certificate authority. Typically, we'll install that on our network. If we're going to self-serve our certificates, be our own CA, we would install that on our network, and then once everything is set up and configured, take that offline so that way it can't be compromised, we're taking the ability to have that root CA breached. We have a root CA that's offline, once it's configured, it will issue certificates to subordinate CAs. We'll also take those offline. this is for a large enterprise, we have disparate networks, we have maybe offices in different locations maybe in East Coast or West Coast, or maybe a global organization, the root CA that sits at the top of everything would issue certificates or subordinate CA certificates and all of those will be taken offline so that they're not compromised. From there, they would issue certificates to down-level CAs, the issuing CAs, those who remain online. That way when clients enroll in the network, they can contact that issuing CA and get a certificate for whatever it is they need a certificate for, accessing a resource, logging into the network, so on. Those things will stay online, but that way, if one of those issuing CAs is compromised, it's only for that small subset, it's not for the entire environment. If the subordinate CA or the root CA were compromised, then it's a much bigger deal, we want to make sure we break this up compartmentalize so we derisk the environment as much as possible. We also make it easier for our clients to get certificates. If someone on the West Coast is logging in, they don't want to necessarily have to contact the root CA, which may be in another part of the world. If we break this up in a hierarchy much like DNS or any other type of hierarchical system, we're attaching to a resource that's closest to where we are.

Smart Cards
Smart cards gives us access control, and it's also a security device. It contains a small chip, or an amount of memory on that card, and that card can contain information about us. It can be metadata about who we are, it could contain medical records, it could contain access, as far as like what doors we can access within a building, also, different levels of authorization or authentication for network resources. So, user permissions or access information. It's also typically combined with multi-factor authentication, such as a PIN or a password. One is something that you have, the other is something that you know. For it to be true two-factor authentication, it has to be from separate categories. We can set it up so that incorrectly entering a PIN or password X number of times can even shut that card down and render it invalid. That way, if it's stolen and someone's trying to just randomly brute force their way in, that will shut things down and not allow that to happen.

User Accounts

Under account types we have user accounts, the basic building block of our environment. User accounts are unique and are used for each person accessing a resource. It's a unique identifier that's assigned to each account. As let's say for instance in a Windows environment, we could have two users, there could be two users with the same exact name. But when I create the first account and the second account, they're going to have a unique ID or security identifier. In a Windows environment that's referred to as a SID. If I delete that account and then add it back again, well, the new account is a different SID. Even though the user account name might be the same, the security ID or the SID is going to be different. Every user should have their own account and be given the least amount of privileges required to do their work. It's known as a concept of least privilege. We don't want to give them more than they need, because that gives them the opportunity to then start exploring, perhaps delete things they shouldn't have access to, access things they shouldn't have access to, install malware, spyware or ransomware.

Account Management

Under account management, there are three main tenants that we want to be aware of. When dealing with shared and generic accounts and credentials, each user should have their own account, but even more importantly, each user should have their own non-admin account. Shared accounts are also too difficult to troubleshoot or audit in the event of a breach. Shared accounts are a no-no. Every user should have their own account, that account should be a non-admin account. That way, if that account is compromised, the person doing the compromising doesn't have that elevated privileges. But because typically, when ransomware, malware, or spyware is installed, it's installed in the context of the user account that installed it. If they're an admin, guess what? That malware or that spyware has admin privileges potentially. Next, when dealing with guest accounts. Guest accounts should be used sparingly if it all. Typically, best practices is to say, disable them. But, if for some reason we need to use them, use them sparingly. In kiosks or other public access locations, they may be acceptable or they may be required. The operating system should be reimaged frequently and locked down as much as possible in these environments. Typically in a kiosk environment, you may want to reimage that machine every day so that if someone goes out and installs software, malware, spyware, each day, well that just gets reimaged and you reduce and mitigate the likelihood that those things will permeate through the system. Next, when dealing with service accounts, service accounts should only be used for, not surprisingly enough, services, not for users, and they should also be unique for each service. That way you can quickly identify what service account is accessing which service or is representing which service. Troubleshooting, audits, and revoking permissions becomes much easier when we understand what that service account impacts. If we use one service account and we give that to everything, 5 applications, 10 applications, and then we need to disable that for some reason, well, we've just disabled potentially 5 or 10, 15, 20 apps, however many we have assigned to that. It makes it very, very difficult to troubleshoot.

Password Complexity
Passwords should be complex enough to be hard to guess, that's a no brainer; however, they shouldn't be so long or so complex that our users need to write them down. That's the

key differentiator here, and I think there's a fine line between usability and security. We want to make them secure enough so they can't be brute forced or easily guessed, but not Much that we have to have them written down to remember them. Passphrases often are easier to remember. Instead of having an eight character password, you might have a complete sentence or maybe a couple words in a sentence, but if it's something that's easy for that person to remember, a sentence, it's long enough to become very difficult to guess, but still easy enough for them to remember without having to write things down. Just something to keep in mind that might work in your environment. Also, we can enforce the minimum length. We have to have a password be at least six characters or at least eight characters, or whatever is appropriate for your environment. With policy, we can enforce those types of restrictions. We can also say you have to have a special character, whether it is an asterisk or an exclamation point, parentheses and so on. By having special characters, again, we're making things more difficult to guess. Also, upper/lowercase. We might mandate that the password contain at least one uppercase letter just to make things more difficult for someone to try to guess or brute force.

Password History
All of these things are used in conjunction with one another to limit or mitigate the risk of someone trying to brute force or guess someone's password. Password history, that's going to dictate how many passwords are remembered by the OS before a user is allowed to reuse a password if they ever are. The minimum amount of time before a user can change passwords is also very helpful. And if we use these two things in conjunction with one another, we have a very secure policy. And how that works is that okay you have to

go through, let's say, 5 or 10 passwords before you can reuse that password again. Let's just say I like the password. P@sswOrd1. Well, when it comes time to change, what do users typically do? it's P@sswOrd2. Comes time to change again, P@sswOrd3. And they'll cycle through until they get back to what they like, which might be P@sswOrd1. If we have a 10-password reuse cycle, they have to go through 10 passwords before they can get back to P@sswOrd1. Well, sometimes if we don't have this minimum amount of time in place, users are a little wise, and they'll sit there and they'll change your password over and over and over and over again. They'll cycle through those 10 different passwords so they can get back to P@sswOrd1, which is the one they like and that's the one they remember. That's a no-no. That defeats the whole password history and the changing your password option. By putting the minimum amount of time that a user must maintain that password before they can change it, we mitigate that risk. If we make it say you have to have that password for two days before you can change it again. They change it to pass from P@sswOrd1 to P@sswOrd2. They try to change it to P@sswOrd3 away, no good. It's going to say no, you have to wait 2 days before you can change to P@sswOrd3. That might be frustrating to them a little bit, but from the company's perspective, much more secure. It prevents that getting around the password history requirement.

Password Reuse
We can define via policy whether the user can even ever use the same password again. If you say no, once you use the password, you can never use it again, you might have a mutiny on your hands, that could be problematic for some users, but a password history of 15, 20 might be even a little bit excessive, but it certainly is doable and much more

workable than saying once you use it once, you can never use it again. I wouldn't necessarily recommend that policy, but we can do all of those things of policy and enforce that across the enterprise. It can be used in conjunction with the password history. We can say it'd have to go through X number of passwords before they can, in fact, reuse that password. Next is password length. We want to make sure we define a minimum number of characters and why do we do that? Well, we don't want it to make easy to guess. We don't want the password to be one or two or A or B, we want them to have a minimum number of characters. Most secure passwords are six to eight characters in length, it can be used in conjunction with complexity requirements to ensure that users have to use uppercase, lowercase, or some type of special character, asterisk, exclamation point, and so on.

Time of Day Restrictions
Another one that may or may not be appropriate for your environment, or every environment, is different, but is time of day restrictions. What this does, it will limit a user's access to files, folders, servers, or the entire network, depending upon the time of day. What it does is it keeps users who have no need to access corporate resources after hours, or from a certain set of hours, from accessing, poking around, and potentially getting access to sensitive company information. It keeps them from having additional opportunities to exfiltrate data. By limiting a user's access to just before and just after normal working hours, you limit that exposure risk by roughly 16 hours a day. That may or may not be appropriate for your environment. As we know, in IT, there are typically people on standby around the clock, depending upon the type of industry in your environment. It may not be applicable, but if so, if it makes sense, then

consider time of day restrictions. That way you can ensure those users who have no need to be in your network don't have access.

User Access Best Practices

When it comes to user access best practices, three things I want to talk about account maintenance. We need to automatically disable temporary accounts after a period of time, periodically audit to ensure group memberships are appropriate as well. What do I mean by that? Well, when contractors come on board, typically, it's going to be for a finite period of time, whether that's a month, 3 months, 6 months. While the day that account is created, we should have an auto expire after some period of time, let's just say 6 months. If we need to extend that, we could have an automated process in place where the manager gets an email says, hey, this account is about to expire, do want to extend it. Reply yes or no, and if yes, then that automated process will extend that account for another 6 months or they may log into a portal and just click on that user account and say extend, but by doing that every 6 months or whatever that period of time is, it ensures that we don't forget about it and ensures that that user account, that contractor account that was created, 5 years ago isn't still active because if it's an account that no one is accessing, then if a hacker continuously tries to get into that account and locks it out every so often why no one is going to notice because no one is trying to use the account. It's very good, best practice in fact, for us to automatically disable those temporary accounts after a period of time. Also ensure group membership doesn't change without our knowledge. Next, we have group-based access control, again important that we assign permissions to groups and not individual users. Well, why is that? Because when we start to assign to individual users, it becomes a nightmare to try to troubleshoot. If a user is a member of five different groups and we know what all those different groups' permissions are, but they still can't access a resource or they're still having some type of trouble, well, then come to find out they have a different level of access assigned to their individual user account, it can conflict potentially with what's assigned at the group level. As an example, if they have deny assigned, they could be a member of five different groups that have full control to a resource, but if they have individually been assigned no access, well that's going to trump everything else. The effective permission is no access, so always assign permissions at the group level. Then location-based policies. As users move from place to place, we need to ensure permissions and access adjust accordingly. Because, we don't want to assign more access and more privileges than the user needs? Always keep that concept in mind of least privilege. If you can always remember that, it's going to go a long way to ensuring users don't have more than they need and it will help mitigate that risk overall.

Permissions Auditing and Review

When it comes to permissions, auditing and reviewing, permissions are not a set it and forget it thing. I had that in quotes. It's not something we should do once and then never look at again. Periodic audits are going to ensure permissions are intact and also still appropriate. What do I mean by that? Well, as a person changes jobs, from time to time, and are given more responsibility, less responsibility, they may change roles, go to different departments, their permissions are going to change as well. As they go to a new role and they get new permissions, new access to different things, we need to make sure we're removing the old ones, the access to the old things. That way they don't start to accumulate things over time. They've been at a company for 20 years, all of a sudden they have access to everything because they've been gathering along the way. It's important to make sure that we have policies in place, automated, if possible, so as they change roles, their group membership will automatically dictate what they do or do not have access to. By periodically reviewing and auditing as well, it's going to give us the opportunity to ensure that additional s haven't been granted or changed without permission. At some point in time, someone gave someone s they shouldn't have had access to, or they may have gotten something temporarily and it was never taken away. By periodically auditing these things, we can ensure people have just what they need to do their work and no more, getting back to that concept of least privilege.

Recertification

Credentials and required clearances need to be audited and periodically recertified, whether that's every 6 months, once a year, once a quarter, floor certified individuals coming into your data center, technicians working on pieces of equipment or having access to resources hardware, software, or data. Levels of access and also the locations being accessed should be periodically audited and they should be recertified because as a company grows over time or they deal with different contractors, different vendors, the vendors themselves will shift personnel around from time to time, well, if that person that was accessing our data center 6 months ago has moved on to another position, or perhaps even another company, we need to make sure we revoke that person's access because if it's left there, guess what, that's an account that potentially is not being monitored, something that a hacker can then use and bang against if he gets locked out every so often, no one cares because no one is trying to use it so no one sees that it's locked out, and then when the lockout resets itself, the hacker can try again and he has the opportunity to potentially bruteforce those accounts, Disable the accounts and revoke access as soon as that is no longer needed. Also, when we deal with equipment or infrastructure, when infrastructure is refreshed where application is updated, we should recertify them again, make sure that the connections, the security protocols, the firewall changes that are in place are still applicable. Do we need more or do we need less? If something changes, an application changes, and it used to use 10 different ports and the updated version of that only uses 1 port, well, there is an opportunity to reduce or mitigate our risk by removing those 9 ports, by closing those 9 holes in our firewall. Periodically, auditing and recertifying infrastructure and applications is definitely a good practice.

Group Policy
Within a Windows environment, we can use group policy to enforce password rules. We can use it to enforce such things as complexity, meaning a user has to enter a password that is, meets certain criteria whether it's a minimum number of characters, it could be uppercase/lowercase, it could have special characters like an exclamation point or parentheses. We can also say, when does that password expire? Is it every X number of 30 days, 45 days, 6 months? If we have contractors, we can set up an automated process that says, every six months that account will expire unless it's automated to extend. Certain environments might say, contractor comes in, you automatically get six months of access, or shorter if you need it, but six months max. Then if the actual company needs to extend that, maybe the person who hired that contractor might get an automated email

that says, password is about to expire. Do you want to extend that? And in a lot of instances, the actual employee or the hiring manager might just simply say approve or just send back an email, that'll kick that workflow off and extend that contractor's account for another six months. But it's a good practice so that things don't extend out further than they need to. We can also enforce group membership via group policy, say who belongs to what groups, and we can also make sure that users don't try to sneak themselves into privileged groups like administrators. It can automatically run and say, these users need to be in this group, let's say the admin's group or domain admin group; or whatever we define as a special group or a privileged group, and if so and so sneaks in the back door, well every 30 minutes or so that's going to rerun through that policy and say, wait a minute, you don't belong in here, and pull him out. That makes sure that we increase our security footprint as much as possible or strengthen that position I should say, so that people don't slip in and try to go in unnoticed. We can also set things like remote access time of day, and then the length of a connection. In other words, let's just say people can remotely access our systems, but if it's after 6 PM, so that shrinks our exposure window by 12 hours. For a 24/7 shop, that's probably not the best policy. And we can also say once you log in, you can only stay connected for an hour, two hours, six hours. By limiting how long they can stay connected, again, we reduce the amount of damage someone could do if they're in here trying to do something harmful to the company.

Expiration

The next thing is password or account expiration. Temporary accounts should have an expiration date set when they are created. The reason I say that is because as an administrator, if we are in a relatively large or very large environment, we're not going to remember to disable that account we created 3 weeks ago, or a month ago, or 6 months ago, just too many of them to manage. If we do that in an automated fashion, and say, every user account that we create, if it's a temporary or a contractor account, as an example, we're going to give them 30 days, or maybe 3 months, or 6 months of access. At that point, it automatically disables unless we extend. There are a number of systems out there, and again it's going to depend on your environment, but there are a number of things that we can due to plug into your directory management or your account management system that will say, 15 days, or maybe, 3 weeks before that account is set to expire, we'll start emailing the account creator, or the hiring manager, and say, this is getting ready to expire, if you want to extend this, just reply back to this email, or log into this website, or send an email to the, the AD, or the directory service administrator, somethings are more automated than others, but by doing that, we automatically guarantee or build in the fact that user accounts, temporary accounts, contractor accounts are not going to extend beyond their useful life That way, after a couple of years, we have 30, 40, 50, 100 temporary accounts that people are long gone, but those accounts are still active, those things become security risks, they are things that are not monitored. It's an attack surface for a hacker, and they have an account that they can bang against and try to brute force or do whatever with it that no one's monitoring, those are all risks that, as security professionals, we need to mitigate. It ensures that administrators don't forget to disable and expire accounts, we covered that. We leave accounts intact, just disabled, that's the differentiator. We don't want to necessarily delete that account, we want to just disable it. It can always be enabled later because if we delete that account, we also delete the security ID, or the SID, associated with that account. If there are encrypted files or things that we need that are specific to that exact account, if we delete it, even if we, even if we recreate with the same username, that SID is different. In effect, from the computer's perspective or from the OS' perspective, it's a different account. So, we can also, extend that account through some type of automated method, so there's no way or wrong way to do that, but just the main take away is we want to automatically or pre-configure that expiration to take place at X amount of days after that account is created.

Recovery
Can users recover their own passwords? Some environments, that's applicable, some it's not. It just depends upon your environment. However, if you have a password recovery process, let's make sure that security questions aren't easily discovered. We want to make sure that they don't put in like their kids names, pets names or favorite vacation spots, so these types of things are more of a training issue than an automated issue, but we need to make sure that users are very well versed in this because as a skilled social engineer and if I realize that most people are going to use their dog's name or their children's name, their favorite car, vacation spot, sports figure, there are a handful of things that most people will use as a password if given the choice. If I sit down and have a conversation with someone, I strike up a conversation at the water cooler or in the break room and say, hey, where you guys going for vacation this week or it's an awesome a picture of your kids I saw on your on your on your desk, what are their names, or I love your dog, what's his name? When you spend five minutes and just have a conversation with someone, you can get very valuable pieces of information that you can then use to try

to guess bruteforce people's passwords, so those types of things should be educated into users in the back of their mind, don't use these things as passwords, or if you're going to do that or if they do it, make sure they replace those characters with special characters and enforce a uppercase lowercase policy. And then policy will define if users need to call the help desk or if they have self-service options, maybe some type of call-in or IVR System, or a web portal they can visit, or they may have to just wait 15, 20 minutes, 30 minutes for that account to unlock itself.

Impossible Travel/Risky Login

Impossible travel or risky login is a security feature many cloud-based applications have, and you may even have it internal to your organization, but in this instance, it will utilize AI and ML, or artificial intelligence and machine learning, to determine what's normal and also what's risky. Logins from IP addresses or locations within a timeframe that is shorter than the expected travel time, as an example, that requires an initial learning period typically like a week or so to understand what's normal and what's not normal, but it allows you to programmatically understand what should be a normal log in. For instance, if someone logs in from the East Coast and then 20 minutes later, they log in from the West Coast well, unless they've developed some type of time portal, and if they did, I don't know why they'd use it the log in from one coast to the other, I'd probably use it for some other purpose, but let's say they did, well then, of course, that would be normal, but assuming they don't have a time travel portal or can't travel faster than the speed of light, then that would be an unusual login., of course, they could use a VPN and log in from different locations, but that would also be part of the learning process. During that learning period, we may learn that user A logs in from a VPN periodically depending upon what they're doing, so that may eventually not get flagged as unusual, but for the most part, that would be flagged as a risky or an impossible travel login. And as an example, if we look at Azure cloud security portal ready for this specific instance, we see there are some alerts generated impossible travel activity for a specific user or a specific service? We flag that and then issue alerts to the administrator and say, hey, there is something suspicious going on, this user logged in what we're flagging as impossible travel or risky log in, here is the information, here are the details, and then the administrator could then take further action, if necessary. There are a number of ways to do this, we could do it manually or programmatically through this cloud app security, as an example, but it's not the only way to do it, but just understand the concept of an impossible travel or a risky log in. We're trying to flag activity for users that would just not be able to do what it is they're doing. It could be indicative of someone trying to hacking account, if someone logged in from the East Coast and then a half hour later or 10 minutes later, they logged in from another country, they couldn't possibly travel that far, well it could be, it could be normal activity via VPN, or it could be someone hacking that account from another country that's trying to get in to that account, so it definitely warrants some additional investigation.

Lockout

A policy should be put in place that automatically locks a user's account after "X" number of times that they incorrectly log into the system or try to log into the system. Typically it's 3-5. You can adjust that up or down, depending upon your environment. But, once an account is locked out, it will typically stay locked out for 20-30 minutes or maybe upwards of an hour. But the key thing here is we want to make that lockout duration long enough to thwart brute force attacks. A 30 minute period is usually good. That way a user can't just continuously run a script or sit there at a keyboard and trying to bang away one after the other after the other, trying to get information or trying to guess a user's password. It will lock out after three attempts or five attempts. Then they have to wait a half an hour.

Disablement
That brings me to disablement, and I talked about this briefly before, but we should disable unused accounts instead of deleting them. And we have already covered the fact that a user account has a security ID, or a SID, under the hood? We look at the user account as lowest X, or lowest one, or lowest two, or whatever, but under the hood, it's some long string of characters alphanumeric numbers that is the security ID. That's what the computer recognizes as that account. If we delete them, they can have a different SID, even if we recreate them with the same username. If that user encrypted documents or did some things that are specific to that user account and then we delete them, we're going to have a much harder time trying to recover that information. Instead of deleting, let's just disable. Once we do that, we can always re-enable it later. In this chapter, we covered three main areas. We talked about identity and all the things associated with a user account, IDPs, attributes, multi-factor authentication. We also talked about various account types and we talked about account policies like lockouts, disablements, impossible travel, risky logins, and various ways to make sure that our accounts are secure as possible.

Chapter 15 How to Implement Authentication and Authorization Solutions

In this chapter, we'll be covering implementing authentication and authorization solutions. We have three main areas again. We have authentication management, talking about passwords, trusted platform chapters, hardware security methods. Some of these terms should be familiar to you. Also authentication methods, talking about protocols and platforms that we use to authenticate users in the environment. And then access control schemes, talking about security settings and methods. When we're talking about authentication management, there's some concepts that you should be familiar with; password keys. We're talking about public key or private key, or it could even be a master key to key vaults. You should be familiar with both PKI infrastructure, public key/private key, and also using them whenever possible, whether it's for SSH connections to servers, whether it is certificate management for various connectivity for communication, transfer of files, or connecting to remote servers, and our master keys to key vaults. And when I say a key vault, I mean a password vault. A secure platform that enables you to store passwords for either automated retrieval or manual retrieval. You can place passwords in this vault to allow users to access them so they don't have to keep them somewhere where hackers or attackers could get access to them easily. A password vault would be a secure area on the network, typically a platform like CyberArk or KeePass as an example. Some are more enterprise ready than others. But you can place your passwords in there and either use them just as a dumping ground, where you have to go in and manually retrieve them, or some of the more full-feature platforms are API enabled Your applications and programs can programmatically access those vaults, the API, and use the passwords within there without having to extract or type those things in manually. Some can also rotate passwords on a predefined schedule, again, removing some of that manual user intervention from the process. Then we've talked before about the Trusted Platform Chapter, or TPM chip, which is a secure area usually embedded on a device, whether it be a laptop, a server, perhaps even a smartphone, they have secure areas within those devices as well, so that's where we can store cryptographic keys to keep them out of prying eyes. Then we have hardware security chapters, or HSMs, and this is similar in form and function to a TPM chip; however, this is on a card that can be inserted into a server and also be used to securely store cryptographic keys. Then we have knowledge-based authentication, otherwise known as a secret question. It's a component of MFA, or multi-factor authentication. In this case, a user's asked a secret question, perhaps what's your favorite dog's name, or where'd you go to high school, or what was your first place that you held a job? These things are good to an extent. Keep in mind if you do use knowledge-based authentication and you have common questions like this, a lot of things out there on social platforms are geared towards getting the answers to these questions. You'll notice on some of the social media platforms they have quizzes and little games you can get into where they'll ask you your high school mascot or test your knowledge about the first place you worked. Well, those things could conceivably be used to gather information that could then be paired with user identities down the road. If they're able to get this information and then pair this up with usernames or passwords that is either stolen from that person or that application directly or combined with other breaches, that can give a lot of information that can answer some of these secret questions. If you have the ability to set up secret questions within your organization, make them such that they're not easily guessable or something that a social engineer would be able to pull from someone just by asking a few innocuous, or at least seemingly innocuous, questions.

Extensible Authentication Protocol (EAP)
EAP, or Extensible Authentication Protocol was defined by RFC 3748 and then replaced by RFC 5247. It's an authentication framework, as opposed to a specific authentication mechanism, but EAP is widely in use across a number of different formats, roughly 40 different formats currently, and some of which you may be familiar with, such things as LEAP, EAP-TLS, or EAP-IKEv2. The takeaway being that an Extensible Authentication Protocol, extensible, meaning it can be added to, you can plug things into it. It gives us a framework that other things can use, whether it's TLS or other authentication mechanisms, perhaps that haven't even been invented yet, but it gives that framework that these things can then plug into very easily.

Challenge Handshake Authentication Protocol (CHAP)
Next, we have something referred to as CHAP, and CHAP stands for challenge handshake authentication protocol. CHAP was originally used to authenticate PPP clients, or point to point protocol clients, to a server, clients dialing in or accessing a remote server. It's a one-way hash based on a shared secret, in this case, a user's password is compared at both the client and the server. Plain text is never sent over the wire, and as an example, we have a client that wants to log into a server. When that client connects to that resource, the server will turn back and say enter your password. The client does not enter or send the password in clear text over

the wire. What it does is it runs a challenge handshake authentication protocol, or CHAP, it hashes the user's password, and then passes the hash over the wire. The server on the other side knows that user's password has it in its database, it's going to run that same hashing algorithm against the password. If the hashes match, then the client is given access to that resource.

Password Authentication Protocol (PAP)
Next, we have something referred to as PAP, or Password Authentication Protocol. This has been deprecated. It's a username and password that's sent in plain text. With a username and password being sent in clear text, it's easy to see why that's no longer used. Again, as an example, we have the client and the server. The client's going to send their full username and password in clear text. Anyone with any type of packet sniffer can pull that information off the wire. What's happening is the user sends their username and their password in clear text, the server's going to check that against its database and then grant or deny access. But as we know, as security professionals, that's a bad idea. Sending things in clear text, very easy to pull that information off the wire using Wireshark or some other type of protocol analyzer or network sniffer. We don't use this specific authentication protocol anymore.

Port Security and 802.1x Authentication
The next concept I want to talk about is port security and 802.1x, securing physical access to the network. We want to control the ability of someone to just walk into our environment, whether it be a kiosk at a retail store, or a library, or a school, or even within our corporate environment, we don't want to necessarily have someone being able to walk up, pull out their laptop, pull out a CAT5

cable, plug it into the wall, and gain access to our network. One way we can do that is through something called port security. This is particularly applicable to things like kiosks, schools, libraries, not necessarily throughout an entire environment, it becomes a little bit unwieldy at that point, but for specialized situations where we want to control specific access to specific ports, port security is definitely a good fit there. What we can do is configure a switch so that it only learns one MAC address per port. We can keep attackers from sending multiple fake addresses. So, in other words, someone can't pull out their laptop, plug in, and then just start bombarding our network with fake MAC addresses. Because if you recall, when we have our devices and it connects to a switch, that very first time it does that, it goes out and tries to get an IP address via DHCP, or it may have one hard-coded, it's going to try to ARP for some resources, it might go to DNS, it might go to whatever the case might be, try to resolve a URL, whatever action is taking place, it's going to put datagrams onto the network. As soon as it does that, the MAC address of that device is attached to that datagram. It's a layer 2 piece of information. The switch, which is a layer 2 device, will learn, or memorize, that MAC address and associate it with that port. And so the switch will learn over time all of the devices that are connected to it, what MAC addresses are associated with which ports, so that way, when information comes in, it knows what port to send that information out of. It's a very directed process. Broadcasts will go out all ports, but if it's traffic between PC1 and PC2, PC1 is connected to the port 1, PC2 is connected to the port 10, as an example, it will only go in port 1 and out port 10. So that keeps things more secure. However, as I was mentioning, we have malicious individuals or malicious activity that can take place where someone could flood a specific port and overrun the MAC table on that switch and bring it down. By sending port security and only allowing certain MAC addresses or one MAC address per port, we negate that ability for someone to do that type of activity. We can also use that in conjunction with something called 802.1x to strengthen security at the wall jack. As I mentioned before with, school setting as an example, or a kiosk, we have something called 802.1x authentication. What that is, is EAPOL, or Extensible Authentication Access Protocol, over LAN, over a local area network. That Extensible Authentication Access Protocol gives us the ability to say, when somebody connects to our wall jack, we're not going to allow them to communicate until they authenticate with the network. They're going to authenticate with something called a RADIUS server. It's an authentication server. In this schema, it's a multi-part process, the client, which is in the terms of this authentication process, is called a supplicant, the client is going to initiate a request that they're going to plug into the wall jack, they're going to say, hey, can I communicate? The switch is going to say no, not until you authenticate. It will only allow EAPOL traffic to pass through that port, it will send it off to the authentication server, all of these things have to be configured in place so that this process takes place, but once it's set up, the port will not be activated until that authentication process is complete. The supplicant will send information to the switch, the switch will then forward it onto the authentication server. Once the credentials are validated and verified, in other words, the client is authenticated, and then the authentication server sends that information back and says, yes, you can communicate, the port is wide open, and of course, the supplicant or the client can communicate on the network.

RADIUS

We have something we refer to as RADIUS, and that stands for Remote Authentication and Dial-in User Service. It started out as Remote Authentication and Dial-In User Service, but people are coming in from cable, from fiber, from other mechanisms, so it's not just referring to dial in, but the concept is the same. It provides AAA capabilities. When I say AAA, I mean three things. It provides authentication, and authentication identifies the user and allows or denies access. We're going to identify that user and either allow them or deny them access. We can also challenge for additional credentials, a two-factor authentication, such as a PIN or a rotating code. They may have a key fob or a dongle. Then next, it's going to provide for authorization, and that deals with providing things like the length of time allowed on the network, access control lists, or ACLs, for various resources, and then on top of that, we're going to provide accounting. Accounting is used for tracking the start and stop time of each session, and it can be used for billing, or perhaps showback, to show how long the user was connected to that service. If we look at an example, we have Alice and she's referred to as a supplicant. We're talking about a RADIUS example where we have a supplicant, we have an authenticator, and then an authentication server, or AS. And you'll also see an AD or LDAP server off in the distance here. That is the actual mechanism that's going to pull up the user account and make sure that they're in the system. Alice perhaps wants to access a resource. She wants to connect to a wireless access point in this example. Well, rather than have each individual wireless access point have her username and credentials, there may be dozens within her environment, they simply are configured to point to a RADIUS server. That way, Alice goes to log in, the supplement to the authenticator. The authenticator is simply going to pass through that request to the RADIUS server. The RADIUS server is what provides the authentication. The RADIUS server's going to contact AD or LDAP, depending on how it's configured, and say, does Alice exist, and what are her credentials? Is she allowed access or not? And if so, we'll reply back positively, replies back to the wireless access point, and she's allowed access. We can further go on, and if we wanted to layer on 802.1X authentication, we can also make sure that Alice's machine can log into that wireless access point as well. We can not just necessarily filter by MAC address or by IP address, we can also filter by account credentials as well. There has to be a valid account on the network before authentication is granted to that wireless access point.

Single Sign-on (SSO)
Next up is single sign-on and single sign-on is a method of allowing users to access all resources that they're going to need, within an environment with a single username and a password. It negates having to remember multiple usernames and passwords. We talked about previously, whether it be a Kerberos realm or Active Directory or some other authentication mechanism or directory service, by having that in place, a user can sign on once to a directory server or an Active Directory server and some type of directory service and then access everything within that environment. Of course, they have to have access granted to them? They can't just login and automatically access everything. Each individual resource is still controlled by ACLs, but they don't need to remember username and passwords for each resource, so it makes it much more secure, mitigates risk by keeping users from having to write down credentials. If you have to remember, 50 different passwords or 100 different passwords for your work environment, it's going to be very difficult to keep those

straight in your head, you're going to have to start writing those things down. Once they're written down, make the task much easier for a hacker to come in and retrieve that information, not to mention the fact that come password changing day, it's a lot easier to change your password once and have it propagate everywhere or have access everywhere rather than having to remember to change your password on 50 different resources or 100 different resources, whatever your environment entails by having to do that each and every time become a very tedious process.

SAML

SAML stands for the Security Association Markup Language, and what this is authenticating through a third-party to gain access to some resource. That resource being accessed isn't responsible for the authentication. You may see this a lot when you're browsing websites out on the Internet, you may go to a website and it asks you to log in, but you're not going to login on that site specifically, you might log in with your Google ID, or an email address, or some type of open ID, or your Facebook account, or your Twitter account. These different things can act as a trusted third-party that will pass through to the site you're trying to access. The authentication requests are passed to that trusted third-party server, the user authenticates to the third-party server, they're issued a token, that token is passed to the target resource. We have a client, we have a resource server that we're trying to get to, and then we have some AS server, the authentication service so that's going to be SAML, in this case. If we look at an example, we have a client, the resource server, and the AS server. The user wants to access a URL, they want to go out to a resource. Well, what's going to happen is that resource server will post to the AS, with an authorization request to the SAML server.

If that user is not already logged in, then they're going to be asked to log in, they're going to log into that AS server, or the SAML server, because there is a good chance you may already be logged into one of these third-party services, and you may be logged into Twitter or Facebook or whatever ahead of time. When that happens, you're redirected to the resource that you're trying to get to with the SAML token and you're logged into that resource server represented with the web page or the resource that you're trying to get to. There are some SAML alternatives. The federated ID concept has several methods that are currently in use. SAML is not the only one. SAML is one that we mentioned, but then we have also OpenID and also OAuth, so they all provide similar features and functionality. However, many of the most popular websites function as the trusted third-party, they use either OAuth or open ID. If you log into a website using your Facebook credentials or your Google ID or your Twitter account, you're using one of those too, probably not SAML, but the concept is the same. I just want to make sure you understand the concept and how it's passed from that trusted third-party onto the site that you're accessing.

TACACS

TACACS stands for terminal access controller access-control system. TACACS was originally developed in 1984 for controlling access to MILNET - the military network. TACACS is not in use anymore, it's been replaced by newer versions, but I just want to give you an idea of where things have come from and where we're at currently. TACACS has been replaced by something called XTACACS, Extended terminal access controller access-control system. This was a proprietary set of extensions to TACACS developed by Cisco in 1990. It added those three additional features that we talked about previously authentication, authorization, and accounting. RADIUS had it, TACACS, at that point, did not. However, the takeaway here is that XTACACS is not backwards compatible with TACACS. We added three things, authentication, authorization, and accounting, and then no backwards compatibility with TACACS.

TACACS+

Next we have TACACS+. This is the most common implementation of TACACS, which is why I wanted to focus in this area, just give you an idea of where we've come from with the other two previous versions. TACACS+ is the most common implementation, it's going to run on TCP over port 49. It also encrypts the entire communication, so that's something new for TACACS+. Previously, it only encrypted the very beginning piece. We encrypt the entire communication, much more secure. It's not vulnerable to the security issues associated with radius. Some key differentiations and I'm going to compare and contrast those two here in just a moment, but remember that, not vulnerable to security issues because it encrypts the entire communication, and it also separates authentication and authorization to allow more granular control. We can split those out to separate servers, so we don't necessarily have to have everything running on one server. As with the previous version, it's not backward compatible with its predecessors. If we look at RADIUS versus TACACs+, there are a couple things we should be aware of. With RADIUS, it combines authentication and authorization, it encrypts only the password, requires each network device to contain authorization configuration, there is no command logging, minimal vendor support for authorization, UDP, which is connectionless, and, of course, the UDP port set operates upon 1645 and 46, 1812 and 13. It's designed for subscriber AAA, not necessarily for administrator or administration.

411

TACACS+, on the other hand, separates all three elements of AAA making it more flexible, it's also going encrypt the username and the password. That's very important to understand. It also allows for centralized management of authorization and configuration, so that's going to give us a lot more flexibility and allow it to scale on a much larger sense. It has full command login as well and it's also supported by most major vendors. It's TCP oriented, which is connection oriented? UDP is connectionless, TCP is connection oriented, it operates off of TCP port 49, and it's designed for administrator AAA.

oAUTH

OAuth is an open standard for authorization. It's commonly used as a way for internet users to log into third-party websites using their accounts at some of the big providers - Google, Facebook, Microsoft and Twitter. But, it allows them to do without exposing their individual password. They can log in or use the login credentials from those bigger services, that's a trusted third-party, and then when you access whatever resource it is you're going to access, they query Google or they query Facebook, and make sure that you are who you say you are and you have the proper authorization. It allows access tokens to be issued to that third-party client by an authorization server with the approval of the resource owner. It's all tied in. As an example, you have a user that wants to access some client applications. They're going to request a service, they're redirected back to the authorization server, and then there's an authorization between user and authorization server, that authorization is granted. They're redirected with that authorization code. It then requests a token with that authorization code, which goes back to the client application. It goes all the way out to the actual resource server, which comes back to the client application, response is sent back to the user, the user requests the service, request for the data with the access token is sent to the resource server, and then it's sent back to the client application and then back to the user. All of this happens behind the scenes, so all you do is click on a resource, you sign in with your Google or Facebook or whatever, Twitter account, that authorization takes place. All of this happens behind the scenes, you don't even see any of this, and all you know is you log into that resource. So, just understand that there are some things taking place under the covers, and that you need to know the basics of the process. However, you don't have control over how Google or Twitter or Facebook mandates their process. Just understand that they're a trusted third-party, and that authentication is used to authenticate to other external resources.

OpenID and Shibboleth

OpenID is a standard, it's an open standard that provides SSO capabilities. The cooperating sites that participate in this OpenID framework, they're called relying parties or RP. A user chooses an OpenID provider, and there are a number, and they use that account to log into any website that accepts OpenID authentication. I'm sure you've seen this before where you go to a website, and it may give you the option of creating an account or logging in with your email address. Or you can log in with your Facebook credentials, Google account, Twitter. It gives you that ability to log in with a trusted third-party ID. And then we have something referred to as Shibboleth, and that's based on SAML, we talked about previously. It provides a free and open source federated single sign-on and attribute exchange framework. It's similar to OpenID in concept. Shibboleth also provides extended privacy functionality, which allows a user and their home site to control the attributes released to each application. You have some finegrain control over what is shared. When you log on it may be configured to just send perhaps your username and email address, or it could send additional attributes as well, whatever is configured within that framework, to share between entities.

Kerberos

Kerberos is, in Greek mythology, a three-headed dog that guarded the gates of Hades, and its applicable here because there's three components when a user or a client wants to access some type of service. It's a network authentication service that was originally developed by MIT, and is used for mutual authentication between client and server. This gives us that dual authentication I talked about before where the client authenticates to the server, the server also authenticates to the client. Some key terminology before we get into the details here. We have something referred to as a KDC, or a key distribution center; we have an authentication service, or the AS; we have a ticket-granting ticket; we have a ticket-granting service; a principal; and an authenticator. If we look at this in a little more detail, I'm just going to cover this at more or less a high level. You don't need to dig down into the nitty-gritty details for the exam, but just for your own information, there are a couple of things that go on here in the background. The client wants to connect to a service. The client needs to authenticate, we're using KDC, or a key distribution center, which in a Windows environment is going to be the domain controller. That's going to contain the authentication service, and also the ticket-granting service to give those TGTs. The client will send that request to the KDC, or the authentication service, the authentication service will generate what's called a session key. It's going to encrypt that session key with the user's password and it encrypts the session key and this user's username, which is also referred to as a Kerberos principal. It's going to create what's called a service ticket and send that back to the client. There's two pieces to that. The client can decrypt the first part, because it has its password. The password, incidentally, is not ever sent over the wire. It's a hash on the client side and it's a hash on the domain controller, so that is used to encrypt, and then it's sent back. The client can decrypt that first part. It cannot decrypt the second part because it doesn't have that, only the service does, but the client will encrypt that second piece along with a timestamp, which is referred to as an authenticator, and it sends that service ticket over to the service or the server that it needs to connect to. The server can then decrypt because, again, it has that information that only it can decrypt, so that's where this mutual authentication is going back and forth. Only the client can do what it can do because it's the only one with the password. Only that server can do what it can do, because it's the only one with the password. If anyone were to capture that in between, it's not going to do much good, because, again, we have things timestamped as well, so that prevents replay attacks. Once all this is done and the service looks up and says, I trust the KDC, the client trusts the KDC, the KDC says, yes, the client is valid, go ahead and grant that service, they connect. Going forward, each time that needs to happen again, rather than having to go through this process for every single connection, you get what's called a ticket-granting ticket. That takes that first part out of the loop, so the next time it needs to make a connection, the client goes to the KDC, to the authentication service, requests that TGT, send that over to the service, and that's encrypted by the session key that was originally set up with that AS. It only has an 8-hour lifespan, Every so often that's going to need to be regenerated. But the point of that is, the very first time it needs to connect to a service it's going to go through the process, encrypt, get those two pieces sent to it, it's going to be able to decrypt one. It'll re-encrypt the second piece along with the timestamp, send it over to the service, the service can decrypt. Next time around, it uses a ticket-granting ticket to shortcut that process so it doesn't have to re-authenticate. It's already valid with a session key that's valid, again, for 8-10 hours, so that way it can just pass directly over to the service and make a connection.

Attribute Based Access Control (ABAC)
Attribute-based access control, or ABAC, it's dynamic, so it's considered more or less the "next-gen" authorization mechanism, and its policies comprised of attributes that can be about anything or anyone. We can get very granular, and it's not confined to a set of predefined rules or a specific type of role. It allows for set-valued and also atomic-valued granularity, and that can be combined for complex Boolean rule sets. Let's take a look at what comprises attribute-based access control. We have three things at the architecture level. We have a Policy Enforcement Point, or a PEP, and that protects the resources being accessed. The PEP generates authorization requests and sends it to what's referred to as the PDP, so that is the Policy Decision Point. The PDP evaluates incoming requests against configuration policies. The PDP permits or denies and may request additional information, metadata in other words, from something referred to as a Policy Information Point, or a PIP. The PIP is a bridge between the PDP, the Policy Decision Point, and external sources of information such as LDAP, specific databases. You can get very granular as to say who can do what. If a person is a specific type of role, perhaps, if they have a certain type of clearance, perhaps, if they're trying to

do a specific type of action. If we look at that in more detail, these specific attributes, we have subject attributes, so that could be anything about the user requesting access. It could be their age, security clearance or their job title. All of these are specific things that you can use to key off of when granting or denying access to a specific resource. Next, we have action attributes. That refers to the action, or actions, being attempted, whether it's read, write, delete, approve, deny. And then we have resource and object attributes, and that describes the object being accessed, the type, the department, the classification, the sensitivity. Much more granular when we start combining all of these things together, who they are, where they're coming from, their age, their clearance, their title, combined with who the user is, what action they're trying to do, what object they're trying to access. Then we have contextual or environment attributes, and this can be things like time, location, or other dynamic aspects. When you combine all of these things together, as you can imagine, you can get a very complex if/then Boolean type of logic around decision making. What it does is it gives us that granular, dynamic ability to provision. We don't have to do things ahead of time. We can let it happened on the fly, depending upon who that user is, where they are, what their title is. As they move throughout the day, move throughout locations, as they change titles, that specific, read, write, delete, approve, deny, all of those things will change, as the attribute about that person changes.

Rule-based/Role-based Access Control (RBAC)
Next, we have rule-based access control, and RBAC is used in two separate context. In this specific one, we're talking of a predefined or a preconfigured security policy and that's going to define and decide access. We could say explicitly

417

deny all of those, except in an allow list, or we could say deny only those who specifically appear in a denial list. It's very much a list-based control mechanism, it's more flexible than MAC or mandatory access control, but less flexible than discretionary access control. That list is configured ahead of time. Then we have another role-based access control, or RBAC, context and that is a role-based access control and that access is based, on the user's role. Group membership determines what a user can and can't do, so that's pretty much how most enterprise operating systems and most enterprise environments are functioning. So once a user changes roles, then their access will change accordingly. As an example, a user might be moving from human resources to finance. So if we have a few folks that are in human resources. If they move over to finance, well they're going to lose access to that human resource document and all those files and folders. However, they're going to gain access to the payroll files. Just by virtue of moving from one group to another, they're going to lose access to their old stuff, but they're going to gain access to their new stuff. It's easy to manage, an administrator doesn't have to go in and specifically give s to each individual person, he can pre-configure those rules and those access s to a group, that way, when people come in and out of that group, they're automatically granted those permissions.

Access Control Methods

There are four main methods of access control that I want you to be aware of for the exam. We have mandatory access control. Or MACs, and that is very inflexible and it's very rigid, but it's also the most secure. Things are written in stone, there is no flexibility, no one can pass your information on to somebody else, it's very, very inflexible. Next, we have discretionary access control lists, and they are a little more dynamic, they're flexible, they're also the least secure so things can change on the fly. Then we have role-based access control, or RBAC. Role-based access control is access based on a role or a group membership. This is what pertains typically in a Kerberos environment, Linux environment, Apple, and also within Microsoft's Active Directory. You place users into groups, you give access to those groups. If you pull a user out of a group, then that access gives away. Then last we have rule-based access control, again, using RBAC, so that's access based on a predefined list. That is saying, if you're on the list you're in, if you're not, you're not. We can either have explicit permit or explicit deny lists depending upon how we have things set up.

Mandatory Access Control (MAC)
Mandatory access control, or MAC, is a predefined set of capabilities and access to information, who can share what and also to whom. As an example, we have a finance folder here we can control who has access to what files and folders, but we can also control, this is written into the program, or it's controlled by a centralized security administrator that says, this person has access to these files and folders, but they cannot share those files and folders with someone else. Even if they create a file, they can't share it, it's very inflexible, and it's very rigid. But it's also the most secure model. But it must be carefully thought out and planned ahead of time because, that lack of flexibility makes it very rigid. If it's not planned properly, it can be a nightmare because people cannot do their work, so it has to be very carefully thought out before it's implemented. But once it is implemented, it's also very easy to spot breaches or deviations because everything is very clearly defined, so if there's any deviation from that, it's very easy to spot.

Discretionary Access Control (DAC)
Discretionary access control, or DAC, that allows users to dynamically share information with others. This is what most environments are comprised of. It's less secure, and it's harder to control information leakage, however, it is how things get done. If I create a file or a folder, I should be able to share that with someone else, that's the general thinking. I may not necessarily be able to share someone else's documents, but if I'm in control of my own stuff, I should be able to say this person can view it, or copy, delete, or this person cannot, I should have control over that. In a mandatory access control environment, there is no flexibility. In a discretionary access, we have that flexibility, but again, less secure, but there is the opportunity for information leakage.

Conditional Access
This is a policy-based access framework based upon if/then type logic to determine the level of access or actions required. We're talking typically around cloud-based services, cloud-based applications, in this case, a software application as a service, or a SaaS application. If it's a certain user or part of a certain user group, or perhaps maybe if it's a certain type of device, or a certain network, or a certain network location, or even a certain application, well, if it's any one of those things, then we could apply policy and say, then either block access, or we could say, then require multi-factor authentication. Let's say, for instance, if a user is part of a specific group, and they're using a specific device, and they're trying to access a specific application, then require multi-factor authentication, or we could say block that, or we could say we're going to require a password change the next time they log in. All of these things can be

done programmatically from the portal or from the configuration tool set, but the takeaway being conditional access is based around an if/then type of methodology. If a user or a device meets these certain set of criteria, and then apply some type of action.

Privileged Accounts

Privileged accounts should only be used sparingly as well. We should use non-admin accounts, non-privileged accounts, for most normal day to day activities. Non-admin accounts reduce the likelihood that something can get installed in our systems and in our environment that we don't want, and if they do happen to get installed, it does with a reduced set of privileges. We should only have these privileged accounts to perform admin-level functions, even admins should have a non-admin account and then an admin account. They would use their lower level account when they want to do day to day activities, and then when they want to do something that is administrative, they would execute that account under that admin account, whether it's an administrator account or pseudo account, it depends upon the operating system, but use those things sparingly. Users, should use non-admin accounts for their daily tasks and their daily activities. Invoke privileged accounts when necessary to perform specific tasks. Separation of those accounts makes things much less likely to be abused.

Filesystem Permissions

When it comes to filesystem permissions improper permission settings on files, folders or even symbolic links, can give attackers unintended access. That means web servers, the files and folders that sit on the web server if they're accessible and they're not properly secured, it could have unintended consequences. We're also talking about database servers, file servers, pretty much any type of file system within our network, if they're not secured properly, it can have unintended consequences and it could be giving away critical information. So, Windows servers typically have read, write, and execute as their permissions. Linux servers can get more granular. But just understand that auditing should be enabled on critical, or restricted files and folders to make sure that these things are secured properly, and also that they stay that way. Because it's possible, for things over time to get changed or shifted either intentionally or unintentionally, and then if we're not aware of those changes taking effect, it could have, unintended consequences, leaking personal information or confidential information, things we don't want others to see, and certainly things we don't want attackers or bad actors to have access to. In this chapter, we covered authentication management, passwords, TPM chips, HSM chapters. We talked about authentication methods, various protocols and platforms that enable authentication across our enterprise. We also talked about access control schemes, security settings, methods.

Chapter 16 How to Implement Public Key Infrastructure

In this chapter, we'll be covering implementing public key infrastructure. We'll talk about public key infrastructure along with the types of certificates, certificate formats, and then certificate concepts. What are a certificate authority and a digital certificate? But just understand that it boils down to PKI, a public key infrastructure, and that facilitates a secure communication between sender and recipient. That communication can be sent over a secure network, something internal, perhaps within a company, or it can be used to communicate over an insecure network, i.e. the internet. By using that public key/private key combination, we can encrypt, as we talked about previously, we can encrypt bulk encryption keys or symmetrical keys we can use a combination of the asymmetrical encryption functions, public key/private key, along with symmetrical functions, which gives us the ability to bulk encrypt, stream large amounts of data quickly, and the combination of the two allow us to securely communicate over that insecure medium.

Certificate Authority
A certificate authority can be internal to our organization or it can be external. As an example, we have one that's external, it's going to live out on the internet, and it will be used as a trusted third party for both Bob and the financial institution, in this case, a bank. They want to communicate. Bob wants to initiate some transaction. So, the certificate authorities that are out on the internet can be Thawte, they can be Verisign. There are a number of major certificate authorities that provide credentials pretty much for the majority of the internet and most of the companies on the

internet. The CA is trusted by both Bob and the bank. When Bob connects to the bank the first time, he's presented with that bank's public key if he wants to establish a secure communication channel. He has the public key that's given to him by the bank. He will use that public key to encrypt session keys that he sends back to the bank. The financial institution is the only one that can decrypt that communication because they have the private key. Bob can be sure that the bank is the only one that can decrypt. Bob can also, if need be, verify the credentials that were presented to him with that certificate authority and make sure that they're still valid. Just like if a police officer pulls you over and checks your credentials, check your license, he's going to trust the state to issue a valid set of credentials. He can check the CRL. He can either go into his mobile terminal or call dispatch and say, let me run this driver's license and see if it comes back as valid. If it does, then he can proceed either giving a warning or a ticket or, whatever he's going to do, but he checks the validity of that credential. Bob can check against the CRL to make sure that it is in fact valid. Assuming that it is, he will encrypt the session key he's used to communicate; he'll send that back. The bank is the only one that can decrypt. It will decrypt that communication, extract session keys, and they have a bulk encryption algorithm they can use to establish further communication over that TLS or SSL channel. It's encrypted, and it's secure.

CRLs

A CRL, or a client revocation list is published by the certificate authorities, and it's used to inform clients that certificates have been revoked or are no longer valid. Where a police officer pulls someone over and checks their license, they're going to check it either on their own mobile terminal, they'll run it against some type of state database, or they'll call into dispatch and say, hey, run this license for me, if that comes back as valid, well then you can go ahead and proceed. If it's been revoked, suspended, it's no longer valid and not in use. If a digital certificate is in fact on that CRL, it can exist in one of two states. We have revoked, which is irrevocable, or we have a hold or a temporary, which means it can be reversed. We have our digital certificate, if in fact it's been revoked, or irrevocable, that means it's done, it cannot be retrieved. Typically that's for a lost or compromised key, so a company can say, I think I've lost this key or I know for a fact it's been compromised, it will be revoked, pulled out of service, placed on that CRL as irrevocable, revoked. That way, no one else can use that certificate or try to initiate any fraudulent transaction. A hold is temporary, that can be reversed. With a hold, we can pull that back off again. Situations there, a client may think they lost their key or they think it may have been compromised, but then they later find out that it has not been, so they either find it or they have definitive proof that it has not been compromised. They can have that hold reversed and that digital certificate placed back into general use.

OCSP

OCSP, or an Online Certificate Status Protocol, and that's used to obtain revocation status of X.509 digital certificates. When we say X.509, we've talked about that previously, that is the format that digital certificates are issued in, it defines what information is contained within those certificates. It's an alternative to CRL, so the client revocation list. The benefits of using OCSP versus a CRL is the fact that OCSPs contain less information, so it puts less burden on the network and the client resources. If you have a very large environment, then you're constantly doing this type of communication back and forth, checking these certificates, using OCSP will contain less information, still gives you what you need, you can tell if a certificate is valid or not, but it contains less information and will put less of a burden, network traffic, in other words, on that network. As an example, so Bob and Alice, they want to exchange communication. Alice wants to communicate with Bob, or Bob with Alice, vice versa. Well, when that happens, Alice will send her public key to Bob, he'll use that key to then exchange communication, he'll create the session key, send that off to Alice, she can decrypt, and then they can communicate over TLS or SSL. Well, what Bob can do in the meantime, however, is once he gets that public key from Alice, he can send an OCSP request to an OCSP responder, that's the terminology used for what these devices are. So that OCSP request goes out, the OCSP responder will check their database to see if that certificate is in fact on there. If it is, they'll respond back and say, hey, you may not want to talk to Alice, she's been compromised, or they'll respond back and say, nope, you're good to go, go ahead establish communication, at which point Bob uses Alice's public key, encrypts session keys and sends it off, and the same process happens as before, communication is then established over SSL and TLS, and they have a secure communication channel from thereafter.

CSR and PKCS Standards
Next we have is a CSR, or certificate signing request, and in this case, an applicant will apply to a certificate authority, or a CA, for a digital certificate. PKCS #10 is the most common type, and PKCS stands for public key cryptography standards, and here is the information that's contained in that request. We have a common name, the business name, department,

city, state, and country, and then the email address. So some basic information about that entity that is, in fact, requesting that digital certificate. Just for your own information, the PKCS standards go through 1 through 15. The ones we've more or less focused on throughout this book would be number five, password-based encryption standards, and also PKCS #10, which is what we just talked about the certification request standard.

PKI

PKI stands for public key infrastructure, and it is the components that enable the usage of digital certificates, and that public key/private key cryptography or encryption, and that's going to include hardware, software, people, policies, and also procedures. Before we get too further along, I want to make sure you understand that when you visit a website, as we've talked about in our previous example, let's say that Bob wants to visit that financial institution. You might ask, well, where do these digital certificates come from? Well, they're built into our web browsers. In Firefox, if we go to Advanced Options, then go down to Options. Each web browser is slightly different, but they all contain roughly the same options. Under the Certificates section, it says requests, When a server requests my personal certificate, I can select one automatically or ask me every time. And then you see Query the OCSP responder. When Bob visits that bank, it's going to query the OCSP responder and say, hey, is this certificate that I'm being presented with, is this public key valid, is that certificate still valid, can I process it? And then we click on View Certificates, and this is all the certificate authorities, they have some pre-made or pre-canned certificates that are issued throughout all of our browsers. That allows us to have a built-in trust up to the root certificates, and there's a number of them. We see the

SHA-256 Fingerprint or the SHA1 Fingerprint, we know where it's issued from, the Common Name, the Organization, when it Begins, when it Expires. We can click on the Details, and then look at the Serial Number, or the Certificate, the Certification Algorithm, it's a SHA1 with an RSA Encryption. We can look at things like the Public Key, so this is the actual public key that's presented to someone that wants to communicate, and if they want to encrypt something, they can use this public key to then encrypt, which the recipient has the private key to decrypt. Getting back into the details of PKI, there are a number of components that make up a PKI environment, that public key infrastructure. The public key infrastructure is comprised of the certificate authority, or the CA. That issues and verifies digital certificates. Next, we have a registration authority, or an RA. That's going to verify the identity of users requesting information from the CA. Sometimes they're referred to as subordinate CAs. We also have a central directory, so that's a secure location in which to store and index keys, so that's going to be typically on an internal network. Then we have a certificate management system, so a method to manage valid certificates, publish CRLs. Then we have certificate policy, which defines who can request, issue, and use certificates, and of course what purpose can those certificates be used for? As you're studying for the exam, it's important that you understand what each of these components are and how they fit into the PKI environment.

Public Key
Public key is something that we should be familiar with at this point, but a public key is one part of a PKI, or a public key infrastructure, used to encrypt or to decrypt data. Remember, a public key can encrypt or decrypt just like a private key can encrypt or decrypt. It's a mathematically

linked key pair that has a corresponding private key. The public key is designed, as the name implies, to be made publicly available to anyone. If I want someone to be able to communicate with me in a secure fashion, I can give them my public key. They can then encrypt communication, a document, an email file, to me that only I can decrypt. Also, they can use that public key to encrypt session keys, so they can instantiate that communication, that TLS/SSL communication going forward. They'll send me those bulk encryption session keys, those symmetric keys. I can use my private key to decrypt, extract those session keys, and then communicate. Just to reiterate, the private key must be kept secret. If that gets compromised, then all bets are off, anything that you have that's been encrypted can be decrypted with that private key. It's very important that that be kept private.

Private Key

A private key is one part of that public key infrastructure, PKI, used to encrypt or decrypt. That's something to keep in mind that I want to say a few times just to make sure it sinks in. A public key can encrypt or decrypt, and a private key can encrypt or decrypt. However, they cannot do the same on an existing piece of data. If you encrypt with the public key, you'll decrypt with the private, or if you encrypt with the private, you'll decrypt with the public. It's a mathematically linked key pair that has a corresponding public key, in this instance, and the private key is, as the name implies, designed to be kept private. That should not be given to anyone.

Object Identifiers (OID)

Object identifiers, or OIDs are incorporated into a PKI, or a public key infrastructure and they're used to assign one or more certificate policies to a given CA, or certificate authority. OIDs are built-in to Active Directory Certificate Services, or ADCS, as an example, can be randomly assigned for internal use only, can also be public or private. An organization can register a public OID to enable that organization's PKI to work with another organization's PKI, so if there is some interoperability that needs to happen there, you can register it publicly so that the OIDs and so that the individual components of that PKI, the certificate policies, can transfer or work between different organizations. If we look at this in a little more detail, an organization can register a public OID, it's a two-step process. One, you would register what's called a Private Enterprise Number, or a PEN. This PEN can be applied for at the address, pen.iana.org, and the following web address, and then once complete, a unique number will be assigned or issued that will be listed at this following web page, iana.org/assignments/enterprise-numbers. And within that there is a numerical prefix that is fixed, that's not changeable, that's 1.3.6.1.4.1, if you're familiar with SNMP and MIBS, it's similar. And then from there you would append whatever your organization's name, that PEN, that Private Enterprise Number, let's say in this example it's 56789, then your OID up to this point would be 1.3.6.1.4.1.56789, and then you would append an additional number or numerical addresses after that for each subcomponent. As it drills down through the organization, you would identify additional numbers, and there are things that you would create or sign internally for your use.

Types of Certificates
Let's go ahead and talk about the various types of certificates. There's a few that I want to cover. We have wildcards, SAN, code signing, self-signed, machine or

computer, email, user, root, domain validation, and extended validation. Each of these we'll cover in more detail. I just want to give you an idea of what they mean and the use cases or where they would be used in your environment. A wildcard is a digital certificate or a public key certificate that is used with multiple sub-domains of a domain. As an example, we may have *.Google.com as our main domain, that's the company domain, but we may have sub-domains within that. Well, rather than have individual SSL certificates for each of these, we can have a wildcard certificate that would allow us to secure all of the sub-domains with that same wildcard certificate. So, in other words, sales.Google.com or support.Google.com, they could all be secured with the same certificate. Next we have SAN, that's a Subject Alternate Name, not SAN as in a storage area network, but within a digital certificate or PKI infrastructure definitions it's Subject Alternate Name, and it's a certificate that allows multiple hostnames to be protected by a single certificate. Not sub-domains like a wild card, this is completely different names, completely different company names, up to 2000, in fact. If you're on a shared infrastructure and you have different hosts and different domain names, that single SAN, or Subject Alternate Name certificate can be used to secure all of those things. Next we have code signing. This is a type of digital certificate that's issued typically by a trusted CA, or certificate authority, and it's used to secure things like downloading code, macros, and objects. Many browsers won't allow code to run unless it is signed by a certificate from a trusted root, Verisign, Thawte, there are a number of them out there that are prebuilt into the browser, but they won't allow that code to run unless it's digitally signed by someone that it trusts. Next we have self signed. This is typically done to provide SSL functionality, or Secure Sockets Layer functionality in a temporary or a test and dev environment for servers that we're going to be temporarily using or in a very low secure environment. It would not be used for something in production, something public facing, but if we need that SSL functionality for testing, this works great. Or if it's in a very low, secure environment, that's internal use only, again, not an issue, just not for public use. And then we have machine or computer certificates. This is used to authenticate, a machine or a computer into an Active Directory environment, as an example. Just like we can verify a sender of a specific document in email, we can also verify, and depending upon how that PKI is used, the domain can verify the machine and also the machine can verify the domain to make sure that both are in fact valid and authenticated properly. Next, email, and that's a digital certificate used, to secure and authenticate email, Used for security, but also for authentication. Then we have a user, and a user certificate is very similar to a machine certificate, but it's used to authenticate users, not machines, but it's used to authenticate that user into that AD environment. In a very secure, or a PKI infrastructure, we're going to not only validate ourselves and we're going to log in with our own credentials, we're going to have our own certificates, we're going to authenticate to the network, but our machine is also going to authenticate to the network. We have two things that are authenticating before we can access resources on that network. And then a user certificate is similar in concept to a machine certificate. It's used to authenticate a user. Just like we talked about with a machine certificate, it's used to authenticate a user in this case into an AD environment. Next we have root, and a root certificate, it's a self-signed public key certificate, we're talking about PKI here, public key infrastructure, so that certificate identifies it as a root CA, or certificate authority.

Typically that's going to be an offline root that will generate certificates that are then put via USB or some removable media into our subordinate or our intermediary CAs. Domain validation is a server security certificate that provides the lowest level of validation available from a commercial enterprise. We can get them pretty cheap out on the Internet, and what happens is the company that's issuing that domain validation certificate will either automate it, or in some fashion contact the point of contact for that domain. When you register you put down this person is responsible for this domain, they'll verify that, quote unquote, wink-wink, and then issue that certificate. It's not very secure and is subject to spam and other types of misuse. Domain validation is a legitimate commercial certificate, but it offers the lowest level of security. Next, we have extended validation, and here it's increased security over domain validation certificates due to enhanced validation process. It's very similar as far as what you need to do to register for one, but the actual validation process is enhanced, "high assurance", meaning they have a human call in, validate that these people are who they say they are. Can it be misused? Of course, we can put in information that is bogus, and someone could validate that bogus information, so it doesn't 100% guarantee anything, but it does provide enhanced security over a simple domain validation.

Certificate Formats

A few certificate formats that we should be aware of. We have PEM, or P-E-M. This is the most common format that CAs issue, and they can have several extensions, .pem,.crt,.cer, and .key extensions. It's Base64 encoded, and it's an ASCII file. Next, we have DER, certificates. This is a binary form of the certificate instead of the ASCII PEM format. It can have extensions of either.der or.cer, and it's very similar to PEM certificates except it's in binary instead of in ASCII. And then we have PFX. PFX certificates, typically encrypted, and it also typically will require a password to open. It can contain almost anything, certificates, certificate chains, or private keys, and it will have the extension of.pfx or p12,.p12. Next, we have something referred to as P7B. P7B certificates only contain certificates or certificate chains, No private keys. Also, Base64 encoded. P7Bs have the extension of.p7b, but it's also known as PKCS#7.

Online vs. Offline Certificate Authority (CA)

We need to make sure that we understand the difference between an online versus an offline certificate authority. An online certificate authority has a couple things. It's typically a subordinate CA, it's not going to be the root. It's going to be typically a subordinate CA, or certificate authority. It can, however, issue certificates. That's typically what it does. It issues certificates either to additional subordinates or further downstream subordinates, or to the actual users or the hosts that will ingest that certificate. Then, it also trusts the enterprise root CA, the enterprise root certificate authority. And then also enterprise CAs need to be joined to an Active Directory Directory Services, or an AD domain. Conversely, offline certificate root authorities, they're a trusted root CA. They're the tip of the iceberg. They are the top of the CA or the PKI hierarchy. And it's often referred to as a standalone root. so that's installed in offline mode. We don't attach the actual root CA to the network. We do that so that it can never be compromised. It's not connected to the network, and it is also not a member of that AD domain, the AD Directory Services domain. We install it in offline mode, we're going to generate that certificate, typically it's going to be put onto a USB drive or a CD or DVD, some

434

removable medium, we'll take that from that standalone root, and then we'll go over and sneakernet it to our subordinate CA. From there, we'll use that certificate to then issue certificates to either other subordinate CAs, or to hosts, or to things within the organization that apply or need that certificate. That way, if it's ever compromised, we can simply take that subordinate CA offline, get rid of it, and anything with it that's been issued from that subordinate CA is compromised, but the entire PKI infrastructure is not compromised. Conversely, if we had a compromise or a breach and the actual root of the entire PKI infrastructure has been compromised, then our entire PKI infrastructure, our entire security throughout the enterprise would be compromised. We purposely don't do that to avoid just that situation.

Stapling and Pinning

Another term I want you to be familiar with is something referred to as stapling. Stapling is also known as OCSP Stapling. It's formally known as TLS Certificate Status Request extension, and we've talked about TLS before and certificates in general before as well. What happens is the certificate bearer appends or staples timestamped OCSP responses to that initial TLS handshake. That gives an added layer of security, and it also removes the need for the client to contact the certificate authority, so it helps speed up the process. Next we have pinning. Pinning is the process of associating a host with their expected x.509 certificate, which is in effect, the public key, that digital certificate. So, more than one certificate or public key for a given host can be possible, and if so, then it's added to what's called a pin set. What we're doing is speeding up the process a bit, and we're also refining or narrowing what we expect that host to have.

Trust Models

When it comes to trust models, a couple things to be aware of. The first model is referred to as a hierarchical trust model, that's a single root CA that digitally signs all certificates. That's for small environments. We don't have a very distributed or a very large PKI infrastructure so that root, that single root CA could in fact sign all of the certificates, not recommended not in use in larger environments, but for smaller environments, you need to know that it exists. And the next model is referred to as a distributed trust model. In this model, we have multiple CAs with one master root CA, That route CA is installed on offline mode and what that does is it limits the risk if one of the CAs is, in fact, compromised before, and then it also distributes the load throughout the infrastructure. As an example, we have our root CA, that's going to be installed on offline mode, and will issue digital certificates, we're going to take that via USB or some removable media, so we'll take that from the offline root, and then use that to configure our intermediary CAs. Those intermediary CAs are the ones that will issue the certificates to clients. One other trust model I want you to be aware of is something referred to as the Web of Trust, or the WoT. That's going to be used in smaller environments or end user communication with no centralized certificate authority. So for the most part, if you're in a small to medium-sized business or anything larger or an enterprise, you're going to have some type of formalized PKI infrastructure, but in instances where there is no centralized CA and a Web of Trust can, in fact, be used. Commonly used with such things as PGP, which is pretty good privacy, is the public key private key encryption mechanism we use to encrypt files or emails, so it's commonly used when communication between two parties, they wish to communicate using what's called self-generated or self-signed encryption keys.

Key Escrow

A key escrow is a trusted third-party that's going to hold the keys needed to decrypt data, so to use in cases where keys are lost or some mandate, i. e. a court order or some situation that requires the decryption of data, it's also referred to as a fair crypto system., as you can imagine, there are some disagreements around the technical feasibility of having a trusted, third-party that can correctly manage access to keys or control collateral compromise if those keys are leaked. We all know that that never happens, I understand, but theoretically, if it did happen, how can we control that if a third-party manages all of our keys or perhaps they manage the keys for a number of different organizations, well, in doing so, we create some risk. There is definitely some historical precedent, it happens more often, cases where organizations are being breached, at record scale, hackers are becoming more and more sophisticated. The idea of having some trusted third-party hold all of our encryption keys, I'm not so sure uncomfortable with that. That's a business decision that you may have, there may be cases where you have to have that again, perhaps a court order or something where it needs to be kept so that law enforcement or whoever can get access to those keys if need be, but That's a case by case basis and something that you, as the security professional within your own organization would need to decide, work with your business units to come up with the best solution.

Certificate Chaining

With certificate chaining, we have something referred to as the path of trust, and that path of trust goes from a user certificate extends all the way up to the root certificate. As an example we have the root CA all the way down to the end certificate. That path of trust extends from that end certificate all the way up to the root CA, or the root certificate authority, and that allows us to ensure that everything is secure from the root down. Conversely, if the root is compromised, everything below that is potentially compromised, we can't trust anything that is valid and has not been tampered with. We made it to the end of the book. In this chapter, we talked about four main areas, we talked about PKI components, we talked about types of certificates, and then we covered certificate formats, and then lastly, concepts around certificates.

BOOK 4

CISSP:
CYBERSECURITY OPERATIONS
AND
INCIDENT RESPONSE

DIGITAL FORENSICS WITH EXPLOITATION FRAMEWORKS &
VULNERABILITY SCANS

RICHIE MILLER

Introduction

IT Security jobs are on the rise! Small, medium or large size companies are always on the look out to get on board bright individuals to provide their services for Business as Usual (BAU) tasks or deploying new as well as on-going company projects. Most of these jobs requiring you to be on site but since 2020, companies are willing to negotiate with you if you want to work from home (WFH). Yet, to pass the Job interview, you must have experience. Still, if you think about it, all current IT security professionals at some point had no experience whatsoever. The question is; how did they get the job with no experience? Well, the answer is simpler then you think. All you have to do is convince the Hiring Manager that you are keen to learn and adopt new technologies and you have willingness to continuously research on the latest upcoming methods and techniques revolving around IT security. Here is where this book comes into the picture. Why? Well, if you want to become an IT Security professional, this book is for you! If you are studying for CompTIA Security+ or CISSP, this book will help you pass your exam. Passing security exams isn't easy. In fact, due to the raising security beaches around the World, both above mentioned exams are becoming more and more difficult to pass. Whether you want to become an Infrastructure Engineer, IT Security Analyst or any other Cybersecurity Professional, this book (as well as the other books in this series) will certainly help you get there! But, what knowledge are you going to gain from this book? Well, let me share with you briefly the agenda of this book. First, you are going to discover what are the most important steps for cyber security operations and incident response, specifically revolving around assessing organizational security. We'll also

440

talk about network reconnaissance and discovery and the various things we can use to accomplish those tasks. Next, we are going to cover file manipulation and the tools we use to do that along with shell and scripting environments. We'll talk about packet capture and replay, data forensics with exploitation frameworks, password crackers, and data sanitization. After that, we'll be covering Appropriate Data Sources to Support an Incident, vulnerability scans and the output, SIEM and SIEM dashboards. We'll also talk about log files and how they can support an investigation or data analysis, trying to figure out what happened, where, when, why and how. Next, you will discover how to use syslog, rsyslog, syslog-ng, journal control and nxlog. We'll also talk about retention for email, audit logs, bandwidth monitors, metadata, and how it changes for different types of files. After that, you will learn how to use NetFlow, sFlow, protocol analyzers and outputs. Moving on, you will discover how to implement Mitigation Techniques to Secure an Environment, how to reconfigure endpoint security solutions, application whitelisting and blacklisting, along with quarantining. We'll also going to cover configuration changes, firewall rules, MDM, or mobile device management, and data loss prevention or DLP. Next you will learn about content filters, revoking and updating certificates, the concepts of isolation, containment, and segmentation and how those can help us secure the environment, along with secure orchestration, automation, and response, or SOAR systems, and runbooks and playbooks specifically. Next we will cover the Key Aspects of Digital Forensics, documentation and evidence gathering in general and why it's very important. We'll also going to talk about acquisition and what we should go after first and why. We'll also cover integrity and a few methods we can use to prove that the data we've collected has not been tampered with, along with preservation, ediscovery and what that means and how it applies to an investigation of data recovery, including the concept of nonrepudiation so the party in question can't deny ownership or a specific action. You are also going to learn about strategic intelligence and counterintelligence along with on-prem versus cloud and some of the challenges and nuances to where that data resides, some things around data sovereignty and applicable laws, depending upon where it's located in the country or in the world if we're doing global business. If you are ready to get on this journey, let's first cover vulnerability scans and the outputs, as well as what we can do with those outputs!

Chapter 1 Data Sources to Support an Incident

In this chapter, we'll be covering an Appropriate Data Sources to Support an Incident. We'll be talking about vulnerability scans and the output, what we do with those outputs. We'll talk about SIEM and SIEM dashboards. We'll talk about log files and how they can support an investigation or data analysis, trying to figure out what happened, where, when, why and how. We'll talk about syslog, rsyslog, and syslog-ng or next generation. We'll talk about the differences there. We'll also talk about something called journal control or journalctl, nxlog. We'll talk about retention for basic things like email, audit logs. Then we'll talk about bandwidth monitors, metadata, and how it changes for different types of files. We'll talk about NetFlow and sFlow, the differences between the two, and then a little bit about protocol analyzers and outputs. When we're talking about accessing all of these different types of data, interpreting assessment results, understanding what's going on, the amount of data that's being created is increasing exponentially, so the amount of sensors, telemetry data.

In this chapter, we'll be talking about Implementing Mitigation Techniques to Secure an Environment. We'll be talking about reconfiguring endpoint security solutions, talking about application whitelisting and blacklisting, how that can help us, along with quarantining. We'll talk about configuration changes, and that deals with firewall rules, MDM, or mobile device management, data loss prevention, or DLP. We'll talk about content filters and also revoking and updating certificates. We'll also talk about the concepts of isolation, containment, and segmentation and how those can help us secure the environment, along with secure orchestration, automation, and response, or SOAR systems, and runbooks and playbooks specifically.

In this chapter we'll be talking about Understanding the Key Aspects of Digital Forensics. We'll talk about documentation and evidence in general and why it's Very important to make sure things are documented properly. We'll talk about acquisition and some things around what we should go after first and why, some of the gotchas if we don't follow those procedures. We'll talk about integrity and a few methods we can use to prove that the data we've collected has not been tampered with. We'll talk about preservation along the same lines. We'll talk about ediscovery and what that means and how it applies to an investigation, along with data recovery, and then a similar concept of nonrepudiation so the party in question can't deny ownership or specific action. And then we'll talk about strategic intelligence and counterintelligence along with on-prem versus cloud and some of the challenges and nuances to where that data resides, some things around data sovereignty, applicable laws, depending upon where it's located in the country or in the world if we're doing global business.

Chapter 2 How to Assess Organizational Security

In this chapter, we'll be talking about operations and incident response specifically around assessing organizational security. We'll be talking about network reconnaissance and discovery and the various things we can use to accomplish those tasks. We'll be talking about file manipulation and the tools we use to do that along with shell and scripting environments. We'll talk about packet capture and replay. We'll also talk about data forensics along with exploitation frameworks, password crackers, and then wrap up with data sanitization. To start off, let's talk about traceroute or tracert. It's a network tool to test connectivity between the host and the target. What it does is allow us to see hops along the way. And when I say hop, meaning we're crossing a router. We're going from one network to another. It allows us to see the hops along the way and then the associated latency with each hop. As an example, when I do a traceroute, what I see is the hop count, and it will go from 1 to whatever number. Typically, it tops out at 30. And then it will show me the round-trip time or the RTT for those three attempts. All along the way, I will see an output that shows me those individual hops and the individual round-trip time or the latency for each of those hops. Whether you're troubleshooting network performance or you're just trying to determine what's in between you and your target, it can show you where things might be a bottleneck, where there may be some type of firewall rule, where things are not necessarily reachable. Just because you've see no response or an asterisk doesn't necessarily mean that there's an issue. It just means that that specific hop is not replying back. It can still pass that traffic through to the destination.

nslookup/dig

Next we have nslookup or the Linux equivalent called dig. It's a DNS troubleshooting tool for Windows or Linux and also for Mac operating systems. They can provide a wide range of information on DNS and associated troubleshooting. Nslookup can be used on Windows and Linux systems; whereas, dig is a Linux and Mac-only command. I can do a number of different things. Like I can say set type=mx, and I'm saying, give me DNS information, and I'm going to put in the domain name of Google. But I'm setting the type to mx, so give me only the mail exchanger records. It returns back when I'm using for DNS. And then it also provides a priority number of which ones that should try first. In this particular instance, it's hosted at google.com. Nslookup and dig can both provide a wealth of information. They can potentially do zone transfers. You can look at all of the DNS information if that specific domain allows those types of lookups. Then to put in the perspective of a forensic examination, these things come in handy when we're doing reconnaissance, trying to figure out where things are going, where they're coming from, perhaps a piece of malware we're trying to track back and get information on the systems that it's touching or reaching out to. All of these different tools, but they help to give us information when we're conducting our investigations or doing reconnaissance.

ipconfig/ifconfig

The next command line told you're probably familiar with is ipconfig or ifonfig. So on the Windows side, that would be ipconfig. On the Linux or Mac side, that would be ifconfig. If I type in ifconfig, you'll see the interfaces, like eth0. Some information about its IP address, its net mask or subnet mask, the broadcast IP address, also its TCP/IP version 6 address. Also, some information about the number of packets received, any errors, and then it's also showing the loopback address. These commands are great for getting your own information as far as IP address, whether it be IPv4 or IPv6. Also it can show you your configured DNS address and, on a Window system, perhaps your WINS Server, not much in use any more. But the point being it can show all the associated information with that specific interface. If you have multiple interfaces, you can bring up information about each.

nmap and nmap demo
Nmap is an open source network scanner and it can discover hosts, it can look at services, it can detect operating systems, vulnerabilities. It's very extensible through the use of the nmap scripting engine, or NSE, and some typical uses for nmap would be device auditing, whether it be host for firewall enumeration, and it can detect vulnerabilities in operating systems, network devices, applications, also, rogue machine detection to identify machines that should not be on a specific network or network inventory. It's a penetration testers tool and network troubleshooting tool that can be used by the good guys, and it's also used very much by the bad guys. Nmap is a very extensible, very powerful program, the full use of which is beyond the scope of the book, but let's just suffice it to say that is a very robust network scanning tool, host enumeration detecting flaws or vulnerabilities that we can then further penetration test, either with scripts that can add or increase the functionality or brute force techniques, or even using other tools that nmap can be a part of, we can use in conjunction with other things. As part of the toolbox that we would use for penetration testing and, of course, what hackers would also use for their malicious activities. We can do threat detections, we can incorporate scripts through the nmap

scripting engine, I can target a specific host, or a subnet, or an entire network. With all of these switches and all of these parameters available to you, just understand that these types of tools should be used in a controlled environment. I would not recommend that you take this into your workplace and start scanning a production environment, that could lead to some bad juju. Your teammates or security folks in other areas perhaps, depending on how big your company is, could see that there are some port scans going on, it could raise some red flags, and then if by some chance it to take down production for some reason, causes congestion on our network, or something bad happens in any way, shape or form, you don't want to be responsible for that. These types of things, should be used in a controlled environment, and then as you develop your penetration testing skills, you can then start using it more in a production environment or in a pen testing engagement if, in fact, you know that's what you're doing at the moment, but just keep that in mind. Keep the usage of these tools to a minimum or in a sandbox environment, at least, until you have proper sign off from the powers that be so that if something does happen, everybody is on board, everyone knows what's happening.

Ping and Pathping
Let's take a look at a few command utilities for network troubleshooting, some things that you should keep in mind, definitely add to your tool bag if you're not already familiar. The first will be ping and pathping. These are two troubleshooting tools, command line tools, for both Windows and Linux., pathping is just for Windows. But ping is pretty much ubiquitous, and that's for Windows or Linux. And that's a network troubleshooting tool to test network connectivity by sending what's called ICMP packets to a host.

Pathping does something very similar, but it also combines the features of ping and traceroute. Next would be hping, and hping is a packet crafting tool that can be used to generate traffic, craft packets (spoofed IP addresses, ICMP floods). Then also Netstat. Netstat displays network statistics about TCP and UDP connections, various ports, routing tables, and also protocol statistics. If we look at ping or pathping, again, a tool to test network connectivity. And ping stands for packet internetwork groper, and it sends ICMP packets or internet control message protocol packets to a host to test connectivity. ICMP, internet control message protocol, and what it does is send an echo, and then it expects back a request. You can think of it as like a sonar, like a submarine that sends out a ping. It goes out and hits an object under the water, and it bounces back, and they can tell that that object is there. A very similar concept here.

hping

Hping, which is hping3 is a package generation tool that can craft packets, it can spoof packets, and configure any number of options as needed. We can do SYN attacks, we can flood the network, we can spoof IP addresses, so a lot of functionality here to test firewall collectivity, to test IDS or IPS systems, also for training with Wireshark to craft specific types of packets We can adjust source ports, destination ports, spoof IP addresses. We can simulate in a very small way a denial-of-service attack on a Linux host. I will be sending packets to another Windows host on my network. I have my Linux host, and then I have a Windows host. On the Linux machine if I issue the command hping3, which is going to invoke that hping program. I'm going to put hping3 -S, which is issuing a SYN packet. I give it the destination address, what port I want it to go over, port 135 in this case, and then I'm going to flood the network. I'm telling it, send it as fast as possible.

```
root@kali:/home/kali# hping3 -S 192.168.10.129 -p 135 --flood
HPING 192.168.10.129 (eth0 192.168.10.129): S set, 40 headers + 0 data bytes
hping in flood mode, no replies will be shown
```

If I go ahead and hit Enter, it's telling me it's going to go into flood mode. No replies are going to be shown because this is going so fast. If I flip back over to my Windows host, you see my Ethernet connection went from zero up to maxed out.

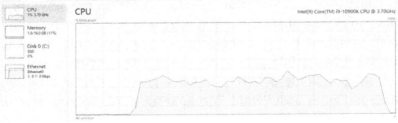

I'm receiving about 40MB per second, 40MB per second of throughput. This is just one machine sending to another. Imagine if we had 10 or 20 or 100 different machines all sending packets to a host on the network. Same thing with the CPU. We can see that CPU jumped up from nothing to about 38, 39, 40% of activity. That's one host attacking. If I had three or four of these, I could very quickly overrun that host machine. Just to go back in my Linux machine, if I cancel that out, Ctrl+C, I stop it, go back to Windows, you can see the activity drops, CPU drops, and then the Ethernet connectivity drops as well.

Each ping is a very powerful tool. It allows you to fire up Wireshark, look at different types of packets. You can craft packets in a number of ways and then, of course, use it for malicious purposes as well.

Netstat

The next one is netstat. And netstat is a command-line utility, and it displays, network statistics, hence the name netstat. TCP, UDP connections, also reports. We can even display the routing table and protocol statistics. Netstat is cross-platform. It's used to troubleshoot and provide network and host information. I can just type in from a command prompt netstat, and it will show me the active connections, the protocol, a local address, a foreign address, and then the state. Then, depending upon what flags you put in, it also gives me the process ID or the PID. That can be useful. You could look into a Task Manager on Windows and see what the process ID is and then associate that with the IP address it's accessing. netstat -a displays all connections and listening ports. If we add -b, that will display the executable involved in creating each connection or listening port. That may be helpful in troubleshooting what is making that connection if you're not sure. -f will display the fully qualified domain name or the FQDN, for that foreign address if it's possible or if it can determine that. It's not always available. But if it is, it will display that. And then netstat -r, will display the routing table. This is another tool added to the toolbox when we're doing network troubleshooting, connection troubleshooting.

netcat

The next one is an application called netcat. netcat is a network troubleshooting or a pen testing or a hacking tool, depending upon who's using it, that can read from and write to network connections, either TCP or UDP. And some common use cases would be port scanning, port redirection. It can be used as a port listener. It can even operate as a remote shell, serving web pages, or even transferring files. It's a very powerful program and can be used in conjunction with other tools like Metasploit. You could install this on a remote machine and then open up a listener on that remote machine and then run commands as if you were local on that machine. You could turn on Remote Desktop. You could do a lot of things that could have some malicious implications. A powerful tool, and like the majority of these types of tools, I recommend highly that you don't do it in a production environment unless you're looking for a new job. But seriously, make sure you do it in a controlled environment. A sandbox is best until you understand what the tools can do because they can kick off a lot of things behind the scenes or a lot of activity that you may or may not be aware of if you're not that well versed with the application. If it's in a production environment, it could certainly pop up on someone's radar. You don't want to draw unnecessary attention or take out an application or cause some type of production issue. Here's just a quick screenshot of netcat. It's included with Kali Linux. Not all distributions of Linux have it.

```
kali@kali: ~
File  Edit  View  Search  Terminal  Tabs  Help
kali@kali: ~                                    ×    kali@kali: ~
root@kali:/home/kali# nc -h
[v1.10-46]
connect to somewhere:   nc [-options] hostname port[s] [ports] ...
listen for inbound:     nc -l -p port [-options] [hostname] [port]
options:
        -c shell commands       as '-e'; use /bin/sh to exec [dangerous!!]
        -e filename             program to exec after connect [dangerous!!]
        -b                      allow broadcasts
        -g gateway              source-routing hop point[s], up to 8
        -G num                  source-routing pointer: 4, 8, 12, ...
        -h                      this cruft
        -i secs                 delay interval for lines sent, ports scanned
        -k                      set keepalive option on socket
        -l                      listen mode, for inbound connects
        -n                      numeric-only IP addresses, no DNS
        -o file                 hex dump of traffic
        -p port                 local port number
        -r                      randomize local and remote ports
        -q secs                 quit after EOF on stdin and delay of secs
        -s addr                 local source address
        -T tos                  set Type Of Service
        -t                      answer TELNET negotiation
        -u                      UDP mode
        -v                      verbose [use twice to be more verbose]
```

You may need to download and then install. With most of these applications, if you do just a -help or double dash and then the word help, you'll get the actual commands that are available to you. Some of them are very basic. Some of them are very complex. Then netcat, like most of these tools, has extensibility and can be used in conjunction with other applications, Metasploit being one of them. Just be careful with them, but definitely understand what they can do. For a deeper dive, I would definitely recommend some of the other books that go into these in a lot more detail. But for our purposes here, just understand what the application is. Its main use cases would be network troubleshooting, pen testing. Hacking, is one of those. But it's a great pen testing tool and allows us to operate in a listening mode or remote shell mode.

IP Scanners

An IP scanner, as the name implies, scans the network, a range of IP addresses. It can discover hosts. It can test for open ports, troubleshoot connectivity. Some of these things we've already talked about can be certainly identified as IP scanners. Then you can have scaled-down applications that

453

just do the IP scanning part. They don't do a lot of the other enhancements, the remote shells, the remote scripting - all those types of things. Some just identify IP addresses, what ports are available. A few to be aware of, Solarwinds being one, PRTG, AngryIP Scanner, Free IP Scanner, and Nmap as we talked about previously. All of these things have IP scanning capabilities. Some are more full-featured than others. Some are free, some are paid applications. Everyone has their preference or their favorite. But just make sure you familiarize yourself with the functionality and be sure to add that capability to your toolbelt.

ARP

Another tool and concept to be aware of is arp, and that stands for address resolution protocol, originally developed in 1982. It's been around for a long time by RFC 826, and it resolves an IP address to a MAC address. A link-layer protocol, so it does not route. Arp stays within the local network. But an IP address is a layer 3, if you recall the OSI Model, to a MAC address, which is layer 2. There's also a thing called reverse ARP. That will derive an IP address from a MAC address. And then we talked previously about ARP spoofing. And that is where a malicious user can intercept and reply to ARP requests, also known as ARP cache poisoning so they can put malicious or fictitious information into the ARP cache and either block connectivity or have connectivity go to an improper host.

Route

The next command is route, and route is used to view and manipulate the IP routing table on either Windows or Linux machines. And when I say Linux, we can general refer to macOS as well. If I just do a route print, it will show me the routing table. And you can see the destination, the net mask, the gateway, the interface, and then the metric. We can also view the routing table if we do a netstat -r. So there are two ways to get to the same information.

Curl and Curl Demo

Next we have a pretty neat command, and that's called curl. And curl can transfer data to or from a server using one of various protocols. But the takeaway here is that it allows us to transfer files, to get web pages, to download things from the internet, as an example, without having to do it from a web page. Web pages are great. They're GUI. They're easy to deal with from a human's perspective. But if we want to script something, we can't script web activity very well. You can't script moving a mouse, clicking on a link. Within curl, you can do the same actions, but from a command line, and allow you to download a file, upload a file, transfer in some form or fashion using it programmatically via scripts. Let's do a quick demo and take a look at using curl to download a file via FTP. So here we are back at our Kali Linux terminal. If I type curl -h, then it gives me the options of what I can do.

I'll go out to a test website that allows me just to test download speeds, and I'll use the -o to give the same name as the one I'm downloading. In this case, speedtest.tele2.net, and we want to download just the sample 10MB file. By using the standard switches, it shows me the download. You can see we use curl to download the file via FTP.

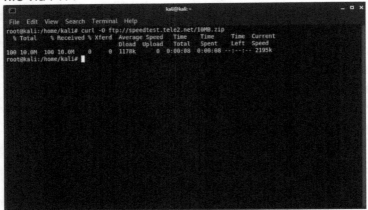

If I change that to a dash pound, you then see it changed the output from a standard download to I'm getting a progress bar. It will show me the progress of the file. And then once that's downloaded, it will finish.

It allows us to do some things that we would typically do via an FTP program or accessing something via the web. We can do that programmatically and incorporate those things into our scripts.

The Harvester

The next one up is another penetration testing tool, and that's called the Harvester. The Harvester is a tool for gathering email accounts and subdomain names from public sources. A quick screenshot showing you the splash page when you fire up the application. I'm going to be running this from Kali Linux.

The Harvester has a number of different options. Two I just want to call your attention to. Number 1 is -d, and that is the domain name to search or the company name. And then -b would be your data source or where you want to look from. And you can pick one source or you can pick all of them. I have a number of things that I can search through, and you can see the list here. If you did a -b and then chose it would search through all of those different sources. Depending upon what of these that you're scanning, you may return a number of records or not much. It just depends on how much information is publicly accessible. But nevertheless, a great tool for information gathering as you work through your initial reconnaissance and pen testing activities. And it can also be used for malicious activities as well because any tool that can be used for good, it can also be used for malicious purposes as well.

Sn1per

The next one up is sn1per and it's another pen testing tool. This one is an automated penetration testing tool and it can operate in stealth mode, it can do a full scan, it can do port scans only, it can scan individual hosts or entire networks, much like some of these other tools that we've talked about, and it's also very extensible with scripting. It can use scripting via nmap or MetaSploit and others, along with creating reports, including screenshots of websites that it goes out and crawls. It also leverages several other testing and exploit tools, MetaSploit being one, nmap, Slack, Shodan, it integrates with these different tools, and it can also brute force all open services on a target system, so a pretty powerful tool, definitely one to take a look at, especially considering a lot of this can be automated, not a lot of heavy lifting. You point it at something, kickoff some commands, and then off it goes. Let's go ahead and take a quick look at installing Sn1per and then a basic scan. As you can see here from the GitHub page, there is a download location, What I would do is go to my Kali Linux terminal, put in that download location. If I jump into a terminal session and then I put in the git clone and then the HTTPS address, write the GitHub address of that Sn1per installation, from there, I would do a sudo command to get to an elevated prompt and then run a bash script that does the install of the Sn1per application, so bash install.sh and that would run me through the actual installation.

```
                                    kali@kali:~/Sn1per                    _ □ ×
 File  Edit  View  Search  Terminal  Help
kali@kali:~/Sn1pers sudo su
root@kali:/home/kali/Sn1per# bash install.sh




+ -- --=[ https://xerosecurity.com
+ -- --=[ Sn1per by @xer0dayz

[>] This script will install sn1per under /usr/share/sniper. Are you sure you want to continue? (Hit Ctrl+C to exi
t)
y
[*] Installing package dependencies...
Get:1 http://ftp.halifax.rwth-aachen.de/kali kali-rolling InRelease [30.5 kB]
Get:2 http://ftp.halifax.rwth-aachen.de/kali kali-rolling/main amd64 Packages [17.4 MB]
Get:3 http://ftp.halifax.rwth-aachen.de/kali kali-rolling/main amd64 Contents (deb) [38.8 MB]
38% [2 Packages store 0 B] [3 Contents-amd64 2,304 B/38.8 MB 0%]                     2,668 kB/s 15s
```

So on my machine, it's about a 7 to 8 minutes installation. On yours, it may be longer, maybe shorter, but rather than have you sit through everything, we'll zip through the installation real quick. Then once it completes, you'll see that it gives us the message saying all done. And then to run the application, you would type Sn1per from your terminal and then, you'll have to give it a target, and then if you have any options that you want it to run, you would put those in as well. As you can see here from the command prompt, if I type sniper -h, it gives me the help file and shows me all the different configuration commands that I can use with the application.

```
                                                        kali@kali ~
File  Edit  View  Search  Terminal  Help
   (   )/ / // / / /    / /
  /   / / / /   / .   /\  / /
    / /

+ -- --=[ https://xerosecurity.com
+ -- --=[ Sniper v9.0 by @xer0dayz

[*] NORMAL MODE
sniper -t <TARGET>

[*] SPECIFY CUSTOM CONFIG FILE
sniper -c /full/path/to/sniper.conf -t <TARGET> -m <MODE> -w <WORKSPACE>

[*] NORMAL MODE + OSINT + RECON
sniper -t <TARGET> -o -re

[*] STEALTH MODE + OSINT + RECON
sniper -t <TARGET> -m stealth -o -re

[*] DISCOVER MODE
sniper -t <CIDR> -m discover -w <WORKSPACE_ALIAS>

[*] SCAN ONLY SPECIFIC PORT
sniper -t <TARGET> -m port -p <portnum>

[*] FULLPORTONLY SCAN MODE
sniper -t <TARGET> -fp

[*] WEB MODE - PORT 80 + 443 ONLY!
sniper -t <TARGET> -m web

[*] HTTP WEB PORT MODE
sniper -t <TARGET> -m webporthttp -p <port>

[*] HTTPS WEB PORT MODE
sniper -t <TARGET> -m webporthttps -p <port>
```

I could run in normal mode just by saying sniper -t and then giving it a target, and then there is a number of other things, a lot of extensibility here. You could go into stealth mode, discover mode, you could run web only, Port 80, Port 443, but at a minimum, it goes in and scans the entire website, all the URLs, all the subdomains, and it puts all of those things into files you can later analyze or look at in more detail, it puts it into what's called a loot folder, and then from there, you can do additional vulnerability testing, penetration testing. A lot of information beyond the scope of this book here to dig into with any detail, but definitely be aware that it's a powerful program for pen testing. Based upon what options you choose when you initiate your scan, some of these things will be skipped, which it goes through a number of different things. It will numerate ports, it will do port scans, it will check the web application firewall if there is one, see if there is any vulnerabilities there, it goes through a number of different nmap scripts, and on and on. I'm just going to zip through this and you can just see there is a lot of information that it scans through, all of the subpages, and it puts all of these things into a file You can go back and analyze it at a later date so that you could go back and do further penetration testing. As you develop pen testing skills, this is a very powerful tool and something you'd want to use quite a bit for doing reconnaissance, but just to play around with, I'm saying, make sure you understand what you're doing before you point it into anything into production. But at the end, and this took about 20 minutes give or take, a scan will complete and then it saves all of those things into a workspace file that's on your machine that you could go back and there is probably 15 or 20 different folders and files that have all the information that was the outputs from these scans that you can then ingest into other applications or read through for further analysis.

Chapter 3 File Manipulation & Packet Captures

Scanless

Another tool that you should be aware of is one called scanless. And scanless is a port scanner that leverages online port scanning services to anonymize scanning a target system. You're not doing it from your own system. You're telling the application to go out and hit a number of websites and have port scans issued from those websites. You can see here, here are the ones that it can go out and target, so Hackertarget, Ipfingerprints, Spiderip, Standingtech. You can read through the rest. But you can initiate these scans from these web-based points of origin. You anonymize where it's coming from. They can't tell it's coming from a specific system. If I want to install scanless on my system, I did a quick Google search and found a link for scanless.

Download scanless:

scanless 1.0.4 can be checked out from it's GIT repository here.

Here it's saying 1.0.4., when I go over to Git's website, it's version 2.1.5 is the latest as of this time. It shows me the install, which is pip install scanless.

	scanless	v2.1.5	last month
	.gitignore	Update .gitignore	4 years ago
	Dockerfile	Dockerfile added	2 years ago
	README.md	v2.1.4, minor fix to web request func	2 months ago
	UNLICENSE	initial commit	4 years ago
	setup.py	v2.1.5	last month

From a terminal session, I'll go ahead and issue that command. It then downloads and installs scanless on my system.

```
                                                          kali@kali ~
  File  Edit  View  Search  Terminal  Help
root@kali:/home/kali# pip install scanless
Collecting scanless
  Downloading scanless-2.1.5.tar.gz (216 kB)
  |████████████████████████████████| 216 kB 2.4 MB/s
Requirement already satisfied: beautifulsoup4 in /usr/lib/python3/dist-packages (from scanless) (4.9.3)
Collecting crayons
  Downloading crayons-0.4.0-py2.py3-none-any.whl (4.6 kB)
Requirement already satisfied: requests in /usr/lib/python3/dist-packages (from scanless) (2.25.1)
Requirement already satisfied: soupsieve>1.2 in /usr/lib/python3/dist-packages (from beautifulsoup4->scanless) (2.1)
Requirement already satisfied: colorama in /usr/lib/python3/dist-packages (from crayons->scanless) (0.4.4)
Building wheels for collected packages: scanless
  Building wheel for scanless (setup.py) ... done
  Created wheel for scanless: filename=scanless-2.1.5-py3-none-any.whl size=218506 sha256=53ca984c2a70971e7a78ef4a6d0039e8afcc13a7a381c75a07
  Stored in directory: /root/.cache/pip/wheels/31/5a/74/f50e9d4d132bfec6a46a6b221b89ea29a2ab9c5c8db1828cf6
Successfully built scanless
Installing collected packages: crayons, scanless
Successfully installed crayons-0.4.0 scanless-2.1.5
root@kali:/home/kali# scanless -h
usage: scanless [-h] [-v] [-t TARGET] [-s SCANNER] [-r] [-l] [-a] [-d]

scanless, an online port scan scraper.

optional arguments:
  -h, --help            show this help message and exit
  -v, --version         display the current version
  -t TARGET, --target TARGET
                        ip or domain to scan
  -s SCANNER, --scanner SCANNER
                        scanner to use (default: hackertarget)
  -r, --random          use a random scanner
  -l, --list            list scanners
  -a, --all             use all the scanners
  -d, --debug           debug mode (cli mode off & show network errors)
root@kali:/home/kali# sc
```

It will upack it, install, and then I'm good to go. So from there, I can do a scanless -h as I talked about before. It gives me the arguments. I can see the current version. I can pick a target, with no additional switches. I can then run the same command again with a -a, which will give me all of the online scanners. And it will run through all of those. It might take a minute or two. And each of the online services might give me slightly different results. Some scan for more ports than others, so you don't get exactly the same results from each. But what it does do, is anonymize those scans.

DNSenum

The next one that I want to mention is one called DNSenum for enumerate. DNSenum is a command line tool, and I just have a screenshot here showing you the help file and some of the switches that you can use.

```
                                                          kali@kali:~
  File  Edit  View  Search  Terminal  Help
kali@kali:~$ dnsenum -h
dnsenum VERSION:1.2.6
Usage: dnsenum [Options] <domain>
[Options]:
Note: If no -f tag supplied will default to /usr/share/dnsenum/dns.txt or
the dns.txt file in the same directory as dnsenum.pl
GENERAL OPTIONS:
  --dnsserver   <server>
                          Use this DNS server for A, NS and MX queries.
  --enum                  Shortcut option equivalent to --threads 5 -s 15 -w.
  -h, --help              Print this help message.
  --noreverse             Skip the reverse lookup operations.
  --nocolor               Disable ANSIColor output.
  --private               Show and save private ips at the end of the file domain_ips.txt.
  --subfile <file>        Write all valid subdomains to this file.
  -t, --timeout <value>   The tcp and udp timeout values in seconds (default: 10s).
  --threads <value>       The number of threads that will perform different queries.
  -v, --verbose           Be verbose: show all the progress and all the error messages.
GOOGLE SCRAPING OPTIONS:
  -p, --pages <value>     The number of google search pages to process when scraping names,
                          the default is 5 pages, the -s switch must be specified.
  -s, --scrap <value>     The maximum number of subdomains that will be scraped from Google (default 15).
BRUTE FORCE OPTIONS:
  -f, --file <file>       Read subdomains from this file to perform brute force. (Takes priority over default dns.txt)
```

If I go in and just scrape down through here, I can get a lot of information about a specific website, its zones and subzones. I can tell it where to scrape from, reverse lookup options or output options. If I just do a DNSenum -v for verbose and then I put in the website, it shows me the web servers, any name servers, mail exchangers. It can go out and, as the name implies, enumerate DNS entries and DNS information about a specific website.

Nessus and Cuckoo

Nessus is a commercial vulnerability scanner. There's three different versions. There's a professional version, a cloud version, and then a free version. The professional version you could install local or have it on your system.

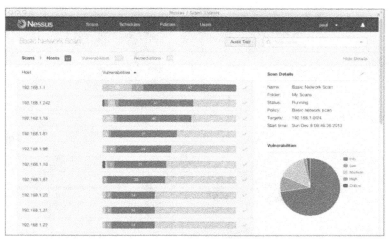

A cloud version, as the name implies, runs in the cloud as a service. The free version will be good for very small environments or for educational use. That's limited to scanning 16 IP addresses. Very limited use, but still gives you a good opportunity to learn about the product. The nice thing about Nessus is it's a very mature product, and it has many built-in templates and scans for common threats, misconfigurations. Definitely one to familiarize yourself with if your organization is looking for a commercial vulnerability scanner. Next, let's talk about something called Cuckoo. Cuckoo is an automated malware analysis platform, and it runs in a sandboxed environment. You would want to run it in the virtualized environment with a sandbox set up so that you can download malware and let that malware execute in that sandbox to see what it does.

More specifically, Cuckoo, it's an open source automated malware analysis tool, and it's designed to be run in an isolated lab environment. It can analyze, trace, and document a piece of malware's actions. It can do tracing of API calls. It can analyze memory and network traffic. It's a great tool to have in a controlled environment. As an example, here we have a Cuckoo host machine. That's going to do our guest analysis management, traffic dumps, and reporting. That's going to be attached, to an isolated network, a virtual isolated network. It's important that we run this thing in a sandboxed environment so that when we do download malware and we run that malware, it doesn't have the potential to escape out onto our production environment. That would be very bad. That's what we call an RGE or a resume-generating event. Isolated network, and in this small example, we have three virtual machines. We have a Windows machine, a Linux machine, and an OSX machine, your virtual environment may be a lot larger, or you may have a different mix of hosts, but you get the idea. Then from there, you could have that host machine go out to the internet you can see if it is, in fact, pulling things down from some command and control server. Or you could have it

466

point to a sinkhole so it goes here. And then you can download this from cuckoosandbox.org and try it out in your own environment.

File Manipulation

Next, I just want to talk about a few file manipulation commands that you can use from a command line. The first would be head. The head command would print the first x number of lines of a file, so the default would be 10. However, that's configurable. Tail is the opposite of that. That prints the last x number of lines of a file. The default is 10. We have the command cat, which would create, display, and also concatenate files or combine files together. And then we have grep. Grep searches plain-text data for lines that match a regular expression. It means globally search for a regular expression and then print matching lines. That's where the term grep comes from, but it's a very, very powerful tool. If you're not already familiar with grep and regular expressions, I definitely recommend you dig into that and learn all about that and add that skillset to your toolbox. From the command line, it's very, very powerful. Next, we have chmod or change permissions on files and folders. We can change permissions on files and folders, again from the command line. And then lastly, logger. Logger is going to create entries in a system log. It provides the shell command interface to the syslog system-log chapter. Back in my Kali Linux terminal, I have a text file here, just as an example, and, inside the file, just some random text. If I go into the terminal and issue a head command, and I can just drag this file in there.

```
 ▢                              kali@kali: ~                        _  □  ×
 File  Edit  View  Search  Terminal  Help
 kali@kali:~$ head '/home/kali/Desktop/ipsum.txt'
 This is the first line.
 Lorem ipsum dolor sit amet, consectetur adipiscing elit.
 Aliquam facilisis metus interdum leo bibendum, id mattis purus tristique.
 Aliquam bibendum consequat dolor at euismod.
 Integer nec enim et nulla cursus aliquet eu vel dolor.
 Etiam aliquam rhoncus lobortis.
 Vestibulum vulputate ullamcorper nibh, dignissim sodales arcu porta vitae.
 Sed maximus tellus purus, pellentesque porta tellus ultrices eget.

 Mauris finibus libero erat. Quisque ac pharetra massa. Duis dapibus tellus risus
 , ut sodales augue ultricies eu.Maecenas pulvinar faucibus ultricies. Nullam non
  enim bibendum sapien ultrices vehicula vel a nisi. Aliquam erat volutpat.Morbi
 elit ligula, dignissim mattis ultrices ut, porttitor quis lectus. Cras in augue
 eget ligula elementum tristique ullamcorper nec metus.
 kali@kali:~$ head -2 '/home/kali/Desktop/ipsum.txt'
 This is the first line.
 Lorem ipsum dolor sit amet, consectetur adipiscing elit.
 kali@kali:~$
```

That will give me the path directly to it. And I can just hit Enter. That's going to give me the first 10 lines of that file. If I want to just say the first one line or, say, first two lines, I could just hit a -2, and it would give me just the first two lines of that file. Conversely, if I type tail, same thing, and let's say do the last two lines of the file and drop that off, there's a space and then the very last line of the file. And if I open it up in the regular text editor, you can see the first few lines of the file and then, down at the bottom, the last line of the file. It makes it easy to work with very large files from the command line, getting to the beginnings or the ends of files. Same type of thing with the cat demand. If I just did a cat and then help, it gives me the flags that I can use. And if I just type in cat and then, let's say, for instance, a n for line number, again drop that file into the terminal window and hit Enter, it shows me then the same file, but it numbers every single line.

468

```
                              kali@kali: ~                              _ □ ×
 File  Edit  View  Search  Terminal  Help
 cAdmptco:
   cat f - g  Output f's contents, then standard input, then g's contents.
   cat        Copy standard input to standard output.

 GNU coreutils online help: <https://www.gnu.org/software/coreutils/>
 Full documentation <https://www.gnu.org/software/coreutils/cat>
 or available locally via: info '(coreutils) cat invocation'
 kali@kali:~$ cat -n '/home/kali/Desktop/ipsum.txt'
      1  This is the first line.
      2  Lorem ipsum dolor sit amet, consectetur adipiscing elit.
      3  Aliquam facilisis metus interdum leo bibendum, id mattis purus tristique

      4  Aliquam bibendum consequat dolor at euismod.
      5  Integer nec enim et nulla cursus aliquet eu vel dolor.
      6  Etiam aliquam rhoncus lobortis.
      7  Vestibulum vulputate ullamcorper nibh, dignissim sodales arcu porta vita
 e.
      8  Sed maximus tellus purus, pellentesque porta tellus ultrices eget.
      9
     10  Mauris finibus libero erat. Quisque ac pharetra massa. Duis dapibus tell
 us risus, ut sodales augue ultricies eu.Maecenas pulvinar faucibus ultricies. Nu
 llam non enim bibendum sapien ultrices vehicula vel a nisi. Aliquam erat volutpa
 t.Morbi elit ligula, dignissim mattis ultrices ut, porttitor quis lectus. Cras i
 n augue eget ligula elementum tristique ullamcorper nec metus.
```

This may or may not be useful for you depending upon what
environment you like to work in. But definitely understand
the uses of them, the flags associated with them, and how
they can be used to in scripting or manipulating files from
the command line.

Shell and Script Environments (SSH, PowerShell, Python and
OpenSSL)
Just to cover some shell and scripting environments without
digging too deeply, making you an expert in any one specific
area, but some things you should be aware of for sure are
SSH, or Secure Shell. It is a cryptographic network protocol
for doing things securely over an insecure network or an
unsecured network. We can do things like remote command
line execution, remote logins. Next is PowerShell. PowerShell
is a command line shell and associated scripting language. It
was originally Windows-only, but has since been made open
source, so its cross-platform. But without digging into the
specifics, PowerShell has a multitude of commands and
functions called cmdlets to access elements of the operating

469

system, to do various functions. Next, we have Python, and Python is a cross-platform interpreted programming language. Meaning you need an interpreter with a focus on readability. It's widely regarded as one of the top three programming languages, Java and C or C# being some of the other ones. Then we have OpenSSL, which is a software library for applications that secure communications using an open-source implementation of SSL and TLS. With TLS 1.3 support added in September of 2018, TLS 1.0 has been deprecated, so make sure that's out of your environment if at all possible. But, TLS 1.3 is the current standard.

Packet Capture and TCPDump

As a security analyst, there's a lot of tools that we need in our toolbelt, a lot of various skills that we need to develop to secure our networks and our applications. When it comes to packet capture and replay, we have a security analyst that's attached to the network, and we have a few other hosts on the network. We have some database and some coding. There's other users on the network. Well, as a security analyst, there's a few different tools that you may use, one of which is tcpdump, which is a command line utility. Another might be Wireshark, which is a GUI implementation. Tcpdump gives you a similar capability as Wireshark, but it's a command line. And then the ability to replay traffic, tcpreplay, and that could be fed into IDS and IPS systems to ramp up traffic to keep it at scale just to give you a bit of an overview of where these things come into play. When we talk about tcpdump, it's a command line packet capture tool to capture and display packets in real time. It can be filtered by IP address, by port, by connection type or protocol. It's a very quick and dirty tool to be able to see what's going on in real time via command line, much like we do within Wireshark, but this is a command line utility. Next is

Wireshark. It's a graphical packet capture utility similar to tcpdump and can be used to troubleshoot network issues, to decrypt communications, assuming we have the proper certificates, and then also to eavesdrop on communications either for a legitimate purpose or an illegitimate purpose. Bad actors can use that maliciously. Then tcpreplay is a command line tool for editing and then replaying previously captured packets. It can be used for troubleshooting, for IDS and IPS systems, intrusion detection systems or intrusion prevention systems, for NetFlow systems. We want to be able to replay that traffic and analyze it in some form or fashion. This is very similar to what we would see in Wireshark. We're capturing packets. It just happens to be displaying in real time in my terminal session. Depending upon what types of tools you like to use, this could be another tool in your toolbelt. Some people prefer command prompt or command line or terminal session. Other folks prefer graphical user interfaces, like Wireshark.

Chapter 4 Forensics & Exploitation Frameworks

When it comes to forensics, there are a lot of nuances within the field. There are different specialties, different areas of expertise. But generally speaking, there are some tools that you should be aware of and some skill sets that you should develop if forensics is, in fact, an area that you want to dig into. Imagine that we have an investigator, and there are a few tools I just want to call your attention. We have the first one being dd, and that's a command line tool to copy and clone disks, partitions, and files. It can be used to erase disks. Some people refer to it as disk destroyer, but it's a very powerful tool, command line tool, built into Linux and allows you to copy, clone and partition files. Next, we have memdump. Memdump can dump either the physical or kernel memory to a file, and it can also be done over the network. You can connect to a machine remotely and do a memory dump to a file and get what's in that system's memory, either physical memory or kernel memory. Next, we have WinHex, and that's a hex editor for examining files, recovering files, searching for specific file types. That can dig into the code underneath of a file or contained within a file to help you look for specific patterns, hidden information, header-type mismatch. And then we have something called FTK Imager, and that stands for Forensic Toolkit, and it's used to acquire disk images and perform analysis for investigations, creating case files. Then we have Autopsy, another forensic toolkit for acquiring disk images and performing analysis and investigations. Two different ways, or two different programs to accomplish the same task. As an example, here we have a screenshot of Autopsy, this is a forensic tool for building cases for investigating systems, gathering evidence.

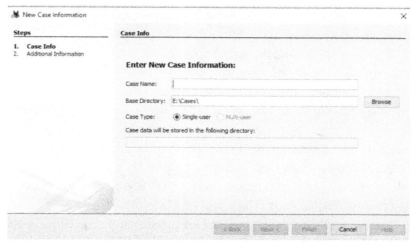

It allows us to create a case, we can name it, add additional information, we can put in the base directory of where we want to store that information. Then once we start the case, there are a number of things that can be automated as it searches through that system. We can do hash lookups.

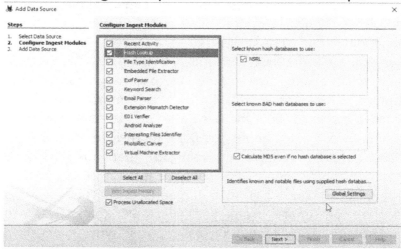

So, if we're looking for illegal images or things we don't necessarily want to have to sift through one by one by one, we can have the application going in and hash all the files on that system and then compare those hashes to a database of

473

known hashes. In other words, if there's a bunch of files that are already known, like child exploitation files as an example, there are large hash databases that have already been compiled by law enforcement that you can subscribe to and then compare those hashes against that. You can very quickly find information without having to sift through each individual file. We can look for file type identification or extension mismatch detector. That's an old school way of trying to hide files. Like you may have a graphics file, but you may change the extension to.doc for a doc file, so that if someone looks at it, they try to click on it, it won't open because it's not associated to the application. By using tools like this, we can very quickly look at the file header and then match it to the file extension. And if those things don't match, it stands out like a sore thumb. It makes it even easier to find those types of files. These types of applications become very powerful. As it does all of these things, it does a lot of it automated. Some of it will be manual process, but some of it is just a matter of you setting things up in the beginning. And then it will go through and analyze that system, build the case file, put everything into proper files and folders, and then something that we've touched on before is the concept of hashing and making sure that hashes match to show that we have two identical files. Well, when we're talking about acquiring forensic images, it's the same process. We have an investigator that would use their forensic toolkit, one of the ones we just talked about, and they would connect it to a target system. They want to acquire an image from a suspect PC to analyze, to investigate. They would typically put a write blocker in between their laptop or their toolkit and the actual target system. That way, it would prevent their forensic toolkit from altering or writing to the target system in any way, shape, or form. It keeps everything pristine. The write blocker would then connect to the target system. Then the forensic toolkit would do its thing. We just saw the screenshot showing some of the capabilities. It would image that system and then write it out to a cloned system. We take all of the data off of the target system and make an immutable copy that's write protected. It may chunk it up into multiple pieces that can be copied out to a CD or a DVD so that it can be then imaged or analyzed over and over again. Then what we can do each time is take a hash of the target system and then a hash of the cloned system. That way, those things match. We know that they are identical, that nothing's changed. That way we can be sure that when we're working off of a cloned system, we're not introducing artifacts or changing data in any way, shape, or form. Those things, as you can imagine, are needed for court, preservation of evidence, chain of custody. All of these things apply when we're dealing with digital evidence, as well as physical evidence, and having a hash value that matches allows us to show when we present that report and say, here's all of the things that we found on that target system. The other side can't come back and say, oh, well, that's not my system. Things have been changed. You added things in there. Well, no, the hash values match. We initially took a hash of the system when we first acquired it, and it exactly matches the hash of our cloned system. Those things go a long way to help strengthen your case. It's a matter of following best practices when we're doing forensic-type work.

Exploitation Frameworks

Exploitation frameworks, and as the name implies, they are there to exploit weaknesses, exploit vulnerabilities in a specific host, or a network, or a system. They are tool sets that can be used offensively or defensively, and they're often used by penetration testers, or pen testers, as well as hackers unfortunately. Popular exploitation frameworks, Metasploit is probably one of the most popular, and it's an open source and commercial, there are both versions available, you can download it for free, and then there's a paid version. It gives you a lot of amazing features and tool sets out of the box, hundreds of different exploits to test, and it's also widely used, by pen testers and also the hacking community. Next is CANVAS. These are just a small list, not an exhaustive one by any stretch and certainly not an endorsement of any one particular piece of software. But CANVAS was a development and pen testing platform originally, and then we have Core Impact, another one, which was designated as the first fully automated pen testing program that's typically used by enterprises and corporate environments primarily due to cost. There's also another one that's called RouterSploit, and as you might guess, that's specifically geared towards routers.

```
rsf (AutoPwn) > set target 192.168.1.254
[+] {'target': '192.168.1.254'}
rsf (AutoPwn) > show options

Target options:

   Name       Current settings       Description
   ----       ----------------       -----------
   target     192.168.1.254          Target address e.g. http://192.168.1.1
   port       80                     Target port

rsf (AutoPwn) > run
[*] Running module...
[-] exploits/multi/misfortune_cookie is not vulnerable
[-] exploits/dlink/dvg_n5402sp_path_traversal is not vulnerable
[-] exploits/dlink/dwr_932_info_disclosure is not vulnerable
[-] exploits/dlink/dir_500_320_615_auth_bypass is not vulnerable
[-] exploits/dlink/dsl_2750b_info_disclosure is not vulnerable
[-] exploits/dlink/dns_320l_327l_rce is not vulnerable
[-] exploits/dlink/dir_645_password_disclosure is not vulnerable
[-] exploits/dlink/dir_300_600_615_info_disclosure is not vulnerable
[-] exploits/dlink/dir_300_600_rce is not vulnerable
[-] exploits/cisco/ucs_manager_rce is not vulnerable
[-] exploits/2wire/gateway_auth_bypass is not vulnerable
[-] exploits/asus/infosvr_backdoor_rce is not vulnerable
[-] exploits/asus/rt_n16_password_disclosure is not vulnerable
[+] exploits/asmax/ar_1004g_password_disclosure is vulnerable
[-] exploits/asmax/ar_804_gu_rce is not vulnerable
[-] exploits/linksys/wap54gv3_rce is not vulnerable
[-] exploits/linksys/1500_2500_rce is not vulnerable
[-] exploits/fortinet/fortigate_os_backdoor is not vulnerable
[-] exploits/technicolor/tc7200_password_disclosure is not vulnerable
```

As you can see here, it runs in very much the same fashion, you can put in a target, an IP address, and you can run a Metasploit-type command set, against this target IP address, and it will run different modules, it'll go through the list, and it will run all of these different types of exploits against that specific router, and it will see where there's a vulnerability or if any exist. And as you can see from the output here, that exploit does exist for a password disclosure, so it says is vulnerable. All the rest in this specific instance is not vulnerable, but it allows you to quickly go through a network and identify all the different routers within a specific subnet or the entire environment, and then run this test against all of those devices, and come back and report and say, hey, here's where we're vulnerable, we're locked down everywhere except, not sure if you knew this, but you're vulnerable here, here, and here. You can very quickly give a report back to management, executive management, or the company that's hiring you to come in if you're a penetration tester, and show them where those vulnerabilities do exist.

Chapter 5 Data Sanitization Tools

Next we have data sanitization tools, and wiping versus deleting, as you may or may not be aware, deleting a file doesn't do much in and of itself. If you delete a file, you're simply marking that file as being able to be overwritten, so the data is still there. There are tons of free tools and commercial tools that can recover that data very easily. If you need to make sure that data is gone and not recoverable, then we need to do something called wiping, Wiping is always going to be better than deleting. Sanitization tools overwrite the data x number of times to ensure that it's unrecoverable, and those number of passes, or that x number of times, is configurable. We'll also talk about SSD disk sanitization. That's going to be different. When we're talking about traditional hard disks, that's a magnetic media, so that's going to be a different method to sanitize than SSDs or the solid state or all-flash drives. With SSDs, each manufacturer typically has a secure erase tool, you'll need to either use that specific tool, or there are also some third-party tools that can work on SSDs as well, so as an example of SSD sanitization. Each manufacturer will have their own specific toolset that is geared toward that specific drive, Samsung, Intel, Corsair, SanDisk, they all make their own different tools. And then there's a third-party tool called Parted Magic, and that includes a sanitization or a secure erase tool as well. As an example, here we have SSD Secure Erase for Samsung drives.

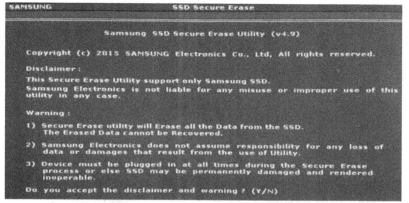

Using the Samsung Magician toolset, we'll create a beautiful drive, either USB or a CD or DVD, and we put that in the machine, and we'll boot into this interface. From here, we just say yes, we want to do a Secure Erase. It'll ask us again, and then within a matter of seconds that drive is securely erased. If we use Parted Magic as an example, it's going to come up first and say, we want to do a secure erase, and it can either be SSDs or it can be NVMe in this case.

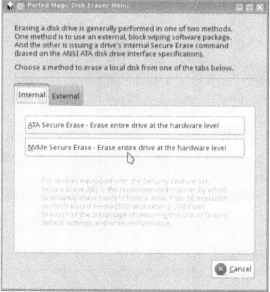

It's going to do a drive-level erase, so Secure Erase issues drive-level command sets to that specific drive and tells it what to do. In this instance, we're going to do a Secure Erase of an NVMe drive. We're going to say, pick the drive from the list. There it is dev/nvme0n1.

It's a Samsung SSD 950 PRO. We're going to say yes, I want to go ahead and erase. From there, it literally takes 2 or 3 seconds, and then it's done. That quickly that drive is securely erased. And it can also generate a log output if you want to review the log settings or review the output, but very quick and much quicker than erasing a magnetic hard disk. When we're talking about data sanitization methods for hard drives, there are a few things or a few standards we should be aware of. There are a couple that I want to call your attention to, and there are others, but these are the main three that you should be familiar with. The first is the DoD 5220.22-M, that's a standard. This is from the Department of Defense, and it is a three-pass write, so it's going to overwrite that data three separate times. Pass 1 writes a zero and then verifies the write, Pass 2 writes a one and then verifies the write, and then Pass 3 writes a random character verifies that write. Once that's complete, that data is not recoverable. The next is RCMP, or the Royal Canadian Mounted Police, an outstanding cybersecurity division. They issue a three-pass write as well. The Communication Security Establishment of Canada, that's what the CSEC stands for. And what we're doing here is writing a one or zero in Pass 1, and then Pass 2 writes the complement of the previously written character, so if the first pass was zeros, then this pass would be a one and vice-versa. Then Pass 3 writes a random character and then verifies that write. Then lastly, something referred to as Secure Erase, and that's a one-pass. That writes a binary one or a zero, very fast, and that's only available for whole-disk sanitization. These other two methods I talked about, they can be used on individual files and folders as well. There are toolsets that you can run within the operating system that will allow you to use those techniques to erase individual files or folders, but with Secure Erase it works only on the whole disk. There are some other ones as well. There's the Peter Gutmann 35-pass, and that was developed back in the mid to late nineties, and back then, 35 passes was thought to be like the most extreme, and that was like super secure. We've found that over time that a subset of that is all you need to have data unrecoverable. It used to be DoD was a seven-pass overwrite, and that was like the most secure. It's going down to three. Same thing with RCMP. They went from a higher level down to three. Then Secure Erase is also acceptable by RCMP as well. That single-pass write has been found to be unrecoverable by pretty much every type of disk recovery software out there. In summary, we talked about network reconnaissance and discovery, along with file manipulation, various shell and script environments. We talked about packet capture and replay, some of the tools that we would use for that, whether they are command-line or GUI based. We also talked about forensics and some of the nuances of acquiring images, making sure that they match, holding up in court. Then we talked about exploitation frameworks, password crackers, data sanitization, and then some demos of various applications.

Chapter 6 How to Apply Policies, Processes and Procedures for Incident Response

In this chapter we'll be talking about applying policies, processes, and procedures for incident response. We'll be talking about incident response plans and process. We'll cover the various testing exercises that you may utilize in your environment. We'll also talk about the various attack frameworks, along with stakeholder management, communication plans, including disaster recovery and business continuity plans. We'll also talk about the continuity of operation planning, along with incident response teams, retention policies, and at the end, we'll put it all together and talk about responding to an incident. But who should read this chapter? Well, we have six main categories. We have computer security staff, people that are implementing this type of stuff day to day; we have computer security program managers, the ones that need to look at things at a little higher level and understand the big risk and also the financial impacts; tech support staff and managers, the folks that make IT run on a day-to-day basis; incident response teams, the ones that are responsible for coming out and handling things when an incident or a breach occurs; system and network administrators, again IT, in general; and then end users, both IT and non-IT. IT security is everyone's responsibility. It's not just for the IT security professional. Everybody is responsible or should be responsible for making sure IT security, information security, cybersecurity, make that a priority. Because, as we know, threats can come both internally and externally. They can come from hackers, organized crime, nation states, but they can also be done internally for things like espionage or to get back at a co-worker or a manager. Then when we look at the actual potential impacts, some things that you should be aware of, drives this home, and the real reasons why you should care, is the fact that companies, both large and small, are constant targets. It makes no difference the industry or the size of the company, not just high-value targets. Smaller victims can play a part in larger attacks. Meaning, you may think to yourself, well, we're a small company of 5, 10, 15 people. We don't have to worry about IT Security as much. Well, that's precisely why you should worry about IT security. The smaller companies that may not have their actual IT network defenses and perimeter defenses as tight and as rigid as some larger companies, they become easy targets. While the information that they possess may not be of a high-value nature to a potential hacker or nation state or what have you, what small company, or your small company, could play a part in a larger attack. You could become part of a botnet or some type of other larger organized or more organized scheme to attack a much larger company or a much larger victim. Don't think just because you're small, you may not play a part in a much bigger attack. Then also such things as loss of data, intellectual property, competitive advantage, or overall consumer confidence. These can all be downstream impacts and fallout from a breach. Then companies can also risk legal action if they're negligent and not properly protected. If there are things that you should be doing but for whatever reason you're not, and then a breach occurs and an incident occurs and consumer data is lost, or personally identifiable information, is leaked, that information, or that fallout could come back to haunt the company in the form of legal action lawsuits, or class action lawsuits. It's very important that we realize that IT security is everyone's responsibility. Everyone should be chipping in. If they see something, say something. Everyone should be playing their part to make sure that their small piece of this larger puzzle is as secure as possible.

Team Models

Let's now talk about the various team models that we should look at developing within our organization. So, we can have a central incident response team, and that means all of our team members are on site, they're in one central location, and they'll handle all incidents for that company wherever they may be. If we have a global presence, however, that may or may not be feasible. In that case, we would have a distributed incident response team, and that means we have incident response teams perhaps spread out through all of our different organization locations, geographically dispersed, either throughout a specific part of the world or potentially globally. And then we have a coordinating team, and a coordinating team would be centrally located. The coordinating team itself, they would coordinate the efforts of the other teams located throughout the various parts of either the country or throughout the world. No matter which of the last two we choose, whether it's distributed or coordinating, it's very important to understand that all of the different teams, whether they are reporting to a centralized coordinating team and they're advising them what to do, or they're distributed and they're each acting as their own entity, they all need to make sure that they adhere to the same sets of policies so a consistent application of that incident response plan and procedures, are in fact implemented and executed, no matter where that's taking place throughout any of the company's various locations.

Incident Response Process

When talking about the phases of incident response we've covered before, the six main phases, the preparation, detection, analysis, containment, eradication, recovery, and then documentation, or lessons learned. This process is a continuous cycle that's refined over time. None of these things are going to be static. It's a living document; it's a living process. Every time we have a breach or an incident, we're going to learn something from that, and we're going to refine our process. Those lessons learned, once you come to the end of that process, we go through preparation, detection, containment, eradication, we get to the end, the documentation and lessons learned, that helps us identify gaps and increase our preparedness for the next time. It would be nice to say there never will be a next time, but unfortunately, that's not the nature of breaches in today's environment. Most companies have hundreds, if not thousands, of breaches or attempted breaches per year. Some companies have thousands per day. It just depends upon the size of your company, the criticality of the information your company has, or the intellectual property or whatever data that's valuable to a hacker, whoever that hacker or hacking organization may be. Then additional resources are brought on line and into that response team's arsenal. It's not a static environment. It's dynamic, and so as we go through this process and we refine, refine, refine, lessons learned, we identify gaps, we close those gaps. We may need additional resources, additional team members with additional skill sets. Every company's going to be slightly different. Every company houses different information, has different potential targets for a hacker or a hacking organization. There is no one set document that will cover everything. There are certainly a guideline and a best practices, but as you go through this, you will identify specific things that are unique to your organization, and correct or add to that arsenal accordingly.

Preparation

When we're talking about preparation, we have a couple things. We need to make sure that we identify team members. It's very important that we identify what skills we need, how many team members we need. One person can't do all of this. It's too vast. There are too many things to do at once. In the middle of a breach, you're going to have multiple things going on at once, detection and analysis, alerting other people, alerting other teams, coordinating with media, coordinating with executive management, identifying the risk, shutting down ports, protocol, and so on. There's going to be a lot of things that may need to happen concurrently or in tandem in the middle of a breach, so it's too much for one person to handle, typically. We'll need to identify those team members. We'll need to identify and define roles and responsibilities. It should be clearly defined who does what and in what order, so in the middle of some type of crisis, we have a playbook or a run book we can go by and say, you do this, I'll do this, he's going to take care of that piece for us. Everybody works in concert and attacks the problem as a cohesive unit. It's very important to have that synergy. Then also develop defense-in-depth strategies. These things should be spelled out ahead of time. You shouldn't have just one lock on the door. There are many things that we can do, so that if a hacker breaches one method of defense, there's still another, perhaps two or three more that they have to get through before they can get into our network and into our systems, make it as difficult as possible. That also gives you time to become alerted, it gives you time to remediate before they penetrate all of the defenses and get at your critical systems.

Chapter 7 Detection and Analysis

In the detection and analysis phases, properly trained teams can assist and expedite all phases of the incident and response process. Having that team in place, properly trained, running smooth, that's going to help all phases of that process. A quick assessment can determine the level of impact and also help direct containment and mitigation efforts. That quick initial assessment; is this malware or is it not? Is this a virus? Is this a hacking attempt that came in through maybe a specific port or a protocol? Or they did some type of SQL injection, or they had a USB stick that was infected and brought into our system, or it was infected laptop. By identifying the source and the type of threat, the type of incident we're dealing with here can help quickly identify the level of impact. Is it going to be a nuisance or is it going to be a multimillion dollar event? Are we going to lose customer information? How quickly can we stem that bleeding? That helps direct containment and the mitigation efforts. Also, analysis of event files, log files, from things like intrusion detection systems, firewalls, routers, switches, directory servers. Anything on our network that can be audited or that creates log files that can be parsed and then correlated across different verticals, we can correlate timing from our routers and switches, our firewalls, IDS systems, access to directory servers, or perhaps pieces of critical infrastructure; if we're able to aggregate and then correlate those events across all those devices at one time, it allows us to quickly get a picture of what's happening, and how it's happening. All of those network systems should be brought into play. That helps us determine the true intent of that attack. So, is your company the clear target? In other words, are you the goal, or is someone just probing? They happened to come across one of your systems, and they're just probing just to see what's there. It's the old hacker mantra: Well why'd you climb that mountain? Well, because it was there. Sometimes people just want to probe and see what they can see. They don't have a specific goal, they're not trying to necessarily steal something or destroy something, and they just want to see if they can get in, more or less as a badge of honor, if you will. Alternatively, was your business the actual target, or are you a side door attack to some other company? And as I mentioned earlier, as far as things being a clear target or just probing, was this a true attack or just someone doing an initial network or resource mapping? They want to come in and probe our network and see how things are laid out. What are our routers and switches? Do we have a single namespace? Do we have different IP spaces for different areas, naming conventions? What type of systems do we have? Are we running Linux, Windows or virtualization. By coming in and doing that network mapping, they can get a good idea of what types of systems are on the network. By having that properly trained team, we can identify and say, is this breach? Are we in all hands on deck mode, and we having to go in and start bringing all of our resources to bear to try to confront this and contain it? Or, was this someone coming in initially? Do we catch them in the very beginning hopefully while they're still doing the network scan, trying to go in and see what there is of value. By being able to identify that, it allows us to quickly attack that in the proper fashion, assign resources correctly, and address that threat appropriately.

Stopping the Spread
When it comes to stopping the spread, we want to focus on a couple things. Containing a security incident is going to help mitigate loss. The quicker we can contain that spread or

that initial infection of that piece of malware or virus focusing on malware here, the quicker we can contain that, the quicker we can mitigate loss. After containment, then comes eradication. Eradication, it may consist of disabling compromised accounts, taking that machine out of service. Also, potentially wiping that machine and reinstalling from scratch. It all depends upon that part of the recovery process that deals with backups. If we can verify them as being valid backups, then we may be able to restore that system from that backed up piece of data, that backup tape. If it's not, however, then we may need to completely blow that system away or wipe that system or reimage that system. Also, check it for rootkits and because we want to make sure that that system is not compromised beyond what we initially thought. When it comes to eradication and recovery, we may need to disable affected accounts. We have to identify how that piece of malware was installed. What user account was used? Is it affecting admin accounts? Is our system set up or is our network set up to have admin accounts disabled by default? If there's a service account that it somehow is able to attach itself to and then spread throughout the network using that service account, we have to identify that quickly and disable that account so it can't spread. It just depends upon the nature of that piece of malware. Next, we have to identify what ports and protocols that piece of malware uses. And shut down those ports and protocols or at least monitor them very closely to make sure that malware is not spreading to other systems across that same transport mechanism, that same port or that same protocol. Next, recover from backup, will verify that the backup is, in fact, good. If it's not, then we need to do a fresh install. It's going to depend upon - the nature of that infection. And then something else that's equally as important, if not more important, and we have to do that very quickly, in tandem with the initial infection as we're going through our identification remediation steps, we need to coordinate with other sites and other locations within our company to make sure they're aware of the breach of the infection and so they can start monitoring their systems as well. That if a spread, in fact, does take place or tries to take place, they can mitigate that as quickly as possible. That goes back to what accounts are being used, what ports or protocols. That information should be shared with other sites and with other locations within the company.

Defining Goals and Expected Outcomes
When we're talking about defining goals and expected outcomes, a few things to keep in mind. First off, we need to periodically test the business continuity, cyber and also disaster recovery plans. We have to make sure and verify that the plans are valid, that they cover the required elements that we want to protect, that we're getting all the critical infrastructure, critical applications and all the critical business functions, and that the plan can be executed when the time comes. Doesn't do us much good to have a very grandiose plan, and we think it might work, but if it doesn't achieve the expected outcome or if it's not even an executable plan, it doesn't do us much good. Many companies have business continuity plans that they've written down, they sound great on paper, but they've never executed them, never tested them. It's important that we do that. Next, we want to make sure we have buy-in from senior management. We must have executive approval, and this should be disseminated, if possible, organization wide so that everyone is aware of what the plans are. We need to make sure that people who are involved with this process know that they're involved with the process and are able to complete and are competent in the roles that they're

assigned. Buy-in from executive management is critical in this regard, and then, if possible, it's going to depend on corporate culture, the size of the organization, but if possible, these plans should be disseminated company wide so that everyone is on the same page. Next, we should have post testing review. After we test our plans, we need to identify what's changed, if anything, because as we test our plan, we might identify, we didn't think of this, or, we thought we had this in place, but it's no longer valid, we can remove that. If anything's changed, we need to document, we need to correct any gaps, and then compare our goals and expected outcomes. We thought we were going to achieve A, B, and C; well we achieved A, B, and F, or we achieved none of it, depending upon the outcome of the exercise. Document, identify those gaps, correct the gaps, and then reiterate, go and test again at some point in time, make sure that it's a working document, it's a working plan that is executable when the time comes. Then also, an important distinction to understand is testing vs. exercises. We want to make sure we don't find ourselves in that situation. A test is a pass-fail scenario. An exercise is much harder to measure in that regard, because some elements of an exercise may be successful, some may not, so it's not an entirely pass-fail scenario. It's also good to put out to the organization, when you're conducting these exercises, make sure they understand it's just that, it's not a pass-fail. It takes some of the burden off the employees, and it also makes them not falsely report because no one wants to fail, so, you don't want them just going through and checking boxes just to check the boxes. If something fails, you want to know it fails realistically, so that you can correct. By letting someone know, we're letting the organization know, we're doing an exercise. This is not pass fail, you're not going to get fired, you're not going to have something drastic. It's going to be a learning experience, we expect some things to not work as planned, that's all part of the process, that's why we're testing. It's much better to find out than to think something worked because someone was afraid to say no or afraid to fail, they checked a box even if they didn't do the exercise or do that specific piece, and then find out when the incident happens where the catastrophe is in full swing, that the plan is not executable, so that's not the time to do that.

Chapter 8 Test Scenarios & Simulations

Testing needs to be realistic. Simply reporting back successful testing results is meaningless if the test is not realistic. Something to keep in mind is, we need to make sure that we test the plan. Don't plan the test. What do I mean by that? We need to make it as realistic as possible. In other words, don't let everyone know, hey, the test is coming. The catastrophe's about to arrive on our doorstep Let's go ahead and plan everything to the nth degree. Let's take everything into consideration, let's have all of our resources lined up, let's make sure we have everything in place because in reality, as we know, catastrophes don't announce themselves. They don't knock on the door and say, hey, I'm going to be here tomorrow at 6:00. Everybody get ready. If you want to test the reality and the validity of a test or an exercise, don't plan it to the degree. Throw in some variability. Make sure that you have some things that throw you off to see how the plan functions in a non-perfect world.

Walkthrough Tests
When we're talking about the various types of testing and exercises, we have five that I want to mention here. We have walk-through testing, or walk-through exercises, we have communications, communication exercises, simulations, we have a partial exercise, and then also a full exercise. Let's take a look at each of these in more detail. For a walk-through, that's a reading through the proposed plan. It's everyone gathering in a room together, or as close together as possible, whether it's over Skype, or some remote communication telepresence, you'll read through the proposed plan, and then you'll ask yourself some questions. Does the plan makes sense? it's a bit of a no

brainer, but depending upon who's reading, sometimes people are afraid to speak up, Everyone should be empowered to say, this doesn't make sense, or this isn't valid, or we're missing something here, go through that, that's the purpose of this exercise. Also does it follow a logical path? Are we doing things in the order that we would realistically expect them to either be restored, contained, mitigated. Also, is it understandable and easy to follow for those that must utilize that plan? If it's extremely complicated, full of legalese or ultra-technical jargon, that people reading that plan may or may not be understanding of or may not be privy to that information, it's important to make it understandable. In the middle of a crisis, the brain isn't as loose, it's tightened down, you're in a heightened sense of awareness, stress levels come up, and it becomes a little harder to focus, Making sure these things are easy to understand and easy to follow is critical. Then also revisions may occur numerous times throughout this process because it's not typically a one and done. As we go through this each and every time, it's understood that there's going to be gaps, there's going to be things that are missed, or things that need to be added, so a few revisions of this plan throughout this process or throughout this exercise is expected.

Communication Tests

Next we have communication tests, we want to make sure or ensure that all relevant personnel, all vendors, emergency responders are identified. We need to verify that we have accurate contact information, critical, it does not stay the same typically, and things can change over time, so a periodic review of this information will pay dividends if and when an actual incident occurs. Also identify backups, otherwise known as deputies, for each key position. We don't want to have just one person identified for each specific key role, we need to make sure we have backups for them in case that person is out, unreachable, or they may be affected by the incident, or the catastrophe, or the event, and they can't reply or respond. We need to make sure we have a deputy in that case. Also identify gaps in response times and availability. As we go through this testing, understand are the people in place and is their response realistic? If we expect someone to be able to respond within 30 minutes, and it takes them 6 hours, well, that's not acceptable for this specific scenario. We need to either mitigate that risk, find another person, or adjust the plan to meet those real-world outcomes.

Simulation (Tabletop) Tests

Next, we have simulations. These are also known as tabletop exercises. The objective here is to be as real-world as possible without blowing up the building or having a tornado sweep through. But we want to make sure that we can make it as realistic as possible in a simulated scenario. To do that, we should inject some variability or randomness into the test before. Maybe not have everybody respond. That way, it mirrors what would happen if that specific person or group of people can't respond because the event is impacting them in some way. Also disasters typically don't announce themselves ahead of time. Injecting some type of variability into that test makes it a little bit more real-world and also shows you and the rest of the organization how you can adapt and overcome, still within the parameters of the plan. Because the goal is business continuity. We want to make sure that business can continue, business functions, business services. By doing this, injecting some variability, we ensure an even greater chance of success.

Partial Exercise

Partial exercises are somewhat intrusive so it's going to require people from various areas throughout the organization. Depending upon the size of that company, you may all be located in one location, you may be spread out within a state, throughout the country, or even globally. There may be some disruption as all of these folks are gathered together. You're going to have to coordinate logistically how to make that happen. Some actions will need to be taken that may disrupt normal operations. That's just the nature of the beast. When possible, do these types of exercises when it's least disruptive to the business, after hours, on the weekends. It just depends upon your business and when your busy times are. The goal here is to prepare for disaster recovery up almost to the point of failing over, but not failing over completely, because that would be a full exercise. But we want to take it halfway or three quarters of the way, gaining a much better understanding of how the operation and how the plan functions, but not a full-blown exercise.

Full Exercise
Full exercises are most disruptive to the business. It's a complete testing of the business continuity and disaster recovery plans. It's going soup-to-nuts, from beginning to end, so a complete failover of systems to ensure continuity, again, a continuity of the business, business services. Then, it should be performed, like we talked about with partial exercises, at times that are least intrusive to the company's operations. It could be after hours, over night, weekends, or it may be certain times of the year, maybe there's a slow period. Coordinate that so it's least disruptive, and then you'll ensure the highest chance of participation and buy in, especially from senior management.

Overall Cost and Complexity of Testing

When we're talking about the overall cost and complexity of testing, understand that each one of these different types have a different dollar amount, amount of time, complexity, associated with them. Starting off, we have a walkthrough exercise. Pretty much free, it's just people in a room reading through the exercises, understanding where the gaps are. Not a lot of dollar value, or time. As far as the five different types we're talking about, this is the least cost and the least complex. Next, we have the communications test. We're going to have to test some of our systems, we're going to have to get people engaged from various parts of the business. A little bit more time, a little more complexity; and then we have simulations, partial exercises, and then full exercises. A full exercise is a complete failover, logistically getting everyone together, staging areas, command center, incident response. It's a lot more to put together, takes a lot more preparation, and it's a lot more complex.

Plan Review and Maintenance

When we're talking about maintaining our business continuity plans, it's very important to review and maintain those plans periodically. Plans should be updated as changes occur, if possible. The size of the organization may dictate that. Well we want to make sure we update these things as often as necessary to make sure the information in the plans are accurate. Business processes, key personnel, vendors and suppliers; all should be updated as things change, because they will change over time. Also, verify contact information. Again, very important, we need to make sure that when we have to go out and call someone, the number doesn't ring back and say, that number's been disconnected, or that's a totally different company because the vendor has changed or has been acquired. It's important that we verify that contact information periodically, update as necessary. Also, site access plans. Have site access plans changed? Have you acquired new buildings? Have you gotten rid of certain facilities. These things need to be up to date as well, and that includes maps, drawings, schematics. All of these things should be included in our business continuity planning, our business impact analysis, disaster recovery documents; and what that does is it demonstrates a continued due diligence. That's critical to insurers, maybe partners you may be working with, interested parties or stakeholders; all of these things show that you have plans in place to recover from a disaster, continue business. You're much more likely to get insurance, to have third-party folks and vendors work with you. Some insurance companies, some vendors, look for that and require these types of documents to do business with you. It depends upon, again, your industry, but it's a great approach to have this and have it continually updated so that you can show, hey, we take this seriously; it's company wide, we have executive buy-in, and we update our documents periodically, it's not a one and done.

Review Process Outcomes

Next, we want to make sure we do a lessons learned. We want to review that process outcome. That's going to ensure the highest probability of success, our implementation and also our recovery efforts. We need to review and constantly refine over time. That shows continued competency. That's very important for our vendors, insurers, third parties, key stakeholders. Also, it will prepare the organization for either internal or external audits that you may or may not be interested in preparing for certification. Maybe ISO 27001 for cybersecurity or 22301 for business continuity. But, if in fact that is a goal or a requirement for your organization or your industry, having this continued refinement and the reviewing of your processes and your plans will help auditing and also help prepare for those certifications.

Intelligence Lifecycle

When it comes to the intelligence lifecycle, we have the six phases: direction, collection, processing, analysis, dissemination, and feedback. You can look at that as more or less of a loop. It starts off with an evaluation of the environment, understanding what the goals are, the roadmap to get there, and throughout that process, there's a feedback loop. We'll do it at the end, but it can also be done at each stage to make sure the process is functioning as intended, and we're getting the results that we're looking for.

Chapter 9 Threat Intelligence Lifecycle

To put that into a different format, we start off with our objectives and our key questions. That's fed from several things, internal sources, technical sources, and, of course, human sources. Some of it may be automated, some of it may be through manual intervention, talking with other analysts as well, seeing what's happening in their space or in their part of the world. All of these things, again, are fed with threat intelligence. That's comprised of the threat intelligence itself and the various security tools, the SIEM tools, and then also analysts, and that will go back and forth. Those two things feed each other, comprised from these different sources, and making sure we're starting off with understanding what it is we're trying to accomplish, what are our goals and key objectives. All of that then turns around and feeds the actual teams that will go out and utilize that information to defend the network. Incident response teams, it could be security operations, it could be a vulnerability management team, risk analysis team, perhaps maybe a fraud management team, and then, of course, security leadership. We talked about the different teams and why that's important and why they need that information, starting off with defending the actual network, the folks that are on the front lines making sure that these threats are mitigated as much as possible or remediated as quickly as possible, security operations, vulnerability, management, patching, all the way up to security leadership so that they have proper data to make informed decisions of where to invest time, resources, money, infrastructure and so on.

Cyberthreat Intelligence Frameworks

Cyber threat intelligence frameworks, a definition would be: it's a structure for thinking how attackers operate, the methods involved, and where in the overall attack lifecycle that event is occurring. More specifically, that cyber threat intelligence framework allows us to be very prescriptive in how we attack a specific situation. It focuses attention on the proper areas to ensure follow up to make sure eradication and mitigation of future threats. It also provides a common language to communicate internally and also externally, regarding threat details, interrelations between events, and correlations with external data sources. It's a framework that allows us to plug in and understand where something is occurring in the process, focus our resources within that small area rather than trying to take the shotgun approach, allows us to be much more laser-focused on the specific area that needs our attention. That way, we don't waste time, waste effort, and resources working on areas that don't necessarily matter or perhaps aren't necessarily relevant.

Cyber Kill Chain

The first one I want to call your attention to is something referred to as the Cyber Kill Chain. This was developed by Lockheed Martin in 2011, and it's based upon the military concept of the kill chain. We have seven distinct areas, and it allows us to understand where in the process a specific attack is occurring, whether it's in reconnaissance, weaponization or delivery, but if we understand where in the process that specific attack is, we can focus our resources and our mitigation efforts, and if they have a proper framework, we can understand what actions need to be taken in that area, We can quickly respond. First off, reconnaissance, the adversary is probing for weakness, so such things as harvesting login credentials, or info that can be used for a phishing attack. Next is weaponization, that is creating the deliverable, the payload, using an exploit as a backdoor typically. Delivery is the process of sending that payload to the victim, it could be a malicious email, it could be a thumb drive left, on a desk or on the floor, someone picks it up and says, what's this, next thing mission accomplished, it's been delivered. Then we have exploits, and an exploit is the act of executing the code on the remote system. Installation is the actual installing of malware on that target asset, and it brings us to command and control, or C Squared, or C&C, that creates a channel or persistence where the attacker can control the system remotely. At that point, they have control of perhaps one system, perhaps a number of systems. Then actions, so that's carrying out the intended goal, whether it's encrypting data, destroying data, exfiltrating data. If we can understand where in the process a specific action is, we know how to focus our efforts to quickly shut that thing down. If we can interrupt the chain, the kill chain, if we break that chain just like you break a link in a real life chain, then the chain breaks apart. You can stop it from progressing.

Diamond Model
The diamond model is a complementary model to the cyberthreat kill chain. This was developed by the Center for Cyber Intelligence Analysis and Threat Research. It was designed to track attack groups over time rather than individual attacks. The diamond model states for every intrusion event there exists an adversary that takes a step toward an intended goal by using a capability over infrastructure against a victim to produce a result. What we see is we have this diamond model set up, and you can see we have an adversary, and that can be certain pieces of metadata that we need to understand about that adversary,

502

their persona, an IP address, network assets, the capabilities that they have, malware, exploits, stolen certificates. We're going to use those capabilities over infrastructure, network assets, devices, domain names to launch some type of an attack on a victim. we need to understand the persona like who that person is, what type of group, what type of industry, role, the persona of that victim, the IP address, network assets. Once we have all these things understood, we can create a persona or an avatar or some type of profile of that person, allow us to understand quickly the types of the remediations that can be put in place to shut those things down. Some of the meta-features that we would also capture to make sure we have data about that specific event in a specific threat group, timestamps, the attack phase, which complements the cyber kill chain, the attack result, the direction, methodology, and resources. Going deep into the diamond model is beyond the scope of this introductory portion, but just understand that these frameworks exist to allow our threat analysis teams to quickly identify where to focus resources and also pass that information on to the defenders that go out and defend against, mitigate or remediate.

MITRE Attack Framework

MITRE is a not-for-profit organization, and they manage federal funding for research projects across multiple agencies. They're responsible for a number of things, some of which you may already be familiar with. For instance, the Common Vulnerabilities and Exposures database, the CVE database. If you've ever done patching, you see the different CVEs that come out and say the CVE and some number attached to it, here's the exposure, here's the vulnerability, here's how you remediate. Also the Common Weaknesses Enumeration or the CWE database. The MITRE ATT&CK

framework has a few complementary things that I'd like to call your attention to as well, one of which is the Trusted Automation Exchange of Intelligence Information or TAXII. What this is a transport protocol that allows sharing of threat intelligence information over HTTPS using common APIs and then also Structured Threat Information eXpression or STIX. This is a standardized format for presenting threat intelligence information. It allows different disparate systems to communicate using a common language and exchange information, all with the common goal of eradicating threats as quickly as possible. Just you're aware, the MITRE ATT&CK, the actual name of the framework, stands for adversarial tactics, techniques, and common knowledge. We touched on it again briefly before, but just to dig in a little bit deeper, it is comprised of tactical categories. There's 314 tactics spread across 12 different categories. We have initialize access, execution, persistence, privilege escalation, defense evasion, credential access, discovery, lateral movement, collection, command and control, exfiltration, and then impact. If we understand where something is happening in the cyber kill chain, as an example, and we're able to identify through our threat intelligence analysis what type of threat group is executing or attempting to execute the specific attack, we can use something like the MITRE ATT&CK framework to understand, that specific group uses these x number of tactics, 3, 5, 10, whatever the number might be.

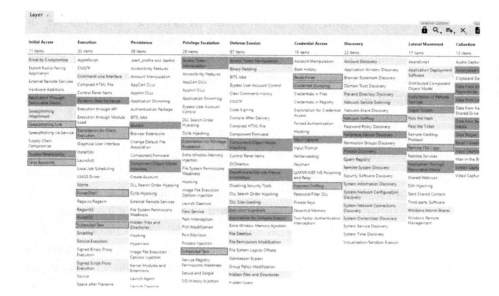

We can quickly focus our attention. We can start enriching that data, pass it on to our defenders so they can go out and do their job of either trying to mitigate or remediate that threat as quickly as possible.

Key Points to Remember

Disaster recovery efforts should be formally started and stopped. People need to know when to start and stop that formal recovery effort. That way they can focus on bringing up secondary systems, recovering full service. If everyone still was under the operating guidelines that it is a recovery effort, they're only going to be focusing on the primary systems. They're not going to be looking at secondary tertiary systems. Once the recovery efforts have stopped, then they can get back to the business of bringing up those other systems as well, and restoring full functionality to the business. Next, tracking systems should also be defined and put in place. Ensure people are accounted for, especially if we have some type of disaster where we have injuries or potentially fatalities. Families notified if applicable, emergency services alerted if required; all of these things should be documented People know how to act, know the steps they're supposed to follow. Then, each tower has a specific area of focus. Executives should address the news media, customers, key stakeholders, as an example. Security will protect corporate assets, our IT admins would bring up key systems, making sure that our data is intact. HR would protect human capital, make sure that those people are accounted for, families notified, hospitals, clinics notified. Then lastly, several call lists should be maintained, and this will go throughout each plan. These things are common to every plan that we develop. That way we can enable quick notification to various groups. We may have an executive call list, then a functional staff, our key people that need to come in away to bring our systems back up and running: managers, supervisors, and maybe a call list for everybody, like a company wide call list. That way we have multiple communication lists that can be triggered or called into action depending upon what needs to be done. We can have different folks focusing on different lists and have them work in tandem. That way, everybody's working in concert to try to get things back up and running as quickly as possible.

Types of Plans
When we're talking about types of plans, there are four categories that we should be aware of. There's incident management, there's business continuity, there's disaster recovery, and then business resumption, business resumption may or could be interchangeable with business continuity, but understand, generally speaking, these are the four categories that your planning will fall into. Plans could be separate and they could be distinct. They don't

necessarily have to be one large document, however they certainly could be. It depends upon the size of your company or your organization, how cohesive the planning is, is it tower by tower or do you have a blanket organizational-wide policy. It just depends upon the individual corporation or the individual company.

Chapter 10 Disaster Recovery & Business Continuity

Disaster recovery plans are similar in scope to business continuity, but it's focused more on information technology. Tasks, action lists, order of recovery. Some of the same things we talked about before, emergency contact information for key personnel, interested parties. Also documentation and references to incident management or command center location because, as we know, information technology, or IT, doesn't necessarily, and quite often does not, sit where corporate sits. It may be in a remote data center, it may be some other location. The things that may be readily apparent to the business, like incident management or command center location, may not necessarily be readily apparent to IT folks. It has to be documented, and we have a standardized way of going through these things. Also, activities associated with people, process, and technology. But again, remember, this is for IT-related activities, not necessarily the initial incident management or initial business recovery efforts

Business Continuity Plan
Business continuity plans deal with the resumption and recovery of business operations once the initial disruption is contained. The incident management plan will deal with the immediate. And then once the bleeding is stemmed, we can move on to business continuity efforts, recovery efforts. How to begin recovery is a key element of the plan, again all of these things will be documented, location of key personnel and key resources, disaster recovery locations or alternate work locations, staging areas. Also, needed resources, whether it be supplies, logistics, interested parties, stakeholders. Also, standardized data collection and

508

reporting templates, forms, portals. How will people start to do their work, do they need to go to a specific location or a portal or fill out a form if they need supplies, how do they request assistance?

Business Resumption Plan

Business resumption plans can be the same or part of the business continuity plan. It doesn't have to be, it can be a separate document, but keep in mind these things could be one and the same. It defines who owns the resumption process because, keep in mind, it may be different than the people who are responsible for incident management or disaster recovery. It may be a separate team. We may have business folks coming in and spinning and owning the business resumption process, processes for determining the replacement of staff, if necessary, perhaps even buildings, depending on how bad the incident was, infrastructure, things could be damaged, compute network storage, power, heating, cooling, HBAC, our heating, ventilation, air conditioning units, also services. It just depends upon the nature of the incident and the scope of damage.

Incident Management Plan

When it comes to an incident management plan, it's going to deal with the initial response to an incident, so that means tasks, and the actions, and the priorities that which things should be addressed. What do I need to do specifically immediately after an incident happens? How do I triage that event? Emergency contact details of key personnel and interested parties, or stakeholders, activities required as it relates to people, process, and technology. This is limited in scope to the things we need to do immediately, not necessarily long term. This is incident management. We need to contain the existing incident, and then we can move on to recovery efforts. Also contact guidelines, internal contacts, media, emergency responders, that's going to include documentation, maps, charts, maybe third-party response details, site access info, especially if we have geo-dispersed locations, and we need to understand how to get into specific locations, what's the best way to get in, get out. Then insurance contact and claim procedures, which is always high on everyone's list of favorite things to do, but dealing with insurance companies, especially if it's a major incident, is particularly helpful if you start documenting from the beginning, so you don't leave anything out or it doesn't get misconstrued.

Data Retention
When it comes to data retention, there's a number of reasons why data may need to be retained, or not be retained, there's various reasons for either side of this coin. It could be for compliance, it could be for eDiscovery, for data mining, to understand customer history, or to improve the customer experience. However, there also may be implications for keeping data too long. Some companies don't want to store data after a certain period of time, just to get rid of data that's no longer necessary, to prune their data to save on storage costs. The longer the data's retained, those costs and storage requirements, they increase, because things start to accumulate over time. Proper data governance helps with this, and when we're talking about data retention, there are a number of options, there's a number of ways to skin the cat, so to speak. Replicating offsite is one option, whether that be a remote data center or a cloud provider, so that can protect against disaster, a smoking hole incident where the entire data center goes out, cyber incidents, ransomware attacks, breaches. If we're replicating to another location, that can help guard against

those types of incidents. As an example, we have a user, and she is accessing using some data, using an application. Well that data is stored in her primary location, her primary data center. There may be primary storage that that network or that system is attached to, and that's fine. She's pulling data off of that primary storage, but, we need to make sure that that's protected. Typically, that storage will be offloaded to a backup device, or backup arrays, so that is off of primary storage, it's on backups, but, it's still sitting in the primary data center. That solves for the problem of if the array were to go out, but it doesn't solve against the problem of what if the data center goes away, we have some type of disaster. We have a couple options. From there, we could backup to a cloud provider. That could be AWS, it could be Google, and it could be Azure. There are a number of options. There are a lot of other providers as well, those are the big three, and then there's hot storage, things that have a higher degree of performance, it's not going to be as good as onsite performance, but it's still there. Or if it's long-term storage, you could even push it down to a lower level of storage within that cloud provider. As an example, AWS has a service called Glacier, which is a very cheap and deep storage, but it's not very responsive, but, it's there for long-term retention. Alternatively, we could replicate to a remote data center. It's something that we own, and in doing so, we maintain that geographic dispersal. If something were to go wrong, a power outage or some type of disaster at our primary data center, we have that data replicated offsite somewhere. A third option might be to have those backups stored on tape, and have those tapes physically transported to a storage facility. The more modern ways, however, will be to replicate either to a cloud or a remote data center.

Putting It All Together

Proper procedures, documentation, and of course, practice, - all of these things together heightens the degree of success when responding to incidents. Because unfortunately, it's not a matter of if something happens, it's more likely a matter of when. It just becomes more and more frequently, unfortunately, more or less as the cost of doing business almost. There are a number of teams that would be involved when dealing with an incident. We have executive management. We have business leadership and the various lines of business. There will be leadership from various areas, not just one group. Typically, it's going to be a number of groups from different types of businesses or lines of business, depending upon the nature of the breach, what applications and services it affects. Then we have IT operations and infrastructure, they're the folks that will be responsible for getting all these things back up and running, and then we have security operations, who will be heavily involved in analyzing and making sure that these things are covered going forward. We have engineering, which may need to change the way that things are done, depending upon, The nature of the breach, the application, maybe there's a hole or something that needs to be patched; and then DevOps, potentially, depending upon the nature of the breach. Do you have to change something in your CI/CD pipeline? All of those types of things. Each of these groups, as you may imagine, have sub components. If we dig into security operations as an example, here we have our CISO sitting at the head of the organizational chart, but there's a number of groups under them: risk management, identity management, security operators, security architecture; and each of those have separate subgroups. Your organization may not necessarily be this large or it may be bigger, it just depends, but there are detection, prevention, incident handling, and even within incident handling, we have forensics and incident management, and incident response teams. Again, if it's a large organization, you may have all of these or more, if it's a very small group, you may have one person wearing all of these hats, it just depends. Digging in just a bit further, we can see we have, under detection we might have security event triage, and security analysts, and then hunt operations and intelligence, threat intelligence analysis, and then we might have security administrators and security engineering. I'm just trying to give you an idea that there's a number of people that may be involved when handling a breach. No need to necessarily understand each of these down to the nth degree, just understand that it's not necessarily just a one person operation unless you're a very, very small company. There's a lot of coordination that takes place when an incident occurs.

Example Process
Let's say unfortunately the inevitable has happened, and a Coffee shop has a breach. So once that happens, a number of things need to take place. Initially we'll have the alert, and that could be from an automated alert from one of our seen systems or some type of monitoring system. We have IOCs, or indicators of compromise, that are observed. It could be an outage that's reported, it could be customer-reported degradation of apps or services, so on. There's some reason why we're alerted to that breach. From there, we're going to have to jump into action and analyze what's taking place. That consists of a number of things, again identifying the issue, understanding what is taking place, take corrective actions as quickly as possible, that's feasible, without going overboard. We need to engage proper teams very quickly to make sure they're aware, they're spinning themselves up, and we begin communications. From there, the communications take place, and that goes amongst a

number of groups. It goes through management, it goes through business partners, peer groups, potentially customers, the media, it could even be law enforcement, and of course vendors. Depending upon the nature of the breach, we may need to bring vendors in very quickly to help us recover or to harden the systems, potentially even bring in additional equipment depending on how big and how widespread that breach is. All of these things are happening in parallel, so this is not necessarily a serial timeline, it's not one after the other, a number of these things will start to spin up in parallel, and you'll have to have someone that sits at the head of that in your command center and coordinates all of these efforts? We've talked about all of these things before, but just understand that there are a number of things that take place at the same time when we're dealing with these types of breaches. So from there, we have to recover and then harden those systems, so that may be rebuilding those systems, restoring from backup, in some form or fashion, we need to recover those systems, validate that those systems are in fact functional, and again that's going to be spinning up a bridge, having all the different app teams involved, having those guys and girls all on the phone saying yes, we're back up online, or yes, I can perform action A, B, and C, so the application is recovered. And then from there, we would take preventative corrections, and then monitor to make sure that things are working, that the corrections work. We want to make sure we don't just bring the system back and leave it in exact same state it was before. We need to make sure that we take preventive action, harden that system, if possible, to make sure if that same type of attack were to occur again, we're protected against that attack. And then we need to make sure that we document and do an AIR, or after incident review, or a peer incident review, or whatever it may be called in your specific organization, but you should do that after the fact, you can review what you've done, lessons learned? Lessons learned, the steps that were taken, also communicate with executives, so they have a level of comfort around the incident, understanding that we have a handle on things, and then and after-incident review, so that we can understand across all the different teams that are involved, what happened, how we can respond better, or perhaps quicker the next time. And then in reality, we want to make sure that we audit the environment. Audit for similar gaps in other systems, and ensure that those corrective actions or corrective measures that we took on that one system or that one application are applied consistently throughout the environment? We want to make sure that we're patching all of our systems that are similar, maybe the same operating system, or the same code level, depending upon what the actual gap was, where the vulnerability was, we need to make sure that we're patching against that across the environment. And then lastly, develop new MOPs, or methods of procedures, so that way we have a documented way of moving forward, ensuring that those best practices are applied when new systems are built and brought into the environment. In this chapter, we talked about a number of things including incident response plans and process, we talked about various testing exercises, walk throughs, tabletops, simulations. We talked about the various attack frameworks, the MITRE framework, Diamond Model. We talked about stakeholder management and also communication plans, disaster recovery, and business continuity plans, along with continuity of operation planning, and then various incident response teams, retention policies, data of retention, and then responding to an incident, putting it all together and understanding all of the various teams that need to be spun up, how things happen in parallel, not necessarily a serial process, and how we get things back up online, communicate properly to all the teams involved, and restore our systems, patching and documenting, making sure that doesn't happen again in the future.

Chapter 11 How to Implement Data Sources to Support an Investigation

In this chapter, we'll be covering Understanding Appropriate Data Sources to Support an Incident. We'll be talking about vulnerability scans and the output, what we do with those outputs. We'll talk about SIEM and SIEM dashboards. We'll talk about log files and how they can support an investigation or data analysis, trying to figure out what happened, where, when, why and how. We'll talk about syslog, rsyslog, and syslog-ng or next generation. We'll talk about the differences there. We'll also talk about something called journal control or journalctl, nxlog. We'll talk about retention for basic things like email, audit logs. Then we'll talk about bandwidth monitors, metadata, and how it changes for different types of files. We'll talk about NetFlow and sFlow, the differences between the two, and then a little bit about protocol analyzers and outputs. When we're talking about accessing all of these different types of data, interpreting assessment results, understanding what's going on, the amount of data that's being created is increasing exponentially, so the amount of sensors, telemetry data. Security tools, analyzers, packet sniffers, all of these things, they generate a massive amount of data. Part of the job is to filter through all of that data and to find out what's relevant, to filter through the noise. Relevance is different for each environment, so it's not going to be a one size fits all. Something that may be normal in one environment could be abnormal in another and vice versa. It's important to understand what is normal for your specific environment. Also, understand what is the goal of the tool or what is the goal of the assessment? What are we looking to gather when we're sifting through all of this data. Then automate where possible. Automation is going to be key here because we want to be able to trigger an alert when a real issue occurs and then filter through all the noise. Filtering through the noise boils down to establishing a security baseline. That's going to help us understand what's normal. This will apply to no matter what the environment is, whether we're doing packet sniffers or a SIEM dashboard or any type of telemetry data. Once we understand what is normal, then we can very quickly or at least more quickly understand what's abnormal. This enables an analyst to quickly see anomalies and deviations from normal. If you understand what's normal, if you see a spike that's not normal, we see a spike in the middle of the night or a spike on a specific port or a spike on a specific type of application that's not normally doing that, then that can alert us to some type of abnormal activity, potentially an indicator of compromise. There are tools that can automate data collection and simplify that task, and we'll talk about a few of those in just a moment. But, we want to alert when a threshold is reached X amount of times within a certain interval. Rather than every single time a threshold is breached, that's going to create a ton of noise because things can spike constantly. If it's an intermittent spike or a one-off, we don't necessarily want to be notified of that. If we have something down the road that becomes a problem, we can go back historically and look for the one-offs and maybe see a trend over time. But every single time something hits a threshold, we don't want to necessarily be alerted by that. By creating these baselines and then setting thresholds or triggers, if X amount of triggers within a certain time interval, that will help us to filter through the noise. One of those tools that can help us is something referred to as a vulnerability scanner, and a vulnerability scanner can determine where there are gaps in defenses. There are a lot of them out there. They all have similar functionality, but some of the more well-known ones are OpenVAS or GVM, Nessus, Retina, Nmap, SAINT. There are a number of other ones as well. I'm not necessarily recommending or endorsing one over the other. Just understand that generally speaking, vulnerability scanners give us a lot of information about our environment. They allow us to scan the environment for vulnerabilities, for gaps in our defenses, if you will. As an example, GVM is a vulnerability scanner that does a number of different things. It gives us a number of vulnerabilities, but it allows us to scan our environment, scan all the different devices within our environment, and then show what gaps exist, if any, on those different pieces of equipment, those different nodes in our environment, whether it's a Linux server, Windows server, some type of endpoint. So from there, once the vulnerability is discovered, we can drill down, see all about that vulnerability, see what the potential severity is, and then potential remediations. It allows us to stack rank what's in the environment and then remediate appropriately.

SIEM

SIEM is the security information and event management system. What this does is do a bit of data aggregation and correlation, doing automated alerting and triggers, time synchronization, event deduplication, and then logs that are in a WORM format or write once, read many. A SIEM platform, is a security tool that allows us to aggregate data from a number of different sources, and it correlates that data to make it easy to identify when things happen. We can look at things from a number of different parameters, whether it be CPU utilization, network utilization. Let's take a look at this in a little more detail. Here we have one called Metricbeat from Elastic, and it's being displayed in Kibana.

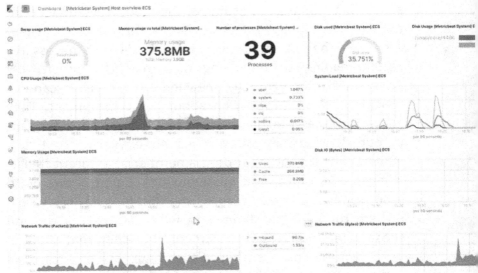

This is a dashboard, and it shows us a number of different things. Memory usage, number of processes, disk usage metrics, and this is for a specific host. But then it also show us the I/O on that specific host, the network traffic, and this can be used to look at individual hosts on a network. It can be used to look at switches and routers, to look at network flow. It gives us a lot of insight into the network, and then we can drill down, and you can see we're looking at the same time slices across all of these different metrics. It allows us to correlate that data and make sure we're understanding what's happening from a global perspective. And if we drill down a bit, we see that we have CPU usage, also system load.

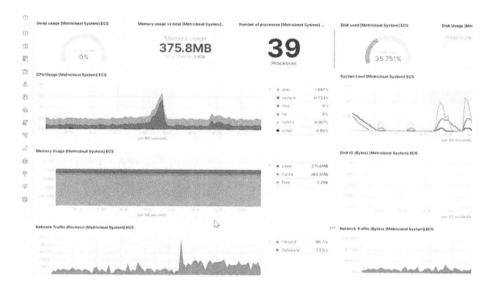

We can see a spike here around 15:15 or 3:15 in the afternoon, and we can see there's a spike. If we click on that, highlight that area and drill down, we can look in the logs for that specific event and see in more detail what's happening. We can search for specific parameters, we can look at anomalies in the network, or we can browse through to see if anything stands out. If we look at this in more detail, we have a graphical representation of a SIEM correlation dashboard. We have application, network, storage, firewall, and compute, and we have a time scale. We can see that is traffic. There's activity on various metrics within this correlated dashboard. Well let's say, for instance, we see this, and then all of a sudden the next day or, let's say, the time slices that we see here represented are the next 12 hours as an example. But we see this generic data. Nothing necessarily stands out. For this example, this could be considered a baseline, and nothing stands out. However, if we then see a spike pop up, and we see a lot of increased traffic, a lot of increased activity, disk I/O, firewall utilization, we can then drill down on each of those specific metrics and see what, in fact, is happening. These could be indicators of compromise. We could see that they could potentially be doing some type of data exfiltration or some type of Smurf attack or amplification attack, some type of breach into the network or least trying to do some type of denial-of-service or distributed denial-of-service attack. These types of things, this correlation engine, allows us to correlate across a number of different metrics and see the trending and then see the aggregate total because if we're looking at just one of these metrics, it may or may not stand out as an anomaly. But if we're looking at it across the board, and we can see well normally it looks like this. But today, for some reason or a couple hours later, it should look like this, but it's jumped up. Those things stand out immediately as red flags. It allows us to go and drill in deeper to see what's going on.

Log Files

Next we have log files, and log files can be a rich source of information. Or they could be ridiculously boring and put you to sleep. It just depends upon how you use the log files, what types of tools you have to parse through them, what automation you may have in place. But, it is a very rich source of information and can be used for many purposes, including audits for discovering IOCs or indicators of compromise. It can be used for forensic investigations, general alerting. There's a number of different types of log files, all of which have various nuances, but we have log files for network traffic, for system utilization, application logs, security logs, web, DNS, authentication logs, log ons, log offs, dump files. We could have VoIP and call manager logs, session initiation protocol or SIP traffic logs. All of these things can prove very valuable when we need to investigate some type of breach or some type of incident. I will say that when you do log, you have to be very careful not to log too much because if you generate just too much noise, then it becomes pretty much just that, noise. By the same token, if you log too little or if you audit too little, then you have a false sense of security thinking that you're capturing the information that you need. But then when something happens, you either don't have that information readily available, or you don't have it in which case, then you start to get calls from VPs and executive management and say, I need that information and you're like oops, well, I don't have it. That, as you could imagine, is a lonely place to be and not somewhere that we want to be. We want to make sure that we proactively adjust and identify what we need to log, that we store it property, that we audit and retain that information long enough so that it retains its value, but not indefinitely so that it becomes, again, just noise or things that we're never going to look at and it just takes up space, which, everything reverts back to things cost money. Storage costs money. Getting back to the previous example, we may see a spike in traffic. We might see a spike of activity, and it's correlated across our network. Not necessarily just on a specific host. It could also be on the network, the firewall. Well, using our logs and analysis tools, we can dig in, pull in event IDs, log files that are stored on the server, in this case a DNS server, and we can see there are a number of hits for two different ports.

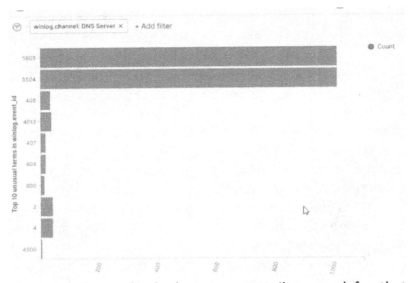

That is an anomaly that's not necessarily normal for that environment. That would be potentially an indicator of compromise and would require further investigation. In this case, it's quite possible that someone's trying to do some type of data exfiltration through our DNS channels or some other type of malicious activity. All of these tools allow us to continually drill in. If we double-click down even further, we can see that in this specific instance, the DNS server encountered a domain name packet exceeding the maximum length in the packet. And it shows the event ID, it shows the IP address. All of these things can be used to identify indicators of compromise. It's not normal, it's not something that we see every day, and it's an anomaly. In this case, someone is trying to breach the network, and it would require again further examination. In the real world when something like this happens, depending upon the size of your organization, you may or may not be doing this yourself. You may be a junior analyst, and you would pass this on further up the chain for further investigation. You might have a network security team. You might have the

524

server admins themselves, the DNS administrators. They may jump in and start trying to identify where that traffic is coming from. You'll have server admins, you might have virtualization admins, the network folks, firewall folks, and, of course, security personnel. You might spin up a war room and have everyone sit around the table and everyone looking at the same thing at the same time. They may all be together trying to understand what in fact is happening. Log files become critical in that case. Everyone can look at the data historically, and you can look back a day, a week, a month, depending upon how long you retain that data, and understand what is normal and what's not normal. Is this something that happens once a week? Is this something that happens once a month? Or is this the first time it's ever happened? By getting a bit of a historical view of events, it helps to identify how serious something may or may not be. It could be just someone probing, just seeing if they can get what they can get, and just doing some general reconnaissance. Or, it could be a targeted attack, which would warrant much more of a response.

Log Management, Syslog, Rsyslog, and Syslog-ng
When it comes to log management, log management can help reduce complexity, it can help reduce cost', and increase speed on ingestion for downstream consumers. What do I mean by that? Well, data quality, normalizing, parsing, and filtering out the noise, the uninteresting traffic, that's a big time saver. It gives us information that is usable, actionable. It also helps with cost reduction. We can optimize our SIEM, we can reduce storage, and also ingestion costs because depending upon the platform that we choose, it can be costly to just bring in data from various sources. If we can parse that further upstream, get rid of the things that aren't necessarily interesting, then we're only

paying for what we're consuming or ingesting. And then also security, we can encrypt data both in motion and also at rest. As an example, here we have a number of things that are producing log files, firewalls, applications, it can be compute network logs, storage logs. All of those things can then be put into a syslog server, a relay or a server, in this case syslog-ng, and then forward it on to whatever applications we want to use or have be the consumer of those specific log feeds, and it could be Splunk, it could be ELK, Kafka, it could be Hadoop, databases, so on, and so on. There are a number of things we can feed those different log files to. syslog-ng, as an example, allows us to do that. If we wanted to install syslog-ng into our system, as an example, here we have a Kali Linux session open, and from a terminal, I can just do a sudo apt-get install, and then choose syslog-ng, and a from there it's going to ask me do I want to do this, and of course the answer is yes. Then it's going to pull down the files, takes a few moments, it'll read through the database, then it'll install the various sub files, and within a matter of, say, a minute or so, we're done.

When it comes to syslog,syslog-ng, and also something called rsyslog, a few things that I just want to make sure that you're aware of. Syslog was developed in 1980, so it's been quite a while, but it's a tried and true mechanism. It was developed initially as part of the send mail implementation for collecting system logs. It was UDP only, User Datagram Protocol, which is a connectionless delivery system, so there's no guaranteed delivery, and it operated on port 514. Years later in 1998, syslog-ng comes out. That extended the functionality of syslog by adding TCP, or Transmission

Control Protocol, which is a connection-oriented delivery mechanism, content-based filtering, database logging features, and also TLS encryption. Then roughly about 6 years later, as a competitor to syslog-ng, rsyslog came out, and that extended syslog functionality even further by adding buffered operation support. If connectivity was lost, it could still buffer on the client until connectivity was re-established. That buffered operation support and then also RELP, or RELP, protocol, which is Reliable Event Logging Protocol, so that made for a much more robust delivery system. It was guaranteed, or at least we knew when messages weren't delivered, so it could retry again. These types of things are used by like the financial industry, things that cannot tolerate dropped messages. Just understand that there are a few different variations of syslogging, whether it's syslog, syslog-ng, or rsyslog, all have the same basic features; however, with each iteration, new features are added.

Journalctl

Next, let's talk about a tool called journalctl, and what journalctl is is a Linux command to view systemd, kernel, and also journal logs, and allows us to parse through those things, configure the output. We can search through all entries, we can look for entries by keyword, by type, by date, and then also output to a file, or also to a JSON format. It gives us a lot of options when parsing through system logs. To use the command, we can open up a terminal, and type sudo journalctl, and we'll want to use sudo in this case, so that we get all the messages, including kernel messages. And if we didn't do sudo, we wouldn't get all of the messages displayed to us.

So from there, sudo journalctl, and from there, we can parse
through all of the entries in the log, and there a number of
options that we can use to show just kernel messages, just
messages since last boot, by a certain date or time, so on
and so on. Let's take a look at this in action and get a little
more detail here. So from a terminal, again, I will run
journalctl, and that gives me all of the current information. If
you do sudo journalctl, and then as new entries are added,
that log file gets updated in real time. I'll open up another
window, and just do a quick check on my GVM setup that we
installed previously. As that happens, you'll notice, as I'm
running commands, and I'll pull it off-screen for just a
moment, but as I run commands, you'll see the log files get
updated. Since I'm following the journal, anytime anything
happens, any entries get put in, it gets updated in real time. I
can also turn around and say journalctl -n, and give it a
number for 10, Just 10 entries, and then put in the output
and make it json-pretty. It formats that output, rather than
the line-by-line that we just saw, and it formats it,
quote/unquote pretty, giving it the proper coding, the
proper indentation. just scratching the surface of what
journalctl can do, but it gives us a lot of flexibility in parsing
our logs, searching for specific events, formatting the
output.

And, as usual within Linux, if there's something that you're
not sure of, or you need to know a command, we can always
do what pretty much every guy doesn't want to do, and that

is read the manual. But, journalctl, journal c-t-l, --help, will give us all the commands that are available.

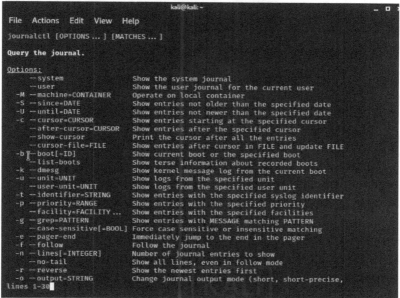

You can see, we can do things like -b. That will give us the current boot or specified boots. We could put a --boot -1 to show us just the kernel messages from the last boot. We can look at things like priority range, or we can grep for a specific pattern. That way we can show messages that only match a specific thing that we may be looking for. We also, -f, or follow, and that will follow the journal. It will show the most recent entries, and then anything new that gets added as we go. we just scroll down, we can keep seeing there are many, many options here available to us. We can do merge, we can output to a file, we can show the disk usage, the total disk usage for all of the journal files. We can vacuum the journal, reduce the size and delete older entries. We can flush the journal from any point in time, and so on. I encourage you to go against your intuition and read the manual on these

529

things, because a lot of times, there's some useful information in here that you wouldn't necessarily know unless you dig in under the covers just a bit. Poke through this when you have an opportunity, and familiarize yourself with the options available.

NXLOG
One other log and aggregation platform that I want you to be familiar with is something called NXLog. This is a multi-OS log aggregation and collection platform. It can collect and aggregate from Windows, from Linux, Mac, even Solaris. And we can also aggregate, filter, and enrich that data and then integrate with other SIEM software. I'm not going to dig into too, too much there, but just be aware that it is a multi-platform collection and aggregation tool and also integrates with SIEM software. It pulls all those different files together, all those log files from different operating systems, collects it, aggregate that data, and then passes it on to SIEM software or some other platform for further usage and consumption.

Chapter 12 Retention Auditing, Compliance & Metadata

We have all of this auditing information, What do we do with it? Retention policies should be defined and may be mandated by certain compliance regulations. When it comes to auditing, we need to determine what is most valuable when auditing that information. If we audit too much, if we collect too much, then it becomes noise, and it becomes limited in value because we just have so much stuff, it's too hard to sift through. That's where taking some time to clearly define what we want to audit and why and then how long are we going to retain that data for. That way we balance between the amount of data that we collect and the amount of time that we're collecting it for. It probably doesn't do us much good to go back 8 years, 10 years for something for a log on or log off. But yet, 2 or 3 days is probably too short. Maybe 2 weeks, a month, a month and a half? It just depends upon your environment. It depends upon what you're auditing for. But you definitely want to make sure that you clearly define it, and it's going to be a group effort here. You might have security folks, you might have administrators collectively understanding what it is we're logging for and how long we're going to keep it. Then we talk about compliance. There are certain things, certain regulatory bodies or local laws that may require data be retained for a certain period of time. That will vary by location. There is no or wrong answer across the board. Make sure you check with your local municipality, local, state, federal, or whatever country may be residing in, make sure that those things are in compliance and that you're retaining that information for the required period of time if applicable. Then for investigations, good data is critical to investigations on incidents, breaches. It could be criminal activity, it just could be malicious activity, or it just could be an anomaly that you need to investigate. Logs, audit data, file metadata, all of these things are very critical when we're trying to determine what happened, who did what, where, when, why, and how. Preservation of evidence is critical. Chain of custody is critical. Not Much just for an internal investigation, but chain of custody becomes crucial if those things ever need to go to court for prosecution.

Bandwidth Monitors

What a bandwidth monitor does, as the name implies, it's going to monitor network traffic and overall bandwidth. It can identify anomalies if we have some type of spike on the network or something that's not normal. We can identify IOCs or indicators of compromise potentially. It doesn't necessarily mean that all IOCs will come through this type of monitoring tool, but it certainly can be a help in that regard. Such things as data exfiltration, we can see things that aren't necessarily normal and identify those trends and those one-offs or the spikes. Then unusual traffic in general, the type, the source, the destination, or perhaps the application. All of these different things can appear once we understand what's normal. If we have a baseline and we establish what is normal, then it's very easy or at least I should say easier for us to identify what is not normal. We can see just a normal amount of traffic, whether it be network, storage, compute. All of a sudden, we see a spike, and then we can go hey, wait a minute. What's going on here? And it gives us an opportunity to then drill down and look in deeper to see what's going on. That's where log files come into play. That's where our aggregation and collection things come into play, our SIEM software. All of these things work in tandem to help us identify IOCs. We'll talk about NetFlow and sFlow here in just a moment, which can also function as bandwidth monitors and help us understand the flows between the different nodes and endpoints on our network.

Metadata

Metadata is data about data. It's data that provides information about other data. That means different things in different context. For email, as an example, an email header can show things like the sender info, the date and time, the IP addresses that it came from or the hops that it went through as it gets from point A to point B, the intermediary hosts. All of this metadata can become important when we're trying to understand where things are coming from. If we're getting a lot of spam, perhaps malicious activity, malware, that metadata around that email can become very, very valuable for investigations. How about for mobile devices? Details about phone calls or messages, perhaps location or GPS information, all of these things can divulge information about a caller, even medical information, associations. When it comes to the web, we can use metadata to optimize for web sites, but it can also be used in a not-so-nice way. It can be used to identify visitors. We can fingerprint their browsers, look at certain things within the screen resolution and the fonts that are installed. All of the different graphical back-end pieces that don't necessarily or aren't necessarily visible to the end user can be used to fingerprint that browser and identify that person. If they visit again using that browser, even if it's from a different IP address, you could identify that person based upon those web browser metadata characteristics. Metadata can be good in a lot of instances. It can be not so good like for advertisers, and spammers. Then it can also be used maliciously to identify things or give away information that we don't necessarily want to become public knowledge or have visible to other users. Then we're talking about file metadata. So file attributes can identify, the owner of that file or the author, the date and time it was created or modified, the word count, even GPS coordinates if it's a photograph and, the type of device used, the type of camera, the f-stop, the aperture, all of these things can be pulled from the metadata on specific types of files. But this EXIF information, the GPS coordinates, it's important to understand that as you upload pictures to social media or send from one person to another, if you don't remove that information, it's quite possible that that actual metadata information gets passed along with that file as well. So keep those things in mind and understand that if you don't want this information to become public knowledge or at least associated with that specific file, then remove those properties whenever possible.

Netflow, sFlow, and IPFIX
NetFlow is a way of monitoring our network, and it takes it a step further, than just looking at typical network monitoring, as it will group the communication between two hosts on a network into flows? It's not just simple packet capturing. It's grouping that into flows to give you a more holistic view of traffic on your network. We have a few things in place here. We have a router, which is typically where you're going to have NetFlow enabled. That's going to be a NetFlow exporter, and that's going to be connecting to various networks, whether it be the internet, remote sites, a LAN, a WAN. Then we're going to be connecting to a NetFlow connector, and we'll have an administrator console where you can see a graphical representation, an application that will take the NetFlow data that's exported from the NetFlow exporter and display it graphically. We also have flow storage that's connected to the NetFlow connector. So, we have NetFlow packets of flow from the router to the collector, and then we also have the administrator that will query the collector. One's feeding data into the collector, one's accessing or querying data from the collector. The collector and the storage itself are collectively known as the NetFlow cache. As we enable NetFlow on the various devices in our network, one thing just to keep in mind is that each device should have its own separate port number. We can have multiple devices in the network reporting into or sending data to a NetFlow collector. Just make sure that each

one has its own port number so that the NetFlow collector can differentiate between. Otherwise, the collector won't know what's what, and it would just group everything together and give you bad data or a bad view of what's happening on the network. Some data that is collected by a NetFlow collector would be the source and destination IP address, the IP protocol field value, source and destination port numbers, also counters, whether it be packets or bytes, timestamps, the start time and end time, and then also where observed, the interface and the direction, whether it's ingress or egress and whether it's unidirectional or bidirectional. And just for your own knowledge, there's two main flavors of NetFlow. We have version 5 and version 9, with version 9 being the newer one. And the other implementations that we'll talk about, sFlow and IPFIX, are based off of NetFlow version 9 as well. There's a similar implementation called sFlow, and we'll talk about some of the differences here. With NetFlow, its Cisco proprietary, meaning it only works or functions on Cisco gear, and more granular collection of IP traffic to create flows. It does it packet by packet. We can get very granular. It only collects IP traffic, however, and we'll notice the differentiation here in just a moment. It's a more detailed collection, but it's also more CPU and resource intensive. Then, if we want to display that data graphically, we'll need a third-party collector such as SolarWinds, PRTG. And it's comprised of two components, the exporter and then the cache or the analyzer. As far as sFlow is concerned, that was introduced by HP in 1991, years after NetFlow came out. It samples packets and counters to create flows similarly to what NetFlow does. But the distinction here being that it's samples, so it doesn't do it packet by packet by packet. By sampling, we're getting more of a trend, but it's also less resource intensive. It potentially scales better. It also can collect traffic from OSI layers 2 through 7. It's not just IP traffic. It doesn't provide as detailed packet-level information as NetFlow, but it samples the data, and that's configurable, how often it samples, so that it has the ability to scale. All devices need to be sFlow compatible, so that's something to keep in mind. Then also, two components, an agent and a collector. There are some similarities between the two. Then we've evolved into a new standard called IPFIX, and that stands for Internet Protocol Flow Information Export. That is a collector export protocol, and it's based on NetFlow version 9. All of the features that you would see in NetFlow, however, it's not Cisco proprietary. It's nonproprietary. It also does packet count, byte count, type of service, flow direction, and routing domain. A lot of good information there. That allows you to monitor your network, see what types of services are running, what are the top sites, the top domains, who's the top talkers? It allows you to go in and get very granular with the network and understand what's going on. If you have lags or if you have applications that are performing poorly, these are, of course, good reasons to use NetFlow or IPFIX. It can be used for network monitoring, for measurement. It can be used for threat detection, and then also, some service providers will use it for accounting and billing purposes as well. All three are great tools. They need to be implemented on the devices in the network, and then all the devices that you're monitoring need to be compatible. You configure the exporters of the agents to report to a collector, and then you can go with an analyzer or a dashboard, and then get all the information that we talked about before about how your network is functioning.

Detecting an Amplification Attack (ICMP echo)
We've talked about Smurf attacks, and we've talked about amplification attacks. What I wanted to talk about real briefly here is how we could use NetFlow or sFlow to help thwart a Smurf attack, or an amplification attack. If you recall, with a Smurf attack, otherwise known as an amplification attack, a hacker would send a directed broadcast with the victim's IP spoofed to a network segment, to the broadcast IP address on

536

a network segment so that everybody on that network would get that request, but instead of replying back to the attacker they would reply back to the victim and flood that person's machine or that server or whatever the intended victim is. So here we have all of the different computers attached to the network. Once that spoofed ICMP echo is sent they all reply back to the victim's computer again, a victim's PC, desktop, laptop, or a server, depending upon what the target is, that can potentially overrun the host system, the amplification attack, if you have enough hosts on that network. Because, again, it could be dozens, it could be hundreds, or it could be thousands of computers all replying back to that specific victim. Using NetFlow or sFlow, or another network monitoring solution for that matter, but since we're talking about NetFlow and sFlow it makes sense to cover that here. What we could do is use NetFlow or, again, sFlow to identify ICMP echo requests or these pings, these Smurf attacks or these amplification attacks to detect that network attack. We could identify the victim using traffic monitoring to identify top destinations for ICMP echo responses. We could identify that within the tool. From there we could use NetFlow or sFlow to filter for the top subnets sourcing ICMP echo responses. We could then identify the port used for ICMP echo response to enter the site or to enter our network by using, again, NetFlow or sFlow to show top router and switch ports, receiving ICMP echo requests and packets destined for that specific victim, and then we can create an ACL filter on the router or the switch port to block ICMP traffic from the source subnet. Just a quick example of how we might use this tool. Automate to some degree, create filters and triggers so if these things happen we can be alerted, and either automate that process and automate that response or at least become aware of it, and then manually investigate and intervene as necessary.

Protocol Analyzer Output

Let's now talk about protocol analyzers and a little bit about what they do. A protocol analyzer is a packet inspection tool, and there are ones out there like Wireshark, which is probably one of most popular ones. It's an open source packet analyzation or packet analyzer tool. Retina, Nessus, Nmap can also be used to map protocols and see what protocols are available, what ports are open. And it can be used to troubleshoot network issues. It could be used to detect or inspect indicators of compromise and even decrypt SSL transmission if you import the certificates into Wireshark and use those to decrypt the traffic that you're capturing. Just to give you an idea though of what it can and can't do, here are some common use cases, and the one that I will draw your attention to is where it says spy on other network users. You can collect sensitive information, such as login details, users cookies depending upon the content and the encryption methods that they may use. A lot of it is done for legitimate purposes. But protocol analyzers can also be used to sniff traffic and gather information on other users. It can be used for good and used for bad. Not intending to make you a Wireshark professional at this point, but I just want to introduce you to the tool. Understand that protocol analyzers can give you a lot of deep, deep information about communication on your network. You can go in and examine packets. You can look at the actual flow of information. You can follow it back and forth. And it gives you a great amount of detail from a security professional's perspective, but also for network analyzation. Network professionals look at it for troubleshooting applications, for troubleshooting network performance, seeing where things might get held up. Maybe packets are dropped quite a bit. I would definitely recommend digging in when you have an opportunity and familiarizing yourself with Wireshark and the other protocol analyzer tools that are available. In this chapter, we covered vulnerability scan output. We talked about SIEM dashboards along with log files, such as syslog, rsyslog, and syslog-ng, how we can use those things to centralize our logging capabilities and then feed those in to other systems. We talked about journal control and some of the flags and some of the commands that can make that a useful tool for us along with an NXLog and then also retention of various types of things, like email and different types of data, and then the different types of compliance or regulations that may mandate that we retain certain types of data for certain periods of time. We also talked about bandwidth monitors and then metadata for various file types and how that can certainly divulge more information than we initially knew about. Then we talked about some network monitoring or optimization tools, such as NetFlow and sFlow, and then wrapped up with a brief look at protocol analyzers and protocol analyzer output.

Chapter 13 How to Implement Mitigation Techniques to Secure an Environment

In this chapter, we'll be talking about Implementing Mitigation Techniques to Secure an Environment. We'll be talking about reconfiguring endpoint security solutions, talking about application whitelisting and blacklisting, how that can help us, along with quarantining. We'll talk about configuration changes, and that deals with firewall rules, MDM, or mobile device management, data loss prevention, or DLP. We'll talk about content filters and also revoking and updating certificates. We'll also talk about the concepts of isolation, containment, and segmentation and how those can help us secure the environment, along with secure orchestration, automation, and response, or SOAR systems, and runbooks and playbooks specifically. When it comes to application whitelisting, that's going to be a list of applications that are allowed to run on a host. All other applications are blocked from running. That makes catching everything much easier. You don't have to know every single thing that could potentially run and explicitly deny that? In a whitelist, you say I have 10 applications that my users can run, Word, Excel, maybe a chat application, web browser of course, and a few other things. That's the 5 or 10 things you can do. That's all you can access. Everything else is blocked. Conversely, you can say blacklisting of an application, you can say, you know what, you can run everything except for these 5 or 10. All other applications are allowed to run. The downside being, if you have enough privileges you can go in and simply rename an executable that was previously blacklisted. As an example, you don't want someone to run regedit so they can't modify the registry. Well, if they have command prompt access or they can -click on regedit, they can browse to it, click on it, and rename it. They can rename that application and then simply run it at that point because it's checking against that file name. Depending upon how you're set up and what types of controls you have in place, it's important to check through these things all the way through, take the mindset of an end user, look at all the ways they can get around the controls you put in place, and make sure the things you have implemented function the way you intend them to.

Quarantine

One method that we can use to make sure that applications don't run, that we don't want malicious applications, malicious scripts, or hosts that perhaps aren't patched or don't meet our specifications before they enter the network, we can do something called quarantine. A quarantine is a proactive blocking of access or the ability to run or execute applications. Hosts that don't meet certain criteria, perhaps they don't have a certain code level, firmware level, patch level, applications or processes that are flagged as suspicious or malicious, we can keep them from accessing the network. Depending upon how our infrastructure is set up, we can identify those machines when they first enter the network and then cordon them off into a DMZ, or a demilitarized zone or a screened subnet, at that point we can make sure that they get patched or updated or somehow remediated to meet our specifications, and then allow them onto the network. Another way of doing that is having applications, whether it be antimalware or antivirus, block applications before they're able to do anything. Popular antimalware applications like Malwarebytes or Windows Defender or Sophos, there's a lot of them out there, McAfee, etc. They can block suspicious activity and they can quarantine downloads, applications before they're allowed to run. Then when we're talking about whitelisting applications, we can also have an allow list. You can see here we can specify certain applications that are allowed to run so that way if the antimalware software blocks that for some reason, we can add it in into a whitelist, so that way the next time we run it, the antimalware software won't block that application. These things are potentially malicious, they're going to be malware, ransomware, cryptojacking software, they would automatically be quarantined because the antimalware software would identify this, whether it be through a signature or some type of heuristics. We can then choose to either keep them quarantined and not allow them to run, or you can check the specific ones that you want to run and it will bring it back to life, and allow you to run that application. Typically not recommended, but if you know for a fact that something is safe, you can go ahead and check it off and then allow it to run.

Firewalls
A firewall is designed to isolate one network from another. It can be hardware or it can be software based. It can be either. It can be a standalone device, or it can be an integrated device, integrated into some other equipment, in other words, routers or switches. Whether you're a small office or a home office, you may have a small Netgear, or a Linksys, or even a Cisco router that combines a lot of functionality together. It can have a firewall. It can do NAT or network address translation, and, of course, routing functionality, as well, perhaps even switching. It just depends on the size of the network, how specific you want to get. There are different devices that can perform very specific functions, or there are integrated devices that can perform a lot of different functions together. If we have a diagram of outside users outside of the firewall, and you see

the firewall denoted by a brick wall. And, incidentally, the term firewall historically came from buildings that were built very close to one another, and in order to prevent fire from jumping from one building to another when they were very close together, think like row homes, for instance, they would build brick walls in between these different buildings to prevent that fire from jumping from one to the other. That brick wall would act as a firewall, to prevent fire from jumping from one building to the other. The same concept is carried, and that's why you typically see a firewall being illustrated as a brick wall. Firewalls are typically used to block or limit outside traffic from entering a network. Whether it's corporate, medium-sized office, small office, or a home office, they all serve pretty much the same types of functions. However, firewalls can also be placed internally, inside of a network, to segment one area from another. For instance, you may have a large corporate environment that has different areas that you don't necessarily want them to communicate, or they shouldn't communicate from one to the other very easily. You can punch holes in the firewall to allow traffic, but generally speaking, these things are cordoned off from one another. For instance, if you have a PCI secure zone, like, say you have a very large enterprise that has some typical day-to-day workers, and you may have an R&D department, you may have an accounting department, a finance department. PCI secure means it contains credit card information and some type of personally identifiable information, you want to have that information cordoned off from the rest of the network. The finance folks don't necessarily talk to the R&D, or maybe the graphics department, just to prevent internal browsing of those resources. A firewall can be put into place between those segments on your internal network as well. It's important to understand, hardware versus software, firewalls can either be hardware or software based. They can be standalone devices or integrated into other devices, like routers and switches. Even if it is a hardware-based solution, it's still going to contain software. You can't just run it on hardware by itself. There has to be some software running behind the scenes. You can drop it onto a server and have that server function providing firewall functionality, or it can be a separate standalone piece of hardware. However, that hardware is still going to contain software or firmware. What are some types of firewalls? Well, we have packet filtering firewalls, and packet filtering firewalls allow or block traffic based upon a specific port, HTTP traffic, as an example, web traffic. That typically comes in over port 80. FTP, or File Transfer Protocol, that's generated on port 21. You can configure the firewall to allow web traffic but don't allow FTP traffic, or allow DNS but don't allow NetBIOS, or time lookups, or whatever the case might be. You can break it down by port by port by port and get very specific, get very granular. Doing it based just on port, there's not a lot of intelligence there. It just simply looks at the port, and then it will either allow or block the traffic at that point. Next, we have proxy firewalls. A proxy firewall's going to be dual-homed, which means is going to have two network interfaces, typically one on each network, or on separate networks. That's going to segment internal users from the outside world, and it can mask the IP address using something called NAT, or network address translation. That gives an added layer of security because the outside world won't know who's communicating. All they'll see is the address of the proxy firewall. The proxy can also cache requests to improve perceived speed. If you have multiple users, as an example, that are accessing the same website while the first person to access that website or that URL will go out and pull it down from the web or from whatever resource it's getting it from. Subsequent requests, as long as that information is still sitting in the cache on that proxy server, so the next user goes out to that same web resource. Instead of going out to the web, or out to whatever resource they're getting it from, they'll get it directly from the proxy server, from the cache. It gives the perception that things are faster and that your network is all of a sudden more responsive. The next type of firewall is something referred to as a stateful packet inspection firewall, or SPI. An SPI firewall examines the packets and keeps the packet table of every communication channel. In other words, it has more intelligence than a simple packet filtering firewall, and it does a deeper dive. It examines what's inside. SPI tracks the entire conversation, so it gives you an increased level of security because it only allows packets from known active connections. If someone's trying to spoof or jump in the middle of a connection or a conversation, an SPI firewall understands that, and they say, wait a minute, I don't know who this is from. I haven't seen this before. This is in the middle of a conversation. There's no initiation. There's no back and forth to establish that connection. This just came out of here, so I'm going to drop that. It drops the packet. It gives you that added layer of security. It's better than simple packet filtering, which only looks at the current packet. However, it's possible to attack by overloading that state table. As we go through all of these different types of routers and switches and pretty much any type of infrastructure or equipment in our network, just understand that nothing is foolproof. There's always going to be a way, and there's always going to be hackers that are trying to somehow penetrate that device, crash it, get elevated privileges. Nothing's foolproof. That's why we're all employed. When it comes to configuring our firewall, we have a couple options. We have firewalls that are built in to our operating systems like we have here in Windows 10. There are other firewalls that are standalone devices, there are ones that are software based, hardware based, like we've talked about before. They all operate in the same fashion. They all allow you to go in and either allow or deny, implicitly deny, explicitly deny, or allow, applications, ports, users, IP addresses. Let's take a look at this. On my Windows 10 Desktop here, I have Windows Firewall open, and this is the Advanced Security? If you go into Windows Firewall Advanced Security, you'll see a number of rules for Inbound Rules and also Outbound Rules, some Connection Security Rules, some Monitoring Rules, and you can monitor in real time, but for this demo, we're going to look at Inbound Rules, specifically around Remote Desktop.

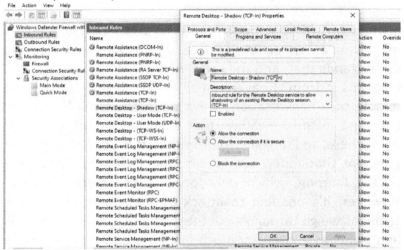

We want to enable Remote Desktop for this workstation. Conversely, if it was already enabled, and we think that might be a threat, we can disable that? Block that. So for here, if I double-click on any one of these, then I have a number of options. I can go in and look at the rule, the description, I can enable that rule, and if I hit Apply, you'll see the checkbox next to that rule. Programs and Services,

546

there are some specific things around that application, Remote Computers. I can say, allow connections from these computers, or skip this rule for these computers. You can think of it as an application whitelist or a blacklist. Same thing for protocols and ports. I can go in and say remote ports, local ports. some of these things, depending upon what it is you're configuring, you may have to change port numbers within the registry, there might be some additional configuration that's needed, but the general gist is here. The Scope, I can say Local IP addresses, allow these IP addresses, or only these specific ones.

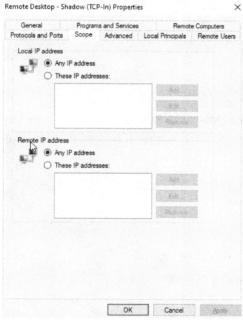

Same thing for Remote IP addresses. I can say Any IP address, or only allow these IP addresses. We're white-listing. Same thing for Advanced. I can say, which profile does this apply to? Is it Domain, is it Public or Private?

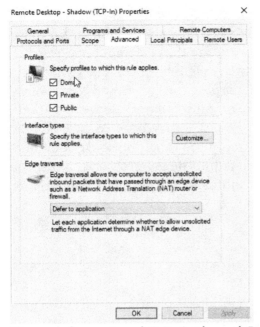

Then as far as Local Principals and Remote Users. I can say Local, only allow connections from these users, or skip this for these users?

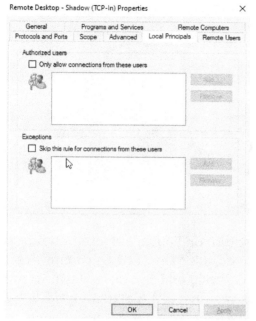

Again, white-listing and black-listing for Local users; same thing for remote. That's one way of doing it. I can go in manually, and you can also start from scratch and just say new rule, and create everything from scratch. If you have a specific application that might be brand new and you want to allow a certain port or a certain IP address, you can do that as well, or you can also configure some of these rules just by turning on, or turning off specific services. If I go and click on my Start button, and go up to System, then I'll see, at the bottom, Remote Desktop. This is one way to get to it. There's always more than one way to get to pretty much anything within Windows, but in this instance, I'm down at Remote Desktop.

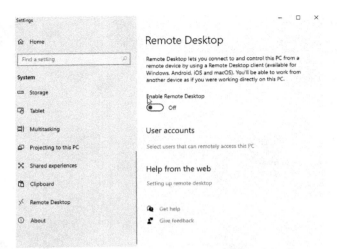

If I open that up and just turn on Enable Remote Desktop, it asks me, do you want to do this? I'm going to confirm, Yes. And if I close that, and Refresh, and I go back down to my Remote Desktop, you'll see those three rules have been enabled.

Remote Desktop - Shadow (TCP-In)	Remote Desktop	All	Yes	Allow	No
Remote Desktop - User Mode (TCP-In)	Remote Desktop	All	Yes	Allow	No
Remote Desktop - User Mode (UDP-In)	Remote Desktop	All	Yes	Allow	No

The same thing I just did before manually, I did automatically just by enabling Remote Desktop. If I go back up, go to System, down to Remote Desktop, and turn that off, I'm going to again, confirm I want to Disable Remote Desktop. Refresh, go back down again, and we see those three things are turned off. Just an example of how to configure a firewall rule, whether I want to allow or deny, based on port, based on IP address, it could be based on user, or it could be based upon application. There's more than one way to do that. You can do it manually, as we did here within the actual Management Console, or I can do it automatically, just by turning on or turning off certain features within the operating system.

Chapter 14 Mobile Device Management

Mobile devices provide users with the flexibility, and they can access work from anywhere, access documents, pretty much anywhere on the planet, and they can conduct business as easily as they could if they're sitting in the office. But with any enterprise technology, security must be at the forefront. It's crucial that these things get vetted and thought through, and designed, and architected upfront with security in mind. We can't allow functions within the business to pick a solution, drop it on our lap. And then say, Hey, make this work. It happens, but if at all possible, we need to insert ourselves into the process far enough in advance so that's not the issue. Such things as insecure access to websites. If we don't make sure we have mobile device management in place, and we don't have some way of controlling what people use their corporate assets for, then they can access insecure websites, download malware, download viruses, data leakage. We have the insecure axis to websites, we have insecure Wi-Fi connectivity. If they're sitting in a coffee shop somewhere and they're accessing our corporate network, if we don't allow them VPN access or give them some secure method to do that, well, everything they type in, everything they browse on with that mobile device could be potentially sniffed from that device, and then company secrets, company proprietary information walks out the door. The other thing is lost or stolen devices housing corporate data. If someone sits at a coffee shop, we'll use that example, they lay their phone down on the table, they get up to go to the bathroom, they go up to pay for their drink or food or something, they turn around and the phone's gone. Well, if that device is not encrypted, there's a high probability that someone can pull that information off the phone very easily. Could be company secrets could be proprietary information, or if you don't have any way of locating that phone or remotely wiping it, there's no way for us to even tell where it is or if it's being used. There are a few things that should be put in place, and we'll talk about those more in detail in just a moment. But then again, geolocation services, if that phone gets lost or stolen, we should be able to figure out where it is. If that phone gets turned back on again and checks into the network, cellular network or Wi-Fi network, it should be able to phone home, and we should able to ping that device and see where it is; and then missing upgrades and security patches. If we don't have any mobile device management in place, we can't limit what they see, we can't make sure they secure their connections. We can't prevent it from being lost or stolen and having that data gone, we can't locate it on a map, and then we can't even make sure that the users install upgrades and security patches. mobile device management is critical on a number of levels to make sure that people are doing what they're supposed to be doing; unauthorized downloads, applications, games, and so on. With iOS devices, iPhones, it's a little easier because everything that goes through the app store meets certain criteria, so there's not as many rogue applications or things like viruses and Trojans, and back doors. On Android devices, their app store is a little more open. The platform is more open, so there's a greater opportunity to have applications or games that may be compromised, that may contain malware and viruses. With mobile device management, MDM software is what enables a company to secure that users BYO device, bring your own device, without compromising their personal information. Some MDM software can partition that phone, that "corporate asset" so that there is a partition that houses company data, and then the rest of it is the user's personal device. here's a couple of companies that can do that, I'm not recommending one over the other, I'm just giving you a couple examples: Good Messaging, Airwatch, and Mobile Iron are three very popular MDM companies that provide software that can allow you to do just that. Someone can bring their own phone, they install this MDM software, creates a separate partition, or it can create a separate partition on that phone, so that way the user can access company assets, company resources, but yet the company is not going to interfere or co mingle with their personal data. They can use it pretty much as a dual device. However previously, if the device gets lost or stolen, the company can at least wipe the corporate partition. They can make sure that any company data, any company secrets, so on can be wiped. They can remotely wipe the entire phone, they can geolocate it, they can require passwords, require patches, and security fixes are upgraded or downloaded and applied in a timely fashion. It gives much more control over that phone, and you can do it in such a way that it doesn't completely hamstring the user and turn that device into only a corporate device, they can use it as a dual purpose asset.

Using MDM to Locate and Secure and Lost Device
Now that we're clear on what MDM software is, the capabilities, let's talk about using this to secure a device, securing a lost device. But we have Alice, and Alice loses her phone, which has very important personal information, as well as corporate data. If Alice is anything like me when I lose my phone, I'm not very happy about it, and I panic quite a bit. Immediately, Alice turns around and calls her good friend, Bob, who happens to be the mobile device management admin. Bob goes ahead and logs into his MDM console, brings up his tracking software, and is able to locate her phone. He's able to remotely access that phone via the

MDM console over the internet. The phone's connected. It's turned on. He's able to access it. It's not somewhere they can readily get to the phone, so they make the decision to remotely wipe the phone. They issue a wipe command. It goes back to its default factory state. There's nothing on there. On the off chance that somebody comes by, let's say, Harry the hacker, and grabs that phone, there is no corporate data, there is no personal data. And that phone can be replaced, and the data is secure.

Chapter 15 DLP, Content Filters & URL Filters

Let's just set the stage here for a moment, and all of the things that we're talking about, we need to make sure that we can implement those things in the event of an incident. Let's just say, for argument's sake, that there's an incident that's happened at the company. It's been discovered that there have been several breach attempts over the last 4 to 6 weeks targeting financial systems, web servers, and potentially customer data. Malware has been discovered on numerous systems, several which have been found trying to connect to C2 or command and control servers, to download additional malicious software. Data exfiltration attempts have also been made using several techniques over common ports, and then reconnaissance-type activity has been observed, and it's currently unclear if corporate web servers have been compromised. Keeping that type of incident in mind, which is not an uncommon scenario, lots of companies have exactly those types of things happen, if not more, and a lot of times those things go undetected for months and months. The average breach is about 18 months, give or take, before it's detected. These things can happen in the background for quite a while. Some additional mitigation techniques that we can use, one will be data loss prevention, or DLP software. DLP software can mitigate data exfiltration, which is what we mentioned in the previous scenario. That data exfiltration can be blocked or that activity can be blocked by DLP software, anything that we deem suspicious. That can be blocked from many sources, whether it be web, email, removable devices, USB drives, as well as suspicious activity such as file access or suspicious user actions. Next, we have content filtering and URL filtering. Content filters and URL filters, we've talked about those before, but they can block access. We can cut that link so that the hosts cannot reach out to those command and control servers. That malicious site that they would typically connect to can download additional software, that link is broken. Whether it's downloading additional software, connecting to botnets, participating in distributed denial-of-service-attacks, all of those types of things can be stopped if we can do content filtering and URL filtering at our own location. Then even further up the food chain, those things can be stopped at the root and the top-level domain servers. Then it's possible to stop that activity at a much larger scale. Then also within our organization, we can update or revoke certificates. Expired or compromised certificates can allow attackers to falsify their identity, they can create trusted applications, steal data. We need to make sure that we revoke certificates, we publish it to a CRL, and those things are updated constantly. We need to make sure we update our browsers, patch when appropriate, as soon as possible, and also patch all the systems very, very quickly. It's also a matter of user training to make sure that users know not to click on expired certificates. If they get a warning that says, that certificate is expired, don't assume that it's just because, well, it was valid yesterday. It's expired today. Someone in IT probably just forgot to renew the certificate, so I'll just go ahead and click on it anyway. Make sure they understand it's all part of cybersecurity training and the culture of security, but make sure they understand that those things are not to be trusted. Trust no one. If you get an expired certificate warning, then take it to heart. Don't click on it. Don't engage in that activity.

Segregation, Segmentation and Isolation

Next, let's talk about segregation, segmentation, and isolation. We have a few security or segmentation models I want to call to your attention. First, is physical. We can physically separate or segment nodes or hosts on a network. We can also do that logically with something called VLAN, or virtual LANs, virtual local area networks. We can also do it with virtualization. It's an isolation model or a segmentation model. Then we also have air gapped, meaning there is no connectivity to the internet or to the network at large. Well, with physical or logical, we have devices that are all on the same segment, the same Ethernet segment, or the same LAN, the same local area network, and in this example, you can assume that they're all connected to the same switch. That is a physical connectivity to the network. Well, we can also logically separate those networks. We can take that same layout, but we can use something called virtual LANs, or virtual local area networks, and group them accordingly. We could have a VLAN10, we could have a VLAN20, and a VLAN30. And what that does is separate those devices out. And what it does is create separate broadcast domains, separate security domains, and it reduces the chatter. Let's look at another example. Now we have a multi-floor building. We have wiring on each floor that goes back to a home run, and it goes down between floors. We have devices on the first floor and a switch, we have devices on the second floor and a switch, and then devices on the third floor and a switch. In this example, and it's not the only way to wire, not the only way to do it, but in this example we have each floor going to a wiring closet. In that wiring closet is a switch, and then the switches are connected via home runs. Vertical up and down wiring goes between floors, so they're all physically located in different locations. Well, we can also group those together, just like we did in the previous example. They don't have to be sitting next to each other. We can group them, again, logically, VLAN10, VLAN20, and then VLAN30. In other words, if we had groups of computers that may be on different floors. Let's say we have finance people that sit on all three floors or HR, or our graphics department, whatever the case might be, we can group them within our switches. We make sure that all the switches have the same VLAN associations, and that way they're grouped logically together. These VLANs can group hosts that are in different locations, into logical groupings. That creates smaller collision domains and reduces chatter. As an example, if you have a very large cafeteria, everyone's talking, it's very hard to understand because everyone's talking. Everyone's clashing into each other. They're colliding, their conversations. If I took all of those people in that cafeteria and separated them out into, say, five different rooms or, in this example, three different rooms, well, I have one third of the amount of people in each room, so the chatter's going to be less, so the collisions are less, so it helps increase efficiency. Then also it can be used to create security boundaries to segment traffic so that one host doesn't necessarily see broadcasts and doesn't see traffic designated for hosts in another VLAN.

Virtualization

Virtualization is the method of segmenting or isolating. We can keep a host in a sandboxed and isolated environment, meaning it's separate from the host that it's sitting on. It can also allow for snapshots. We can quickly revert changes, we can use virtualization to isolate our segment. We can do all of our testing. We can test changes we can even test viruses or malware to see what it does without affecting the rest of the network and without affecting the host that it sits on. It also separates the guests from the host, the guest from the hypervisor. If we have Hyper-V or VMware, or KVM, or VirtualBox, whatever our virtualization technology is, this allows us to keep those individual guests separate from the host. Other devices can be virtualized as well. We can virtualize other infrastructure, such as routers, switches, load balancers, firewalls. But the nice part is those things can be instantiated or spun up on demand. As a load increases, we could spin up additional load balancers or, if we have applications that need specific firewalls, instead of having to go through the normal change process and buying the equipment, and racking and stacking, and all the things that are associated with physical infrastructure, we can do it virtually very quickly, spin that device up, use it while we need it, and then we can tear it down just as quickly.

Air Gaps

An air gap is a method of isolating a computer or a network from the internet or from other external networks, or other networks aside from the one you're on. It doesn't necessarily have to be just from the internet. It could be from other networks within your company. If you have a very highly secure environment that you need to make sure that there's no chance of malware or viruses being introduced, then you would set up an air-gapped network. As with anything, there is no 100% guarantee, as we've seen in the past, with things like Stuxnet and some other very highly visible and highly cited instances where malware has jumped into air-gapped environments, nothing is 100% certain. But anyway, it's used for critical infrastructure, SCADA systems, as an example, and I refer back to Stuxnet, where the SCADA systems were still compromised, highly secure classified networks. There are some advanced techniques, however, to jump air-gapped networks. That's been demonstrated. Emanations, there's a technology, and it's been completely demonstrated, where they can view the emanations coming off of a computer, whether it is the sound of the hard drive whirring, or even the heat being generated by the hard drive

559

spinning up. If you're close enough to that device, you can pick those things up from the device and discern what's going on. You can read data from that device, pretty scary stuff, pretty advanced stuff. It's not something the average hacker I can do. But just understand that an air gap is a very good way of isolating the network, but it's not 100% foolproof. In fact, the US government and other agencies around the world have specific guidelines to create additional security. The US uses something referred to as TEMPEST, which protects that room, has to be certain thickness of walls and has to have additional coating and protections, Faraday cages, and things that just prevent emanations and monitoring from nearby locations. Emanations, FM frequencies, even some hard drives that have a small LED light on the front that shows activity of that drive. You don't see that too much anymore, but it is possible that if you have a line of sight visibility to that light going on and off as the hard drive writes, you could read, almost like Morse code, what's going on with that hard drive and read data from that device.

Securing the Environment using Isolation, Containment and Segmentation
Now getting back to our previous example, and we're talking about this incident that occurred and how we want to secure the environment, we can use these three technologies and techniques to secure the environment. We need to make sure that we air gap a network. If we have automation in place to create an air-gapped network, great. If not, and it's a manual procedure or we need to shut down ports, then, so be it. But if we're able to air gap that network, we can keep attackers out or keep compromised systems from spreading. There should be plans in place, and we'll talk about runbooks and playbooks here in just a moment, but there should be

some things in place defined so that if and when an incident happens, we have the ability to isolate when possible or where possible, especially as I mentioned around our most critical environment or most critical assets. Next, containment. Virtualization can separate hosts from guests and also guests from each other. We can also use that technology to revert to an earlier snapshot. If we find that we're compromised, we can revert that machine back. We can clone systems as necessary, spin up additional systems or additional resources. We can also use that cloning technology to clone a system, take it offline, and then forensically investigate that system or do whatever investigations are necessary to help us track down what happened, where, when, why, how. Then also, segmentation. We can use VLAN technologies I talked about before to create separate subnets, separate logical subnets within our environment that help to mitigate the risk from ransomware, malware. By creating those logical separations, we can break the connections between the two. We can isolate or contain, if necessary, if we have VLANs set up or we can also very closely watch or tighten down our firewalls, tighten down our routers, and we only allow certain types of traffic through. We can allow critical things to allow business to operate, but not necessarily everything through. We can ratchet that down or turn it up as necessary. All of these technologies can help us secure an environment in the event of a breach and also proactively if we suspect something may be happening.

SOAR and Runbooks/Playbooks

Next, we have something referred to as SOAR, and that stands for Security Orchestration, Automation and Response. What this does is complement your SIEM software. They do have some overlapping capabilities, but it complements SIEM software versus replacing it. It's going to allow us to aggregate all of the tools within a SOC, or security operations center, and then provides automated playbooks. We can script a lot of these actions together, not just within our SIEM software, but it may also kick off ticket creation, case management. It also has integration with third-party products. There's numerous things that it can integrate with, and then it automates, it orchestrates and automates that response. The SIEM software will collect all this data, it'll generate alerts, it'll do all of its things. It can bring in other sources to help enrich that data, and then it can help kick off investigations, open cases, open tickets, take remediation steps. It provides a full toolbox of capabilities. Imagine if we have a SOAR platform that sits in the middle. We're going to have different things on the left here. Events are coming in, our SIEM software, our endpoint detection, endpoint detection and response software is all going to be generating information and data. All of that stuff can then be fed into the SOAR platform, which can then do other things like ticketing, IT ticketing, change control, and it can also integrate with other controls, alerting, whitelisting applications or whitelisting protocols, and then also are third-party tools. You can think of it as the glue that holds a number of different applications and capabilities together and allows them to talk and integrate with each other, orchestrating and automating that interconnectivity. Getting back to the earlier incident, we've experienced some incident, and we need to have these different tools and technologies to help us secure the environment. We can leverage the SOAR platform to help us with orchestration and automation, the whole point of the platform. But these things are all predicated on us having very clearly-defined runbooks and playbooks so that we understand what needs to happen, in what order it needs to happen, who needs to be alerted. Let's take a look at this in a little more detail. These runbooks and playbooks, and this is just an example, this is not an exhaustive list, but some things that need to be defined and then put into the SOAR platform where possible to help us automate some of these actions. What tickets are to be created? What changes need to be implemented and also in what order? Depending upon the size of the environment, you may have a very complicated or a very wide-reaching change management system. A lot of different systems that are integrated, some things feed other things. You might be a 24/7 organization. You might have a lot of public-facing customers. You might be mandated by certain regulations and compliance mechanisms. All of these things have to be carefully vetted and also orchestrated so that they happen as quickly as possible, but without creating additional disruption to the business. What tickets need to be created? What changes have to be implemented? And in what order is critical. Also, what teams need to be engaged? What management teams need to be alerted and when? Also, what additional resources should be added? Whether that be monitoring resources. Do we need to spin a site up? Do we already have a site? Are we in the cloud and we need to spin up additional resources? Also callouts; do we have additional resources, vendors, third-party labor that needs to be engaged, also vendor engagements? Most of these systems are provided by some type of vendor, we should engage them as well to get their subject matter experts on task as quickly as possible. And then some additional items that should be defined, network changes. Are we going to look at isolation or containment or segmentation? Some of these things can be automated. Are we going to be taking clones or reverting from snapshots? Again, failing over to a remote site or up to the cloud. Do we have a dark IP space that's air gapped that we can move things over into or we may have been synchronizing with? Our most critical systems may have been synchronizing in the background and then logically air gapped. Well, do we need to spin up that dark IP site and revert to a last-known good configuration, or a last-known good set of data? Then from an investigation standpoint, spinning up investigations, who do we contact? What types of things do we preserve? Do we need forensics in place? Is there a preservation of evidence or a chain of custody that needs to be maintained? All of these things should be defined ahead of time. We don't want to be flushing these things out in the middle of a breach or in the middle of an incident. The more planning we have in place ahead of time, the more documentation that we have, and that everyone knows what the roles and responsibilities are, and then the runbooks and playbooks can then run that much more efficiently. We can automate where possible. The SOAR platform, this orchestration and automation is a big piece of this puzzle. It's the glue that holds all of these things together. The more planning we do ahead of time, the more successful the outcome. In this chapter, we talked about reconfiguring endpoint security solutions like application whitelisting and blacklisting. We talked about quarantining, whether it be applications or processes or downloads and. We talked about configuration changes like firewall rules, MDM, wiping devices remotely, DLP. We talked about content filters and also revoking or updating certificates. We also talked about isolation, containment, and segmentation and how that can help us secure the environment. Then we talked about SOAR, which is Secure Orchestration, Automation and Response, along with runbooks and playbooks and how those things will help us be successful in the event of an incident.

Chapter 16 Key Aspects of Digital Forensics

In this chapter we'll be talking about Understanding the Key Aspects of Digital Forensics. We'll talk about documentation and evidence in general and why it's Very important to make sure things are documented properly. We'll talk about acquisition and some things around what we should go after first and why, some of the gotchas if we don't follow those procedures. We'll talk about integrity and a few methods we can use to prove that the data we've collected has not been tampered with. We'll talk about preservation along the same lines. We'll talk about ediscovery and what that means and how it applies to an investigation, along with data recovery, and then a similar concept of nonrepudiation so the party in question can't deny ownership or specific action. And then we'll talk about strategic intelligence and counterintelligence along with on-prem versus cloud and some of the challenges and nuances to where that data resides, some things around data sovereignty, applicable laws, depending upon where it's located in the country or in the world if we're doing global business. But what is computer forensics? Well, it is the analysis of digital data in a very simple term. A forensics-level investigation would be something a lot more sophisticated and typically a lot deeper than simply just logging into someone's computer and reading through their internet cache or their internet history. The mere fact that we log in to someone's computer and try to check those things, we tamper with that data. It renders the investigative process, or the probative value, it renders it more or less useless. We have to make sure that we do it when we do investigations in a very controlled, predetermined fashion so that we don't either knowingly or unknowingly tamper with or contaminate the evidence that we're trying to preserve.

It's an analysis of digital data, and that can be computers, it can be smartphones, USB drives, it can be the internet activity taking place, text messages between two people or groups, game consoles, and more. Everything that's connected to the internet, even the Internet of Things, whether it's a refrigerator or, all of those things generate information. They generate data that can be used to either put someone at the scene of a crime or at least help to corroborate a chain of events. Who uses computer forensics? But, anyone who has a need to gather and retain digital evidence. Anyone, whether it's a small mom and pop shop and they may hire a third party to come in and do that, a criminal or computer forensics investigation, or it can be a very large company, a corporate enterprise, a Fortune 500 or a Fortune 150 global organization, they may have an entire team of forensic investigators that they can either dispatch anywhere around the world or they can work remotely anywhere in the world. A small business investigating an internal data breach, a large corporation investigating a hacking attempt or data theft, so anyone from small to the very large has a need for computer forensics. Also, law enforcement investigating a crime. It doesn't necessarily have to be an internal group or department within a company, law enforcement oftentimes will do some type of computer forensic examination, and that's becoming more and more prevalent as time goes on. 10 - 15 years ago it was relatively unheard of to have each department have a specific computer forensics lab or a computer forensics division. Nowadays, pretty much every department has either one or two, or maybe an entire department devoted to computer crime investigation and computer forensics. Additionally, we have private detectives, investigating spouses and insurance fraud.

Order of Volatility

Computer evidence is stored in a number of locations. It can be stored on a magnetic disk, it can be stored in a flash, it can be stored in RAM. Some locations are very temporary. RAM, or random-access memory, is one of those. Everything that your computer does, when it interacts, the CPU, or the brains of your computer or your smartphone or your game console or whatever it is, all of those things have a CPU of some sort. That CPU cannot communicate directly with the data on disk or the data on a flash drive or what have you. It has to pull that data into RAM. That's the intermediary, or the staging area. That is the place where the CPU talks to when it needs to do something of a process. The information in RAM is fresh, it goes in and out very quickly. There's only a finite amount of RAM, and things that come into RAM, if it's already full then it will cache out or swap out or page out, depending upon the operating system that you're using. It'll take that data out of RAM and place it on the disk. Well, that RAM can go away very quickly if the computer is turned off or if it loses power. That's one thing we have to be aware of. Some locations are longer term, Even after deletion that information or that data remains. Magnetic hard disks are a good example of that. If you delete a file from a disk, in other words you just simply highlight it and then click Delete, that file is not deleted. What it is is it takes off the master file table, or again, or it depends upon the operating system how that functions, but there's some table of contents, that has all the pointers to where those files are located. When you delete a file you simply remove that marker. You ultimately say, hey this file is capable or able to be over written. This location of data is no longer needed. It takes the pointer away, so it makes it look like the file is no longer there, but the data itself remains until it's overwritten. This pertains to hard disks. Flash drives are a little bit different. But for magnetic hard disk, if you delete something it doesn't go away. Some locations, are long term, but once deleted they quickly become irretrievable. This specifically refers to SSD or flash drives. With magnetic disks we can place our 1s and 0s, or our bits on the disk. And if we erase that or we mark it for deletion those bits remain. With an SSD, you can't overwrite information in an SSD. If I have information there and I mark that file for deletion I can't simply just overwrite it because it can only have two states, on or off, it's a flash drive. I need to erase that and set it back to 0s so that it can then be over written. When that happens I'll mark the file for deletion, and then very quickly behind the scenes there's a trim process or a garbage cleanup function that takes place and it will then clear that data out. Once you delete it off an SSD, sometimes within minutes, sometimes within half an hour or an hour, depending upon the type of flash drive and what functionality it has, that data will be deleted and it's irretrievable. From a forensics perspective, where that data is stored has some type of bearing on how quickly you need to access it and the order in which you should access it. With the order of volatility, data should be gathered based on the life expectancy of that data. The CPU, cache, and register content, okay the things that are closest to the CPU that need to be there, or need to have power there for it to exist and continue to exist, that is the top of the priority list. We want to try to capture that information first because that information, most often than not or more often than not, will have the most probative value. But it's also the easiest to disappear. If we turn the computer off that information is gone. Next, we have the routing tables, ARP cache, process table, kernel statistics, again, all things that are very volatile. Memory, RAM, all of these things, temporary file space, swap space, data on hard disk, remotely logged data, data contained on archival media. It goes from the things that are very ephemeral, where if we power that computer off it goes away. Those things need to be captured, if at all possible, first. There are tools we can hook up to a computer, we can attach either locally or remotely that allow us to capture that data without contaminating it. Then we can do the same thing with routing table, ARP cache, and memory. The remaining things, temporary file systems, swap space, we can capture that because it's written to disk and the data on the hard disk. We can do that in a slightly more methodical, deterministic fashion. With the data in that volatile space, memory and RAM, that's a little more difficult to capture, but it also provides, a lot of times, the most value because it shows us exactly what was happening just within a few moments ago.

Chapter 17 Chain of Custody & Legal Hold

There's something that can be critical to an investigation, and it can also sink an investigation. Even if it's the best, most meticulously conducted investigation on the planet, if it fails during the chain of custody, if and when it ever has to go to court, that could sink the investigation. When collecting evidence, maintaining that chain of custody is crucial. We want to make sure that we have no gaps in the chain of custody because why? Well, because that can destroy a case. If in other words, if there's a gap and we collect all of our evidence, we do all of our due diligence, we get our search warrant, we go in and we take possession of equipment, we document, and do all the things that we're supposed to do, but then we bring that back to our headquarters or to our office, and we don't document where that evidence goes, whose hands it changes along the way, where it's stored, and so on, it's very easy for a defense attorney, at that point, to interject and say, well, wait a minute. How do we know this wasn't tampered with during the process? How do we know that this wasn't swapped out or something wasn't manipulated or tainted in some fashion? There's hours, there's days, there's weeks where no one had eyes on this specific equipment. How do we know this is even my client's computer or hard drive? You don't want to have that discrepancy come into the investigative process. Evidence can become contaminated, if we don't have it accounted for each and every step of the way. It also introduces reasonable doubt. The defense attorney can turn the tables on an investigation. It's important to lock this thing down tightly and do not leave any room or any chance for error. When we're dealing with custody logs, it should accompany each piece of evidence. Everything that we secure, everything that we take away from a scene, should have a chain of custody tag attached to it, an evidence tag, depending on how your specific department or organization works. That chain of custody tag should have who acquired it, who received it or who it was received from, the date, and the time. That should account for everything, including when it's logged into an evidence locker, when it's removed from an evidence locker, so, there is no gaps in time. Every time the evidence is logged in or out of evidence or an evidence locker or some type of containment facility or changes hands in any form, that should be documented, the date, the time, the location, the person checking it in, checking it out, and then seals and/or tags on evidence bags. If an evidence bag needs to be opened, then it should be written on there why that seal is broken and when a new seal is applied, and, of course, initialed. That way everything is accounted for from the moment it is acquired to the moment it's no longer needed.

Legal Hold

Legal holds is data that has been identified as material to an investigation. It's copied or moved to an immutable location. Immutable means it can't be altered in any way. That way it's write protected, so that way it helps us maintain a continuity of evidence. there are different applications out there that will do a lot of this for us, so all actions, access, anything that's done to that data, if anyone accesses it, moves it, uses it in any type of searches, all those things will be logged. There are a number of applications and application suites or tool sets that will do all of that for us and automate a lot of this process. Something else to keep in mind is the fact that it's not subject to typical retention policies, so it may in fact be held indefinitely. Your organization may have, say, a 30-day, or a 3-month, or even a 3-year data retention policy, or 5 or 7 years, depending upon the type of data. Well, legal hold data will be held indefinitely until that specific case is over, and in some instances, that data may be held indefinitely. Some companies may keep that data in an immutable location on a higher class of storage or a higher tier of storage while the case is active, and then archive that off to something else, whether it be DVD or some write-once media, or it might move to tape backup or some type of archive location, so that way it can be held indefinitely but then recalled, if need be, whether it's part of its own case, or it may be part of some other case.

Chapter 18 First Responder Best Practices

The first responder can be on scene, or you can image your computer remotely over a network, again, depending upon the role that you play, whether you're law enforcement or an internal corporate investigator, whether you work for a state or a local, or the federal government. Each of these different tiers, have different capabilities. Once you're there, you need to photograph the computer, photograph the scene. It's critical to get a good understanding of how things are, again, if you're local to that scene, if you're not doing it remotely. If you're on scene, photograph the computer and the scene. That way, you know exactly from beginning how things are laid out, how things are connected. Then if the computer is off, do not turn it on. The simple act of you turning on a computer and booting it up changes thousands of files, changes the timestamps, the last access, last modified on a number of files, hundreds of thousands of files, just simply booting the operating system. That can have a negative effect on your investigation. It can wipe out some things that could be extremely valuable down the road. It's off, don't turn it on. Then if it's on, don't turn it off, at least not yet. We want to photograph the scene, make sure we have everything in place. Then, if you have the proper tools, again, you can connect to that computer, whether it's USB, whether it's some other type of method, and you can image, you can write block the computer, and then image it without contaminating anything. You can capture the information that's in RAM, that's in all the volatile areas that we talked about in addition to imaging the actual disk itself. That way you can get an exact duplicate of the data that's on that computer and the state that it's in when you come across it. You want to turn off if you have the tools available to do that type of imaging. Then, depending upon your role, whether it's IT security or whether you're law enforcement, will dictate whether you can or can't put your hands on someone, if you're law enforcement and you're doing the search warrant, you want to make sure you separate that person from the device. Because if they have the chance to get to the computer, start erasing files, turning it off, or doing something to manipulate the device. In some instances, there have been cases where people have their computers hooked up to explosives, they have degaussing coils, so if they flick a switch they can turn around and wipe their hard drive instantly. Some extreme cases, but depending upon your role, you want to separate the person and the computer, image it on site. That's not always possible, but these types of things are best practices that allow you to get with the least chance of contamination the data that you need in a format that will stand up and hold up in a court of law, if it ever has to go through an investigative process and it ends up in court. I don't want to get off on a tangent too, too much, but, again, you'll separate the person, then you'll collect live data. You want to start with the RAM image. You want to get all that data that you can off the computer in its live, volatile format so that you can look at and parse through what that person was doing at that exact point in time. Because if they just had a chat conversation with someone, or if they were just logging into a website, doing some type of hack or a breach, the things that they typed most recently in that conversation, the data that's passed through the computer will be stored in RAM. That gives you a high-value target. Then you want to collect a local image of the hard disk using forensics tools, and there are many tools out there, so this is not an endorsement of any one product. But there are tools like dd, Helix3, EnCase, F-Response. There's a number of tool. AccessData is

574

another. There are a lot of ones out there that can give you a forensic bit-by-bit copy of a hard drive without writing to that drive at all. Takes an exact copy, bit-level copy, creates a hash against that copy, so it does a hash on the original, does a hash on the copy, and those hashes will match up. It gives you the ability to say definitively, yes, that's exactly the same data as what was retrieved or what existed on the suspect computer. Once that's finished, then you can unplug in the power cord from the back of the computer or remove the battery. The power cord is the best way to go, or removing the battery. There have been instances where the power button has been wired to a degaussing coil or some type of explosive, in some cases. If you flick that power button, you have the potential to not get the desired result. So removing the power cord, removing the battery if it's a laptop, is the best option. That way it shuts it down ungracefully, doesn't write to the swap file, any of those things. It just shuts it off at the point in time that it was. Then once we're done, we want to diagram and label all cords, document all devices themselves, model numbers, serial numbers. That part of an investigation is very time consuming. It's certainly not the most glorified part of the investigation, but it is critical because all of those things need to be documented properly, so they can be reconstructed, if necessary, or at least very accurately describe the scene as you found it.

Capture a System Image
A system image can be captured locally or remotely using special software or devices. There are applications that can do it via software, but there are also other applications or devices that can do it through a hardware connectivity. It will write-block the computer or the device in question, and when I say write-block, you're not able to write to that disk

at much like read-only, but better. That way, even if it's read-only, there are still some things that could be accessed just by the nature of you interacting with the file system. When you write-block the computer, you literally turn off its ability to write at all. That way you can image that disk, you can create a forensic image, a bit-level, bit-by-bit image of that disk, even the slack spaces on the drive, is then copied to a duplicate. When you're done, you would run a hash, and if the hashes match up, you know it is an exact duplicate of the suspect device or the suspect file, folder, disk. There are live USB or CD/DVDs, whatever your media of choice is, and when I say live, what I mean is that these are ISO images that are on the USB or a CD or a DVD. That computer will boot up, but it boots up completely off of the USB drive or the CD. Nothing is written on the hard disk, and there are a number of devices out there. Kali Linux is one but there are literally dozens of different distributions and programs from encase, access data, and there's lots of them out there that can give you these live, bootable images that can give you forensic capabilities on a target PC, laptop, etc. Something else to keep in mind when talking about capturing a system image is to make multiple copies of the imaged data. The reason for that is that we want to make sure we have a copy that we're working off of, never the original data. We don't want to work on the original image or the original PC or laptop, simply because, that will contaminate the data. We make multiple copies; that way, we can work off of a copy if something goes wrong, or we need to in some way destroy it or go through some type of destructive analysis, we can always go back and start with a new or a fresh image to copy the next time we have to do something again. That way, we're always working off of a copy that we can verify via that hashing algorithm. We can verify it is an exact duplicate of the original. We never want to use the actual target hard drive, simply because it contaminates the data. Forensic software will log and timestamp every action that we take during the investigation. That way, we can build what's called a case folder to aid in the documentation and the reporting, because if we're simply trying to determine what happened, if it's a breach, if it's someone that's trying to hack into our system, we may never have any desire to take this to court, or we know it's not going to go anywhere from a legal standpoint, but we want to understand what happened, how we can harden our defenses. In that case, it's not as important. But if we're talking about a criminal case where we think, or there has the potential for that case to go to court at some point in time, it is crucial that we maintain proper evidentiary procedures, and making sure we maintain chain of custody. But having that documentation again is critical, because it's very important if it ever goes to court, we want to make sure that we can recall that testimony and make sure that we can understand, very systematically what we did, and it may be six months, a year, two years down the road before that goes to court. If we're not aware of what we did, we don't have a photographic memory, that documentation is going to be extremely important.

Chapter 19 Network Traffic and Logs

The next thing that you want to look at, or a potential for digital evidence would be network traffic and logs. If you think about it, every single thing that's attached, whether it be a local network, a small office, home office network or a SOHO, SMB, small- to medium-sized business, or a corporate enterprise, again, a Fortune 500 or Fortune 150, every single device that's connected in any fashion generates logs, generates traffic. Network traffic, including IP addresses, the data that sent, the actual websites we're browsing or the photos that we're accessing, the data that we're either copying or saving, the protocols that we use, all can be used to investigate a crime or a hacking event. An IP address, for example, can be used to locate the source and the destination of an event. It can help us to narrow down where a suspect is located. It could be on our internal network. We could be in a corporate environment trying to identify who a suspect is, who's accessing files. It doesn't necessarily mean that we know exactly who that person is because, again, someone could be sitting at that person's computer. Same thing if we're investigating a crime from a law enforcement perspective as well. Just because we have someone's IP address doesn't necessarily mean we know exactly who that person is. That gives us an idea, that gives us a start, but that only begins the actual investigative process. Once we have the IP address we can narrow it down, we can potentially see where they're coming from, what, perhaps, hops they're taking to get from where they're located to their destination. They may be trying to hide where they're located, we can backtrack and see if that leads us to the end, or to the suspect, rather. Sometimes it will go to a dead end, if they're smart enough and they jump through enough hoops. It doesn't necessarily always mean we have a person of interest. It can help place the suspect behind the keyboard, but, that's just a piece of the puzzle. We have to have more than just that. Then logs themselves are generated by a variety of devices. If you think about desktops and laptops, there's lots of logs within the actual computers themselves as to what they're doing, when they're doing it, the registry on a PC, there's configuration files on Macs and Linux devices, lots of log files that are generated and saved, typically for troubleshooting. But it also identifies when files were accessed, when system parameters and variables were changed, when people logged on, or when they logged off. All of these things can help us to build a case. Routers, switches, and firewalls on our corporate network, or even if it's in a home and we're trying to identify what's taken place from my location to a corporate location. In other words, someone's outside of our corporate network and trying to come in. Routers, switches, and firewalls, both within our own environment and potentially within a suspect environment, can all create log files, syslog files on routers, switches, the firewalls themselves. All of these things should be gathered and then correlated. Once we have all this information, we then need some way of either feeding it into a big data analysis type of tool, something like Splunk or some type of other big data analysis tool so we can correlate all of these different pieces of information, log files from here, switch files from here, configuration files from here, and put them all together. Then we can correlate the times and get an idea of what's going on. Smartphones, gaming consoles, some other things that people typically don't think of, but, they all generate logs. Smartphones have diagnostic information. We can tell when it was used, what was installed. Gaming consoles, whether it be an Xbox or a PS3 or PS4, all of these things get

IP addresses that they connect to the internet. They generate log files and generate data. Everything, if you take it and put it into a combined case folder, can lead to a pretty precise picture of what happened and when.

Capturing Video
Video can be a crucial component to documenting an investigation. It can be taken of ourselves or of yourself as you're in your investigation, You can wear a camera to record your movements or you can simply just video the scene itself you have a good picture of how things were laid out, where they are, record what's on the screen, the position, the location of various components, and so on. Also, video can be from a surveillance camera, whether it be on site or perhaps outside of a business or a specific data center or a location. Do we have evidentiary value or do we have evidence from video cameras inside of our data center about an office or a remote site, the entrance or an exit of a building. Video can be something that we take or it can be taken from an outside, third-party source that we can then use to help build our case. Video can be used in a number of different fashions.

Record Time Offset
When I talk about recording the time offset you might say, well why is that important? Who cares? Well, it's extremely important when we're trying to corroborate and correlate all these different log files that we have. There's something referred to as UTC. That stands for Coordinated Universal Time. It stands for Coordinated Universal Time. It's the mean solar time at the Earth's prime meridian. 0 degrees longitude located near Greenwich, England. The time zones from around the world are expressed as positive or negative offsets from the UTC. Why that's important? Well, we may

have people, whether they're suspects or even within our own corporation or our own corporate networks, that are global. Or they may be at least within different time zones. If we don't have the proper offset and we're not sure that everything is in sync then it's going to be very hard to try to build a case based on time. We could have multiple breaches within a corporate network, that take place across multiple time zones. It could be globally. If we're not able to correlate exactly what happened when it's going to be very difficult for us to then match up, Person A, our suspect, was at their location here and they hit our PC or our network here. Well if the times are completely offset and they're not accurate it's going to be much more difficult for us to lineup than if we can see that on the suspect computer at exactly 15:15 it did this, and here it is 15:15 on our systems as well and here's where the breach occurred. It's going to be much more difficult if everything is out of whack to try to correlate that. It's just, it's important for us to make sure that within our own systems that we have control over that we have all of our systems in sync pointing to a network time server. Okay? They can either be internal or it can be external. We can point our devices, routers, switches, PCs, we can point them to an external time source so that way everything is in sync. Typically in most environments, whether it's, a Linux environment or an Active Directory environment, more than likely you'll have the Active Directory server or, some component within your Active Directory environment, point to a time server. They will coordinate time and push out the proper time for all the computers within that environment. However, your switches and everything else, routers, they need to be in sync as well. That way it's very easy to corroborate and correlate time.

Taking Hashes

When we're talking about hashes, a hash can be an MD5, SHA1, SHA256 or SHA512, it's a mathematical algorithm that's applied to a file folder or an entire disk that verifies the integrity of the evidence. The hash is taken prior to imaging. If we arrive on scene and we take possession of a suspect computer, we have a device we can either connect externally or we boot up using some type of write-blocking software, we're going to connect to that target PC locally or remotely. We will then run a hash against that target hard disk, typically it's going to be the entire hard disk. We'll run a hash against it. It will come back when it's finished and spit out a number, a long string of characters and numbers telling us this is a unique fingerprint for that specific drive. When we're done, we'll then take an image of that hard disk and we'll run that same hashing algorithm against the copy. If both of those numbers come back the same, we know beyond a shadow of a doubt that they are absolutely identical. If one letter, as an example, if we were to hash an entire dictionary or an entire encyclopedia or the entire Library of Congress, whatever it is you want to focus on, if you took a hash of that entire body of work, let's just say a dictionary, well, if we changed one letter in that dictionary from a lowercase to an uppercase, the hash would be completely different. In other words, if we were to make the analogy to a computer, if we went to a computer and just simply turned it on, accessed some files, logged in, things are going to change, timestamps, file access, whether we're read, write, modify, anything that we do at that point to that computer changes something. When that happens, it would then change the hash, and if those hashes are different between our target and our copy, well, then it's no longer valid, and in a court of law that would be thrown out.

Chapter 20 Screenshots & Witnesses

A screenshot of what is on a suspect's computer, on their screen at that moment in time, gives us an idea or a good indication of what they were doing, what they were working on, perhaps before they had a chance to destroy evidence. especially if we don't have the opportunity for the tools to take a proper image and grab what was in RAM and volatile memory, if we don't have the ability to capture that information, then our second best option is to take screenshots., again, we don't want to interact with the actual computer itself. If we have no other choice than yes, something is better than nothing; however, remember back to what I said if we have to go to a court of law and it depends upon the type of investigation, but we don't want to tamper with the original suspect PC if we can help it, but if you can't then taking screenshots can help. An alternative would be, either video or to take pictures and physically take a picture of what's on the screen at that point in time. Depending on what's on the screen, it may outweigh the risk, losing that information.

Witnesses
Something else that we want to not overlook for sure are witnesses. Witnesses and witness accounts can be crucial to an investigation, and more often than not, a witness can help or kick off an investigation. A lot of times crimes, attempted crimes, breaches have been solved by tips from witnesses from the general public. Don't overlook the fact that there are always a second set of eyes, that can be crucial to your investigation. When taking statements from a witness, always try to ascertain the general who, what, where, why, and how, but also the date and time, what else

was going on at that point in time, who else was there, because you may be able to have follow up witnesses. Maybe that person that you initially talked to didn't see everything or they weren't there long enough, but if they can also say who else was in the room or who else was in the general area and you're able to contact those people, you maybe able to get additional information as well. Also, what other equipment was present, because that may give you more things that you want to search, especially if you're going to prepare a search warrant and you want to make sure you include everything in your search warrant, but you don't want to be overly broad because as you take things before a judge, if it's overly broad, a lot of times they will shoot that down and make you go back and rework that search warrant you're wasting valuable time depending upon the nature of the crime. If you can pinpoint it, narrow it down, and get it the first time, then that's going to expedite your ability to get that warrant and go and get that evidence and then, you want to make sure you capture the who, what, where, when, why, and how. But if you capture all of these things and you touch all of these points when you're doing your interview, you're going to capture the majority of information that you need.

Chapter 21 Preservation of Evidence

As an example, let's say we have our target system. We have a couple of options. We could attach to it with a laptop and we could use software where I protect that computer. We could also use a USB or bootable disk we could boot into that system and boot to that live CD instead of allowing the system itself to boot. Because if you recall, the actual act of booting that system changes hundreds, potentially thousands of system files, access times, dates, so it tampers with that evidence. We want to use something, some device to write-protect that target system so that it's not tampered with. Alternatively, we could use some type of hardware or software device to connect, a USB token or a specific, or an actual device specifically built for forensic purposes that allows us to attach to that machine via USB or some other connection, and write-protect that system, and from there we would take a bit-level copy and we would create, in essence, a cloned image. Typically we'd take that bit-level copy, that entire computer, and copy it to an image file. That image file is then what we would work from. We would then take our forensics workstation, and we would work from that cloned image, we would not work on the actual target system. We can use a hashing algorithm to hash the original system and then hash our cloned working copy or copies and make sure they are identical. That way we can prove that nothing's been tampered with or have been added or changed in any way. But we always want to work off of an image. That way the original target system is preserved.

Recovery
When it comes to recovery from a forensics' perspective, data can be recovered forensically if it hasn't been

overwritten. That's it at the end of the day. If the data has not been overwritten, it can be recovered using forensics tools. If it's been wiped, in other words it's been overwritten by multiple passes, that's going to make it very difficult, if not impossible, to have that data recoverable. If it's an SSD, if those NANDs have been reset, there are some tools, both from the SSD manufacturers and also some Linux tools from third-party tools that allow us to reset those SSDs so you can wipe that entire drive in a matter of seconds. If that, in fact, happens, recovery of that data is very, very difficult, if not impossible. Additionally, the media itself needs to be intact. If someone were to take a drill and drill through those hard drives or drill through the SSDs or otherwise break them apart, degauss them if it's a magnetic media, something where it physically destroys that disk, it's going to be very difficult, again if not impossible, to recover the data. Depending upon what it is, the nature of the investigation, and who's doing the recovery, impossible is a relative term. There are some Three Letter Agencies that have access to tools and toolsets that the average person and the average company does not have. Impossible is not necessarily a finite term, but for all intents and purposes for the average company, for the average person doing forensics recovery, if the media is physically damaged, broken apart, drilled through, scratched beyond repair, that data is going to be unrecoverable.

Strategic Intelligence / Counterintelligence Gathering
Whether we're talking about strategic intelligence or counterintelligence, it's done to allow the person or the company commissioning those actions to make real-time, actionable decisions. The actions are going to be proactive based on real-time data. We're not looking at historicals, we're not looking at trends, this is real-time data, it's very

fluid, it's real-time analytics, active logging activities that will typically have clearly defined rules of engagement and allow us to make very quick decisions based upon real-time data. Next, it relies on human interaction, as well as automated methods. Human reconnaissance or boots on the ground, as well as active logging and automated toolsets to gather that intelligence. We're not looking at logs and looking back historically, we're not looking in the rear view mirror, and we're looking at real time and looking forward to make these actionable decisions on how to act proactively. Then it can also be either defensive, which is our intelligence gathering, or offensive, which is counterintelligence. Intelligence information can be used to defend a company's or a country's interests or they can be offensive, and that's done to neutralize an adversary or an adversary's intelligence gathering capabilities. The mandate of most counterintelligence agencies are to go out and actively pursue, actively neutralize, or try to neutralize, an adversary's intelligence gathering capabilities. We're trying to thwart their ability to perform espionage, exfiltrate data from us.

Chapter 22 Data Integrity

Data integrity is part of the CIA triad, confidentiality, integrity, and availability, but with regard to digital forensics, just a few things to clarify. With data integrity, we have a couple of ways to provide data integrity, one of which is hashing. And as we know, hashing is a mathematical algorithm that maps data of an arbitrary size. It can be a variable, it could be short, it could be long, to a hashed value of a fixed size. It's pretty much deterministic. Every time we do a hash of a specific piece of information, we're always going to get the same result. It's a one-way function that's infeasible to reverse or inverse. There are a few different hashing algorithms, MD5, various flavors of SHA, SHA-1, SHA-256. So from a forensics perspective, you can hash the files on a drive and get a specific value. Then when you're done, when you've done your investigations or if you have a copy of that data, you can run that hash algorithm again. If those two hashes match, that means that the data has not been altered in any way. Next will be checksums. It's very similar in functionality to hashes as far as what the end result is, and it's used to verify the integrity of data, but not the authenticity. We can run checksums against a piece of data, and we do this with error-correcting code, with RAM, we do it with checksums when we're sending packets on a network, and we can do the same thing here. A checksum would allow us, so to test before and after, and if those checkssums match, then we know the data has not been tampered with. We can't necessarily prove the authenticity, but we can prove that the data itself is the same. Then we have the concept of providence, which is the metadata that documents the inputs, the changes, to data and provides a historical record of the data and also its origins. In essence, it allows us to track who created the data, any changes to that data throughout its lifespan. It's a way for us to verify the integrity of data and to get a bit of a historical view on what has happened to that data since its origin.

Non-repudiation

Next we have nonrepudiation, and nonrepudiation is an accountability concept. It is an inability to refute an action or an ownership. It says the person that we think has done this or owns this or has interacted with this, they can't reasonably say no, it wasn't me. Cryptographic nonrepudiation we can think of as digital signatures. That provides the inability to refute something. If a person, as an example, has a public key/private key and then they sign something with that certificate, then that proves that they are who they are. Of course unless someone steals their certificate, then of course all bets are off. But as long as that secret is kept safe, that PKI certificate is kept safe, then that would prove that that person is who they say they are. We can also have network nonrepudiation, and center around the generation of enough data of activity so that it can't be refuted, so the action itself cannot be refuted.

On-prem vs. Cloud Challenges and to Audit

Let's talk about some of the on-prem versus cloud challenges. We have three things to cover. We have the -to-audit clauses, we have regulatory and jurisdictional issues, and then data breach notification laws. Auditors will typically routinely access on-prem data centers to perform audits as needed. It can be regulatory or compliance mandates. It can be investigations of breaches. It can be contractual, annual, or biannual audits. You could have customers and your customers need some type of certification or understanding that you are providing security controls and that you're doing things effectively, best practices. If that's the case, you want your customers to be able to have documentation and proof that these things exist. But having things in the cloud can pose unique challenges to auditing, because cloud providers typically don't allow auditors in, just because of their sheer size. Cloud providers typically have thousands or potentially tens of thousands of clients or tenants, and if those tenants were routinely allowing auditors or having auditors come in to audit their infrastructure, it would get very unruly, very quickly, and the cloud provider wouldn't be able to get anything done, like business-as-usual, day-to-day work, because they'd have auditors in there, inspecting things 24/7, 365. There are ways around that, though, and you can still prove that you are, in fact, following best practices and having your security controls in place. Let's say, for instance, we have a data center or a cloud provider, a co-location facility, and in there, we have a number of tenants who have IaaS and SaaS, infrastructure as a service, software as a service, virtualization equipment. Well, we need to be able to provide a way to have those things audited and show definitively that we're following best practices, our security controls are in place. There are two organizations that I just want to call to your attention. One is SSAE 18, and that stands for the Statement on Standards for Attestation Engagements, number 18, and then internationally, we have ISAE 3402, that provides similar guidance. Those certification bodies have three different types of reporting. We have SOC 1, SOC 2, and SOC 3, and SOC stands for Service Organization Control, or SOC reports? There are three different types: SOC 1, 2, and 3. SOC 1 deals with financial reporting controls, SOC 2 deals with security controls, and then SOC 3 is publicly accessible. What these do is they ensure that data centers, channel partners, and vendors, utilize the same security controls as the data center or hosting provider? And all of these things are in place. Then there are two different types. Within SOC 1 and SOC 2, there are two different types, which we'll talk about here. Type 1 is an attestation of controls at a service organization, at a specific point in time. An auditor will give their opinion and say, they have these controls in place, but they don't verify or validate their effectiveness; they don't test them. It's a point in time. Type 2 reports is an attestation of controls at a service organization over a minimum six-month period, so it's a much more involved type of report, but they go through and not just validate that the controls were there, but they test them, and make sure that they're workable, they're effective, and they do what they say they're going to do. Two types of reports; 1 is easier to get or get certified against; Type 2 is more comprehensive, as you may guess, but once you're certified, your clients, customers have a strong understanding of what controls are in place and that they're effective. Then the SOC 3 type of report, those types of reports have the basic information, but the details, the under-the-hood type of things, are stripped away, and that's made publicly accessible, so that anyone can look and see what controls are there or what types of controls are there, but not the details, not the inner workings.

Chapter 23 Jurisdictional Issues & Data Breach Notification Laws

As a business, once you start to put things into the cloud you run into some potential issues, not necessarily every time, but some things to definitely think about. Data sovereignty and accessing that data, who owns or maintains or has jurisdiction over that data, can vary from country to country. Some countries are stricter, they have stricter laws, while others are less restrictive. It just depends upon where that data is stored. That can impact the ability to access the data, to audit data. So, data sovereignty, that states that the legal restrictions of any jurisdiction where data is collected, stored, or processed can apply. Depending upon where your information is stored, what region, what part of the world, different jurisdictional laws can apply. It's important that you know that. As an example, let's say we have a global business. We're doing business all over the world. We have customers all over the world. We may have a data center in one part of the world, maybe another data center somewhere else, and then another data center somewhere else. If we're a cloud provider or we're using a cloud provider, it's important to understand that cloud providers typically will have data centers all over the world. They do that purposely, so they can disperse that infrastructure globally, provide for geo redundancy and failover. Data can potentially be copied, stored, or processed anywhere globally. SoData is often copied between data centers in different regions. ? They might stay within a specific country, but it's copied within regions to make sure you have that redundancy, high availability. But it could potentially be copied somewhere else. ? Be sure to know where your data's stored. If it's copied between regions or between geo dispersed regions outside or into other countries, make sure you're aware of the applicable laws that may be in play. Also, if you have customers in other countries then data might be stored local to that region. An investigation or a breach or some type of audit could be impacted by that specific country's data privacy laws, data sovereignty laws.

Data Breach Notification Laws
They were first enacted in 2002, roughly almost 20 years ago. All 50 states have data breach notification laws, although it took probably 15-18 years to get all 50 states on board. But individuals and companies affected by a data breach must notify their customers. That's the general gist of the laws. Then they must also take specific steps to remediate any deficiencies. If a breach occurs and we identify why that happened, the companies must make sure that they're doing the proper steps to remediate and get rid of those issues, fill those gaps and make sure it doesn't happen again. Something also worth noting is that there's no federal data breach notification law currently. There are certain regulatory mandates that have certain industries disclose breaches, but not across the board of federal notification law. There are also data breach notification laws in other countries, so it's not just a US thing. Australia, China, the EU, Japan, New Zealand, etc., they are examples of other countries that have similar data breach notification laws. Then there are certain regulations that can affect customers or companies globally like GDPR, California's CCPA, there are a number of other ones in other countries as well. But just understand that just because you reside in a specific location, if you do business globally or if you utilize a cloud provider you may potentially be subject to other countries' laws, data sovereignty laws, or to privacy, to notification laws. It's very important that you understand all the

nuances, and then wherever that data resides, if it's processed, collected, stored, there are applicable laws that may impact how you do business, depending upon where it's located. In this chapter we talked about documentation and evidence, the acquisition of that evidence, how to collect it, the order of volatility, where you should start collecting data first. We talked about the integrity of data and how we need to ensure that it hasn't been tampered with, and we can prove that. We talked about preservation and e-discovery, along with data recovery, non-repudiation, being able to certify or attest that something is what they say it is or some action was performed as we suspect it was performed. We talked about strategic intelligence and counterintelligence and then some nuances and challenges on-prem versus the cloud when it comes to storage of data, data acquisition, data sovereignty.

BOOK 5

CISSP
CYBERSECURITY GOVERNANCE
AND RISK MANAGEMENT

POLICY CONCEPTS & DEPLOYMENT
WITHIN
ORGANIZATIONAL SECURITY

RICHIE MILLER

Introduction

IT Security jobs are on the rise! Small, medium or large size companies are always on the look out to get on board bright individuals to provide their services for Business as Usual (BAU) tasks or deploying new as well as on-going company projects. Most of these jobs requiring you to be on site but since 2020, companies are willing to negotiate with you if you want to work from home (WFH). Yet, to pass the Job interview, you must have experience. Still, if you think about it, all current IT security professionals at some point had no experience whatsoever. The question is; how did they get the job with no experience? Well, the answer is simpler then you think. All you have to do is convince the Hiring Manager that you are keen to learn and adopt new technologies and you have willingness to continuously research on the latest upcoming methods and techniques revolving around IT security. Here is where this book comes into the picture. Why? Well, if you want to become an IT Security professional, this book is for you! If you are studying for CompTIA Security+ or CISSP, this book will help you pass your exam. Passing security exams isn't easy. In fact, due to the raising security beaches around the World, both above mentioned exams are becoming more and more difficult to pass. Whether you want to become an Infrastructure Engineer, IT Security Analyst or any other Cybersecurity Professional, this book (as well as the other books in this series) will certainly help you get there! But, what knowledge are you going to gain from this book? Well, let me share with you briefly the agenda of this book. First, you are going to comparing and contrasting various types of controls, including managerial, operational and technical, and physical controls. We'll also talk about deterrent,

596

preventative, detective, corrective and recovery, and then compensating controls, the methods and procedures, along with the logical and physical ways that we can restrict access and deter the bad guys from trying to get into our systems. Next we will cover applicable regulations, standards, or frameworks that impact the security organization. We'll also talk about key frameworks, benchmarks and secure configuration guides. After that, you are going to discover how to implement policies within organizational security, as well as personnel and the associated issues with managing, maintaining, and keeping things secure. We'll also cover diversity of training techniques, along with third-party risk management, data classification, governance, and retention, and then we'll talk about various credential policies along with organizational policies. Next, we'll review the risk management process and concepts such as the risk types, risk management strategies, risk analysis, along with disasters, and business impact analysis. Moving on, you will learn about privacy and sensitive data concepts and considerations as well as organizational consequences of privacy breaches, notification of breaches, and the various types of data and how they're classified. We'll also cover privacy enhancing technologies, roles and responsibilities, information lifecycle, impact assessment, terms of agreement and privacy notices. If you are ready to get on this journey, let's first comparing and contrasting various types of controls!

Chapter 1 Threat Types & Access Control

In this chapter specifically we'll be talking about comparing and contrasting various types of controls. We'll be talking about the various categories, including managerial, operational and technical, and then physical. Managerial, operational or technical, and then physical control types, we'll be talking about deterrent, preventative, detective, corrective and recovery, and then compensating controls, the methods and procedures, along with the logical and physical ways that we can restrict access and then deter folks from trying to get into our systems. The goal of this chapter is threefold. Number 1, I want to make sure that you understand the threat types and understand that not all threats are created equal. No one control type can deter or prevent everything. We need to have multiple arrows in the quiver or tools in our toolbox, but the point being, make sure you have enough tools available to take care of threats from various types, various groups. Next, realize that different groups have different motivations. What motivates one hacker or one group may be completely different than another, which is why multiple control types are needed. Things that may deter one group may not deter another. Even a technical control that may deter or prevent one group may or may not prevent another, depending upon their skill level, their motivation, how resilient they are, the amount of resources or money. Thirdly, I want to make sure I reinforce the importance of defense in depth. one size does not fit. Multiple layers of defense are required to properly deter and prevent breaches. We won't have multiple locks on the door. It doesn't do us much good to have this super strong door, this thick, impenetrable door and then have a window on the side of the house wide open. We have to make sure we have multiple layers of defense at all access points so that a properly motivated attacker doesn't bypass one control and go in through one that's may be less complicated or less restrictive.

Threat Types
As far as threat types go, we have script kiddies, which are not necessarily that sophisticated, but they can cause some damage. We have hacktivists, which a lot of times are maybe politically or motivated by a specific cause. We have organized crime, which everyone knows more or less what organized crime does. They're motivated a lot of times by financial gain or some type of power. We have nation states and advanced persistent threats, or APTs, and they're motivated quite often by power, control, espionage, country secrets, proprietary information as far as technology is concerned. Then we have insiders, and they may be motivated by money or to get back at a specific person or a boss or management or the company in general. They might be motivated by some type of revenge. Then we have competitors. They're looking for espionage, looking for competitive advantage, some type of proprietary information that might give them an edge over you or other competitors. All of these different types of attacks and all these different types of threats require different levels and different types of deterrents and control types.

Types of Access Control (Managerial, Operational, and Physical)
To make sure that you understand the various types of access control, let's go over a few of those. We have managerial, otherwise known as administrative, and these are the policies, the standards, the processes, various procedures, guidelines, risk management policies, account

management policies, and various regulatory controls that mandate certain things be put in place and also things that we can do or we can administer, or manage, to make sure access is restricted in some form or fashion. Next are operational controls, otherwise known as technical controls, and these things revolve around endpoint protection, antivirus software or anti-malware software, anti-ransomware, various methods of encryption, whether at rest or in transit, access control in its various forms, intrusion prevention systems and intrusion detection systems, along with firewalls. Then we have physical, as the name implies. That would be locks, fences, mantraps, CCTV, guards, and things that are physically put in place to deter or prevent access to a system, to a building, a datacenter

Deterrent
When it comes to the actual control types, a deterrent is a system or signage that's designed to discourage people from doing something, so accessing a network as an example, entering a restricted area. It could be to keep them from accessing some type of information, or it could be to prevent them from getting hurt or injured, so it could be for their own safety as well. Then it can also alert those people, those trespassers, to the potential of additional controls, cameras, or guards.

Preventive
Preventive controls are something that's designed to keep someone from doing something. Some of these control types overlap, and a specific type of control can fall into multiple categories. As an example, guards, fencing, locks on doors windows or cabinets. We're preventing someone from accessing an area. We're preventing them from doing something. Whether it's a physical control or administrative

control or technical, they could all be preventive, so there is an overlap on some of these.

Detective

Detective controls are controls that detect activity and initiate some type of action. It could be an event manager or some type of intrusion detection system or prevention system. It could sound an alarm. It could send an alert, whether it's to management, administrators, police. It can also record the activity for later analysis. It doesn't prevent the access, but it can assist in analyzing and investigating. It doesn't keep anyone from doing something, but it can send alerts, and it can also record for later analysis or investigation.

Corrective / Recovery and Compensating

Corrective and recovery go hand in hand. Depending upon where you read about them, these might be two separate categories, or they may be one, so I'm just going to include them both here. It's a type of control used to get a system back to normal, so that could be restoring from a backup, it could be updating antivirus or antimalware software, it could be installing patches or fixes or firmware updates. This is something that we would want to do as an administrator or as a security professional or some type of IT staff member. We're going to be doing something to help get a system back online. We're going to correct some deficiency, or we will recover from some type of crisis. On the recovery side, a disaster recovery site is an example, or in HA, or high availability site, is another example. Also we have system and data backups. We're going to recover or restore from those backups to get our systems back up online. Compensating controls are controls that provide an alternate or an alternative solution to a countermeasure that's either too difficult or potentially impossible or just too expensive to implement. As an example, we might choose to install a gate or a swipe card system instead of paying for guards 24/7. We may decide that updating all of our operating systems is too expensive, too time consuming, to technically challenging, We're going to just application whitelist. We're going to create lists of only the applications that can run in hopes of covering some type of maybe operating system deficiency, as an example. We can substitute one control for another in hopes of achieving the same result. In this chapter we talked about several categories of controls, such as managerial, operational, and technical, and then physical controls. Then we talked about the various control types, including deterrent, preventative, detective, corrective and recovery, and then compensating. In essence, the various ways we can protect our systems, our files, folders, data from unauthorized access.

Chapter 2 Applicable Regulations, Standards, & Frameworks

In this chapter, we'll be talking about applicable regulations, standards, or frameworks that impact the security organization. We'll be talking about regulations, standards, and legislation. We'll talk about key frameworks and then benchmarks and secure configuration guides. The challenge is the global nature of the internet can cause communication and expectations of privacy to vary widely throughout different parts of the world. Behavior that is totally acceptable in one part of the world can be a capital offense in another. The nuances of these laws and these regulations, especially if you travel globally, are very important to keep up on and make sure that you're familiar with. When we're talking about doing business in a global economy, a few things you need to keep in mind. The United States used to traditionally set the tone for data privacy laws. Up until recently, the last 5, 10 years or so, the US more less led that initiative. However, other countries have stepped out and taken the lead, specifically countries throughout the European Union. More restrictive regulations aimed at consumer privacy and protection, so a lot more geared towards privacy of the consumer. The whole data protection laws and regulations that are coming out both in the UK or the European Union and also the US and other parts of the world are again geared towards protecting that consumer information or that customer data. The onus is being placed on the organizations or the companies to make sure that that data is protected. Companies must comply with the laws of each country in which they do business. This is where it can get a bit cumbersome because the laws will change or vary from region to region. They may be very restrictive in one area and not so restrictive in the other. But as you can imagine, the best bet will be to comply with the most restrictive policies. That way you ensure that you're covering all bases. Let's take a look at some of the privacy compliance challenges. Data security requirements come from all angles. Data privacy laws, cybersecurity regulations, trade secret law, customer-specific contracts, consumer protection statutes, all of which can vary depending upon jurisdiction or location. These things can potentially overlap depending upon where you do business or, in some cases, may be slightly contradictory. It's important to thoroughly understand all the regulations in the areas in which you do business. Deletion of data is another big one. Understanding what data a company has in its possession, where it resides, and how long to retain that data is a major challenge. As companies grow, and we have terabytes upon petabytes, potentially exabytes of data, and that data is accumulated over a large period of time, user files, application files, data files, logging that grows and grows and grows. We have separate environments within our infrastructure. We have production. We have testing, dev, QA. And you may have multiple copies of that data. As things grow, data grows. A lot of times in a lot of situations, we don't understand, at least at a macro level, what all that data is because, there are copies of copies in many instances. We may delete the primary copy of that data, but there's like 5 or 6 or 10 other copies in lower environments or in test and dev, QA environments that exist that we may not necessarily be fully aware of. Data governments is a big one. Also, documentation, keeping up with requirements, especially with global companies. It's becoming increasingly complex. Requirements between various countries and even between states, local, federal, etc., they can sometimes overlap or even become slightly contradictory if you don't understand the nuances of those specific regulations. Some other ones to keep in mind, ethics and compliance. Collection of massive amounts of data from an ever-increasing number of sources, that can create, as you can imagine, privacy and also security challenges. Big data aggregation and analysis can create PII or personally identifiable information from disparate sources. What does that mean? Well, it means then we have pieces of information that by themselves don't necessarily identify someone. But when I start doing data aggregation, data analytics specifically, I can start pulling all these different pieces together and build a profile of someone that is very accurate. Those individual pieces of information become very telling of who a person is when looked at the whole body of information. Also, inadequate data management, defining who owns the data. Who's the data owner, or the governor. This also includes data lifecycle, how we delete, how he manage, how long that data is processed, analyzed, and secure. This entire conundrum becomes more and more complex. Then also we have insecure infrastructure. Data environments are often designed for speed or for scale, but not necessarily for security. In many instances, security is a bit of an afterthought as we know. It's not necessarily designed with that in mind from the beginning. A lot of companies with their dev and engineering departments, they view security as no as a service and that's changing luckily, the perception at least is changing. Security is an extremely important part of the entire ecosystem, and it has to be thought from day 1. It can't be an afterthought. It can't be a bolt on. The insecure infrastructure is creating major challenges because we have to go back and try to retrofit a lot of these environments. IoT devices or the Internet of Things devices, posing a major challenge because these things, again, are a lot of times consumer devices not necessarily designed with enterprise-type security in mind. When you bring those devices into an enterprise, you start to crack fissures in the security infrastructure, and you're fragmenting the security posture.

GDPR and Key Terminology

Next, one of the ones that gets a lot of attentionadays is GDPR, or the general data protection regulation. It's a privacy and security law that originated in the European Union in May of 2018. It imposes obligations onto organizations anywhere. This has reached beyond just the EU, Long as they target or collect data related to people in the EU. Just because you're located in the United States or maybe somewhere outside of the European Union, it doesn't necessarily mean you are not impacted by GDPR. What type of data does the GDPR cover? Well, it provides individuals, which are known as data subjects, more control over how organizations process or control the processing of their data, such things as names, locations, patient data and health records, email addresses, photos, essentially any data that could be used to identify a living person. Let's look at some GDPR key terminology. When it comes to personal data, let's say we have Mary here. Anything that could identify her, such as names, ID numbers, dates of birth, email addresses, online identifiers, photographs, religious beliefs, location data, and a number of other things, anything that can be used to uniquely identify her is covered under GDPR. So keep those things in mind when you're collecting data from customers. Do you have a legitimate use to know all of these things? As an example, are you collecting someone's date of birth, but you never have any need for that data? You're not going to wish them happy birthday. You're not going to send them a birthday card. It's not used for loyalty purposes or anything. Well, that might be ruled then as an unnecessary piece of information and you could be subject to regulation under the GDPR. It has to be specific. The Use has to be relevant, it has to have a purpose for being collected and also maintained.

GDPR Key Terms and Data Processing Principles
Processing is any operation, whether automated or a manual process, that is performed on personal data. A data processor is responsible for the processing of personal data on behalf of what's known as a data controller. A data controller is the person or the thing that determines the purpose and the means by which personal data is processed. as far as GDPR is concerned, there are six data processing principles. When we're collecting all this personal information, we need to make sure that they fall under these data processing principles. There needs to be lawfulness, fairness, and transparency. We have to have a lawful or a legal reason to gather that information. Purpose limitation, a specified use and explicit use and specified limit of time. Data minimization. We're only collecting what is necessary. If we're collecting someone's date of birth and we have no need for that data, then why are we collecting it? If we can't demonstrate and document why we need that data, then we could be subject to those regulations. Also accurate and, where possible, kept up to date. If we're gathering someone's information, they have the to update their own information. They have to have access to it and see what we're keeping on them. But also it needs to be kept up to date if it all possible. Also, storage limitation. Keep only as long as necessary. If we're keeping data for an indefinite period of time, we could be liable to GDPR regulations. If we only need that data for 6 months, then only keep it for 6 months and delete afterwards. Most importantly, we have to document and be able to show that that data is being

deleted. We just can't say it. We have to have processes in place and documentation in place to show that. Then integrity and confidentiality. Just like we have for any security tenant, the triad confidentiality, integrity, and availability, well, same thing here. We need to make sure that the data is kept secure. We have to demonstrate via documentation and the systems we have in place that we're making a best effort to keep that data secure. If we fail any of these six tenets, these six data processing principles, then that company can be held liable under certain parts of the GDPR.

Six Legal Grounds for Processing Personal Data
We have six legal grounds for processing personal data. We have to make sure we have that person's consent, it has to be explicit, and they have to be able to opt out just as easily as they opted in. There also has to be a legitimate interest. We need to be able to demonstrate and document that we have a legitimate interest to that data. Is there some contractual obligation that we process that data? Then a legal obligation, are we legally bound to either gather and process that data? Public authority and this one goes without saying. a lot of the things of the GDPR, public authorities aren't necessarily bound by those same underlying principles. Then vital interest is a matter of life and death. Whenever a company processes a customer's or a user's data, it has to fall under one of these six legal grounds as to why they're processing that data, consent, legitimate interest or some type of contract, a legal obligation, you're a public authority, or it's a vital interest, a matter of life and death. If you can demonstrate, and, This all has to be demonstrated and documented, it can be subject to audit of course, if one of those six things are being addressed, and typically it's going to be the top three that

you'll see consent, legitimate interest, or some type of contractual obligation, most companies will utilize those three as one of their legal grounds for processing, then you've met, at least on the surface, the grounds for GDPR processing of data.

GDPR Compliance and Penalties
But what happens if GDPR compliance is not met? Well, the GDPR provides for significant fines for non-compliance. There are two tiers of fines depending upon the type of infraction. Let's take a look at these. GDPR penalties, there's two tiers. A less severe infringement can go up to €10 million or 2% of the firm's worldwide annual revenue, whichever is higher. Not whichever is lower, whichever is higher in this instance. The second, more serious or more egregious infringements, can result in fines of up to €20 million or 4% of the firm's worldwide annual revenue, whichever is higher. It can be, very significant.

Compliance Frameworks
What is compliance? It is the adherence to a set of rules pertaining to people, process, and technology as it relates to policies, standards, regulations, laws. Let's look at some examples of compliance frameworks. We have HIPPA, the Health Insurance Portability Accountability Act. We have the GLBA, the Gramm-Leach-Bliley Act. And the other is PCI-DSS, the Payment Card Industry Data Security Standard. These are all very structured, very detailed compliance frameworks. A single business can, in fact, fall under the purview of multiple different types of regulations, depending upon where they do business with in the world. There are two different types of security compliance drivers. There's legislative mandates, things that must be done, and they're external to the organization, and then good business practices. That's what

we should do or what should be done, and they're typically internal to the organization. Let's look at how these two things interact. We have external requirements, and we have internal requirements. External might be legislation like GDPR as an example or various laws or policies throughout, different parts of the world. Those things are all going to have external forces or external pressure on the company, and that's going to drive some of the internal requirements to make sure that they're complying with external requirements. We have enterprise security management. We have an overarching mandate or an overarching guideline. That's going to drive our enterprise security compliance requirements, such as policies, standards, procedures, and guidelines. Those things then have a direct impact on internal operations, security operations and other operations. They fall under that larger umbrella. The enterprise security compliance requirements also drive external operations as well and how we deal with partners, how we deal with vendors, how we deal with contractors, customers. All of these things are done to make sure the business operates in a good fashion or in an ethical fashion. We're driving revenue. But then it also makes sure that we are in compliance with external factors that could, if not followed properly, have a very negative impact on our business, a risk as great if not greater than any type of security breach, depending upon the severity of the non-compliance. If it's an egregious event that keeps taking place over and over the fines could be so great that it could put a company on a business. It's very important to take these things seriously and to devote the proper resources to make sure that they are adhered to properly.

NIST and the Cyber-security Framework (CSF)

NIST stands for the National Institute of Standards and Technology. And what they do is come up with frameworks for a number of different things, all different types of things related to IT in IT security, how things are deployed, best practices. And this specific one refers to a presidential executive order, and that's executive order 13636, that was designed or relegated to improving critical infrastructure cybersecurity. It's an important one for you to become familiar with. You can download this and read through this at your leisure. But a lot of companies, it's not just applied to a specific type of IT company, companies in all different types of industries that have any type of cyber security needs are adopting this framework as the basis of their own internal policies. It's a framework that was originally created in February of 2014, it was revised in January of 2017, and it consists of three parts. It's beyond the scope of this book to dig deeply into each of those three parts, but I want you to be aware of what they are. We have the framework core, we have the framework profile, and then also the framework implementation tiers.

PCI-DSS

PCI standing for payment card industry data security standard, hence the DSS. That protects, cardholder data. The IT impact, various levels of controls depending upon how a company interacts with credit card data. The more they interact with that data, there's different levels of controls that may apply. It gets deeper and more complex. Self-assessments, on-site audits, and also quarterly network scans are typically required to make sure you're in PCI compliance. Depending upon the size of the company and the things that you deal with, the level of transaction, you may have on-site auditors from PCI, on site to do these types of things, on-site audits, quarterly network scans, to make sure that cardholder data is not being exposed, is not being compromised, or doesn't have the potential to be compromised. We need to make sure we have the security controls in place. Organization types, merchants, banks, credit card processors, and others, anybody that deals with PCI-related data or credit card information. If you deal in one of those industries. PCI is probably familiar to you as well.

Enterprise Security Framework (ESF)
Next up, let's talk about enterprise security frameworks, what it is. An enterprise security framework, or an ESF, is a guide that we can use to create all of the documentation, the reporting within our organization. There are a number of free and existing guides already out there, we don't have to start from square one. Use existing guides where possible as a starting point. A great example comes from the National Institute of Standards and Technology, or NIST. They have a publication SP 800-53 that is a great guide to act as a starting point. It's recommended security controls for federal information systems and organizations, but it doesn't apply just to federal organizations. It's the standard enterprise security framework that's used by organizations of all types, all sizes, not necessarily just federal organizations. Another good one is ISO 27001/27002, also COBIT, which stands for control objectives for information and related technology. There are a number of guides out there that gives us structured documentation around planning, assessments, and also monitoring. These guides are very comprehensive, and in some cases, they may not be comprehensive enough. It depends upon your organization, but at least it gives you a good starting point.

NIST SP 800-53 and ISO 27001

The NIST publication SP 800-53 is comprised of a number of categories, a number of families, and each of those families have a number of subsets or controls. There are 18 different categories or IDs, access control, awareness training, audit and accountability. Each of these are broken down into subsets that have definitions and parameters around each of these subsets, each of these individual controls, that you can then used to formulate your own enterprise security frameworks within your own organization. Let's take, for instance, we take one of these IDs or one of these families. If we break it down a little bit further, we can see security assessment and authorization or configuration management. Each of those has subsets. As an example, security assessment and authorization policies and procedures or security assessments or how about information security connections. If you further drill down, each of those has a number of processes and procedures that need to be followed or should be followed. This is a guideline. It's not a hard fast rule. But these are guidelines of best practices that should be followed to make sure that your organization is secure. And what this does is it allows you to provide due diligence and say, hey, we've done the research. We're following best practices. We have a guide in place that shows every aspect of our business, every aspect of our information security controls, our security posture, and here's what we're doing to address any issues that may come up. Another good example is ISO 27001. It has similarly a number of different controls, a number of different IDs, or, in this case, references and then a number of controls within each. Information security policies, organization of information security, human resources security. And then each of these, you'll see in parentheses is the number of controls that apply to that category. Again, a slightly different approach, but the same net effect. It gives us a guideline that we can use to formulate our own framework for our organization. If we drill down as an example into, let's say, A.9, Access Control, it has 14 separate controls within that group. If we take a look at that under Access Control, these are all the different things, and each of these has additional parameters and additional guides and best practices under each of these topics that we can use to follow and draft our own documentation, our own policies, how we monitor things. And then, depending upon your organization and how you want to formulate your own plan, you may map one to the other. You may have NIST controls, or you may have the ISO 27001 controls, but you may have a plan, or you may be following compliance guidelines by some external regulation that says you need to map to one or the other. Well you can show by saying, hey, under the category of least privilege, AC-6, under NIST, this is what I'm following. But it also maps to ISO 27001 under A.9.1.2, 9.2.3, and so on and so on. You can show that you have controls in place that will put you in compliance with various regulations.

Cloud Security Alliance (CSA)
The Cloud Security Alliance or the CSA have defined a number of categories for Security as a Service offerings. I just want to list these out you have an idea of what types of services or the breadth of services that these Security as a Service providers can offer to customer organizations. So business continuity, disaster recovery, continuous monitoring, data lost prevention, email security and encryption, identity and access management. Also, intrusion management, network security, security assessment, the SIEM service that we talked about, vulnerability scanning, and web security. That's pretty much everything or at least a very large part of the security services that a company would

want to have in house. If you're a small company or a mid-sized company and you don't have the expertise and the personnel to handle all of these things, Security as a Service would definitely be a viable option to take a look at.

SSAE 18, SOC 1, 2, and 3

To mention risk assessment frameworks without getting into the weeds too, too much, I want to make sure that we're aware of SSAE 18, which stands for Statement on Standards for Attestation Engagements., it's an accounting framework, and that governs the way that organizations report on their various compliance controls. Our own environment, if we're SSAE 18-certified, we understand that all of our security controls are in place. Or if we're dealing with a hosting or a cloud provider, if they are certified, then we know that their controls are up to snuff and also the vendors that they deal with. Let's take a look at that in a little more detail. When talking about geolocation or hybrid cloud security, as an example, let's say, for instance, we're not going to stand up our own data center, so we want to stand up our infrastructure, our applications, web servers, and also customer-facing applications. We want to instantiate those things at someone else's data center, so a colocation facility. Since we're a security-minded organization, we want to make sure that the people we deal with, the colocation facility, we want to look for that SSAE 18 certification. We're talking about Infrastructure as a Service, Software as a Service, and also their virtual infrastructure. It also applies to bare metal, but in this instance, we're talking about as a service type of applications. All of those things, we're looking for that certification. That certification has three main components. We've got SOC 1, and that deals with compliance on financial reporting controls. Then we have SOC 2, certification, and that deals with actual security controls themselves. That's what we're most interested in, making sure that the facility is as secure as possible. And then there's SOC 3, which is like SOC 2 certification, but it leaves out the specifics, the specific systems. That way, that information can be publicly accessible without giving too much information about the actual systems and the underpinnings behind the scenes, of how things are run. It allows someone who's evaluating a hosting provider or a managed service provider. It can look and say, they're certified, they have SOC 3 certification, but it doesn't give the nuts and bolts as to what applications and what systems are running behind the scenes. And what this also does is ensures the data center's channel partners and vendors also, very important, the channel partners and the vendors also utilize the same security controls as the data center and the hosting provider because, as you may or may not know, a lot of times they will subcontract out certain work, whether it's working in the data center. There may be contractors that are doing the racking and stacking, the cabling. It could be power and cooling, the HVAC folks. All of those different subcontractors and vendors and also the vendors from the actual hardware, whether it's network, compute, or storage, when those vendors come in, it makes sure that they are also certified to the same level that the data center is certified, and it gives you the added layer of confidence that you're dealing with a secure facility.

Chapter 3 Benchmarks & Secure Configuration Guides

Next we have benchmarks and secure configuration guides. Some things that I want you to think about are web servers, or public facing servers, operating systems, application servers, and then network infrastructure devices. All of these things I talked about just a moment ago, are ways that we can either keep people out, or if we don't lock them down enough, they are ways that they can get in. Web servers are public facing, that's one of the biggest targets because it's publicly accessible. People can bang against those types of servers all day long, and if we don't have safeguards in place and we don't become aware that people are doing that, they can spend a lot of time brute forcing their way into those servers, and from there it's off to the races if they're able to elevate privileges, execute some remote code, crash the system, or gain, administrative or root level privileges come in, pivot, go through our network. We don't want to allow that to happen. Same thing with operating systems. We want to lock it down as much as possible. We want to make sure that we disable services we don't need. We want to make sure we harden the services that are there to limit that attack surface or reduce that attack surface as much as possible. Application servers, again, are very critical as well. Applications need to be constantly updated, just like we update the servers themselves with operating system updates, security patches, firmware updates, BIOS updates, HBA or NIC drivers. The applications themselves also experience issues, vulnerabilities, so the applications have to be patched and kept up to date, just like everything else. And then network infrastructure devices, our routers, switches. All these things need to be patched, updated as much as possible. We need to make sure we establish a routine a lifecycle management, a patch management process, whether that's weekly, monthly, quarterly. But then also a process in place for out-of-band updates. If something comes out as a critical or zero-day, you need to make sure we have processes in place to alert everyone and then also to push those changes out as quickly as possible.

Systems Hardening
Some concepts that apply to all of the things, systems hardening, disabling or uninstalling unnecessary services. Make sure we use secure protocols. Don't use Telnet, use SSH. Use FTP Secure instead of FTP. Use HTTPS when possible instead of just HTTP. Encrypting when possible, using secure protocols when possible. We also want to make sure we use least permissive or least privilege principles. Don't give people more access or more so than they need. If all they need to be able to do is read something, don't give them the ability to maybe modify or delete. The more we give them, the more chances they have to exploit those extra privileges. Least permissive/least privilege. Also, set up monitoring and alerting. Things that are not monitored are not payed attention to that just increases our risk. Disable the things we don't need, and the things that are left, make sure you monitor, you set triggers with thresholds, whether it's through machine learning and you learn over time what's normal or what might be an anomaly, or you just set up thresholds and triggers. If it hits a certain percentage, a certain number of failures in a period of time, there needs to be some type of alerting set up. Logging and alerting, logging so we can go back and identify trends, and then alerting so that we can become aware away when these security breaches or potential breaches are in fact incurred. Also, you have to establish baselines. If we don't have a baseline, we don't have a way to determine what's normal

and what's abnormal. If all we know is the server is running at 85%, or we have 500 failed login attempts a day, or we have whatever the case might be, if we don't know that well, 500's normal, every single day it's the same way, we have thousands of people in the environment, yep, 500 people a day mistype their password or they fail a login, we might think that's ridiculously high and spend a lot of resources trying to dig in when it's not necessary, or we may think it's low, and we may think we have thousands a day, and we only have maybe a dozen, but on this specific day there's 500, well, if that doesn't raise a flag with us and we don't start investigating, that could have been someone either attempting or getting into our system and breaching our defenses, and we did nothing about it. Having baselines in place allow us to very quickly determine, it raises the red flags when something is not. Then also periodically audit. It's important that we periodically go through and establish new baselines, update when appropriate, what's the new normal, and also audit all of our different systems to make sure we're not missing anything or to make sure people are not trying to cover their tracks. Because if we had insider threats, people inside the company, they can, do their dirty work, and then if we don't monitor closely and periodically audit, well, then they can come in and cover their tracks very effectively, making it much more difficult for us to try to track anything down.

Vendor and Control Diversity

With vendor diversity, we want to utilize more than one vendor. We reduce impacts of vulnerabilities, upgrades, and patching potentially. If we have only one provider of all of our switches or all of our servers or all of our network cards, if we only have one of them, we're locked in. If we have a breach or a vulnerability, that vulnerability is potentially

619

everywhere. If we have multiple vendors, well, yes, you have multiple vendors to deal with, but you also limit the impact of a specific vulnerability because maybe only a third or a quarter of your environment may be impacted. Some other things that are the intangibles from an IT security perspective, things that the IT security professional may or may not think about, is also vendor diversity gives you some leverage when dealing with those vendors. You get better pricing. You might get better attention from that vendor, so they're updating their systems more often because they want to earn your business. They don't just think that they're the only game in town. If they realize they're competing with other vendors for your business, they're going to be a lot more attentive typically. There's some intangibles there as well. Also control diversity. More gates for a hacker to get through. The more locks on the door, the harder it is for them to accomplish their task. A lot of times they're going to say, well you know what? I'm going to spend my time on something that's a little bit easier of a target. So control diversity, again, for the same reason we talked about vendor diversity, control diversity gives us the best of breed in a number of areas as well, not the least of which is additional protection against vulnerabilities. In this chapter we covered regulations, standards, and legislation. We talked about several key frameworks that you should be familiar with, and then benchmarks and secure configuration guides to make sure our systems are as secure as possible and some of the ways that we can either automate or templatize that process.

Chapter 4 How to Implement Policies for Organizational Security

In this chapter, we'll be talking about Implementing Policies within Organizational Security. We'll be talking about personnel and the associated issues with managing, maintaining, and keeping things secure. We'll talk about diversity of training techniques, along with third-party risk management, data classification, governance, and retention, and then we'll talk about various credential policies along with organizational policies. Let's first talk about the importance of policies in reducing risk. Policies provide standards for use and behavior, such things as a privacy policy and acceptable use policy. It could be security policies, or it could be things like mandatory vacations, job rotations, separation of duty, or things like the concept of least privilege. Guidelines provide advice on how to proceed. They're not necessarily hard-fast rules. They could be rules within an organization, but typically they're just guidelines on how to proceed.

Job Rotation
When we talk about job rotation, what it does is keep one person from becoming so ingrained in a specific role that they can easily hide their tracks. That helps to mitigate against things like embezzlement, fraud, espionage, data, exfiltration? So one person doesn't sit in a job Long and just think or assume they're going to be there forever so they can go ahead and do whatever they want. They know they're going to be rotated out every so often. That keeps them from doing things that may or may not be on the up and up because they realize they're going to be out of that position before too long. Then also, when folks are moved or rotated

621

from one job to the next, be aware of job creep or responsibility creep. That's where people retain s and privileges as they move from one role to another? Over time, people have the potential to accumulate things they no longer need. So by having things set up via group policy or some type of automated method so when they change roles or change jobs they're pulled out of one group, those s go away automatically, and then when they're added into a new group, they have new sets of s provisioned. Even if for the most part they're the same s, it's a good idea to remove them from one group and then put them into a new one. That way there's no guessing involved, and there's a much smaller chance for things getting missed. Then provide least privileges, making sure they only have enough to do their current job. These things prevent things like snooping, inadvertent access, accidental deletion of files or folders, and that could be potentially hundreds or thousands or even millions of files and folders. If someone were to accidentally delete or rename a root folder, all of the things underneath could potentially disappear, depending upon if that's a share or a group folder. So having just the amount of privileges that someone needs goes a long way to help prevent these types of things.

Mandatory Vacations

When it comes to mandatory vacations, some of the reasons behind requiring that is it keeps personnel away from company assets for a period of time? That enables anomalies to be discovered much, much more easily because things like fraud or theft or even collusion, when we have a fresh set of eyes, we can see things that may otherwise be overlooked or potentially hidden. When someone else comes in and then sees how that person previous was doing things, they can uncover potentially unscrupulous activities, things that are against company policy, or potentially down illegal? So having mandatory vacations helps uncover some of these potential pitfalls.

Separation of Duties
This is a security practice that doesn't allow one person to control all facets of a transaction, checks and balances you can think of it as. Writing checks versus cashing checks, approvals for expenditures, bookkeeping and accounting? We don't want people who write the checks to be able to also cash the checks. There's no oversight at that point? We need to make sure that things are able to be audited and not easily hidden or covered up. Another way of putting it is it keeps one person from wearing too many hats.

Least Privilege
Next, we have the concept of least privilege. This is providing a user with the least amount of privileges they need to do their work. Providing just enough that it helps mitigate the risk, installing applications that they shouldn't, malware, spyware, viruses. Keeps them from accidentally accessing stuff they shouldn't be accessing or deleting a renaming files and folders that they shouldn't. It also helps mitigate configuration drift issues in that it prevents users from installing or updating drivers. Firmware, patches? Those types of things typically should not be done by the user themselves. It should be pushed out by IT administration, or IT security, or whatever centralized group would be responsible for provisioning.

Clean Desk Policies
If you think about it, it can go a long way to reducing data theft? It can discourage prying eyes, and it also may be compliant with various regulations? Enforcing that policy,

you should have that documented in writing, part of their onboarding or new hire presentation or new hire packet, and then also do random checks. Making sure they don't have excess clutter all over the place. They don't have usernames, passwords, confidential information, account numbers written on sticky notes or written on pieces of paper that can be easily observed by others. And then also, when they leave their workspace, make sure those things are locked up in a secure drawer or some type of secure location. A little bit of common sense, just making sure that confidential information or things that should not be seen by others are not lying around on the desk. So keeping a desk nice and orderly and clean goes a long way. When you leave, you just clean your desk for the night, put things that should be secured in a secure location.

Background Checks, NDAs, and Role-based Awareness Training

A few additional personnel management concepts would be background checks. Ensure employees are appropriate to work in a specific environment, adhere to company policies. Some organizations, some companies require background checks, others do not. But background checks go a long way in helping to make sure that the people that you hire either have the credentials that they say they do or have the ability or the permissions, the clearance to work in a specific area. Depending upon the nature of your environment, if it's classified or highly secretive information, background checks very well may be in order. Next we have nondisclosure agreements, or NDAs. It's an agreement, usually at the time of hire that employees will review and sign and agree not to disclose company secrets, proprietary information. An NDA may also be given by third parties or vendors that you deal with so they can review new information, things that may not necessarily be publicly available yet, like road map items or new technologies, so that you have an opportunity to try them out or at least plan for them. They may have you sign an NDA at the time of the meeting or the presentation, or you may have in NDA on file with that company or with that vendor that covers any of those types of presentations. Next is role-based awareness training. These are simulated situations to ensure that employees know how to respond appropriately in a specific scenario or specific situation. It could be failover testing for applications, like in a DR, disaster recovery, or business continuity setting, application testing. It could also be things like even an active shooter situation for things where the building may be compromised or breached. It could be phishing campaigns. IT security may put out some scam emails or phishing emails to make sure employees know how to recognize them and then report them to the proper location. Role-based training periodically is a great idea to help reinforce concepts and to make sure that people are adhering to company policies and procedures.

Chapter 5 Monitoring & Balancing

Let's talk about monitoring in general and why a company can do that, why they should, and perhaps why they shouldn't. Use cases for monitoring. Number 1 would be to boost productivity. That may or may not be true depending upon your company, but boosting productivity. You can track time spent on social media, on web surfing, non-related work activities. Number 1, the company can be aware of what's happening. Number 2, the employee knows if they're monitored, and if those activities are looked at, they will typically do less of that with the hope being spend more time on actual work. Next, deter or detect criminal activity. Detect intrusions or breaches, criminal activities such as threats and harassment or illegal behaviors. employees doing things they shouldn't be doing, whether it's out illegal or if they're harassing other employees or using it for non company-related activity that may come back to the company and cause ill will or cause harm. And it can also be used to track employees location. In this case, we would ensure that remote workers are adhering to company policies, working at their prescribed locations, traveling safely. We have the opportunity or the ability to monitor where they're at so that if they say they're going to be a location A, we can look at our GPS tracking software and say, yep, they're at that location, they're at that job site. If they're traveling to or from a specific job site, especially if they're in a company vehicle, then you can potentially track the speed that they're going, the direction they're going, making sure they're taking main roads versus back roads or tolls. It's also possible to geofence locations so that if they leave a specific area, you get notified. Or if they enter a specific area, you're notified. Then, lastly, to protect IP or intellectual property, you want to ensure that proprietary company, employee, or customer data is secure and not being removed from the company. We can monitor things like data exfiltration. You can monitor ingress and egress, firewalls, DLP or data loss prevention systems, intrusion detection and prevention systems. All of these things can work together in tandem to make sure that your intellectual property is protected. A company, again, has the opportunity or the ability, not necessarily saying it's or wrong, it's going to depend upon your location, your part of the world that you live in, and, of course, the company that you work for, but they have the ability to monitor an employee. That would typically be monitoring desktop activity or laptop activity, what they do on that specific piece of equipment, because, again, it's company owned, the company has the to see what data is on that device and how it's being used. It could also be email - typically it will be work related email, but depending upon your location and your jurisdiction, a company may also be able to access personal email. If you're using a corporate device to access personal email, then they may have actual rights to see that personal email. So keep those things in mind. Then it goes without saying, a smartphone, especially if its company issued, all of the transactions on that smartphone could be monitored by the company. Even if it's a BYO device, depending upon the MDM software, the mobile device management software on that smartphone, they may be able to view or should be able to view content on that phone that is corporate or company related, not necessarily personal information. That's the nice part about some of the MDM software, it can partition a smartphone between a corporate side and a personal side so that it can be wiped or remotely access only the corporate data. And then activity logs. Coming and going logging on, logging off, entering a building, exiting a building. GPS activity on cars, locations, speed, all that good stuff. All of these things can potentially be monitored, not saying that they are or that it's. Again, it's going to be jurisdictionally based and also, to some extent, based on industry.

Balancing What's Reasonable

All of that comes down to balancing what's reasonable. A defined privacy and acceptable use policy goes a long way. We need to make sure that the employee knows from the beginning what is acceptable and what's not. And they also understand what can be monitored and what not, and they sign off on them. Then we're balancing that with an employee expectation of privacy, like what is reasonable for an employee to expect is private versus public or versus corporate viewed, and making sure everyone is on the same page. Then, making sure we have BYO devices and remote employees covered as well so they understand if it's a BYO device, if you're accessing corporate resources, then the corporation or the company has access or should have access to that data. If it's personal data, then maybe not. But, again, depending upon the MDM software that's installed, the company may have the ability to see only the corporate-related information, be able to wipe that device remotely.

New Tools Are Constantly Developed

It's important to understand, however, that new tools are constantly being developed, and we can monitor things like login time, logout time, overall productivity, social media postings, again not saying it's or wrong, but the ability is there, emails, full content of emails, keywords so you can check to see if specific things are being talked about or mentioned in emails, also live stream of users desktops.

Depending upon the company that you work for and the software they have installed on desktops, it is possible with the tools to bring up a user's desktop and see what they're doing in real time, livestream what that user is doing, and then remotely lock screens, or covertly install or uninstall agents to do additional features and functionality, additional monitoring, security-related things. Then also display messages on users desktops so that you can get the word out about specific security initiatives, or company initiatives, or just general company branding.

Monitoring Social Media

When it comes to monitoring social media, it's worth noting that 26 states currently in the U.S. have passed laws barring employers from forcing employees to provide access to social media accounts. But it is worth noting that over half the states in the U.S. have in fact passed laws barring employers from that, and then 16 states have barred academic institutions from forcing students to provide access, refusing to admit or otherwise disciplining for social media posting. It gets back to that balancing act between what is public or what is personal versus company related. As far as social media is concerned, the law is starting to lean more to the side of the user.

Employee Protections

That leads us into our next topic, and that is employee protections. The Fourth Amendment protects against unlawful search and seizure here in the US. It applies to the public sector, which is government and law enforcement, but it does not apply to the private sector. That's a key distinction that people may or may not necessarily be aware of. Companies are free to monitor employees. That can be work-related or personal, email, communications while at work. You're at the office, and you're using the company network, using the company Wi-Fi, resources, potentially laptop or desktop, mobile phone. All of those things are, in fact, company assets, so they have the right to monitor those assets to make sure they're being used appropriately.

Onboarding / Offboarding

Processes should be defined for both onboarding and offboarding, so that users should have a clear understanding of what's acceptable, what's allowed, and what is expected. This should be in writing. It should be presented during that onboarding process, and then they should sign some documentation stating that they've read it and understand. Additionally, companies should ensure they take possession of all company assets when an employee leaves. That way, secrets or data or confidential info, doesn't walk out the door. They should also conduct what's called an exit interview, so they understand why the employee is leaving, was there a gripe, was there some grievance? In other words, what was the reason for them leaving the company? The company can address those issues if valid, and improve their overall process and procedure.

Culture and Creating a Culture of Security

Culture is the set of shared attitudes, values, goals, and practices that characterizes an institution or an organization. When talking about creating culture, where do you start? Well, first and foremost, focus on the weakest links. Individuals are the weak link in that they have access to the business' systems, computers, networks. Make sure we understand where we focus on our people. Part of that is bringing in diversity, disparate groups to share experiences. This enables executives, managers, and also individual contributors to all share and learn from one another's experiences and understand each other's needs because not everybody is going to look at things the same way. They're not going to experience things the same way. If all we do is surround ourselves with people that are just like us, then we develop a bit of an echo chamber, and we never change. We're never able to grow and develop other ideas, other opinions. By having that diversity of thought, you bring in expertise, you bring in opinions, viewpoints from different directions. By having all these differing views, it benefits the collective. It makes everything better. Then also, ensure that training is timely, relevant, and interactive. Engaging training that is applicable to a person's job or function is much more likely to be interesting, memorable, and actionable than some cookie-cutter presentation that deals perhaps with an industry they're not even in or with a highlight reel from 30 years ago with technology that doesn't even exist anymore. Make sure that the training is relevant. It applies to that specific industry. And if it can be customized specifically to that company, that's even better.

Chapter 6 Awareness & Skills Training

Setting the stage as far as understanding what is appropriate, what types of training, what types of skills need to be developed. You can put this on a map and say, here where we are today, and here's where we want to get to in the future. You can plot your current level of awareness. And then after meeting with senior management and getting an understanding of what their expectations are, you can say, here's our desired level of awareness. In between there is the gap. That's the gap analysis. That allows you to list out and create a skills matrix, of what's necessary. What skills, resources, and infrastructure may be needed to make these things happen, and then devise a training plan to achieve those awareness goals. Everyone's on the same page. We understand where we are today, where we want to be tomorrow, the skills and resources and infrastructure that's needed to make that happen. And then once the plan is in place and we set in motion, we understand it's an iterative process, it's continuous improvement. This can also span suppliers, vendors, stakeholders, and, of course, key customers. Everyone's on the same page, and they all have the ability to contribute to the overall success.

Awareness Training
When it comes to delivering this training, the awareness training, we need to understand who the intended audience is. Are they individual groups, or is it company-wide? Are they internal only or suppliers and also key customers? Then talk about the methods of delivery. That could be posters spread throughout the company, it could be company swag

with a mission statement, it could be on the company intranet, via newsletters. All of these things should reinforce that common message so that the target audience sees that message over and over again. Then make sure we have clearly defined expected outcomes. What is success? It's very hard to understand if you're successful if you have no idea what success means. Having these things clearly defined goes a long way to understanding when you've hit the mark.

Skills Training

When it comes to skills training, we have goals and objective. We need expected outcomes and success criteria. We need to make sure we define those things we understand what is success. We also want to make sure that we adhere to company standards. Also, a big part of creating and delivering quality training and making sure that we're covering all the bases is proper funding. Executive buy-in and participation is also key. Next, when we're talking about the specific skills, we need to make sure that we define the intended audience. Different training based on different groups, so not necessarily a one size fits all. There may be instances where training fits across the board, but make sure it's as individualized as possible. Then identify gaps in skills and create training to level up employees to make sure that they have the skills they need to do their jobs. Also, it's beneficial to create varying methods of delivery, whether it's classroom, online, study groups, or it could be CVTs. Then lastly, we have metrics and KPIs. We have to make sure that we measure the effectiveness. That also makes future funding requests much easier because you can go ahead and show the actual benefits and results of the training that you've delivered. This also has the byproduct of continuing awareness, and it builds upon itself. There should also be a continuing effort, whether that be monthly, quarterly, or yearly, it's going to depend upon your organization and your needs, but it should be an ongoing effort. Then gamify things where possible, contests or games to help measure participation and also make things competitive. People tend to perform better when there's some type of competition involved.

Funding and Executive Buy-in
How is the awareness and skills training funded? It could be department funded. It could be cybersecurity or business continuity budgets. It could also be company-wide if it's a much bigger endeavor. Then when it comes to presenting our idea and making sure we have executive buy-in, do we create the training internally, or do we contract third-party training materials? Measurements of effectiveness are critical to long-term success, especially when we're reporting back to executives and key stakeholders. They want to make sure that the funding they provided is effective and they're getting some type of return on investment. Then, lastly, create mechanisms for feedback and for constant improvement, a feedback loop, as much of real-time feedback as possible, but then make sure that feedback is acted upon. It doesn't necessarily do a lot of good to gather all this information, all this feedback, and then do nothing with it. Take the information that's given and then tweak the training. Next time around, make it a little bit better. Constantly improve, continuous improvement.

Continuous Improvement
You need to identify needs, design the training, deliver the training, do assessments, and evaluate. That's a continuous loop. The goal is long-term awareness, increased readiness, and continuous improvement. We're not training just to train people, we want to have specific skills developed to

help improve the security posture of our organization, developing methods to obtain feedback, metrics, and KPIs to measure effectiveness. Then refine that over time and act on the feedback, fix what doesn't work, and strive to constantly improve. It's a never-ending process, it's not a one-and-done, it's an iterative, ongoing process.

Chapter 7 Technology & Vendor Diversity

When it comes to diversity, technologies, vendors, cryptographic keys even, security controls, all of these things will benefit from diversity. The more diversity that you have, you typically get best of breed, you get differing opinions, different ways of looking at things, different ways to solve problems, and then with security controls, you're not as reliant on any one specific technology or vendor. As far as technology diversity is concerned, utilizing more than one type of technology to accomplish a given task. The thought being that it would safeguard against a bug or a vulnerability being able to take down an entire system. If you have more than one technology in play, if one is affected by a bug or a specific vulnerability, it doesn't necessarily affect the rest. It also provides a method of failback or failover in the event of an incident.

Vendor Diversity
Next when it comes to vendor diversity, vendor diversity helps safeguard against supply chain attacks, also vendor lock-in, more financial leverage. If you have all of your eggs in one basket, with one vendor, than they potentially have more financial leverage over you and could be less willing to negotiate on price. And there is a real business risk of having all systems, data, technology, and knowledge in the hands of a single vendor. It's not necessarily a bad thing. If the vendor's good and they represent more than one company and you're getting diversity of thought, that's not necessarily a bad thing. But generally speaking, vendor diversity in and of itself helps safeguard against those things.

Service-level Agreement (SLA)

SLA or a service level agreement is a legal document that you need to be put in place before you engage the services or interact with third parties. That way you clearly identify a number of things. It identifies and defines things like uptime, reliability, and response times and then also penalties for non performance and spells out things like vicarious liability if, in fact, the folks that you do business with subcontract some of their work out as well. That liability may pass down to their contractors as well.

Memorandum of Understanding (MOU) and Master Services Agreement (MSA)

An MOU, or a memorandum of understanding is a letter of intent, it's not a formalized contract, and it specifies mutually accepted expectations between two or more people, typically not legally binding and more flexible than contracts. Then also, certain legal remedies like liquidated damages, vicarious liability may not be available. Just something to keep in mind, though, regardless of how cautious the authors might be, MOUs pose risks. In a business environment, these informal agreements lack the formality and the standardizations of a contract that would protect both parties during a project. As a result, legal remedies might be nonexistent in the event of a nonperformance issue or a lack of adherence to the MOU. While these things may be good or good enough to get the ball rolling, I would recommend contracts and SLAs in place wherever possible. Next, we have something referred to as a master services agreement, or an MSA. This is a contract reached between two parties in which the parties agree to most of the terms that will govern future transactions and future agreements. We're trying to expedite future transactions. Most of the terms are negotiated ahead of time, and then that way only terms specific to the transaction at hand need to be negotiated. Everything that's pretty common across the board can just be referenced in the MSA. That way, every time you have a new engagement with your vendors and suppliers, instead of having to renegotiate pricing and margins and all that good stuff, and performance penalties and SLAs and all the things that may be pretty much standard across the board, you can negotiate those things out ahead of time. Then for each new engagement, only the things that are specific to that engagement need to be negotiated. Everything else can just have a pointer or a reference to the MSA.

Business Partner Agreement (BPA)
Next is the BPA, or a business partner agreement. This defines the roles on each side of a manufacturer and reseller relationship, also, the decision making process and the management style, how capital is to be distributed, salary, distributions. All the things between business partners that should be spelled out so there's no confusion. There's no, I want this and I want that, but we never talked about it. There's some type of confusion. No, all of those things should be spelled out and defined ahead of time via a BPA. That way, that confusion gets taken out of the equation.

EOL / EOS
EOL and EOS, stands for End of life and end of service. Maintaining documentation of contracts and service dates, it's critical here, so it helps with budgeting and with long term planning. We have to understand when our equipment hits the floor and when it's going to leave the floor, so that way we can budget properly and that way, we're also not at risk. Because if we don't plan those things, then we're going to invariably get hit with some type of funding surprise, we're going to have extended maintenance fees at the end of our contract. In other words, let's say we bought 500 desktops and at the end of a 5-year period, if we're not prepared to buy brand new, typically the vendor will extend maintenance, but at an uplift or an up charge, so it's going to be more than it would be if we bought

new. But if you don't have the capital to buy new, all we have is opex, not capex, we have to extend maintenance, that could be a surprise, that could be a hit to our budget and create a shortfall that we're not necessarily prepared for. Also, there is some increased risk as the vendors gain leverage because they understand that, hey, we need to refresh our equipment or we're at risk of things failing or if the equipment is not just end of life, but end of service. We can't even get service on it anymore, and they realize we have to upgrade, well, they're are a lot less likely to negotiate because they realize they don't have to. By maintaining end of life and end of service documentation, proper planning, all these things help reduce that risk to help reduce budgetary surprises and also helps reduce headaches for you down the road when management comes knocking and saying, you have that LRP for me, that long-range plan, I need to understand what's our budget looks like for next year and you don't have that, well, that's not a necessarily good place to be, so always make sure you have documentation, it's kept up to date, and you understand when things hit the floor and when things were set to leave the floor.

Data Retention
All of this boils down to data retention, so the continued storage of an organization's data for compliance or for business reasons. Data retention policies are created often as a collaboration between legal, IT, and business owners. You may have a company-wide policy that says you're going to maintain data for X amount of months or years, or it may vary depending upon the type of data or by department. But generally speaking, creating a data retention policy and adhering to that policy can reduce an organization's storage costs by purging old data or by moving that data to lower tiers of storage.

User Account

639

User accounts are unique and used for each person accessing a resource. That should be common knowledge, but just to make sure. A unique identifier is assigned to each account. As an example, in a Windows environment, every user account gets what's called a security ID, or a SID. The computer systems identify the user by the SID. The user account name is a human readable one that we can remember, but the SID is what's used to identify that user. Every user should have their own account, and as we've talked about before with the concept of least privilege, the users should have the least amount of privileges required to do their work.

Shared, Generic, Guest, and Service Accounts
We have shared and generic accounts and credentials. Each user should have their own non-administrative account. Shared accounts are too difficult to troubleshoot or audit in the event of a breach, so, we should avoid them whenever possible. Do not share accounts between people, because if you think about it, if you have 10 or 15 or 100 people using the same account, how can you possibly know who logged in, who logged out, who accessed the file? You might be able to see the username, but you don't know who that user belongs to, who that username references. Make sure everyone has their own account. That way, you can lock individual people out if necessary, or if you do have to go back and audit, you can tell who accessed the file and when. Next is guest accounts. Guest accounts should be used very sparingly, so kiosks and other public access locations are fine, typically, but the OS should be reimaged frequently and locked down or hardened as much as possible. The takeaway here is guest accounts for the most part are a no-no. We should not use them. Again, it's very much the same as a shared or generic account because we don't know who's using the account. Using them in a very specific situation or scenario is but generally speaking, disable them whenever possible. Next, we have service accounts. A service account

should be used only for services, as the name implies, but not for users, and unique for each service. Troubleshooting, audits, and revoking permissions when necessary are much easier if we have clearly defined service accounts. The service account name references what service it's using, and then we maintain individual ones as much as possible. That way, auditing becomes much easier. Otherwise it can turn into a nightmare.

Privileged Accounts

Privileged accounts should be used sparingly, only to perform admin-level functions. Even administrators should have a regular user account that they use typically throughout the day. If they need to do something on an administrative level, then they can invoke that privileged account when necessary to perform specific tasks. But, otherwise, generally speaking, use that non-admin account. That helps with the spread of malware, worms, all types of ransomware, because typically those types of malicious programs will operate in the context of the user that's logged in. If you're logged in as an admin, and you have the ability to do pretty much anything, well, then does that piece of malware. If you're logged in as a regular user who doesn't have a lot of privileges and you download or accidentally download a piece of malware or ransomware or what have you, there's a lot less chance that an actual piece of malicious software can do as much harm.

Chapter 8 Change Management & Asset Management

The ultimate purpose of change management is to reduce risk, it's also an administrative and a technical control. What we're doing is coordinating changes throughout the environment. We also need to ensure that procedures are followed, such things as established change or maintenance windows and also documented methods of procedures, or MOPs. Then, if something were to go wrong during a maintenance as an example, if we have a properly documented MOP, or an M-O-P, then they should have backout instructions as well, so that if something goes south halfway through the maintenance, we know how to back out of that and get back to a last known good state. Along those same lines, change management should have approval, an approval chain to document understanding and compliance. Has the change been tested? Is there a rollback or backout procedure documented, that should be included in the MOP. Has it been peer reviewed or is it just the person implementing the change? If it all possible, it should be peer reviewed so that code can be looked at, a second set of eyes can catch mistakes, reducing risk wherever possible. Then lastly, have affected users been notified? It's very important that users understand what's happening, if their servers need to be rebooted, if their service is going to go down for a period of time. All of these things should be communicated way ahead of time so that they have ample opportunity to reduce risk on their side and then also have someone available to validate changes, validate success once the maintenance is complete. Then lastly, when it comes to documentation, we need to make sure we document the work to be performed, any downstream systems that might be affected, servers, storage, network, applications. Also make sure we notify everyone involved or everyone that needs to be notified when that change begins and then notify when the changes end. And then if we have a maintenance call or a maintenance bridge setup, the teams that need to jump on and verify and then validate their applications and make sure that everything is back up and running before that maintenance window comes to a close.

Asset Management

It's very important from a compliance standpoint we understand how many of any one thing we have in the environment. As an example, if we have 5,000 servers, but we only bought 3,000 licenses or we have 500 instances of an application, but we only bought 2 copies, when it comes time to do a true up, that company comes in and asks to audit our environment. If we're not compliant, there could be a big, hefty fine associated with that or we have to quickly come up with the money to pay for the licenses and make things whole or remove those things out of the environment, which could create even more work and more effort. So it's important that asset management is properly maintained. Same thing when it comes to patching and updates. We need to have a clear understanding of how much of any one thing we have in the environment, whether it's Windows servers, Linux servers, IoT devices. All of these things need to be documented and understood in some type of asset management software so that we can quickly, at a glance, understand where we're deficient from a patching level of perspective, from an updates perspective. All of these things help to mitigate risk in the environment. It's hard to monitor what you don't know about. Asset management is a critical, critical component to a successful and secure system and an overall secure environment. In this chapter, we talked about personnel and the various things that we need to have in place to make sure our personnel is managed and administered properly. Also, we talked about the diversity of training techniques, third-party risk management, data classification, governance and retention, along with credential policies, and organizational policies, change management, asset management.

Chapter 9 Risk Management Process and Concepts

In this chapter, we'll review the risk management process and concepts. We have a few main areas. We have risk types, risk management strategies. We'll talk about risk analysis, along with disasters, and then business impact analysis. When it comes to risk and managing risk, I want to make sure that you and I are on the same page, and that we understand what are the various types of risk and where do they come from. You can generally categorize risk in one of six categories. There are some others, but these are the main ones. We talk about external risk. That's things that are external to the company, things you don't necessarily have control over. That could be man-made disasters, that can be a terrorist attack, it could be a bomb, it could be a plane running into the building, it can be a multitude of things that are not within your direct control, they're outside or external to the company. Next, there's internal risk, and that can be inside the company, whether it be hardware or software faults. It could be faulty equipment, it could be a power outage, or it could be insider threats. It can be hackers or internal bad actors. It doesn't necessarily have to be hardware related or power related, it could be personnel related. Then we have legacy systems, and by legacy, we mean old. A legacy system is something that's aging out of its useful life. For instance, if you have a 3-year or a 5-year lifecycle on equipment, and perhaps it's 6, 7, or 8 years that that piece of equipment or piece of infrastructure has been on the floor, well there is risk being injected into the environment because you're at a greater risk of things failing, components failing, hard drives, internal components, motherboards. Additionally, not just referring to the hardware components, but the actual systems themselves, if they've been around for a long time, if a legacy platform, as an example, has been around for 5, 10, 15, 20 years and has not been updated, it might be a homegrown application or something that was developed in-house, well that person may not even work for the company anymore. By having those things in play and not having a good way to support them, that introduces risk into the environment. Next, we have multi-party, and as you might guess, if you have multiple parties or multiple folks, multiple vendors or multiple applications that are responsible for something, then you have multiple people that can point fingers back and forth, it takes a while to figure out whose responsible for what, and that again can add additional risk into the environment, especially if folks are not on the same page, or if you're the middle of a crisis and you need support and then you get a bunch of finger pointing, that certainly adds additional risk and frustration into the environment. Next, we have IP theft, and, intellectual property is big business. That's one of the things that potentially differentiates one company from another, provides competitive advantage. IP theft, or theft of that intellectual property or that critical data, can be very problematic to a company. It can be their lifeblood, and if it's stolen and given to someone else, that could have huge impacts and huge ramifications to the bottom line, to reputation, to a company's overall viability,. That's a big risk. And then we have software compliance and licensing. As we get further into the chapter and talk about asset management, if we don't keep track of what we have in the environment, especially if we're in a big environment and we have software compliance and licensing issues, that could end up introducing a big risk to the company. For instance, if you have 10,000 copies of a piece of software, but you're only licensed for, say, 5000, or 500, even worse, when it comes time to true up, and that can potentially happen and does happen quite often where software vendors will ask to come in and audit a company's environment to make sure they're in compliance, so if you're not in compliance, that could be a hefty bill that you either have to pay, negotiate down, or remove that software from the environment, all of which introduce their own version of risk into the company or into the environment. As you might guess, it's very important that we focus on each of these different areas to make sure that we're keeping the environment as clean as possible and as secure as possible, but also de-risking as much as possible.

Managing Risk

There are multiple ways, of managing a risk. We can do one of several things. We can accept certain levels of risk. We understand it's never going to be 0, we'll reach some type of posture and say, we're going to accept this level or this threshold. We can also transfer risk and say, we're not going to accept that. We don't want to necessarily take the burden of trying to constantly mitigate that ourselves. We'll transfer that, let's say, to a third party. We can also implement controls to reduce risk as much as possible. Then in some instances, we can avoid it altogether. Every company is different, and as such, each has a different tolerance for risk. That's what this boils down to is, what is your risk tolerance?

Risk Management Defined

Risk management can be defined as the identification, the assessment, and the prioritization of risk, along with the mitigation and the monitoring of those risks. As an example, when dealing with computer hardware and software, risk management is also known as information assurance, or you may see the abbreviation IA. And that will depend upon the company's risk tolerance, your risk tolerance, and that can vary by industry, a government versus a tech startup, as an example. Also, the value of the data that you're protecting. If it's something that's maybe ephemeral, it's not going to last very long, or it's not a high value piece of data or dataset, well then you're not going to do a lot to protect that necessarily. If it's something that's extremely valuable, critical to your business, then you're going to invest time, resources to make sure that that data is protected. Then, lastly, the ability to recover that data. If it's something that can be easily regenerated, well then the risk of it going away is not so high. Maybe the risk of it being stolen is great, but if it's capable of being recovered or regenerated quickly, then the controls in place to allow that regeneration to take place don't necessarily need to be as complex or perhaps as costly.

Risk Management Concepts
When we talk about risk management, there's several concepts I want you to be aware of, and that is the concept of risk transference. If we transfer risk to a third party as an example, we may insure our datacenter or insure some part of our business so that if disaster strikes, well, insurance will protect us. And all of these things tie into compliance because a lot of these different things are components of being compliant with various regulations. If you're wondering where these things tie together, all of these things go hand in hand. We have to make sure we're doing things in an ethical way. We have to make sure we're during our business in a standardized fashion across our footprint, whether we're in the US or the UK or anywhere abroad. And then we have to make sure that everyone is acting under the same guidelines. And then next we have risk acceptance. What's the cost of removing the risk versus dealing with the issue if and when it occurs? And that's what we talked about

before. That's going to vary upon the type of data, how quickly it can be regenerated, recovered. Is a business critical, or is it business necessary, or is it just something that's nice to have, or perhaps even scratch data. And then risk mitigation and deterrence. What level of reduction is acceptable? We talked about that risk posture. What controls can be put in place to effectively minimize that risk? And then we also have something referred to as risk avoidance. She's very upset and wants to avoid that risk at all costs. Many organizations will simply opt to not do something, deciding that the risk is too high. An example might be deciding not to patch a certain piece of infrastructure. And you might say, well, why wouldn't we do that? Well, in some companies, in some environments there is infrastructure that's been there for Long, it's been up and running, and it's working, so it's like if it's not broken, don't fix it. If it's a critical patch, well, that's a different story. But if it's just a patch and just because its patch Tuesday and it's that time, well, we may not want to take that piece of infrastructure down because we're not sure if it's going to come back up again. In certain cases, it may be better to not do something. How about migrating to a new platform? If the risks of migration are too great, there's a potential for downtime, and it's an application that needs to remain up at all costs, well, that risk might be too great at this point in time, We're going to avoid that risk altogether. Also perhaps launching a new site or a new service. If we're not ready, if we don't have the infrastructure, if we're afraid we're going to launch it and then it immediately crashes because we're going to get too much traffic, and then that will hurt our brand or our reputation, well, then that might be a risk that's worth avoiding at the moment. Regroup and then come back with a different plan. It all depends upon the situation, but risk avoidance is in fact, a mitigation strategy that you can add into your overall processes.

Strategic Options

Some strategic options we can look at it, we have something we need to understand how we're going to address this issue. There's a risk that we've encountered, if we start it left to, we can go should we avoid or terminate, share or transfer, reduce or modify, or accept or tolerate? Let's expand this out a bit. If we avoid or terminate, if we say no, well, then the next thing is, do we share or transfer, if we say no, do we reduce or modify it. If we avoid or terminate and we say yes, well, then let's cease activities that create the risk. If we can do that, then it drops down into, is it acceptable? Is that an acceptable level of risk? And if it is yes, then say that residual risk will be monitored and we'll just accept it and just keep an eyeball on it. If we go over to share and transfer, again, if we decide that's the book that we want to go, we can say, let's move that over to a third-party and allow them to manage that risk. And same thing, is it acceptable? If so, yes, then we'll just simply monitor and go forward, and you get the idea. Same thing with reduce or modify and accept or tolerate. Each has its own yes or no fork, and we can make subsequent decisions based upon which way we choose. All of these things lead themselves, when we're talking about actual security, when we're talking about compliance. The thing that we're driving towards or the things that were driving toward are the three core principles of IT security at the end of the day, and that is confidentiality, integrity, and availability, otherwise known as the CIA Triad. This is the basic fundamental purpose of implementing security within our system. We want to make sure that our data is confidential, that it's available, and that the integrity is there, so it's not tampered with. If we can do those three things well, then we're going to be in compliance probably 99% of the time, because if in fact those things are done properly, and there's no breaches, there's no inappropriate access, there's no data unavailability, the bulk of most compliance mandates will be met.

Chapter 10 Risk Register, Risk Matrix, and Heat Map

The first thing I want to cover, we have what's referred to as a risk register or a risk matrix or sometimes referred to as a heat map. You may hear it referred to as any one of these things. They're all the same concept. What we have here is a matrix, and it's showing us that we can rate a specific risk from likelihood of occurring on the left with a vertical axis, you'll see the likelihood of that thing happening. It's Rare, Unlikely, Possible, Likely or Almost Certain.

		Consequences - Maximum Reasonable Consequence				
		Insignificant	Minor	Moderate	Major	Catastrophic
Likelihood Rating	Almost Certain	Medium	Medium	High	Extreme	Extreme
	Likely	Low	Medium	Medium	High	Extreme
	Possible	Low	Low	Medium	High	High
	Unlikely	Low	Low	Low	Medium	High
	Rare	Low	Low	Low	Low	Medium

And then on the horizontal axis, we have consequences. What's the maximum reasonable consequence? It's either Insignificant all the way over to Catastrophic. As an example, if we have a specific risk, and we can take any risk that we want, and we can say, well, it has a rare chance of happening, but a Catastrophic if it did happen, well, then that risk will be rated as a Medium. We can see where they intersect on that axis. Conversely, let's say we have a likelihood rating of Unlikely, but catastrophic if it happened. Well, that would give us a rating of High. You get the idea here. If it's almost Certain, and it's Catastrophic if it happens, then that would be Extreme. That takes us from one end of the spectrum to the other.

Risk Control Self-assessment (RCSA)

Next, we have a risk control self-assessment, or RCSA. This is a process by which management and staff of all levels collectively identify and evaluate risks and associated controls. So, everyone that's involved with a specific process, a business process, line of business, they would all get together from individual contributors up through management, and they make sure that they identify and prioritize business objectives, assess and manage high-risk areas of business process, self-evaluate the adequacy of the controls that are in place. This is a time to be brutally honest. We want to be very self-aware and very honest about what works and what doesn't work. If we have gaps, we need to identify these gaps because one of the points of this entire process is to inject risk assessment and risk awareness into business processes. When we develop our business processes, we have that risk awareness in the back of our mind, and we understand where we need to mitigate and, hopefully, de-risk the environment as much as possible. Moving on, we also want to make sure we develop risk treatment action plans. We have to not necessarily just identify the risk, but how are we going to either transfer, mitigate, or somehow get that risk out of the environment? And then ensure reporting consistency across all levels of the organization. It's important that everyone is reporting the same language, the same metrics so that we can gauge what's effective and what's not effective. As an example, the RCSA workflow may go something like this. We select our participants, who is going to be in this process, who is going to collaborate? We're all going to get together and discuss all of these things. We want to make sure we get a cross-section of everyone involved. We need to identify the risks. This is a collective process. Everyone together identifies the risks. Assign risk against business objectives. We say, which is most important? What aligns with our business objectives and what doesn't? Then we identify controls to mitigate those risks. We assess those controls. And then actions if those controls fail or they lapse. What are we going to do if something doesn't work, in other words? And then we continue to monitor that and then report the results. And then, finally, take corrective action. This is a looping process, that we continuously look for risks. We continually look for ways to get those risks out of the environment and make things as smooth as possible because, again, unplanned downtime, outages, failures, just having to redo work over and over again, unplanned work, all of these things add to our cycle time. They add to our ineffectiveness, and that's the opposite of what we want to do. We want to increase effectiveness. We want to make our processes more effective but also more secure.

Risk Awareness (Inherent, Residual, Control, and Risk Appetite)

That brings us to risk awareness. Understanding what types of risks exist in the environment, that's part of that risk assessment we just talked about, but just understanding what the different types are. We have inherent risk, which are things that are, as the name implies, inherent in the process, inherent in what we do. It might be a dangerous process. It might be a very complicated process. There are some things that just inherently have some risk to them that we may end up having no choice but to just accept or transfer maybe to an insurance company or something else. We reduce that risk as much as possible. But it may not be feasible to remove it completely. And then we have residual risk, and that's risk that's carried over from some other process. If we're going through all of our steps to derisk that environment, and there's still some left over, and that carries forward into other processes, that could be

654

considered a residual risk., just understanding how to control risk. What controls can we put in place? Are they technical controls? Administrative controls? Can we do it via people, process or technology? What are the different ways that we can control risk? These are all things that factor into risk awareness. And then risk appetite, what is our actual appetite or our tolerance level for risk? Are we very adverse? Are we okay with some certain levels of risk? Are we going to just accept certain pieces of it and have it be residual risk that will carry forward? Or are we very risk adverse, and we're willing to spend whatever it takes to get that specific risk out of the environment? All of these things need to be known and understood so that we can formulate plans accordingly.

Chapter 11 Regulatory Examples

Let's go and take a look at a few examples of regulations that may affect your ability to do business, depending upon what region you do business in, where your company resides, where your customers reside. Starting off, the Gramm-Leach-Bliley Act, the GLBA, and we'll cover each of these in more detail in just a few. Also, the Health Insurance Portability and Accountability Act, otherwise known as HIPAA, Health Information Technology for Economic and Clinical Health, otherwise known as the HITECH Act. Also, Sarbanes-Oxley Act, otherwise known as SOX. And then one of the newer ones that have been getting a lot of press lately is General Data Protection Regulation, or GDPR. And then a bit of a US version of that regulation, the California Consumer Privacy Act, or CCPA.

Gramm-Leach-Bliley Act (GLBA)
To start off, the Gramm-Leach-Bliley Act, GLBA, also known as the Financial Modernization Act of 1999, and what this does is specify that financial institutions must secure any and all personally identifiable information, or PII, so tax agents, mortgage brokers, banks, credit unions. And then there are a few sub-bullets, within that regulation that provides additional regulations, as an example, the Safeguards Rule. This stipulates that financial institutions must implement security initiatives to protect confidential information. The Financial Privacy Rule, this stipulates that financial institutions must provide a privacy notice to the customer both when the relationship is established, and on an annual basis. You may notice that you'll get pop-ups or information from your banks and your financial institutions once a year saying, we've updated our privacy rules, or here is a

reiteration of our privacy notices, just You're aware. And then we have pretexting protection. This prohibits access to personal private information without proper authority. What this is supposed to help with is things like social engineering, where a hacker or bad actor would call into a company, pretend to be someone in the know or someone that has a legitimate interest for information, and ask probing questions to try to get information out of the unsuspecting victim. This type of regulation helps put some guard rails around that, some training, and also just awareness around the fact that these types of things need to be protected and they need to be protected at scale throughout the entire company.

HIPAA

Next we have the Health Insurance Portability and Accountability Act, otherwise known as HIPPA. This is also known as the Kennedy-Kassebaum Act, implemented in 1996, and the one that we are concerned with, or probably most applicable, is Title II: Preventing Health Care Fraud and Abuse; Administrative Simplification; Medical Liability Reform. What this has is two main sections. We have the Privacy Rule, which defines patient medical records or protected health care information, PHI, and then also the Security Rule. The Security Rule defines security measures required to protect electronic protected health information, or EPHI. Without digging too much into any one of these specific regulations, because, quite frankly, each one of these would be probably a couple day book in and of themselves to fully understand, in most cases very complex, but the thing you need to understand is, if you're dealing with these types of situations and you're doing business and you're maintaining health records or financial information, or you're dealing with business outside of the country, it behooves you to dig in and start understanding the nuances of all of these different regulations and how they apply. There are rigid sentencing guidelines, up to criminal prosecution can result for violating HIPPA rules. Very important that these things are followed to the letter.

HITECH Act

Next, we have the HITECH Act. The HITECH Act is the health information technology for economic and clinical Health act. It became law in 2009, and in 2013, provided updates to HIPAA based upon the HITECH Act, so that included additional reporting requirements around significant harm and also removed the requirement that there needed to be actual proof that harm was done. At this point, it's just possible to prove that harm could have been done and that would satisfy the requirement. Before this, you had to prove that harm was done. As long as it's reasonable to believe that harm could have been done, the regulation provides for penalties. Additionally, it also added business associates of parties handling medical information or medical data are included. Not just the primary business, but business associates are covered under this HITECH Act as well. And then the length of time that PHI, protected health information, is protected was shortened from forever, which is, as we know, quite a long time, down to 50 years, which for the most part is the majority of a human life or at least a human adult life. A few HITECH considerations, Wilful neglect can result in significant penalties and we're talking up to $250,000 with repeat or uncorrected violations extending up to $1.5 million, Not an insignificant amount of penalties for non-compliance. Very important that these things are followed as much as possible. Also, penalties can extend, to business associates. As a covered entity, you must get assurance from any business associate that you do business with or whom you share EHR or EPHI that they will protect that data. If not, you can be held liable, HITECH Act considerations, very important to understand the nuances of all of this. And then also, breach notification, patients must be notified of any unsecured breach. If 500 or more patients are impacted, health and human services must also be notified. The media must be notified. So breach notifications are not optional, it's a mandatory thing that must occur if patients are, in fact, impacted.

Sarbanes-Oxley Act (SOX)
Next let's talk about the Sarbanes-Oxley Act, or SOX. The actual title of the regulation is the Public Company Accounting Reform and Investor Protection Act of 2002. Sarbanes-Oxley, the names of the people that presented or introduced the legislation created primarily to protect investors and improve the accuracy and the reliability of corporate disclosures around security laws, so on. The CEO and the CFO are both required to certify financial reports. It provides for greater accountability, and holds them accountable for inadequately protecting IT systems responsible for financial reporting. After such corporate meltdowns and debacles such as the Enron fiasco of years ago, Sarbanes-Oxley was designed to prevent those types of things from being able to happen again. If you're involved in these types of corporations or companies or organizations that are around finance, investing, securities, people that are responsible for that specific part of your organization I'm sure are very familiar already with the Sarbanes-Oxley Act, but if you are not in that scope specifically but within that company, I still would recommend that you familiarize yourself dig into the nuances of these acts, and that should go enterprise-wide or company-wide, everyone is driving the same objectives, and also making sure that the accounting is

done properly. When the books are messed with and accounting is not accurate, there's a huge potential for investor loss, so this type of legislation is designed to help prevent that. When it comes to SOX compliance, what are the main areas that the regulation is looking to cover? Well, first off, maintain data integrity and confidentiality. In other words, keep the data safe and secure, remember, SOX compliance, the CEO and the CFO need to sign off that these controls are in fact in place; that they're there, they're documented, they're demonstrable, we can show that they exist and they are protecting the data, keeping it safe and secure. These deals with financial systems, access to files, access control lists, auditing who can access what. Also, track any attempted security breaches, and also, what are the actual resolutions. What happened, and what did we do to prevent it or mitigate that risk going forward. Next, maintain event logs and make available for independent audit. That's one of the key takeaways. This is not one of those things where you just have a checklist and you're checking the boxes, you put it into a folder and put it on the shelf. These things need to be able to be audited every so often, and they will in fact be audited every so often, and if those controls are not in place and they're not demonstrated that they are working and functional, then you can be found not in compliance document that compliance and be able to show the prior 90 days. Since we don't know when the audits are coming, what does that mean? Well, that means we need a running log of the previous 90 days pretty much at any point in time. The moral of the story, friends, is keep the systems functioning, make sure they work, make sure they're documented and also demonstrable, make sure logging is in place, we track any attempted breaches, we know who's trying to access what files and when, who they are, and if they try and fail, that's logged as well. All of these things have to be in place and be able to be shown at a moment's notice when those auditors come knocking on the door.

GDPR

Next, one of the ones that gets a lot of attention days is the GDPR or the general data protection regulation. It's a privacy and security law that originated in the European Union in May of 2018. It imposes obligations onto organizations anywhere, so this has reached beyond just the EU, Long as they target or collect data related to people in the EU. Just because you're located in the United States or maybe somewhere outside of the European Union doesn't necessarily mean you are not impacted by GDPR. What type of data does the GDPR cover? Well, it provides individuals, which are known as data subjects, more control over how organizations process or control the processing of their data, such things as names, locations, patient data and health records, email addresses, photos, essentially any data that could be used to identify a living person.

Chapter 12 Qualitative and Quantitative Analysis

A qualitative analysis is an assessment that assigns a numerical value to the probability of a risk and the impact it can have on a system or network. The point to take away here is that no monetary value is assigned for our assets or the possible losses when we're talking about qualitative analysis. As an example, we would assess a risk of not installing; let's say, for instance, an antivirus application on our end user systems. We would range that or give it a range from, let's say, 1 to 100, and that range is arbitrary. We can assign it whatever number scale we want. For this example, let's just go 1 to 100. The probability of risk of an infection at some point, if it's an outwardly-facing system, again, if people have access to the internet, the probability of risk is, let's just say, 99. The amount of impact, we'll rank that at an 80. Again, arbitrary because there's a 20% chance that our systems would still be functional even if we caught a virus or a piece of malware. So, we may be able to still do some work, but it's going to be significantly slowed down. Our ability to get things done is going to be impeded. We'll give it a ranking of 80. If you multiply that 99 times 80, that gives us a ranking of 7920 or 7,920 out of a possible 10,000. Because if we took our 1 to 100, both of those categories would have a maximum value of 100. If we took 100 times 100, that would give us 10,000. That's where we get the 7,920 out of 10,000. That's on the high end. It's in the top, the top quarter or the top 25% of risk. That's, relatively speaking, it's a high risk. The flip side of that is a quantitative analysis. Quantitative, it signs an exact monetary value to assets and then attempts to give expected yearly loss in dollars for any given risk. What that does is allows us to prioritize based upon the financial losses to be incurred versus the cost of protecting. As an example, and it's comes down to a business decision, but if we said, we have 10 systems, and it's going to cost us, let's just, hypothetically speaking, cost a $1,000,000 to put antivirus on those 10 systems., it's not going to cost that much, but just for this example. It costs us a $1,000,000 to protect them, and the systems themselves only they cost $1000 or $1500 a piece. They only do very minimum amount of work. And if they all were compromised and went down, it would cost us maybe 30 or $40,000 in damages. Well, it's not worth spending a $1,000,000 to protect $30,000. So, in that instance, we could say the financial loss is not as great as the cost of protecting.

Risk Calculation
The risk calculation is the process of identifying the likelihood of a threat, the impact from the threat, and then how quickly our systems can become operational again. The likelihood is, as the name implies, how likely is that threat? Is the vulnerability likely to be exploited? The other thing is the ALE, and that's the Annual Loss Expectancy, and, how much do I expect to lose throughout the year if I combine my Single Loss Expectancy and my Annualized Rate of Occurrence? That's the total amount that I expect to lose throughout the year. There's an algorithm or a formula that's applied to get to that value. The impact is as the name implies, it's the impact of having that threat exploited. Is it downtime, is it complete loss of data, is it loss of customer confidence, it just depends upon what the asset is. The Single Loss Expectancy, or the SLE, is how much will that single loss if that threat is exploited, how much will I expect to lose on that single occurrence? Then the Annualized Rate of Occurrence is how often do I expect that to be successfully exploited throughout the year. Just understand

that these things are combined to give us a formula on how much we can expect to lose throughout the year.

Likelihood of Threat

The likelihood of the threat is the possibility of the threat initiation. It can be ranked qualitatively or quantitatively. Just because a vulnerability exists doesn't mean that it can necessarily be exploited. If it's an internal system that can't be reached from the outside world, then some type of external facing threat, we don't necessarily need to be concerned with, we may or may not want to take the time and effort to patch that. I just want to make sure you're aware that understanding the risk enables proper prioritization. Everything cannot be the highest priority, and everything, can't be the lowest priority, We have to rank our likelihoods and our threats so that we can remediate those things appropriately.

Impact of Threat

The next thing is the impact of the threat. If the threat is successfully initiated, then what's the impact? Could it be systems are slow and unresponsive or completely offline? Does it mean data loss? Does it mean destruction of systems or data, customer confidence, downstream effects? Downstream effects meaning if one system goes offline, does that then affect five other applications or five other systems? And it does it have dependencies that can create a much bigger outage than just the threat itself? All of these things have to be planned, and that's why it's very important to do planned maintenance versus unplanned outages.

Loss Calculation Terms (ALE, SLE, and ARO)

Some loss calculation terms that we use to calculate some of these things, are the annual loss expectancy, or the ALE, the monetary measure of how much loss you can expect in one year. The single loss expectancy, or the SLE, is the monetary measure of how much you can expect to lose at any one time, so single loss. That's calculated by the value of the asset by the exposure factor, AV times EF. Then we have the annualized rate of occurrence, or the ARO. That again, gets back to the likelihood, and that's usually determined with historical value of an event occurring within a year. We're going to go back and look, what's the realistic number? How many times did we get hit with this last year, for the last 2 years, the last 5 years. You look at some type of historical trending You get an idea of what's the likelihood I'm going to be hit with this specific, either vulnerabilities going to be exploited or I'm going to have some type of threat. Then when you do that, you times the SLE times the ARO of the single loss expectancy times the annualized rate of occurrence and that's going to give you your annual loss expectancy. As an example, let's say we have an ecommerce company that generates $100,000 in sales per hour from their website. The probability of the server failing during the year is 30%. If it's a highly functioning ecommerce site, it's not going to have a single server, but it's going to have a server cluster, load balancing. The probability of that server failing during the year is 30%. The failure would generate 4 hours of downtime and $6000 in components to repair. We may have to put in new hard drives, maybe a new motherboard, a new power supply. It's going to cost us 4 hours of downtime plus $6000 in components. The SLE, the single loss event, or expectancy is $406,000, $100,000 per hour because we're going to be down for 4 hours, plus the $6000 in repair for the parts. So our ARO is determined to be 30% because we said the probability of the server failing during the year is 30% so that's our ARO. If we then calculate the ALE, or the annual loss expectancy, it's going to be

$121,800. That's how much we can expect to lose each year, or this year, we can expect to lose $121,000 because we have our $406,000, which is the single loss expectancy, times the actual annualized rate of occurrence, What's the likelihood of that happening?

Threat Assessment (Disaster)
There are three main categories. First off we have the environment or natural threats. These are threats that can come from natural disasters such as a hurricane, an earthquake, a fire, flood, and so on. These things there are impossible to predict, but you can look historically to see how many times has each of these or any of these happened to that environment, to that building. If you're in an area that floods once or twice a year, then you need to put more prioritization on those types of threats. If your datacenter or your environment's out in the middle of the desert, as an example, you probably are not going to be flooding all that often, but you may have other natural disasters such as fire, earthquake. Next will be manmade. These are intentional attacks, such as breaches, viruses, malware, spam, and the distributed denial-of-service attacks. We can look historically and say, how many times have I been breached in the past? How many attempted breaches do I have per day or per week or per month? There is no way to predict necessarily what may happen in the future, but it can give you a rough indication of how much that specific environment gets targeted. You can also look at an industry standard and say, I'm in the healthcare industry, or I'm in the construction industry. You can look at the industry as a whole and get some approximation of how often that specific industry is targeted as well. Then next we have internal versus external. Internal would be internal to the company or inside an organization. External will be from the outside, hackers.,

depending upon which study you read, most threats are coming from internal, or that's the biggest threat, because these folks have the most intimate knowledge of your environment, where things are located, naming conventions, infrastructure, what operating systems are run, what applications are run, and so on. It's important to understand that just because our perimeter defenses might be shored up very tightly, we may have very good defenses against the outside world, if we don't also check and audit and monitor our inside environment as well, we put ourselves at risk.

Additional Risk Calculation Terms (MTBF, MTTF, and MTTR)
When it comes to risk and risk calculation, what exactly is that? Well, risk calculation is the process of identifying the likelihood of a threat, the impact from the threat, and then how quickly systems can be operational. There's three terms I want you to be familiar with, and that's MTBF, or the mean time between failures, the MTTF, the mean time to failure, and then also MTTR, the mean time to recovery. Let's take a look at each of these individually. When we're talking about the MTBF, or the mean time between failures, that is the statistical average a device or a component lasts between failures, and that's referring to things that are repairable. If things are not repairable or they're so insignificant we just rip them out and put in a brand-new one, then this doesn't apply. But for things that can be repaired, what's the average a device or component lasts between those failures? Then we have the MTTF, the mean time to failure. That is the average of how long a component lasts. That refers to things that will be replaced rather than repaired. We want to get ahead of that and replace those things before they fail. That's always our goal here, is to understand when we can proactively get in and have planned downtime, as opposed to unplanned downtime. Then the MTTR is the

mean time to repair, so the statistical average of how long it takes to repair that failed component.

As far as BIA, or business impact analysis is concerned, there's some key terminology. We're talking about maximum tolerable downtime, or MTD. That is how long can something be down before it has a significant impact to the business? That ties into our mean time to repair and the mean time between failures, also the RTO and RPO. All of these things combine so if we know the maximum amount of time that we're allowed or we should be able to be down before we start seeing a significant impact, then we can work backwards from there and adjust our policies accordingly. The mean time to repair, or MTTR, is the mean time that it's going to take to repair a specific piece of equipment. If something fails, and it's going to take us 6 hours or 6 days or 6 weeks to repair that, and our maximum tolerable downtime is only an hour or 2, well, then, we're going to have some issues if that were to go down. That stresses the importance of having planned downtime and planned outages we can make sure we periodically and preventatively take these things offline We can fix them, repair them, replace them without having an impact to our business. Next, we have mean time between failures, or MTBF, and that is a calculation of how long a specific piece of equipment will be in service before it fails. That allows us to calculate should we take this thing offline during a planned outage or a planned maintenance versus unplanned? Planned is always better than unplanned. Having an idea of what the MTBF for specific components within our infrastructure is, whether it's disk drives, storage arrays, computer servers, desktops, laptops, switches, routers, the individual components themselves, the line cards, the supervisors, all these things have their own individual MTBF metrics. By knowing what those things are, we can plan accordingly. Then, next, is our recovery time objective, or our RTO. How long does it take us to bring that specific piece of infrastructure or that specific piece of data back online? Next is the recovery point objective. How far back do we want to go? This revolves around data protection and backups. But we could do a recovery time objective. It might take us a half an hour to get that data back, as an example. But a recovery point objective is we want to recover up to an hour or if it's 5 minutes, that's going to have an impact on our RTO as well. What you can take away from that is the RPO and RTO, the recovery time objective and the recovery point objective, as those things slide closer to zero, the expense is going to go up. But, again, it depends upon the industry. If we're making millions of dollars a second per transaction, as an example, then it's going to be worth spending that money to have a very short RPO and RTO. Conversely, if it's something that doesn't have a large impact on our environment, maybe some archival data or just some log statistics and, well, then our RPO and RTO can slide way to the left. It could be hours. It could be days. We don't have to spend as much money to get that information back as quickly as possible. Next, we have work recovery time, or our WRT. It might be best if you look at this in a chart format just to see how all of these different terms tie together. Here we have a situation where we have some type of disaster, when disaster strikes. We have our RPO, RTO, our work recovery time, and then something else referred to as our maximum tolerable downtime, or MTD.

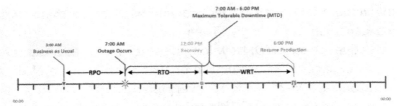

At 3 a.m., business as usual, cooking along just like we do every other day. Well, at 7 a.m., some type of outage occurs. Well, our RPO gives us a 4-hour window. We have a 4-hour recovery point objective. We would have the actual outage occur at 7. We're going to go back 4 hours. That might be the first earliest backup. That's the earliest that we can recover information based upon the RPO in this specific example. These things are fluid. Our RPOs and RTOs could change depending upon the parameters and the acceptable limits that we set as a business. In this example, 4 hours. So outage occurs at 7 a.m. Our RPO is 4 hours. We're going to go back and recover up to 3 a.m. Well, from 7 a.m. until 12 p.m., that's our recovery time objective. That means that's how long it will take for us to get that information back either off tape, VTL data domain, Avamar, or some type of backup device, some type of backup appliance is going to bring us back to 12 noon. From 12 p.m. to 6 p.m., that's our WRT, or our work recovery time, that's the amount of time it's going to take us to bring all the various teams in, have them validate their applications, make sure the log files and databases are intact, all of the things that we need to have in place before we're live in production. The maximum tolerable downtime is from 7 a.m. until 6 p.m. That's an 11-hour window. The work recovery time is the MTD minus the RTO. That work recovery time is how long we have to validate before we exceed our maximum tolerable downtime. If our MTD was, for instance, say, 7 hours, well, if our RTO is 5 hours, it takes us from 7 a.m. to noon to bring that information back, well, then we only have 2 hours for our work recovery time. We only have 2 hours to validate and get back online, get back in production before we exceed that maximum tolerable downtime. WRT is the difference between the RTO and the MTD.

Mission Essential Functions

Let's talk about mission essential functions. What we are talking about here are operations that are core to the success of the business. It's imperative that we, as IT professionals and security professionals, understand which ones are absolutely critical, essential to the functioning of the business. Revenue generating applications, billing applications. Every environment's going to be different. Every business will be different. Some will have two or three core applications. Some may have dozens or more. But as a security professional, it's critical that we understand what those systems are, how they interoperate with other systems, and make sure we secure them as much as possible. Not just the application itself, but understand what applications feed these applications and also what other applications these core ones feed into. We have to make sure we secure all of those systems appropriately because if there's a chain of applications and one breaks down, well, then that has a cascading effect. All of the other systems, all of the other systems go offline as well. If it takes 5 minutes or 5 hours or 5 days to get that one system back up in that chain, and it feeds information to subsequent systems, the entire system has the possibility of being down as well. To that effect, are those systems backed up or protected? Are the highly available? In other words, if one system goes down, can we bring up another one, or can we fail over to another one instantly or quasi-instantly. And are they redundant? Are all the sub-components within these different systems redundant? Do we have multiples so that if one goes down, we're still up and running? And then disaster recovery or BCP. Do we have disaster recovery in place so that if we have a "smoking hole" scenario, where our data center or our supply closet or whatever the situation might be, where we're housing our data and our infrastructure, if that goes away, do we have another place that we can bring those systems back up? Is there business continuity planning, or BCP, in effect? And disaster recovery and high availability, these are all components of a larger BCP plan, a business continuity plan. All of these things should be taken into account and audited, making sure they're documented, stack ranked by order of importance, and then remediated appropriately.

Chapter 13 Identification of Critical Systems

Next we're talking about the identification of critical systems. A full audit of the environment can turn up application dependencies that you may or may not know exist. How does data flow through the network? Don't just assume that an application is in a vacuum in and of itself, it's its own tower. Most applications and most systems will either feed data into something else or get data from some other system. There's going to be a flow of data through the network. When a customer visits a website, as an example, and they put information in some web portal, that gets stored in a database in some multi-tier application, it goes through a number of different systems, and may go to order a processing and customer attention and analytics platform and data lakes and so on. All of these things apply or supply data to and from our critical systems, quote-unquote. I can guarantee you that when something goes offline that you didn't necessarily deem important and you didn't even know all the different systems that it feeds, well, it's going to have downstream impacts and you'll very quickly understand the interdependencies at that point. You might ask yourself, well, how does that happen? I mean, I know everything in my environment. Well, that might be true. For small environments or midsize environments that might be very true. But as things grow over time, they grow organically, things come up as skunkworks projects or little side-of-desk or side-of-table projects that eventually grow. Sometimes when things are not funded, but all of a sudden, hey, that's pretty cool when everyone starts using it, and it never gets properly architected, properly backed up, and as it grows and grows and grows, it morphs into a critical system. Here you end up having something that the business relies on that's not fault tolerant, redundant, backed up. A full audit of your environment periodically will prevent those types of things from happening. And is each system or application in that chain that we spoke about, do they all have the same level of availability and redundancy? Because again, we can't say that a system is a tier 1 or class 1 or whatever classification system you use within your organization, you can't say it is a top-tier application just because the application itself is top-tier infrastructure. If all the things that it feeds or the power grid that it sits on, or all of the different interdependencies are not also class 1 or tier 1 your classification is, then that application or that system is not at that level either. Because if something breaks down and it's critical to feeding that application or that system, well then that system's going to go offline, just as easily as the downstream or the weak link in that chain goes offline. A full audit of the environment is critical, understanding what these systems are and how they all interrelate.

Single Point of Failure (SPOF)
Having two of something doesn't necessarily mean that it's redundant. The fact of the matter is just because we have two of a certain component, a server, or whatever, it doesn't mean we have redundancy, or it doesn't mean it's still not a single point of failure. As an example, a dual-port HBA, or a host bus adapter, connects a server to a Fibre Channel network or to a Fibre Channel storage array. Well, if we have a single HBA in that server, it's a dual-port HBA, and we have two ports coming out, one to each fabric, we have dual fabrics, we have a server, and we think we have two paths of storage, well, we may say to ourselves or think, everything is covered. We're redundant. We have two of each. But the reality is, as you can guess, is no because it's a single HBA. There may be two ports coming out of it, but if that HBA

were to fail, you'd have lost connectivity to both fabrics. You're much better off to have two single-port HBAs. That way, in case one of those ports goes down, the other is still functioning. Same thing with two servers connecting to the same line card on a switch. We may have two servers clustered together. But if they're both connected to the same line card in a switch, well, if that line card goes down, both servers are down at the same time, so that becomes a single point of failure. You see where I'm going with this. We have to break these things down and look at the individual components and make sure that there is no single point of failure in any of those sub-components as well. Power and cooling, making sure we're not on the same power grids, all of the servers. If power goes down on one side, it doesn't take down the other. Multiple server paths to storage, we could have some type of multipathing software in place, whether it's PowerPath or MPIO or some native multipathing. But if the configuration files are not set correctly, well, there's a good chance we may not be using multipath. We still may have only one path to storage. It just depends upon your environment, what equipment you have in there. But I encourage you to go through an audit and make sure that you identify and understand what your applications and your systems are made of and that the components then to that level are, in fact, redundant. We do this by fully auditing and documenting the environment for potential risk. Then we rank in order of importance and, remediation. That way we know where we need to focus our resources for first because typically with any IT department or any business in general, there's only a certain amount of resources. So by prioritizing, you know where to put those resources first.

Chapter 14 Order of Restoration

Let's talk about the order of restoration. We have to get our information back online. What do we need to do? Well, a few things. We need an understanding of that application's full stack. Define what network, what storage, and what compute components make up that application or service. That sounds like a no-brainer, but as these applications grow, or if it's a very large environment, you may or may not necessarily know all the things, all the interrelations, all the interconnections, all the teams that are involved, what applications feed into it, what applications that specific application feeds out to. A full understanding of everything that's required to bring this application either down or back up is critical. Next, what teams need to be involved? Typically, more than one team manages the various components of that application or that service. The assumption is going to be that we're going to do this in a very controlled fashion. There's going to be some type of bridge set up. You have all the teams connecting. They're all dialed in. They're all either in a board room or they're going to dialed in remotely. They're all going to be aware of what's happening, and things will be brought down and then brought back up again or vice versa in a very programmatic fashion. That way there's consistency with data, there's no corruption, and also we have everyone on site if something were to go wrong, and they can quickly jump in and help get things back online. And then, ensuring backups can be recovered and restored. This is also a bit of a no-brainer, but not necessarily that something is done all the time. Test backups and restores prior to bringing that application up or down. Test backups and restorations of the application or the service before a crisis occurs, that's the critical component here, before the crisis to ensure that that required data is available.

Phased Approach

We need to have a phased approach when we're talking about tackling some of the issues that we have at hand. We have to identify what's critical and then do things in a very systematic approach. We can't do everything at once. We can't boil the ocean. We need to identify what is most critical, and that deals with infrastructure, with applications, with people and skills, all of these things, understanding what fits in with our grand vision, what's in alignment with business objectives, business outcomes. Then out of these things, infrastructure, application, people, skills, what's most critical? What do we have to tackle up front? Let's make those things a top priority. Again, ensuring alignment with business objectives, and then also revisit these periodically to make sure they're still valid because, guess what? If it's a brand-new business, we simply don't know what we don't know. There's no necessarily tried-and-true proven roadmap. Maybe there is to a certain extent but not typically across the board. There are always going to be variables. There are always going to be bumps in the road. By re-evaluating and understanding that this is a fluid document, a fluid process that's going to change over time, it allows us to pivot our objectives or, as we achieve objectives one, two, and three, we can add some additional ones to that list so that we have a rolling list of objectives or tasks that we want to accomplish as we drive towards getting this business up and running and making it as secure as possible.

Identifying Most Critical Systems First

We need to identify what services and what products that we're providing. As a brand new business, what is it that we want to bring to market, provide to our customers? Provide that list and rank them by criticality. Revenue generating, business critical functions. Next, identify what is required to provide those services or products to customers. That can be our computers, our servers, networking. We decide whether we're doing on-prem or cloud. How about digital or physical? Are we going to be doing things completely in the digital realm? Do we have physical products and services? Do we need physical infrastructure? All of these things have to be stack ranked in criticality we can understand where we need to focus our resources first. Next, define how to secure that infrastructure and that data that encompasses that service or those services, or those products. Firewalls, encryption, multi-factor authentication, understanding what in-house expertise, what we need to outsource. A lot of things to consider. There are a lot of things that can revolve around starting up a business. A lot of times we think of only the product or the service and not all of the underlying nuts and bolts on how to make that thing a reality. It's important for us to understand how to rank these things so we can drive most efficiently. Next, identify and document any compliance or regulatory requirements. This is critical depending upon the industry that you're in. So, healthcare, finance, are going to be much more regulated, have a lot more compliance and data governance issues, data governance is very, very important and can be the actual undoing of a business if it's not done and managed properly. It varies by industry, but some examples could be the California Consumer Privacy Act, it could be GDPR, it could be HIPPA, SOX. There are a number of different compliance frameworks, regulatory frameworks that may apply to you in your specific industry. Then lastly, rinse and repeat for the remaining applications and processes. go through that list for revenue generating and back-office functions, and then also document any gaps that exist because you may or may not want to necessarily address that specific thing here and, but by documenting it at least allows you to table that effort for the moment and then come back to it when you have time and resources available.

Risk Assessment

We need to make sure that we are identifying potential risks that are most harmful throughout the entire business, not just one area. What is the most harmful, and then what do we need to do to mitigate against that specific risk. The risk assessments are useful, but understand, they may not account for everything. It's very difficult to understand every tiny piece of a business from top to bottom. Understand that you potentially, may miss some things. That's why testing, that's why going through this process is so critical, because as things are missed, it's a living document, we're going to go through an iterative process, and we're going to measure those risks over, and over, and over again. We'll take a first pass, we'll get everyone together from Legal, Accounting, HR, Finance, IT., all these people together, and we'll flesh it out, and we'll figure out does this work, does that work, if this happens, what are you going to do, if this happens, what are you going to do? And everyone chimes in, and then you'll go through an iterative process and you'll understand over time what works, what doesn't, and what needs to be adjusted, so it goes back and forth.

Chapter 15 Continuity of Operations

That all revolves around something called the continuity of operations. All areas of the business are connected. That's just a fact of business. Every area of the business relies on IT in some capacity. If you're in HR, Finance, Accounting, Marketing, you name it, every area relies on IT whether it's for your PCs, your smart phones, telecommunication systems, and it all revolves around that central hub. So have an understanding of that and the reach of IT itself has throughout the entire business helps you to understand what areas will be most heavily impacted, a mitigation plan, and we can understand where we need to focus resources, and then rate them and go from an order of priority going forward. Continuity planning centers around what alternatives exist to keep the business running in the event of that disaster. We have fault tolerant systems, we have redundant systems. Well, what if they fail? What if we can't get those things to come back online? That's where continuity planning comes into play. We need to have alternates or a plan B.

IT Contingency Planning
We want to put things into play or into place so that we can mitigate risk. We can either have redundancy or fault tolerance and just skip over that blip in the network if you will. But there are going to be times, for whatever reason, that we can't do that. If that disaster strikes and that uninterrupted continuity is not an option, then we have to have a contingency plan or a plan B. Procedures for relocating operations to a new location is an example. Minimizing disruption and downtime is, always our main mandate. But just for your own information, the federal

government has some guidelines, as they do, NIST. There is a special publication, SP 800-34 that outlines the methods and gives guidance for providing alternative methods for infrastructure, for telecommunications, and for mainframe systems. I definitely recommend that you review this publication. It's great information. It covers all the main areas that you need to be concerned with. And it gives you some guidance from high level all the way down to some granular step-by-step instructions on how to protect these things and how to set up your own policies and procedures within your company. The discovery process can identify gaps and potential remediation steps. That's going to be a process in and of itself that can help us mitigate risks, and we can identify, Oh, we don't have enough resources here, or we didn't realize the impact of this specific area on the rest of the business. We saw them sitting there in the corner. We never knew what they did. But we understand, wow, they have a huge impact on every area of the business. You might find these things out through your process. In doing that, you identify the gaps. You can add additional resources. You may need to buy new equipment or additional pieces of infrastructure, maybe to have duplicates if you're going to have a hot site, adding resources, and increasing resiliency. And then on top of that, you may identify gaps in training. Will all the necessary personnel be available to relocate? What happens if you have 500 employees locally, your disaster site is, let's say, 2000 miles away or 1000 miles away, and all those 500 people cannot or will not or, for whatever reason, can't relocate from one location to the other. Are there people available in the new location that you can bring on board relatively quickly? How long will it take to train those people? Does the new location have available personnel at all? You might be in an area where there aren't 500 people that you could bring on at a moment's notice. All of these things need to be taken into account when we're doing our BCP and our business impact analysis and our contingency planning so that we have the bases covered. That's the name of the game is we want to make sure we have as little disruption to the business as possible in the event of some type of downtime. In this chapter, we talked about risk types. We talked about risk management strategies along with risk analysis, different types of disasters, and then business impact analysis, and how all of these things collectively allow us to become more aware of risk, how to integrate risk awareness into our processes and planning, and then, of course, also devise ways to remove risk or de-risk our environment as much as possible.

Chapter 16 Privacy and Sensitive Data Concepts

In this chapter, we'll be talking about privacy and sensitive data concepts and considerations. We'll be talking about organizational consequences of privacy breaches, notification of breaches, the various types of data and how they're classified. We'll talk about privacy enhancing technologies, also roles and responsibilities, information lifecycle, an impact assessment, and then terms of agreement and privacy notices. So let's talk about some company obligations to protect security, again, getting back to whether it's the US laws, UK laws, or elsewhere in the world, a lot of countries are adopting similar regulations. Physical security goes without saying, we need to make sure that we're providing adequate protections against physical break-ins, people crossing into the barriers of our workplaces doing physical harm, but then also breaking into our data centers and accessing data inappropriately or without authorization, then computer and network security, making sure we're putting things in place so that our computers, our networks are secure, we have policies in place like password complexity issues, two-factor authentication, if possible, different types of encryption, encryption at rest or in transit. And then also network infrastructure security to make sure that our routers, switches, and the perimeter devices that may be accessible from the outside, anything that's public facing or internally facing, assuming someone more to breach our perimeter and get physical access to the building. Is our network infrastructure secure? Do we have such things in place so they can't just plug into a network jack and gain immediate access to our network and then proper training of employees. This is an ongoing thing, it's not a one and done.

We must periodically make sure that our employees are all on the same page, they all understand that security is everyone's job. They also understand what's expected of them, what's an acceptable use, and what's, of course, unacceptable, and then also understand to the extent that they're potentially monitored so that they have a proper expectation, or perhaps depending upon the location, no expectation of privacy. If they're using corporate resources, laptops, phones, well, then they should be properly trained to understand that anything on those devices could potentially be accessed by the company at any time. That lack of expectation of privacy will go a long way to making sure that they're using those corporate resources for corporate purposes.

Potential Damages from Mishandled Data

If we don't have things properly set up and we don't have the systems in place to make sure that we're protecting our data, what can possibly go wrong? We could have loss of intellectual property Proprietary information, data or programs could be stolen, used by competitors, or in one form or fashion, bring damage to the company. Intellectual property as we know can be a key differentiator, it can be a competitive advantage, so if that goes away, if that goes out the door, then that potential competitive advantage may go out the door with it, so it's very important that the company does, in fact, safeguard this data. Next, we can have loss of revenue, financial loss due to disruption of business, loss of, the competitive advantage. These things can happen very, very quickly up until the point where it could force the company out of business, depending upon how great the loss is. Next, we have loss of brand and reputation. That could be loss of consumer confidence, investor confidence, employee trust. It takes a long time to develop trust, to develop a brand, and develop a company, a persona that people want to do business with and interact with. It takes a long time to build that. It takes a very short amount of time to lose it if things aren't secured properly, if there is a customer breach and sensitive information is leaked out into the public, or proprietary information is gone and competitors can potentially do what you do, maybe even better, so those things have to be secured as much as possible.

Chapter 17 Incident Notification and Escalation

Next is incident notification and escalation. We need to make sure that we quickly assess and triage as appropriate. Triage means we handle the most important things first, just like an ER nurse or an ER doctor would do in the emergency room. You have a bunch of patients coming in; they're going to quickly assess the damage and treat the most critical patients first. We need to do the same thing when we have a breach or an incident in our IT environment. We have to handle the most serious things first. Depending upon the nature of the attack, different groups may need to be notified, and those things will hopefully become apparent as we're doing our quick assessment. We're handling the most critical things first and notifying the appropriate groups. Some of those might be security teams. That might be your own security team, or there may be other teams within the environment, within the company, that should be notified. We could also talk about executive management. Again, depending upon how serious it is, the CEO, CTO, CIO, or the CISO, they all may need to be notified. Also, human resources, public information officers or public affairs, all of these groups may need to be contacted so the damage can be handled as quickly as possible. Also we have a legal team. If it's PII or something that may have customer impact or proprietary or sensitive information, legal teams may need to be notified so they can start working on damage control as quickly as possible as well. Then we also have social media teams. We live in the age of social media. When things happen, almost instantly, it's known around the world, and if it's something bad, we want to make sure we get ahead of that. If you don't have a social media team in place, you may want to consider having one on staff or on retainer full time.

First and foremost, when good things happen, let's not focus on the bad things for a minute, but when good things happen, you should be putting that out there on your social media platforms. Every social media outlet available, you should be pushing that information out so that everyone knows about the good work that you do. But by the same token, those teams should be in place and ready to activate when bad things happen. They need to be able to get in front of that so that the company image, reputation, customer satisfaction can be managed and damage control can be done as quickly as possible.

Notifying Outside Agencies

When it comes to notifying outside agencies, we're talking about law enforcement, and that could be local, state, or federal, U.S. government agencies if we're talking about a breach in some type of government agency, they may need to contact US CERT, which is the United States Computer Emergency Readiness Team. If it's a critical infrastructure or a government entity, then more than likely US CERT should be notified. Their website is www.us-cert.gov. You can check them out for more information. Then when it comes to the communication itself, if we rely solely on email as our form of communication, well, what happens if your internal email system is the one that's compromised? You're dead in the water at that point. We need to make sure we establish out-of-band communication methods. We need to understand the location of our war rooms where we can all congregate, have all the different teams that are involved all meet in a central location. If email is our only place or Skype or some type of Webex, or if we all rely on technology, and that main technology is the one that's impacted, then how do we communicate? How do we coordinate our efforts? We need the location of these war rooms we can all meet in person, face to face, everyone working on the issue in real time. Management can get updates very quickly that way. It ensures everyone is on the same page. A centralized location, also for information dissemination. It could be done electronically. It could be done via some network operation center where things are done over a phone line or a landline. There also needs to be a centralized location for information dissemination, both internally and externally, whether that's voicemail, website, social media.

Chapter 18 Data Classification

Next, let's talk about data sensitivity, labeling, and handling, or data classifications. When we classify data, it's important that we do it properly so the data can be secured properly. We make sure only certain people have access to it, and then also it's disposed of properly in the proper fashion as well when it comes time to get rid or purge that data. We have a couple different types or a couple different classifications. Confidential is material that is meant for internal use only, and it could cause damage to the organization if disclosed. This is the stuff that we don't want getting out to the public. Private is compartmental data that must be kept private for various reasons. It could be regulatory compliance. It could be HR data. Its things that should be within specific departments or compartments within an organization. It's not just for anybody within the organization. And then we have public and that's the least sensitive data type, and that can be used for various purposes. Marketing, just general release to the public, website data. Then we have proprietary data, and proprietary is data that should be disclosed on a limited basis, as it contains information that could diminish a company's competitive advantage, technical specs on a specific piece of equipment or infrastructure, some type of patent they're working on or what have you, something that gives that company an edge. That proprietary information, if it were to get out, a competitor got a hold of it, it could diminish that company's advantage. Next, we have such things as PII, or personally identifiable information. PII is any data that could be used to distinguish or trace an individual's identity. And an interesting point to take away is that PII is not a single set of data. Non-PII or non-personally identifiable information could become PII when additional information is combined and used to identify an individual. Things that are not necessarily in and of themselves, PII, but if they're coupled together and we have three or four different pieces, we start to paint a picture. Collectively, once they're all aggregated together, that could, in fact, become PII. It's not just a rigid set of data. It's a fluid line in the sand that you have to keep your eye on if you're managing or dealing with PII in your workplace. Next, we have protected health information, or PHI. PHI is protected health information, and that's defined as part of HIPAA regulations, and it's a subset of health information that could be linked to a specific individual. That includes any information about health status or provision of healthcare or payment for health care, anything that's collected by a covered entity or a business associate of a covered entity and can be linked to a specific individual. You see the recurring theme here, things that can be deanonymized or refer back and traced back to a specific individual. Anything around their health status or care they've been given or payments for health care, any business that collects that type of information or other businesses, third-parties that work with health care providers there in that loop, and they potentially have access to that information, they should be wary of PHI regulations as well.

Chapter 19 Privacy-enhancing Technologies

Let's now talk about some privacy enhancing technologies. One is data minimization. What this boils down to is only keeping what is necessary. When you collect data, anything that's not pertinent to what you need to market or use to identify someone or process an order or any of those things, that data should then be removed, deleted, destroyed. Next is data masking. Data masking we've talked about before, and that's replacing one piece of data with another. Next are tokenization, which we've talked about previously as well, and then anonymization, and then pseudo-anonymization. Let's dig in for just a moment. And data masking where we can mask data by removing or masking things that are used to identify someone. While using data masking techniques, we can replace that with asterisks or some type of wildcard. That way we still retain the essence of the data, but the sensitive information has been removed or masked. That way someone viewing that data does not get access to that critical or that sensitive information. Next is tokenization. But tokenization is replacing sensitive data with a non-sensitive equivalent. The token can be a single use, a multiple use, it could be cryptographic or non-cryptographic, and it also could be reversible or irreversible. It just depends upon the use case and the technology being implemented. High-value tokens, or HVTs, can be used to replace things like primary account numbers on credit card transactions, they can be bound to specific devices. Then we have low-value tokens. They can serve similar functions, but need the underlying tokenization system to match it back to the actual primary account number. Two systems that do the same type of thing.

Anonymization and Pseudo-anonymization

These entire things boil down to anonymizing data, Protecting private or sensitive information by erasing or encrypting identifiers that can connect an individual to stored data. We have anonymization and then also pseudo-anonymization. Anonymization we've talked about, data masking, it could be tokenization, all of those things are ways to anonymize data. And then pseudo-anonymization, that's a data management technique where it will deidentify data. We're taking off identifiers and replacing them with fake identifiers or pseudonyms. So, we could take a person's name and replace it with something else or any other identifier for that matter. We could replace it with something else. What it does is it preserves the statistical accuracy and the data integrity. It allows that data to be used for training, for development, for testing, for analytics, while still protecting data privacy.

Chapter 20 Data Owners & Responsibilities

Data is not typically owned by individuals. We want to give ownership to the enterprise itself. Data is owned by the company or by the enterprise or the organization. Owners are assigned for management, compliance, and accountability. Within your organization, you'll typically have a data owner, a data steward. But it's done for accountability and also for management. When it comes time for compliance, we need to know who owns that data, who's responsible for maintaining it.

Data Controller and Processor
Processing is any operation, whether automated or a manual process, that is performed on personal data. A data processor is responsible for the processing of personal data on behalf of what's known as a data controller. The data controller is the person or the thing that determines the purpose and the means by which personal data is processed.

Data Steward / Custodian
A data steward and a custodian, sometimes those terms are used interchangeably, although they do have some distinctions depending upon the role or the size of the organization, but a data steward or custodian is responsible for maintaining data quality. They incorporate processes, policies, guidelines. They're going to define the terms and the metadata that they will steward. We're talking about databases; we're talking about business analytics. There's going to be terminology. There are going to be classifications within the data. We have tons of data coming into an organizational, a lot of unstructured data, a lot of database type data. Well, the fields themselves and the types of data

and the metadata need to be defined ahead of time. They need to be a strict set of guidelines as to what type of data can be used, where it can be brought in, how it's classified. That way, that data can be managed. It can be mined and analytics run against it. That ensures that the data is relevant and also fit for use. That means it's data that can become actionable. It doesn't do us much good to take in tons and tons of data, terabytes or petabytes of data, if we can't do anything with it. It just becomes a waste of space at that point. By proper data management by a steward or a custodian, it ensures that the data coming in can then be analyzed properly, can be mined, can be categorized so that it's actionable and of value to the business.

Privacy Officer
Next, we have a privacy officer, and a privacy officer oversees all the ongoing activities related to the development, the implementation, and the maintenance of an organization's privacy policies. Everything you can think about regarding PII and PHI and sensitive data and the different types of data classifications, all of those things fall under the auspices of a privacy officer or a chief privacy officer. Depending on the size of the company, it may be a single person, or it may be an entire team. They also may wear multiple roles working with legal, compliance.

Chapter 21 Information Lifecycle

Next, let's talk about the information lifecycle. So, what we're talking about here is how we collect and what we do with the data once we have it. The lifecycle itself, depending upon where you read you may see some additional steps, there may be some other ones thrown in there, but generally speaking we have the steps that I have outlined here. We have collection, and then we have access, usage, storage, the transfer, and then deletion or destruction. Going through that we're going to collect data some way, somehow, whether it be a form, whether we collect data behind the scenes when someone visits a website, take some action. Somehow or other we're getting data. And then we should define how we access that data and then how we use the data. All of these things should have a defined process and rules around them. And that's part of our transparency policy, our privacy policy. Our terms of agreement we'll talk about in just a moment as well. That way we're making sure that it's kept secure. Confidential information remains confidential. Do we interact with third parties or share that information with other folks? And then once it's no longer needed, how do we get rid of it? The deletion or destruction. All of those things should be spelled out and then the process adhered to. And then on top of all of that, we need to have data protection in place to make sure that that data is safeguarded from prying eyes, from data breaches. What that does is maintain compliance with various regulations, as an example GDPR. It also ensures that data is collected properly, used, and stored in accordance to policy, our defined policies, and destroyed once no longer needed. It also helps us build consumer trust, the overall brand and reputation. So by letting users know what we're doing, how we're doing it, and what goes on behind the scenes, what we're doing with that data, it just increases the level of trust, and it ensures that they understand that the data is being protected, or we're doing everything we can to protect that data. And lastly, the point of all that is to help guard against breaches, unauthorized access. As a security professional, one of our tenants is CIA, the confidentiality, integrity, and availability of data. All of these things go a long way to making sure that that stays intact.

Privacy Impact Assessment
This is used to identify and manage privacy risks arising from new projects, new systems, processes, or even business relationships. When these things spin up, we're starting something new, whether it is internal, whether it is technology based or process based, maybe starting to partner with another company or another vendor, all of those things should require that we do a privacy impact assessment. It's a self-directed assessment to make sure things are secured properly and that we're baking that privacy into the process, or it's not a bolt-on after the fact. The privacy impact assessment achieves three main goals. It's going to ensure compliance with applicable legal and regulatory laws. It also identifies and evaluates risks of privacy breaches or other incidents. We'll go through our various systems, our relationships, technologies, applications and identify what risks exist. And then we'll stack rank them to make sure that we understand what are the ramifications if one of those breaches were to be, in fact, successfully executed so that we can then plan and direct resources appropriately. And then, identify appropriate privacy controls to mitigate those unacceptable risks. We talked about risk before, so there are some things that you probably would be willing to accept, and it is what it is. We're not going to spend the money to necessarily mitigate those things, but there are certain risks that are unacceptable. We then need to identify, how are we going to de-risk that environment? How are we going to take those risks out of the equation? And that boils down to time, money, resources, people, process, and technology. We need to direct resources in some fashion or maybe all three

696

of those things to implement a control or a piece of technology or software to mitigate that risk. We need to stack rank in order of importance so that we would focus our resources on the most important things first and then work our way down from there.

Terms of Agreement and Privacy Notice

Two additional terms that I want to make sure you're familiar with. First one is terms of agreement. This ensures that the specific terms of a relationship are spelled out, discussed, and agreed upon prior to beginning that relationship. A lot of times it's one of those things where you go to a website and it'll flash up a little end user license agreement or terms of agreement, the things that no one ever reads. Well, in there typically will be what type of data is collected, how it's used. All of those things are there to protect both the company and also to inform the user. And then next is a privacy notice. That's one of those things you may have gotten in the mail before, email, saying, hey, we've just changed our terms, here's a link to our new privacy policy. And it's one of those things where you probably don't read, most people don't, but I would encourage you to go through it and look at that next time you see one, because it's there for a reason, and it provides easy access to information for users, customers on how data is collected, what it's used for, how it's stored, and if it will be shared with other folks, third parties. The privacy notice is important, and it should be accessible from websites, from places that you visit and places you do business with, so that you understand how your data is being collected and being used. In this chapter, we talked about organizational consequences of privacy breaches; we talked about notifications of breaches; along with various data types; also privacy enhancing technologies, various roles and responsibilities around data privacy; along with the information lifecycle; an impact assessment; terms of agreement; and then lastly, a privacy notice. That wraps up this book. We made it to the end. I'm so happy that you took this journey with me. Best of luck with your training and certification endeavours, and thank you very much for completing this book.

Conclusion

Congratulations on completing this book! I am sure you have plenty on your belt, but please don't forget to leave an honest review. Furthermore, if you think this information was helpful to you, please share anyone who you think would be interested of IT as well.

About Richie Miller

Richie Miller has always loved teaching people Technology. He graduated with a degree in radio production with a minor in theatre in order to be a better communicator. While teaching at the Miami Radio and Television Broadcasting Academy, Richie was able to do voiceover work at a technical training company specializing in live online classes in Microsoft, Cisco, and CompTia technologies. Over the years, he became one of the top virtual instructors at several training companies, while also speaking at many tech and training conferences. Richie specializes in Project Management and ITIL these days, while also doing his best to be a good husband and father.